Learn Haskell
by Example

PHILIPP HAGENLOCHER

MANNING
SHELTER ISLAND

For online information and ordering of this and other Manning books, please visit
www.manning.com. The publisher offers discounts on this book when ordered in quantity.
For more information, please contact

    Special Sales Department
    Manning Publications Co.
    20 Baldwin Road
    PO Box 761
    Shelter Island, NY 11964
    Email: orders@manning.com

Manning Publications Co.
20 Baldwin Road
PO Box 761
Shelter Island, NY 11964

Development editor:	Katie Sposato Johnson
Technical editor:	Alexander Vershilov
Review editor:	Radmila Ercegovac
Production editor:	Kathy Rossland
Copy editor:	Christian Berk
Proofreader:	Jason Everett
Technical proofreader:	Timo von Holtz
Typesetter:	Dennis Dalinnik
Cover designer:	Marija Tudor

ISBN: 9781633438934
Printed in the United States of America

Dedicated to my parents, Hildegard and Martin. Love you always!

contents

preface

Haskell is a language that, from the outside, may seem shrouded in mystery, academic vocabulary, and foreign concepts. While some of that is true, I fully believe you don't have to have a PhD in mathematics to get things done with the language. It's only a matter of the right introduction. It's possible to start writing real programs very quickly with Haskell, and that is what this book is primarily about.

I will let you in on a little secret: the first time I tried learning Haskell, I failed miserably. No language ever felt this confusing and strange to me (except for Prolog and Uiua, maybe). It took me many years to revisit Haskell, and I couldn't be happier that I did!

What changed the second time around was the introduction. I already had a few years of experience with other functional programming languages at that point and was fully entrenched in the academic jargon commonly found in Haskell discourse. First and foremost, I understood how to apply it, and since a language only makes sense once you can meaningfully apply it to a problem you are facing, I think this aspect is vital to learning the language. In this book, I want to highlight exactly that.

But why even learn Haskell? What do we get out of it? Other than bragging rights, we learn a whole new way of structuring programs and thinking about problem-solving. Haskell is a pure functional programming language, and it will teach us to minimize state and make our programs fundamentally easier to understand. Apart from that, knowing how to apply Haskell to real problems will give you one more tool in your toolbox and make you a better programmer. Learning other functional languages after learning Haskell is also usually much simpler. Whether you want to learn Haskell to write more correct software, just out of curiosity, or because you want to broaden your horizons, this book will serve as your guide into the deep and wonderful world Haskell can be.

acknowledgments

No book is just willed into existence out of thin air by a lone author in an afternoon (oh, I wish!), and the book you are reading right now is no exception. It would not have been possible without the tireless work of many people and invaluable input by many, many more.

First and foremost, I want to thank the people in my life closest to me: my parents for their continued support throughout my life. Without you, I would not be where I am right now, and I will forever be grateful. Additionally, I want to thank Ali for always listening to my monologue-ish rants about programming.

Next, I want to extend my gratitude to the team at Manning, especially my editors, Patrick Barb and Katie Sposato, for their encouraging words and patience with me and this book. Thanks are reserved for Alexander Vershilov for directing my focus on the technical aspects of Haskell in this book. Alexander has worked for the last 15 years as a software engineer, has a PhD in Physics, and now leads a team of Haskell engineers who are building an educational product. Many thanks also to Ivan Martinović for his support on the technical side of the book writing process. Special thanks to Timo von Holtz for the technical proofreading of this book. This project would have never been brought to fruition without all your guidance.

Thanks also go out to the countless reviewers of this book: Alex Mason, Alexy Vyskubov, Andy Jennings, Ankit Mittal, Anton Rich, Cameron Presley, Clifford Thurber, David Paccoud, Damian Esteban, Dan Sheikh, Ernesto Bossi, Ernesto Garcia, Frans Oilinki, Gowtham Sadasivam, Gregorio Piccoli, Gunnar Ahlberg, Jack Kelly, Joel Holmes, Juraldinio Shikin, Kai Gellien, Katia Patkin, Kristof Semjen, Keith L. Mannock,

Kevin Cheung, Magnus Therning, Manzur Mukhitdinov, Marco Perone, Mark Elston, Michael D. Roach, Paul Silisteanu, Patrick Regan, Richard Tobias, Satej Kumar Sahu, Stefan Turalski, Stefano Paluello, Thad Meyer, and Vinicios Wentz. Your suggestions helped make this a better book.

Finally, I would be amiss if I didn't thank the wonderful Haskell community, not just for breathing life into this language but for continuously innovating with tireless commitment. Haskellers are some of the smartest, most talented, and well-meaning people I have ever met, and I hope this book introduces some new people to this awe-inspiring community.

about this book

Learn Haskell by Example aims to teach Haskell from the ground up by building practical applications instead of tiresome exercises. Too often, Haskell is regarded as a purely academic language. Away with this preconceived notion! Haskell is as practical as we need it to be.

By setting the focus on the application of the language, the reader will get a better understanding of its inherent and fundamental strengths as well as how its beautiful abstractions are not just a thought experiment but a real tool for real work.

Who should read this book

This book is for programmers and software engineers who already know at least one programming language and want to dip their toes into functional programming with Haskell. Prior exposure to functional programming is not required. While this book does not serve as a comprehensive study of the language, it serves as an entry point that will enable the reader to, first and foremost, write their own code.

How this book is organized: A road map

This book covers nine different software projects throughout 15 chapters.

Concepts of the language are explained when they are needed. The chapters are divided as follows:

- Chapter 1 is an introduction to Haskell and the book. It covers some history and the very basics of functional programming without going into the specifics of Haskell code.

- Chapter 2 starts with an introductory project: Caesar's cipher, an ancient encryption algorithm.
- Chapter 3 and 4 introduce a clone of the `nl` tool to number lines of text input, which serves as the first executable program introduced in this book.
- Chapter 5 and 6 are more focused on handling data and designing algorithms with an algorithm to solve the word ladder game.
- Chapter 7 and 8 introduce a practical tool to parse, serialize, search in, and modify CSV files.
- Chapter 9 is focused on property testing, covering practical tips on how to write test suites for our software.
- Chapter 10 and 11 cover writing a software synthesizer with a built-in domain-specific language for composing music.
- Chapter 12 and 13 introduce a library to parse image data and provide a parallelized image transformation pipeline.
- Chapter 14 and 15 cover working with exceptions in a file synchronization application.
- Chapter 16 and 17 teach the reader how to write a server for a REST API using JSON, a database for persistence, and an automatically generated client application.

In general, each chapter builds on the knowledge acquired in previous chapters, so chapters should not be skipped. Even if a project isn't necessarily for you, you should still understand the core concepts of a chapter before moving on to the next.

About the code

This book contains many examples of source code both in numbered listings and in line with normal text. In both cases, source code is formatted in a `fixed-width font` `like this` to separate it from ordinary text. Sometimes code is also **in bold** to highlight code that has changed from previous steps in the chapter, such as when a new feature adds to an existing line of code.

In many cases, the original source code has been reformatted; we've added line breaks and reworked indentation to accommodate the available page space in the book. In rare cases, even this was not enough, and listings include line-continuation markers (➟). Additionally, comments in the source code have often been removed from the listings when the code is described in the text. Code annotations accompany many of the listings, highlighting important concepts.

You can get executable snippets of code from the liveBook (online) version of this book at https://livebook.manning.com/book/learn-haskell-by-example. The complete code for the examples in the book is available for download from the Manning website at https://www.manning.com/books/learn-haskell-by-example, and from GitHub at https://github.com/phagenlocher/learn-haskell-by-example.

liveBook discussion forum

Purchase of *Learn Haskell by Example* includes free access to liveBook, Manning's online reading platform. Using liveBook's exclusive discussion features, you can attach comments to the book globally or to specific sections or paragraphs. It's a snap to make notes for yourself, ask and answer technical questions, and receive help from the author and other users. To access the forum, go to https://livebook.manning .com/book/learn-haskell-by-example/discussion. You can also learn more about Manning's forums and the rules of conduct at https://livebook.manning.com/discussion.

Manning's commitment to our readers is to provide a venue where a meaningful dialogue between individual readers and between readers and the author can take place. It is not a commitment to any specific amount of participation on the part of the author, whose contribution to the forum remains voluntary (and unpaid). We suggest you try asking the author some challenging questions lest his interest stray! The forum and the archives of previous discussions will be accessible from the publisher's website as long as the book is in print.

Other online resources

There are many great resources online that you can additionally check out:

- "What I Wish I Knew When Learning Haskell" by Stephen Diehl (https:// github.com/sdiehl/wiwinwlh)
- The Haskell Wiki (https://wiki.haskell.org/Haskell)
- *Haskell for Imperative Programmers* by yours truly (https://www.youtube.com/play-list?list=PLe7Ei6viL6jGp1Rfu0dil1JH1SHk9bgDV)

about the author

PHILIPP HAGENLOCHER holds a master's degree in computer science from the Technical University of Munich with a strong background in formal methods and functional programming. He is a full-time Haskell developer, working on distributed systems with a need for absolute program correctness. Philipp has been passionate about teaching and educating others on functional concepts for a long time, and from experience, he knows the difficulties a reader might have. His YouTube video series "Haskell for Imperative Programmers," has amassed over one million views.

about the cover illustration

The figure on the cover of *Learn Haskell by Example*, titled "Femme de Saint-Pierre," or "Woman of Saint-Pierre," is taken from a book by Louis Curmer published in 1841. Each illustration is finely drawn and colored by hand.

In those days, it was easy to identify where people lived and what their trade or station in life was just by their dress. Manning celebrates the inventiveness and initiative of the computer business with book covers based on the rich diversity of regional culture centuries ago, brought back to life by pictures from collections such as this one.

Introduction

1

Complex software is all around us, and we, as programmers, need tools to construct it. Mainly, we need programming languages that can facilitate and ease our development process and Haskell, a state-of-the-art language providing a mix of various cutting-edge technologies, is exactly that. Featuring an impressive amount of language features mixed with a certain elegance that few other languages can achieve, Haskell has become shrouded in legend and myth ... and we are going to take a look behind the curtain!

In this book, we will cover the implementation of various small (some might even call them *tiny*) projects. Some of them are just for fun, some of them are useful tools, and some of them were chosen to specifically show you, the reader, how to effectively use Haskell to create fast, safe, and reliable software. In following along

1

with these projects, you will learn the ins and outs of writing software using some of the most elegant and elaborate programming models.

If you have researched Haskell before and thought, "I don't know where to start" or were unsure about the practicality of it, don't worry. This book does not require any prior knowledge about any of Haskell's features or functional programming in general. We will start slowly with simple algorithms and end by writing our own web servers!

So jump in. The journey is worth it!

1.1   *What is Haskell?*

If you have picked up this book, there is a good chance you already have some idea of what Haskell is. You know that it is a programming language, you most likely know that it is a *functional* programming language, and you probably have heard of the unique nature of some of its features. But why would you use Haskell, and what is it that makes it special?

1.1.1   *Abstraction and theory*

Firstly, Haskell features many high-level abstractions, such as algebraic data types, type classes, and monads, all of which will be explored in this book. These abstractions allow us to write neat, composable, and clean code that lets us generalize complexities into reusable functionalities. Why is that a good thing? It saves time and avoids a lot of headaches when debugging. It is very common to implement algorithms only once in Haskell and then reuse them in different contexts over and over again. Why write a sorting algorithm for multiple different data types, when you could just write it once?

A special property of Haskell is its direct connection to academia and contemporary programming language research. Other languages typically are born from an industrial need. This is reflected heavily in their architectural design. Java serves as a prime example, since many low-level design decisions were first made due to the advertised *write once, run anywhere* promise. Later, specification changes came with the *Enterprise Edition*, promising a well-designed API for web services and distributed computing. Haskell, on the other hand, doesn't have such a background. It was built with modern results from type theory and programming language design, focusing on simple concepts from which the language was built. This makes Haskell much more focused on program correctness than other languages, leading to design decisions that heavily favor safety.

However, that does not mean that performance has been neglected in Haskell. Its compiler is an *optimizing compiler*, which means it will try to analyze the source code and perform rewriting steps to decrease its execution time. In certain situations, aggressive optimizations can even lead to code with a performance comparable to low-level languages, such as C! Haskell also features powerful libraries for parallelism, concurrency, and asynchronous computations, making it simple to write multithreaded code to improve performance even further—all the while, you, as a programmer, do not have to worry about pesky details, such as memory management, since the runtime uses a garbage collector.

Haskell is not an ordinary functional programming language but a *pure functional programming language*. By *pure*, we mean that functions we write in our programs are much like functions in the mathematical sense. They have input and produce some output but have no *side effects*. This means functions can only work with the data we put into them and cannot, for example, read additional data from files or the network. Is that helpful? *Yes!* It makes Haskell programs easier to analyze and understand just by reading the code itself and generally leads to fewer bugs and more reliable software. We will explore this concept at great length in this book, since it forces us to think about programming differently than we normally do.

1.1.2 A safe place

So how does Haskell compare to other languages, keeping the aforementioned design decisions in mind? An important attribute of programming languages is their *strength of assertions*, meaning how many rules on the programming semantics the compiler or interpreter of that language enforces. This brings about two qualities in programming languages: *freedom* and *safety*. *Freedom* specifies how unrestricted the programmer is in their ability to modify the program state and work with resources such as memory, files, sockets and threads. *Safety* specifies the likeliness of a written program to be inherently free of undefined behavior and bugs. Both have an inverse correlation. If the language allows many dangerous operations its safety decreases, but if these operations are simply forbidden the safety increases while the freedom to do dangerous things decreases since these operations are either impossible or have a much higher implementation overhead. This relationship is represented in figure 1.1.

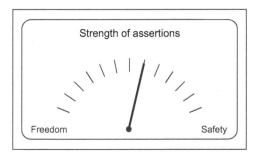

Figure 1.1 The Freedom-Safety relationship

Programming languages have to make compromises when it comes to these qualities. Many dynamically typed scripting languages, like Python, allow almost everything that you could want. As a result of this design decision, the inherent safety of these languages is very low. It is easy to write scripts and it is even easier to write scripts that fail on execution. Statically typed, compiled languages try to increase safety by letting the compiler perform sanity checks, which forces the programmer to adhere to the type system's rules to produce programs that are allowed to be executed. The stronger the assertions the compiler makes are, the less error-prone the language becomes but the harder it also is to write a program that the compiler allows. For example, Python allows for values of arbitrary type to be passed to any function which makes it very easy to write polymorphic functions but also is prone to errors since you can not necessarily be sure of the types the arguments of your functions have. In a language like C, your compiler at least checks if the types of variables match, but it gives you free rein over the memory, which makes it easy to manipulate data on a low level but might lead to undefined behaviors. Java uses a garbage collector as an abstraction to deal with this problem but still lets you share object references across processes, which can lead to race conditions. A language like Rust disallows such behavior, ruling out many types of unexpected behaviors, but still allows for mutable state. Haskell is a language on the *safe* side of programming, having many restrictions like enforcing immutable data and not allowing side effects without the usage of special programming models.

In figure 1.2 we can see how we can understand the process of compiling programs as a pipeline. The programmer writes (syntactically correct) source code which is then used by the compiler (or interpreter) to create executable binary code. The stricter the compiler enforces rules the "harder" it becomes for the programmer. However, this filters away many programs which might eventually fail while executing. So if the compiler is very strict there is a good chance that if the program compiles it produces the correct result and does not crash while executing or produce undefined behavior. This means that the compiler makes sure that the programmer's intent is correctly reflected by the executable code. Haskell falls into this *safe* category. To help you understand the uniqueness and helpfulness of Haskell's safe paradigm, we will start with a little bit of background.

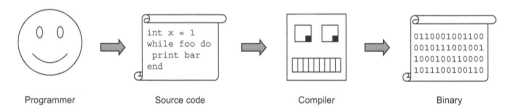

| Programmer | Source code | Compiler | Binary |

Figure 1.2   The programming pipeline

1.2   *The pure functional way*

Since the dawn of programming, we have been confronted with a question that is easily stated but almost impossible to solve: *How do we know that our programs are correct?* With this question, we don't just want to know that our programs don't crash but that they indeed have the intended behavior we as programmers specified. Many resources are used for quality assurance and testing in software development. This makes it seem like we simply can't trust the programs we wrote. Why is that? When we write a function, don't we know what it does? For the most part, we do! However, there is one thing that often cannot be correctly accounted for: *state*. When a program is running, it has some internal state, which consists of the data the program is working with (e.g., the values of our variables) and the execution context (e.g., what system the program is running on and what its environment is). In the last 50 years, many attempts have been made to work with state in a more manageable way. One answer was to split up the state and package it into objects, associated with some interface to work with that state in a controlled manner. That is essentially what object-oriented programming is. However, there is another way of dealing with this problem.

1.2.1 A declarative recipe

What if, instead of trying to split up the state, we tried to simply *minimize* it? The less of that pesky stuff around, the better, right? This idea is at the heart of *pure functional* programming used by Haskell!

For the uninitiated, here is a little excursion into the world of functional programming. What is it? First, let us think of how nonfunctional programs usually work. Such a program can be thought of as a sequence of instructions, like in a recipe. They tell you the steps you need to take to arrive at a finished result. That might look something like this:

1 Melt *butter* in a pan on low heat.
2 Add *chocolate*.
3 Beat *8 eggs* in a bowl.
4 Add *flour, sugar,* and *baking powder*.
5 Mix well with a hand mixer.
6 Add the *butter and chocolate mixture*.
7 Pour the *chocolate cake batter* onto a baking sheet.
8 Bake for 25 minutes at 200°C.

In the end, following the steps will result in a chocolate cake! But what if we now want to create a lemon cake? It's possible that the recipe would look almost identical to our chocolate cake but will vary in step 2, where we don't add chocolate but something lemony. So if we wanted to write a lemon cake recipe, we would need to copy most steps. This poses a problem. Which steps do we copy? We realize that steps 1 and 2 have nothing to do with making a generic cake batter—they are additional steps. Step 6 is also highly specialized and cannot be copied into other recipes, since you need a butter and chocolate mixture to add it to something. This is a problem of *state*! After completing each step, you have changed the state (the finished products in your kitchen in this case), and some steps depend on this state. An instruction like "mix well" only makes sense when you have something to mix!

So what would a *functional* recipe look like?

- A *butter and chocolate mixture* consists of melting *butter* and *chocolate* over low heat.
- A *cake batter* consists of *8 beaten eggs, flour, sugar,* and *baking powder*.

- A *chocolate cake batter* is a *cake batter* mixed with a *butter and chocolate mixture* using a hand mixer.
- A *chocolate cake* is a *chocolate cake batter* baked in an oven for 25 minutes at 200°C.

We immediately see a profound difference. The recipe doesn't tell us what to do, but how our intermediate results are defined! However, from this, we can easily infer the steps we need to take to produce the finished *chocolate cake*. We first have to create the chocolate cake batter, for which we need the general *cake batter* mixed with the *butter and chocolate mixture*. Both, in turn, have their own definition. So by recursively looking at the definitions, we arrive at the most basic steps (adding basic ingredients), from which we can then produce the desired result. So what if we wanted to create a lemon cake recipe? It's easy! We need to switch out the *butter and chocolate mixture* in the third step with something lemony, and we are done! The definition of a *cake batter* stays the same. We have no state in our recipe; we only have definitions for intermediate results. This also means this recipe doesn't have a fixed order. It doesn't matter if you first create the *cake batter* or the *butter and chocolate mixture*. You, as the baker, can decide which is more convenient for you!

1.2.2 *From cake to program*

So how does this relate to programming? If we imagine the ingredients, mixtures, and cakes to be variables, we realize that in the imperative recipe, they change over time, being modified by our instructions. In the functional recipe, they never change; they are produced once. The steps are not reliant on the state of those variables but only on their existence. Once a variable is needed, we can evaluate it. In the functional recipe, some steps contain information on *how* to perform transformations, like *baked in an oven for 25 minutes at 200°C*. In software, this would be represented by a function, which, in turn, can be parametrized. This is one of the main properties of functional programming: functions are *first-class objects*. They can be passed as arguments to other functions!

This type of programming is also called *declarative* programming, since the program can be interpreted as a single, big definition made up of other smaller or even recursive definitions. This approach makes it much easier to create reusable code, since the same definition might be used in different contexts. This makes it clear that we don't want to have mutable variables, since they don't follow a clear definition but change over time. However, some functional programming languages allow mutable state. Those languages might be *functional*, but they are not *pure*. For a programming language to be *pure*, functions cannot have side effects. A *side effect* is any interaction with the state of the program outside of a function while being inside that function. This means functions are not allowed to do several things:

- Input (reading)/output (writing) of
  - Files
  - Network sockets

  - Threads or other processes
  - Databases
- Values that change between accesses
  - Random numbers
  - Information on the current time
- Access memory
  - Reading from memory directly
  - Writing to memory

Of course, there is a way of doing all these operations in pure languages, by controlling the effects using a variety of software design patterns. In Haskell, the chosen paradigm is called *monadic programming*, which we will eventually go into. This way of programming is very different than the programming you are probably used to and forces us, as programmers, to rethink many concepts we have taken for granted. Interestingly, modern programming languages employ an increasing number of functional concepts and features—be it Java, TypeScript, Python, or even C++. Additionally, many new languages designed by large companies leave behind historically popular paradigms, like imperative or object-oriented programming, instead focusing on a more functional design. F# (Microsoft) and Reason (Facebook), which are two direct descendants of the functional programming language OCaml, serve as two examples. Understanding functional concepts is an important step to future proofing yourself as a developer.

1.2.3 *It's all for simplicity*

Additionally, Haskell uses a large number of exotic and foreign concepts as its main language features. Some of them include the following:

- Monadic programming
- Type classes
- Lazy evaluation
- Software transactional memory
- Generalized algebraic data types

But why? What is it for? In software engineering, we have figured out many concepts to help our architecture stay maintainable—*keep it simple, stupid* (KISS) and *don't repeat yourself* (DRY) are two examples. While we try our best to fit our implementations to follow these rules, we, as software engineers, often have to fight against the programming languages we are working with to achieve these goals. Sometimes, we just have to copy code from one class to another because otherwise, we would need to refactor our class hierarchy, and sometimes, we cannot keep our procedures short and simple, since there is no way to further break up the process we are trying to describe. Haskell's declarative approach mixed with its high abstraction potential doesn't just make it simple to follow clean coding principles but actively aids the developer in creating maintainable code, which is why the language has become more and more popular within the software industry. Haskell's academic roots show in almost every language feature it presents. These features were not just created as fun thought experiments but have practical value if you know how to use them.

Haskell's pure nature makes it easy to write tests for our functionalities. If the specification of our functionalities is clear, tests can often reflect that specification exactly. We don't have to write adapter classes to plug our code into some test framework; we rarely need to set up fake environments to reflect a real production environment, and we generally have an easier time determining good code coverage than in other languages. All we test are functions without side effects. Observing a function's behavior is as simple as looking at its output directly.

Industrial applications and testability aside, Haskell also has a passionate open source community that actively develops tools and libraries for the language. This passion might be fueled by intellectual curiosity or the need for a quicker and easier way to develop software, but I think there is a much more important reason: Haskell is fun! It's that easy. Once you've gotten the hang of it, Haskell feels like a powerful magic wand, just waiting to be activated with the right spell, unleashing its magic on the digital realm. Developers making a career of writing Haskell code often cite a passion for program correctness, simplicity, and applied theory as their motivation, but I believe this all boils down to something much simpler: the joy of constructing complex and intricate software components that never feel overbearing, never seem too complicated, and always have the potential to be made *even easier* to work with. In short, it's the *joy of programming*. I know that my colleagues and I do it, at least partially, for this exact reason.

1.3   *Usage of abstraction*

It is clear that no programming language is universally useful. Haskell is highly abstract. It *redefines* what a high-level language is. This means that the source code the developer writes is far removed from the actual instructions run by the processor in the end. This has clear upsides and downsides.

1.3.1   *The good parts*

Abstraction shines when complexity becomes overbearing, and modern software is full of complexities. Haskell makes them manageable, which makes it a prime candidate for usage in cryptographic and distributed systems. By minimizing state, the developer minimizes the possibilities for bugs and unexpected behavior, which is why implementing security-related protocols and web server logic is almost stress free. Declarative languages are generally very definition heavy, which is great if the program logic is mostly based on definitions. This is true for compilers, transpilers, and programs for file conversion.

However, Haskell is a general-purpose programming language. Generally speaking, any program could be written in it. The vast number of libraries available allows the language to be used in a wide variety of industry applications. Haskell truly shines in building large software with varied data sources, since its fundamental core is *composition* of disparate software components. After all, the whole is greater than the sum of its parts.

As beginners to the language, we might ask: What projects can we complete in this language? Good choices make tools with well-defined input and output. Think of UNIX tools. They follow a simple philosophy: do one thing, and do it *well.* They often read their input, process it, and produce some output. Haskell's pure nature is ideal for such tools. Even if the actual task becomes slightly complicated, like computing advanced statistics on a bunch of data, it often can be modeled very easily. A nice example of such a tool is *Pandoc,* an open source tool used for the conversion of documents of varying file types. It can take documents in, for example, HTML, OpenDocument, or LaTeX formats and output equivalent documents in other formats, such as DocBook, EPUB, or PDF.

Somewhat different from many other languages, Haskell was born in the world of academia, not the industry. Thus, it is no wonder that many programming projects in Haskell (by hobbyists and professionals alike) revolve around building compilers, interpreters, and domain-specific languages. What could be more fun than programming in a language someone else wrote? Programming in a language you yourself wrote! Haskell allows you to define your own operators, which lets you create your own domain-specific language components within Haskell itself. The language's academic roots are also shown in the many proof assistants and automatic reasoning tools written in it. These applications can be used for mathematical proofs or testing software specifications.

Haskell's ability to simplify complex software architectures makes it a popular choice in backend software for data analysis or complex data management. It is used by large companies, like Facebook, Target, Barclays, Standard Chartered, and NASA, in data-intensive applications, and there is a good reason for it: Haskell code tends to be more reliable, easier to refactor, and much simpler to test and verify. If you need a "safe bet" when writing software, Haskell is an excellent choice.

I find Haskell to be an excellent choice for rapid prototyping because it is easy to create simple applications with just a few lines of code and then extend those lines, often without the need for any refactoring. You can turn a single-threaded processing model into a multithreaded one with just a few lines of code and no additional changes. You can often switch out configuration file structures by simply switching from one parser to the other without any other major changes. You can prototype an application with file input and then, much later down the line, switch to network input, often without changing most parts of your system. Haskell applications often grow very naturally with your changing needs.

1.3.2 The bad parts

Abstractions are great. However, Haskell is as far removed from low-level code as a space shuttle is from the Mariana Trench. This has a profound downside: as a programmer, you are never fully in control of what is going on in your program. Between your intentions and the actual hardware sits a runtime you have little to no control over. Threads are being handled by it. Memory gets allocated whenever the runtime pleases. The garbage collector starts acting whenever it deems it necessary. Of course, in some ways, this makes the developer's job easier, but it also makes the language largely unsuitable for several applications:

- Real-time critical applications
- State-heavy programs, such as video games or multimedia applications
- Device drivers or operating systems

It is in no way impossible to write such applications with Haskell. However, it will likely prove a challenge and require careful study of the technical aspects of Haskell, which is outside of the scope of this book.

1.4 The things we learn

Some people claim you need to have studied mathematics to learn Haskell. This book tries to once and for all break this stereotype by explaining the fundamental concepts of the language in an easy-to-understand manner. You don't have to have any prior exposure to functional programming at all! However, you should be familiar with procedural or imperative programming (C, Java, Python, etc.) and have a basic understanding of algorithms and data structures as well as operating and file systems. The ideal reader has

- At least one to two years of programming experience
- Worked on different (small) software projects and knows the problems that can arise in real-world applications
- Some basic knowledge of operating systems (specifically UNIX)

Much different from other materials, this book will not give you a crash course on the most advanced techniques and concepts in Haskell but highlight fun, creative, and useful projects, showing you how to tackle certain problems that arise when writing real applications. The chapters will also present best practices and explain why they are important. Haskell can be an ocean of foreign concepts, and this book is not trying to give you a deep dive. It, rather, tries to be the diving instructor showing you the safer, shallower depths of this ocean. By the end of the final chapter, you should then feel comfortable to board a submarine and explore the deepest depths yourself. It's going to be an amazing journey.

This book is designed to cover a wide variety of projects. We will begin by writing beginner-friendly tools, like a simple (but clever) artificial intelligence for a special variety of the game "word ladder" and a CSV tool capable of neatly formatting a CSV file and printing it as a table in ASCII form as well as providing additional features, like searching. Later in the book, we will cover more data-intensive work, like working with audio and image files and how to manipulate them within our software, even creating our own musical synthesizer and multithreaded image processing library. Of course, no book on software would be complete without trying to emulate the big boys by creating our own microservice—a web server capable of answering requests by performing actions and storing data in a type-safe manner! All the while, we will have a chance to look at some advanced Haskell libraries in action!

We will mostly focus on writing applications used on UNIX-like systems, like Linux, BSD, or macOS. If you want to use Haskell on Windows, that is possible by using Windows Subsystem for Linux (WSL). The projects will consist of applications running on the command line or terminal. This is a deliberate choice, since it simplifies the development process, allowing us to focus and concentrate on minimal user interfaces without needing to worry about GUI programming.

After reading this book, readers will feel comfortable using Haskell, implementing real-world projects, and avoiding the pitfalls beginners typically fall into. Additionally, readers will know how to apply the learned functional concepts universally to other languages.

Summary

- Haskell is a pure functional programming language, focusing on safe and composable code.
- Safe code disallows dangerous operations, which translates to fewer bugs and undefined behavior, thus better reflecting the programmer's intention.
- Haskell has strong roots in academia and presents many results from contemporary programming theory in its feature set.
- Haskell is a garbage-collected and compiled language, featuring native support for parallelism and concurrency.
- Pure functions are functions with no side effects, only consuming some input and producing some output.
- Functional and declarative programming focuses on the definitions of intermediate results instead of providing a sequence of instructions.
- A side effect is any interaction with the state of the program outside of a function while being inside that function.
- Haskell's declarative approach mixed with its abstractions aids the programmer in following clean coding principles.
- Haskell's abstractions simplify complex software architectures, making it a popular choice in backend software for data analysis or complex data management.

Ancient secret keeping on modern machines

In the last chapter, we learned what Haskell is and discussed its peculiar language design decisions. We also learned some specifics on pure functions and how pure functional programs, such as the ones we write with Haskell, are structured. Although it is essential to understand these concepts, it's not much use talking about them, without getting our hands a bit dirty. You can't learn the application of theory without applying anything. So let's get down to implementing our first project!

When learning any programming language, one has to start somewhere. While I could bore you with mathematics or some other highly academic exercises, the topics in this book are a bit more playful. Some people might even call them fun; however, you don't have to go that far. This chapter is mainly an introduction to Haskell's syntax and how to go about writing programs. Since Haskell's main principles are somewhat foreign (compared to other programming languages) it would be good if you could unlearn some of the patterns you know from programming. Mutable variables? Static data? Imperative control flow? You should forget about these things for now, since the world we will travel to knows no such dark magic.

This description has been somewhat colorful, so let me explain: Haskell's *pure functional* design can be intimidating at first. If you have no prior experience with functional languages, the concepts in this chapter might seem strange. This stems from the fact that this kind of program language design is much different from languages you might be used to and feel familiar with. For example, Haskell has no loops! Of course, there are many ways around this limitation. Truthfully, we don't need any loops, but this means we need to rethink many things about programming.

While this might seem intimidating at first, it is a journey that is well worth it. The concepts in Haskell are universal and can be implemented in almost any other language. Learning pure functional programming means learning a wholly different way of thinking about writing programs and ensuring whatever you write is correct!

This chapter will begin by showing you how to set up a new Haskell project, using the interactive mode of the Haskell compiler to prototype some code. Then, many fundamental data types of Haskell are introduced in conjunction with how to specify types for our functions and expressions. An introduction to writing functions in Haskell is also given. Following that, working with lists and strings will also be discussed. The discussion on functions will be further elaborated by learning the usage of guards and pattern matching. The chapter will conclude by introducing and using the built-in `map` function.

2.1 A primer on Haskell

Modern computer systems are almost always reliant on an external network to be used effectively. Be it for timekeeping using NTP or PTP, storing data in distributed NoSQL databases, or just streaming video footage of cats in 4K resolution in the evening, the possibilities are endless. However, with this, comes a profound cost: the need to protect our personal data being sent over public networks. We can't just scream our bank details into the woods and hope nobody hears it!

As you might have already guessed, the solution to this problem is *encryption*. This is usually achieved by using a procedure that encodes information with a secret key that parties share. Cryptography has become an ever-present part of our lives, and its research field keeps presenting us with algorithms and procedures of ever-growing complexity to make it possible to keep a secret.

The encryption scheme we want to tackle is called *Caesar's cipher*, a rather primitive way to keep secrets. While it is not relevant for real-world usage, it will teach us about the basics of functional programming, nonetheless.

2.1.1 Caesar's cipher

How does this ancient algorithm work? The cipher substitutes each letter in an alphabet with another letter by shifting the original alphabet by a certain offset. Thus, you encrypt the letters by choosing a new letter that has a certain distance, based on the positions of those letters in the alphabet. You can imagine the alphabet as a wheel, where all letters are ordered in a circle. Starting on a letter and turning this wheel by a certain offset will give you a new letter. This idea is illustrated in figure 2.1.

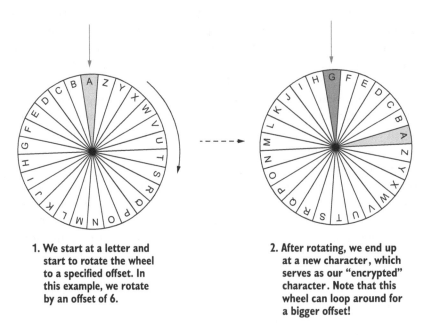

1. We start at a letter and start to rotate the wheel to a specified offset. In this example, we rotate by an offset of 6.

2. After rotating, we end up at a new character, which serves as our "encrypted" character. Note that this wheel can loop around for a bigger offset!

Figure 2.1   Letter substitution wheel

By transforming every single letter in a message, we can encrypt it! The offset used for the transformation is the *encryption key* for the algorithm and needs to be known by the communicating parties. When decrypting the message, one can do the same process backward and get the old message back. You can see an example in figure 2.2, where a little message is encrypted with an offset of 5.

When only encrypting letters from the basic Latin alphabet (and treating uppercase and lowercase letters with their own alphabets), we can observe an interesting symmetry. When using a rotation offset of 13, the encryption and decryption cancel out, meaning you can use the exact same method for encryption and decryption. This special case of Caesar's cipher is known as *ROT13* and is commonly used as a type of word scrambler, since it's easy to implement. Some editors, such as Vim and Emacs, even have ROT13 built in! Vfa'g gung arng?

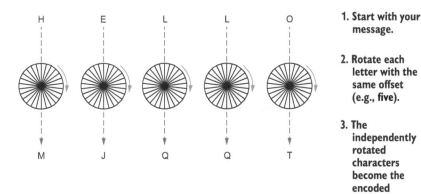

1. **Start with your message.**

2. **Rotate each letter with the same offset (e.g., five).**

3. **The independently rotated characters become the encoded message.**

Figure 2.2   Encryption with Caesar's cipher

WARNING   For the love of your and everybody else's data, *never* use this encryption in any of your applications!

2.1.2   A new project

So let's start by creating a new project with stack. If you haven't already installed stack, please refer to appendix A. Once the toolchain is running on your computer, you can open a command line on your operating system. On macOS, this could be iTerm, while on Windows, it might be cmd, and on Linux, the choices are much more varied. Then, we can start by navigating to your desired workspace location and running the following command:

```
stack new caesar
```

This will create a new directory called caesar, which already contains a premade project structure for our Haskell project.

Let's go over the folder structure introduced by stack, which can be seen in listing 2.1. It contains files with meta information, like the changelog, a license text, and a README file for usage explanations if this project were ever to be released. caesar.cabal, package.yaml, and stack.yaml are important for configuring dependencies and compilation options of our projects; however, we are not going to touch them in this project.

Now comes the meat of the project: the app and src directories. The app directory has modules that contain the program's entry point, called main. This is where compiled executables would start, much like in languages such as C or Java. The src directory contains the library code, meaning all the modules, types, and function definitions that can be used in a standalone library. This allows us to use the same functionalities across multiple executables or compile the project as a library alternatively to an executable. The last directory is test, which can be used to bundle testing suites with our library and executable code. We will explore this later in chapter 9.

Listing 2.1   The project structure for a new stack project

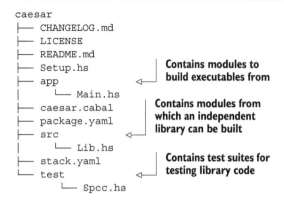

```
caesar
├── CHANGELOG.md
├── LICENSE
├── README.md
├── Setup.hs
├── app
│      └── Main.hs          Contains modules to
│                           build executables from
├── caesar.cabal
├── package.yaml            Contains modules from
├── src                     which an independent
│      └── Lib.hs           library can be built
├── stack.yaml
└── test                    Contains test suites for
       └── Spec.hs          testing library code
```

The only file that is important to us right now is Lib.hs. We will use this file to write our functions and use them in the interpreted mode of the Haskell compiler. Speaking of which … let's try out the read–eval–print loop (REPL) to get familiar with some of Haskell's syntax. You can use

```
stack repl
```

This will fire up GHCi, the interpreted mode of the Glasgow Haskell Compiler (GHC). The prompt looks like this:

```
ghci>
```

If your current working directory is a project created with stack, the modules and definitions are automatically loaded into GHCi, so you can try them out. Now, we can start typing some Haskell! Let's try out some basic arithmetic:

```
ghci> a = 1 :: Int
ghci> b = 2 :: Int
ghci> c = a + b
ghci> c
3
```

As we can see from the evaluation of the terms, we can define *variables* in our code to associate values with names. Each input we make in the REPL is being evaluated. The evaluation of an assignment has no result, while evaluating a variable results in its value. Also, we see that values have types, which we indicate in Haskell using : :.

NOTE   When putting expressions like 1+1 into GHCi, they will evaluate to 2 but, additionally, give us a warning about defaulting type constraints. These will almost always pop up when we don't specify types in an expression. To disable these, you can use : set -Wno-type-defaults.

It's now time to put the *function* in *functional programming* by defining some functions. Their semantics are comparable to the semantics of other languages. The basic syntax for functions is very simple. A name is followed by a parameter list, which is followed by an equals sign (=) and a definition. Let's look at an example:

```
square x = x * x
```

This defines the function `square` with a single argument that is being multiplied by itself. Function applications look like this:

```
square 2
```

Neither in the definition nor in the application are parameters surrounded by braces or separated by commas, like in many other languages. By typing a function application like `square 2` into the REPL, we make it evaluate the function and print the result. Let us type the definition into the REPL:

```
ghci> :{
ghci| square :: Int -> Int        Starts a multiline
ghci| square x = x * x            input in GHCi
ghci| :}               Ends a multiline
ghci> square 2          input in GHCi
4
```

The type given for `square` is not strictly necessary, but omitting would cause warnings to appear. This should give you a starting ground for experimenting with Haskell. Feel free to spend a few minutes in GHCi to get a feel for things to come.

While the REPL is good for prototyping and rudimentary code testing, it can quickly become cumbersome to work with, especially when writing bigger functions. This is why we want to turn our attention to Lib.hs in our project, where most of the implementation will reside.

2.1.3 The first module

The file will have a very basic structure and highlight the most basic aspects of a Haskell *module*. Modules contain our code, consisting of definitions and implementations. They provide us with a way of structuring our projects by grouping related code. In general, their name has to be equal to the file path (except for Main, depending on the project's configuration). In this simple case, the module lives on the highest level of the src directory, so its name is just the filename without the file suffix. Additionally, modules can define an *export list*, which indicates which definitions should be made visible to other modules, since modules can also import other modules. The file will likely look something like the following listing.

Listing 2.2   A simple example module created by stack

```
module Lib            ⟵————— Defines the module name
    ( someFunc       ⟵—┐
    ) where              └── Specifies the export list

someFunc :: IO ()              ⟵————— Gives the type signature
someFunc = putStrLn "someFunc"   ⟵—┐
                                    └── Provides the definition
```

This module serves no real purpose but to be an illustrative example of how a module can be constructed. We see a single definition of an *IO action* with the name someFunc. This definition is exported by the export list in parentheses after the name of the module. We will learn what an IO action is in chapter 3, but for now, we are not concerned with it.

The most basic way of importing another module is with the import statement. This will import every definition from the module that was specified in its export list (or simply *everything* if no export list was specified). This is generally good if you import some utility module that provides unique functions but can lead to clashes of names otherwise. In that case, we can simply prepend the name of the module with a dot to choose the correct implementation. So instead of writing x, we would write ModuleName.x.

We now turn our attention to Main.hs, to see how the Lib module is imported and how the "main module" looks. This module is our entry point in the program, since it contains the main action. For now, we are not interested in what this action is; we can just think of it as a function that is called. This *main* is the first code that is called in our program on execution. The Main module contains an import statement importing our Lib module. Thus, someFunc is present in our Main module, since it occurs in the export list of the Lib module. The code will look like this.

Listing 2.3   A simple main module created by stack

```
module Main where

import Lib        ⟵—┘ Imports the module

main :: IO ()     ⟵————— Defines main action
main = someFunc
```

This project will be implemented solely in the Lib module and tested with GHCi, so we can ignore the Main module for now. Just so that we can make the executable compile and your IDE doesn't throw any weird errors, we change the Main module to not import Lib anymore and make its main action simply to print Hello World. This implementation looks like this:

```
module Main where

main :: IO ()
main = putStrLn "Hello World"
```

Let's go back to Lib.hs and get a bit more familiar with Haskell. We can delete the export list and `someFunc` for now. The module then looks like this:

```
module Lib where
```

Nice and empty—a fresh start! We can leave GHCi behind when defining functions and write them down in that module. In addition to defining our function, we need to export it by writing it down into an *export list*, which comes after the name of our module:

```
module Lib
  ( square,
  )
where

square :: Int -> Int
square x = x * x
```

After saving this file, we can now load it. To do that, we navigate within the command line to our project and run `stack repl`.

> **NOTE** Don't forget to add functions and types you want to expose to other modules to the *export list* of the module the definition resides in. Otherwise, the definition will not be found. While you could, alternatively, expose everything by not writing down an explicit *export list*, this is considered bad style and leads to unmanageable code later on.

The module will automatically be loaded. After that, you should be able to use the functions in the newly opened GHCi. Keep this GHCi session open, as we will use it for prototyping!

2.2 *Typical types and fantastic functions*

To structure our project properly, we should start thinking about what kinds of data we want to work with. More precisely, this means we have to think about the *types* of our data. Types are invaluable in a language like Haskell. Like some other languages, Haskell is *statically typed*, which means types are already known at compile time and cannot dynamically change. If a variable has a certain type, this type cannot change during run time. Additionally, Haskell uses *type inference*. If types are not written down, Haskell will try to figure them out from the context in which functions and variables are used. For the most part, this works flawlessly; however, in certain instances, it's necessary to tell Haskell the explicit types. This type inference enables us to write down the functions as we did in GHCi in the module, *without* writing down any types.

However, it is good style to explicitly write down types for definitions we create on our module's top level. We can do this by using *type expressions*. A basic type expression looks like this:

```
name :: type
```

It provides some type for a name (sometimes called an *identifier*). In turn, these names are a simple mapping to some values. So we are specifying that certain values should have certain types. Usually, a type expression is immediately followed by the corresponding definition, even though this is not strictly enforced. Type expressions are an interesting counterpart to the typical *semantic expressions* that make up our program. We have already seen these semantic expressions; something like x * x is a semantic expression. On cvaluation, this expression must produce some *value*. When a semantic expression has a type expression, this means the produced value has the type given by the type expression, not the actual semantic expression. We will see this difference later, when examining functions.

2.2.1 *Types on the atomic level*

So that's the primer on type expressions, but what do types look like? The easiest ones are *atomic types*. These are the most common types for our programs. Table 2.1 describes some of these.

Table 2.1 Common atomic types in Haskell

Name	Description	Examples
Bool	Boolean truth values	True and False
Char	UNICODE characters	'a', 'A', '1'
Integer	Integers with arbitrary size	-1, 9999999
Int	Integer with fixed size	-1, 10
Float	Real floating-point number with single precision	3.1415, -1, 1e2
Double	Real floating-point number with double precision	1e-2, 9.99999

As you can see from the examples, the numeric types share some values. When using these somewhat ambiguous values, Haskell's type inference kicks in and tries to infer the correct types. Knowing about these types, we can start thinking about how to implement our cipher.

Looking at figure 2.3, we can start thinking about how to implement the wheel rotation. Since every step in rotating the wheel is a discrete move from one element to the next, we know that our encryption key will be a simple Int, since it is unlikely that we need the arbitrary size from the Integer type. Our message to be encrypted will be simple letters, so a collection of `Char` values. The function we will create for this project will need to work with these types.

Rotating is a discrete movement through the letter substitution wheel in one direction.

Moving 3 steps from A ends up at D.

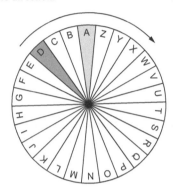

Figure 2.3   Letter substitution wheel

Something important to note about atomic types is that the provided types themselves are type expressions! So we can give a value (or semantic expression) of this type, which looks something like this:

```
kilo :: Int
kilo = 1000

mega :: Int
mega = kilo ^ (2 :: Int)

nano :: Double
nano = 1e-9
```

Here, we define values for three unit prefixes. By assigning the identifier `kilo` the type `Int`, we explicitly define it to be an integer, while `nano` is a floating-point number of type `Double`. We see that `mega` is defined by performing an operation on `kilo`, namely the exponentiation `^`. Thus, it has to be of the same type as `kilo`, since numeric operators typically consume and produce values of the same type.

2.2.2 Lists and tuples

Simple atomic types are not enough to construct useful data structures. In our case, we need something to represent a collection of letters. Luckily, Haskell features some more complex types, which we will go over in detail here.

The first one is *lists*. They are an essential building block, not just in Haskell but in many other functional programming languages as well. A list is really simple. It is a *homogenous* sequence of values, meaning that all these values have the same type. We can write down such a list as comma-separated values surrounded by square brackets. Lists have no size limit and can grow dynamically. Here are some examples:

```
intList :: [Int]
intList = [1, 2, 3]

boolList :: [Bool]
boolList = [True]

floatList :: [Float]
floatList = []

doubleList :: [Double]
doubleList = [1, 1 + 1, 1 + 2]
```

The type expression of a list is given by another type expression surrounded by square brackets, similar to how list values are written down. Since all the elements of a list must have the same type, the type arising from the bracketed type expression is the internal type of the list. The values (or expressions producing values in that list) have to have this type. In the examples, we can see that even an empty list (like `floatList`) can have a certain type. The type of a list tells us that any value from the list has a certain type, but it makes no assertions about the existence of any values in that list. Additionally, with `doubleList`, we see an example of a list containing some expressions, which later, have to evaluate to `Double` values. Here, we also see Haskell's type inference at play. The `doubleList` can be used in Haskell programs, and the compiler will correctly deduce that all the elements are of type `Double`. But why? `1` as an expression could also be an `Int`. So how does Haskell know that this value should be a `Double`? It's because of the type of `doubleList`! Haskell knows that its type is `[Double]`, so it knows that all the values in this list need to be of type `Double`!

Lists are a "bread and butter" data type of functional programming. The programming languages ML, Lisp (short for *list interpreter*), and languages derived from these two languages use lists as one of their essential data types. So learning about lists in Haskell is a skill you can transfer to many other languages, even nonfunctional ones.

Another important data type is the *tuple*. Much like lists, tuples are a sequence of values but with two differences. First, the length is fixed, and second, tuples can have multiple types! Tuples are comma-separated values surrounded by parentheses. The type expressions are also similar to the value expressions, just like they worked for lists:

```
intPair :: (Int, Int)
intPair = (0, 1)

intFloatPair :: (Int, Float)
intFloatPair = (0, 1)

intCharDoubleTriple :: (Int, Char, Double)
intCharDoubleTriple = (1, 'a', 2)
```

```
septuple :: (Int, Float, Int, Float, Int, Float, Char)
septuple = (1, 1, 1, 1, 1, 1, 'a')
```

As we can see, we can construct complex types from many different types. We are also not bound by how many different values we want to use, but we have to use at least two. This type is very helpful when constructing an association between different values.

2.2.3 Function types

Let's look at the last (and perhaps most important) data type for now: *functions*. Yes, that's right. Functions are a data type! Not just that, but *functions are values!* So far, we have written down expressions and values for basic, mostly numeric, types. Something we haven't talked about is why our previous definition of square even resulted in a function we were able to evaluate. We created a value, which we then associated with the name square. First, let's examine how to write down functions without giving them a name. These functions are called *anonymous functions*, for obvious reasons. We write them down with a so-called *lambda abstraction*. They look like this:

```
\x -> x * x
```

This is our square function from before. It takes a single argument x and produces an expression x * x. We can associate this function value with a name:

```
square = \x -> x * x
```

Here, we arrive at our previous function again! Our square function from before was the same, just written a bit differently. Let's see what the type for this value looks like:

```
square :: Int -> Int
square = \x -> x * x
```

The type expression is very similar to how the actual functional value is written down. Similar to how a function maps a variable (like x) to a value or expression (like x * x), the type makes a similar statement. The function maps an Int to another Int.

This is the type expression for a *unary function*, meaning a function that only takes a single argument. Let's look at how a *binary function* is constructed:

```
add :: Int -> Int -> Int
add = \x -> \y -> x + y
```

If a function takes some variable and produces an expression, this expression could be a function as well! We can highlight this by putting parenthesis around the "inner" function:

```
add :: Int -> (Int -> Int)
add = \x -> (\y -> x + y)
```

However, writing functions like this would not only be cumbersome but also hard to read, which is why we can use some syntactic sugar:

```
add :: Int -> Int -> Int
add = \x y -> x + y
```

Here, we see a lambda abstraction with two arguments, but we can make use of even more syntactic sugar:

```
add :: Int -> Int -> Int
add x y = x + y
```

Here, we arrive at how we usually write functions in Haskell. The arguments from a lambda abstraction can just be pulled over to the side of the function name. In many other languages, one might think about a *function signature* consisting of types for the arguments and a return type. Haskell's function-type expressions can be interpreted in the same way. The first types are the arguments, and the last type is the functions "return" type. This is highlighted in figure 2.4. The word *return* is put into quotes for a deliberate reason. In functional programs, you should not think about functions in the sense that they are *returning* a value. They are *evaluating* to a value.

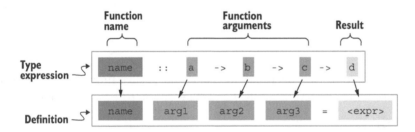

Figure 2.4   An example type expression for a function with its matching definition

2.2.4   Adding types to math

Now that we have some insight into how types are written down, we can see how `Int -> Int` would be a valid type for the `square` function. But why are we using `Int` and not some other numeric type? The truth is, there is no reason; however, we cannot just freely change the types. The `(*)` operator works with all numeric values; however, the usage of this operator forces us to use the same type for both arguments. If we were to supply the function with values of different types, we would encounter a type error:

```
ghci> a = 1 :: Int
ghci> b = 2 :: Double
ghci> a * b
```

Specifies a variable to be of type Int

Specifies a variable to be of type Double

```
<interactive>:4:5: error:
    • Couldn't match expected type 'Int' with actual type 'Double'
```

```
• In the second argument of '(*)', namely 'b'
  In the expression: a * b
  In an equation for 'it': it = a * b
```

The error description is exactly what was expected. The expression a * b produces a type error, since the usage of a forces b to be of type Int, which it is not.

Thinking back to our encryption algorithm, we can already surmise that we will need some function that can rotate a single character by a specified offset, so we will need a function of type Int -> Char -> Char. However, since we need to handle lower-case and uppercase characters differently, we need to think about how to reason about our used sets of characters and the alphabet.

2.3 A little help with the alphabet

To construct our algorithm, we need to think a bit more about how the Caesar cipher works. As we can see from figure 2.5, we *substitute* each letter with another one, which is why this cipher is a so-called *substitution cipher*. Since we want to implement this cipher, we should ask an important question: How do we work with letters and alphabets?

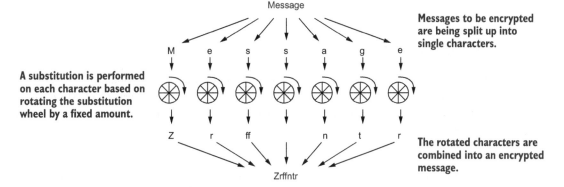

Figure 2.5 Overview of Caesar's cipher

We have already started thinking about what *types* we are working with. We need a way of specifying some offset, which could be positive or negative, so an Int will probably be fine. A message consists of some letters, so String might be fitting for it.

2.3.1 Synonymous types for readability

Wait, String? We haven't seen that before. Well, luckily, we implicitly have. Here is the full definition for the String type in Haskell:

```
type String = [Char]
```

The type keyword defines a simple synonym for a type. So String is just a synonym of a list of Char! But how do we define a String value?

```
string1 :: String
string1 = "Hello World"

string2 :: String
string2 = ['H', 'e', 'l', 'l', 'o', ' ', 'W', 'o', 'r', 'l', 'd']
```

Haskell, much like many other languages, has an explicit syntax for strings, which is simply a nicer way of writing down an instance of a list of chars. The two strings from the preceding example are, thus, identical!

Now that we know what types we are working with, we can start thinking about what we require to write this algorithm. Whatever the solution will be, the function we will write needs to produce a substitution for single characters. First, we need some utility functions to make our life easier. When encrypting messages, it is very helpful for us, to know what we are working with. We want functions telling us if a character of a String is an uppercase letter, lowercase letter, digit, or none of these. We can imagine their types to look like this:

```
isUpper :: Char -> Bool

isLower :: Char -> Bool

isDigit :: Char -> Bool

isMisc :: Char -> Bool
```

Implementing these functions requires us to decide if a Char belongs to a certain set of characters. We will call these *alphabets*. To make that clear, we want to first define a new type synonym for alphabets, which essentially are just lists of chars:

```
type Alphabet = [Char]
```

It might seem funny that the types of strings and our alphabet are completely identical. However, the types are supposed to indicate what the values of that type should be used for. A String is something we print to the screen and (for the most part) represents human-readable text. Our new type for alphabets is meant to imply that the value is a collection of characters we want to use in our substitution cipher, which can be rotated as shown in figure 2.1.

Now that we have a type for our alphabets, we can start defining them. Here is an example of the lower Latin alphabet:

```
lowerAlphabet :: Alphabet
lowerAlphabet = ['a', 'b', 'c', 'd', 'e', 'f', 'g', 'h', 'i', 'j',
➡ 'k', 'l', 'm', 'n', 'o', 'p', 'q', 'r', 's', 't', 'u', 'v', 'w',
➡ 'x', 'y', 'z']
```

But writing that is a bit verbose and cumbersome. Luckily, Haskell has a shorthand syntax for *ranges*:

```
ghci> [1 .. 10 :: Int]
[1,2,3,4,5,6,7,8,9,10]
ghci> [1, 5 .. 100 :: Int]
[1,5,9,13,17,21,25,29,33,37,41,45,49,53,57,61,65,69,73,77,81,85,89,93,97]
ghci> [0, -2 .. -10 :: Int]
[0,-2,-4,-6,-8,-10]
```

As you can see, even step sizes are supported. The great thing about those ranges is that they also work for `Char`. With that, we can define our alphabet, seen in listing 2.4.

Listing 2.4   Definitions for different Latin alphabets and digits

```
lowerAlphabet :: Alphabet
lowerAlphabet = ['a' .. 'z']

upperAlphabet :: Alphabet
upperAlphabet = ['A' .. 'Z']

digits :: Alphabet
digits = ['0' .. '9']
```

I hope you still have your GHCi session open, because now we can inspect our alphabets! After saving these definitions in Lib.hs, you can reload your GHCi session. This will re-import modules that might have changed and, thus, make the changes we made to the file instantly accessible to us:

**Reloads modules and makes new versions
of modules available after the reload**

```
ghci> :reload            ⟵┘
[3 of 3] Compiling Lib          ( .../src/Lib.hs, interpreted )
Ok, three modules loaded.
ghci> lowerAlphabet
"abcdefghijklmnopqrstuvwxyz"
ghci> upperAlphabet
"ABCDEFGHIJKLMNOPQRSTUVWXYZ"
ghci> digits
"0123456789"
```

If you have closed the pevious session, don't worry. Just save the alphabets in Lib.hs, and call `stack repl` in the project directory again.

> **WARNING**   When using `:reload` in GHCi, all local definitions and values will be deleted! The command acts like closing and reopening GHCi.

As you can see, the alphabets contain all the characters we want. However, why are they being printed as `String` values? Didn't we specify them to be of our special type for alphabets? Let us double-check that within GHCi, using the `:type` command:

```
ghci> :type lowerAlphabet
lowerAlphabet :: Alphabet
ghci> :type upperAlphabet
```

```
upperAlphabet :: Alphabet
ghci> :type digits
digits :: Alphabet
```

Indeed, they are of our custom type. However, since alphabets are a synonym for lists of chars and, in turn, they are almost always used as `String` values, Haskell prints them as such by default. When using type synonyms, they can be used interchangeably. This might raise a question: Why would we create type synonyms in the first place if they are treated identically? The short answer is *readability*. If a function takes an `Alphabet` type as an argument, we can infer that the function treats this list of characters in a special way. In this case, we can infer that we have written the function ourselves and that we are treating those values in the context of the cipher.

> ### The FilePath type
> Such usage of types for readability can be observed in the standard library as well. A special type for file paths exists, called `FilePath`; however, when observing it in GHCi, we find something interesting:
>
> ```
> ghci> :info FilePath
> type FilePath :: *
> type FilePath = String
>         -- Defined in 'GHC.IO'
> ```
>
> This special type is nothing but a normal `String` (which, in turn, is just `[Char]`)! However, this improves readability for many functions. If a function has a `FilePath` as a parameter, it is much clearer that it expects a `String` in a certain formatting. Using type synonyms this way can make your code much clearer!

When trying to figure these types, `:info` can be used to obtain information on how and where they are defined.

NOTE Instead of `:reload`, `:type`, and `:info`, you can use `:r`, `:t`, and `:i`, respectively!

2.3.2 *The kinds of letters*

Now that we have our alphabets, we can get to writing the functions that decide if a character is part of one of them. We can use a function called `elem` for that. `elem` is a *binary* function, taking two arguments: the element and a list we want to check for the element. It will return `True` if the element is present in the list and `False` if not. We are allowed to use this function on our alphabets, since their type `Alphabet` is a synonym of `[Char]`. Using this function is straightforward:

```
ghci> elem 'a' lowerAlphabet
True
ghci> elem 'a' upperAlphabet
False
```

```
ghci> elem '1' lowerAlphabet
False
ghci> elem '1' digits
True
```

Haskell has a little syntactic trick up its sleeve when using binary functions, making them a bit more readable:

```
ghci> 'a' `elem` lowerAlphabet
True
```

Any binary function can be used in an *infix notation*, using backticks! Now, we can actually read our code out loud. The expression is equivalent to the question, "Is *a* an element of the lower alphabet?" Putting everything together results in the code shown in the following listing.

Listing 2.5   Helper functions to check alphabet membership

```
isLower :: Char -> Bool
isLower char = char `elem` lowerAlphabet          ◁——| Returns True if a character
                                                       is a lowercase letter

isUpper :: Char -> Bool
isUpper char = char `elem` upperAlphabet          ◁——| Returns True if a character
                                                       is an uppercase letter

isDigit :: Char -> Bool
isDigit char = char `elem` digits             ◁——| Returns True if a
                                                   character is a digit
```

Let's test these functions in GHCi:

```
ghci> :r
[3 of 3] Compiling Lib              (.../src/Lib.hs, interpreted )
Ok, three modules loaded.
ghci> isLower 'a'
True
ghci> isLower 'A'
False
ghci> isUpper 'A'
True
ghci> isDigit '5'
True
```

2.3.3   Logical combinations

But how do we decide if a character is miscellaneous, meaning it is not part of any of these alphabets? For that, we can use Boolean operators:

```
isMisc :: Char -> Bool
isMisc char = not (isUpper char || isLower char || isDigit char)
```

The Boolean operators we can use are the logical OR (||), AND (&&), and NOT (not). They have the types one would expect from these operators:

```
ghci> :type not
not :: Bool -> Bool
ghci> :type (||)
(||) :: Bool -> Bool -> Bool
ghci> :type (&&)
(&&) :: Bool -> Bool -> Bool
```

The parentheses around the operators are needed to interpret them as functions, since that is what operators in Haskell are: functions written in infix notation. We could also write them in prefix notation:

```
ghci> (||) False True
True
ghci> (+) 1 2
3
```

Returning to our `isMisc` function, we can see that while the function is correct, it is not easy to extend further. Let's assume we would add another alphabet. Then, we would need to create another helper function and add its result to the disjunction. We don't want that. So maybe it's more helpful to check if the character in question is not an element of all the alphabets we have. This raises the question of how to combine our alphabets. The answer is the append operator for lists (`(++)`):

```
ghci> [1,2,3] ++ [4,5,6]
[1,2,3,4,5,6]
ghci> "Hello" ++ " " ++ "World!"
"Hello World!"
```

Note that this operator works on `String` values as well, since they are just lists! We can use this operator to combine our alphabets. Additionally, a function is provided that is the negation of `elem`, called `notElem`! Combining these functions yields the code shown in the following listing.

> **Listing 2.6   A helper function that determines if a character is neither a letter nor a digit**

```
isMisc :: Char -> Bool
isMisc char = char `notElem` lowerAlphabet ++ upperAlphabet ++ digits   ◁─┐
```

**Returns True if a character is not part of either
the lower or upper Latin alphabet or a digit**

There we go! Much better. Extending this function by providing more alphabets or characters that are not considered miscellaneous can now be achieved by simply appending another list to the expression that creates the list of characters we check.

2.4   *Rotating the wheel*

Now that we have our helper functions in place, we can think about implementing our cipher. We want to focus on understanding how to perform concise and appropriate case distinctions for our algorithm.

The following steps still have to be taken care of:

1 Get the index of a letter within an alphabet.
2 Get the letter at a certain index within an alphabet.
3 Transform a `String`, character by character.

2.4.1 *Finding an element's index*

Let us start with the first subtask: finding the index of an element in a list. This will require us to do two things: first, go through the list, and second, keep track of our index. However, there is a little catch—Haskell uses *immutable* data. You cannot change a value after setting it. It might seem like it's possible in GHCi, but that is actually not true. When "changing" a value, you are overwriting it. Such a thing is not possible in our functions. Furthermore, we do not have a concept of loops. So how is it possible to go through a list? The answer in pure functional programming is *recursion.*

Functions are allowed to be defined in terms of themselves. When this is the case, a function is calling itself. This is the concept of recursion. Since we are unable to use loops, we have to somehow be able to apply the same definition over and over again on different parts of some data.

Let us look at how to recursively implement a function that determines the length of a list. Assuming there is a way to split a list into its first element and the rest of it, we could define the length of the list to be the length of the rest of the list plus one. The length of the rest is then determined recursively. But how can we split a data structure?

This can be achieved with something called *pattern matching*, a powerful language feature that allows us to write function definitions for different "patterns" of data. Let us first look at how to implement a function that determines the length of a list. A list for which we always know its length is the empty list:

```
listLength [] = 0
```

Here, we specify that if the input has the structure of an empty list, the result will be 0. This function is now a *partial function*. This means there exist inputs for which it does not have a definition. We can test this:

```
ghci> listLength []
0
ghci> listLength [1,2,3]
*** Exception: .../src/Lib.hs:...: Non-exhaustive patterns in function
⇒ listLength
```

Here, Haskell tells us what's wrong. There exists an input for which we have not specified a pattern, hence it is nonexhaustive. How can we make it exhaustive? To understand this, we need to understand that lists have two *constructors*. These constructors are used to build lists. The two constructors are `[]` and `(:)`. We already know `[]`, which is simply the empty list. `(:)` is a prepend operation that takes an element and an existing list and prepends the element to that list.

Here are examples of these constructors:

```
ghci> []
[]
ghci> 1 : []
[1]
ghci> 1 : [2, 3]
[1,2,3]
ghci> 1 : 2 : 3 : []
[1,2,3]
```

These constructors are what we use for pattern matching. We are already using [] in our definition. To have exhaustive pattern matching, we need to add the second constructor as well. This leads us to a pattern matching frequently seen for lists, shown in the following listing.

Listing 2.7   Function displaying the usual patterns for pattern matching on lists

```
listLength [] = 0            ← Matches if the list is empty
listLength (x:xs) = ...      ← Matches if the list is built
                               from the prepend operation
```

It might look strange, but in Haskell, you can create partial function definitions for different patterns, for which we essentially define completely different behavior.

NOTE   For lists, the two patterns we have introduced are always exhaustive!

In the definition for the (x:xs) case, we use x as the variable for the first element (head) and xs as the rest (tail) of the list that was given as an argument. In figure 2.6, we can see how a list would be split up into two variables. Note that for a list with a single argument, xs would be [].

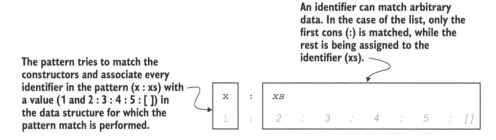

Figure 2.6   Pattern matching of a nonempty list

So how do we compute the length of the list? It is clear that the length of an empty list is 0, but what about the case where the list consists of an element x and some rest xs? As we have already discussed, it must be the length of xs + 1, since x is an element in the list (so it must be counted) and the rest of the list's length is determined recursively on the rest of that list (which is xs). Here is how we can do it:

```
listLength [] = 0
listLength (x : xs) = 1 + listLength xs
```

Here, we have our first *recursive* function! This function terminates if the list supplied as an argument is finite, since that means its definition will end in an [].

Similarly to the function determining a list's length, retrieving the index of a certain element can also be done recursively. In the case where we have a list with at least one element, it is rather simple. If the one element we have is the element we are searching for, we have found our index, but what if the element is not the one we are searching for? Let's start with this:

```
indexOf :: Char -> [Char] -> Int
indexOf ch (x : xs) = if x == ch then 0 else 1 + indexOf ch xs
```

This function starts at the beginning of a list using this pattern. Thus, if the first element we find is the right one, the index must be 0 (since indices always start at 0). If we need to keep searching, we are searching in the tail of our current list. The result in this recursive call is offset by exactly 1 (the element we have ignored in the recursive call). Thus, we increment the result. For this, we, of course, assume the recursive result is correct. Now the important question is this: What do we do in the case of the empty list? There is no correct result! Thus, we will explicitly keep this case *undefined*. This implementation is shown in the following listing.

Listing 2.8 Function to compute the index of a character in a list of characters

```
indexOf :: Char -> [Char] -> Int
indexOf ch [] = undefined                                      ◁─── Throws an exception in the case that
indexOf ch (x : xs) = if x == ch then 0 else 1 + indexOf ch xs      the input list is empty or the end of
                                                                   recursion has been reached
```

Throws an exception in the case that the input list is empty or the end of recursion has been reached

Recursively computes the index of the character in the list

However, this way we must always ensure that the character we are searching for is present in the list. Otherwise, our program will crash:

```
ghci> indexOf 'a' lowerAlphabet
0
ghci> indexOf 'f' lowerAlphabet
5
ghci> indexOf 'f' upperAlphabet
*** Exception: Prelude.undefined
CallStack (from HasCallStack):
  error, called at libraries/base/GHC/Err.hs:75:14 in base:GHC.Err
  undefined, called at .../src/Lib.hs:... in main:Lib
```

NOTE   Explicitly using `undefined` is very bad style. We will learn other ways of working with such problems in chapter 3. The proper function that returns the index of an element in a list is `elemIndex` from the `Data.List` module.

Since we are in control of how this function is used, this is fine for now. Nevertheless, we should make it more obvious that this function should be used on an alphabet and not any arbitrary list of characters, so we can change the type:

```
indexOf :: Char -> Alphabet -> Int
```

2.4.2   *Finding the element at an index*

Now that we have a way of getting the index of an element in a list, we still need a function that retrieves an element at a certain index. Luckily, this function exists and is called (`!!`). It can be used in infix notation like this:

```
ghci> [1,2,3] !! 0
1
ghci> [1,2,3] !! 2
3
ghci> [1,2,3] !! 3
*** Exception: Prelude.!!: index too large
```

> **Exercise: Writing the (!!) function using pattern matching**
> Try to write this (`!!`) function yourself using pattern matching and a recursive approach. If the index is too large or negative, you can use `undefined` to make your function throw an exception.

Just like our indexing function, this one has the problem of some inputs not producing valid results. Thus, we have to be very careful when using them! However, now, we can write functions that perform the rotation we specified in figure 2.1 for the uppercase and lowercase alphabets! Given a character and an offset as an integer, we can retrieve the correct character from the alphabet:

```
upperRot :: Int -> Char -> Char
upperRot n ch = upperAlphabet !! ((indexOf ch upperAlphabet + n) `mod` 26)

lowerRot :: Int -> Char -> Char
lowerRot n ch = lowerAlphabet !! ((indexOf ch lowerAlphabet + n) `mod` 26)
```

We are computing the new index by adding the offset to the index of the old character. To achieve the cycling of the wheel, we use `mod` to compute the modulo of the new index with 26 (the length of the respective alphabet). As we can quickly surmise, even negative indices work this way:

```
ghci> upperRot 3 'Z'
'C'
```

```
ghci> upperRot (-3) 'C'
'Z'
```

However, the two functions are essentially one function that we duplicated. We can make the definition more general by having another helper function that receives the alphabet as an argument. The finished code is shown in the following listing.

> **Listing 2.9   Rotation functions for general alphabets and uppercase and lowercase letters**

```
alphabetRot :: Alphabet -> Int -> Char -> Char          Defines a general rotation
alphabetRot alphabet n ch =                             on an arbitrary alphabet
  alphabet !! ((indexOf ch alphabet + n) `mod` length alphabet)

upperRot :: Int -> Char -> Char                         Defines a rotation function
upperRot n ch = alphabetRot upperAlphabet n ch          for uppercase letters

lowerRot :: Int -> Char -> Char                         Defines a rotation function
lowerRot n ch = alphabetRot lowerAlphabet n ch          for lowercase letters
```

We have arrived at a very general definition for a rotation function for any alphabet!

2.4.3   *Guarding control flow*

Now, we can write a general function that transforms an arbitrary character using our helper functions. What we'd like to do is either not use any transformation (e.g., for a digit or whitespace) or use one of the previously defined rotation functions based on whatever the input was. Thus, what we need is some kind of case distinction. A way to do this is using *if-then-else* statements. Common in almost any programming language, the if-then-else construct is used to provide *control flow*, based on predicates in our code:

```
ghci> x = 10 :: Int
ghci> if x > 5 then "x is larger than 5" else "x is not larger than 5"
"x is larger than 5"
```

However, this construct does not work like in many other languages. In Haskell, it is not possible to have an `if` ... `then` *without* `else`. That's because an if-then-else statement is just like any other expression. It needs to be evaluated to a value. However, an `if` without an `else` might not evaluate to a value, so it's forbidden. Now, we can write a function that uses the correct rotation function based on its input:

```
rotChar :: Int -> Char -> Char
rotChar n ch =
  if isLower ch
    then lowerRot n ch
    else
      if isUpper ch
        then upperRot n ch
        else ch
```

While this function is correct, it has a problem with readability. Using nested if-then-else statements has many downsides. First, it becomes hard to read once the expressions within the if-then-else statement become very large and complicated. Second, it's just not possible to keep going on with more and more cases if you have a lot of them. Eventually, you will have to become very creative to keep a readable style this way. Luckily, the if-then-else construction is somewhat of a rarity in Haskell, since there is a much better approach: *guards*!

Before we go into detail, let's see what our function would look like, rewritten with guards. This is shown in the following listing.

Listing 2.10   Rotation function for arbitrary characters

```
rotChar :: Int -> Char -> Char
rotChar n ch
    | isLower ch = lowerRot n ch
    | isUpper ch = upperRot n ch
    | otherwise = ch
```

Checks if the argument is a lowercase letter and applies the lowercase rotation function to it

The same as before but with uppercase letters

Evaluates to the unchanged character if it wasn't a letter

Guards give us a neat way of specifying predicates and their fitting definitions, much like pattern matching did! However, we are not matching on patterns but on Boolean expressions. In general, *any* Boolean expression is fine as a guard.

> **NOTE**   Guards and pattern matchings are done *in order*. So if a pattern or guard matches before another one, it will always take precedence, which is why cases that always match should come last.

But then, what is `otherwise`? Funny enough, it is a synonym for `True`! Because (for the most part) we want functions to be defined for all input values, the last guard we use should always be `otherwise`, since it is the *default case*, a catch-all.

Let's test our implementation:

```
ghci> rotChar 13 'A'
'N'
ghci> rotChar 13 'a'
'n'
ghci> rotChar (-1) 'A'
'Z'
ghci> rotChar 10 '1'
'1'
ghci> rotChar 10 ' '
' '
```

2.5   *Transforming a string*

Now that we can rotate single characters, we just have to figure out how to do it for all characters in a given `string`. Since a `string` is just a list of characters, we just have to apply our `rotChar` function to every element of that list. How can we change anything in a list if all data is *immutable*? The answer is easy: we cannot change any values but must create new ones! We will encounter this pattern often when working with pure functional code. Instead of modifying the old list, we have to create a new one. We can exploit the pattern matching we have used before to create a function for Caesar's cipher:

```
caesar :: Int -> String -> String
caesar n [] = []
caesar n (x : xs) = rotChar n x : caesar n xs
```

An empty list remains an empty list, while a list with a first element x and the rest being xs is a new list that begins with the transformed x and has the transformed xs as its new tail. This function is our cipher:

```
ghci> caesar 13 "Caesars Cipher!"
"Pnrfnef Pvcure!"
ghci> caesar 13 (caesar 13 "Caesars Cipher!")
"Caesars Cipher!"
```

Let's take a closer look at what we tried to achieve with the caesar function. We wanted to apply some transformation (rotChar in this case) to a list, but there might be a possibility of generalizing this concept.

2.5.1   A higher-order mapping

In the real world, this kind of transformation happens very frequently in pure functional programs, so it is a good idea to investigate this operation further. When doing an element-wise transformation of lists, we can think of our operation to *map* from one value to another, without changing the order of elements. This is graphically shown in figure 2.7. Of course, this logic is valid for any values and any transformation.

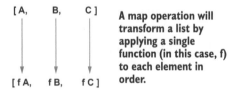

A map operation will transform a list by applying a single function (in this case, f) to each element in order.

Figure 2.7   A mapping of values

If we want to generalize our caesar function to a general transform function, we need to make the function an argument. Remember that functions are just values, so we can use them as arguments too!

  Looking at the function, we can see that the n argument is unnecessary for a general case, since it is related to the rotChar function. Speaking of which, we need to replace rotChar with an argument, which we will simply call fun. This argument is a stand-in for some functions consuming a single element from our list and returning a new element that will take its place. This results in the following function:

```
transform fun [] = []
transform fun (x : xs) = fun x : transform fun xs
```

This is a *mighty* function! Let's look at some examples of what this function can do:

```
ghci> transform (\x -> x + 1) [1..10] :: [Int]
[2,3,4,5,6,7,8,9,10,11]
ghci> transform (\x -> x > 5) [1..10] :: [Bool]
[False,False,False,False,False,True,True,True,True,True]
ghci> transform (\x -> if x == 'e' then 'u' else x) "Hello World!"
"Hullo World!"
```

When data is represented as a series of values in a list, we can use this function to change the data without having to manually take the list apart and put it back together. It is a nice example of a family of functions that only specifies *how* to work with a data structure and is parametrized by another function. In general, functions that receive other functions as arguments are called *higher-order functions*, which are a vital part of functional programming, since they allow us to provide general descriptions of algorithms that will be later used in concrete definitions.

2.5.2   *Parameterizing types*

This should make us wonder: With a function so general, how would its type look? It must be just as general as its definition. When inspecting its type in GHCi, we see the following:

```
ghci> :type transform
transform :: (t -> a) -> [t] -> [a]
```

These types look strange. t? a? Here, we see an example of *parametric polymorphism.* The types for this function are not fixed but parametric, meaning we can substitute arbitrary types for t and a. However, when we do that, we must substitute the same types for *all* occurrences of said parameters. So when we want to replace t by a concrete type, we have to replace every t in our type expression. However, t and a can be different types (they don't necessarily have to be).

> **NOTE** The names of type parameters are somewhat irrelevant. t could be called b and a could have been called foo.

What exactly is this type expression telling us? It specifies that transform has two arguments, with the first being a function taking a t argument and returning an a value. The second argument of transform is a list of t values. The function then returns a list of a values. Let's say we have a function like this:

```
f :: Int -> String
```

If we use it as the first argument for `transform`, then `t` is replaced by `Int` and `a` is replaced by `String`, which means the second argument has to be of type `[Int]` and the return value of the function will be `[String]`:

```
ghci> :{
ghci| f :: Int -> String
ghci| f n = show n
ghci| :}
ghci> g xs = transform f xs
ghci> :t g
g :: [Int] -> [String]
```

Here, we also see the type inference of Haskell doing its job. The substitution we have done in our head can be performed by the compiler as well! This type of polymorphism is present in almost every function and data type we will encounter in the rest of this book, so getting familiar with it is essential. It is one of the most basic concepts to write abstract, composable, and general code.

> **NOTE** Parametric polymorphism can be compared to the concept of generics in many other languages, like Java or Go. In our case, type variables would be generics with a completely arbitrary interface. In chapter 5, we will learn how to restrict the assumed nature of our type variables when we discuss type classes.

Higher-order functions depend on this polymorphism to be useful. We do not want to write the same function over and over again for different types. On the contrary, we want to find the most general type we can to reuse the functions multiple times. The `transform` function we have created is a very general and important building block for creating algorithms on lists.

2.5.3 A finished cipher

As a matter of fact, this `transform` function is so important that it is already built into Haskell and is one of the most important functions we will learn about: `map`. It receives a function used for element-wise transformation as its first argument and the list to work on as its second argument. Since our cipher is supposed to perform a rotation of characters on every character in our string, we can use `map` to describe our `caesar` function. This is shown in the following listing:

Listing 2.11 Functions that perform Caesar's cipher and ROT13

```
caesar :: Int -> String -> String
caesar n message = map (\ch -> rotChar n ch) message   ←─  Defines Caesar's
                                                            cipher by applying
                                                            the character rotation
                                                            function to each
rot13 :: String -> String                                   character in a message
rot13 message = caesar 13 message   ←─ Performs ROT13
                                       encryption by using
                                       the Caesars cipher
                                       with a fixed offset
                                       of 13
```

Here, we arrive at our cipher! Of course, the cipher is parametrized by the offset we used for the character rotation. Thus, the special case of ROT13 can easily be constructed from Caesar's cipher itself. Now, we can encrypt our communication just like the Romans!

Exercise: The ROT135 cipher

ROT13 is nicely symmetrical; however, we needed to omit the rotation of digits because that would have made it asymmetrical, since sizes for the alphabets are different. However, the rotation by an offset of 5 makes the rotation for digits symmetrical again! Your task is to combine ROT13 and ROT5 (for digits) to a combined ROT13.5 to have a symmetrical encoding for Latin letters and digits!

Write a function, `rot135`, that performs this encoding!

Make sure two applications of this function cancel each other out:

```
ghci> rot135 "Hello 1 2 3 ... 7 8 9"
"Uryyb 6 7 8 ... 2 3 4"
ghci> rot135 (rot135 "Hello 1 2 3 ... 7 8 9")
"Hello 1 2 3 ... 7 8 9"
```

And there we have our "totally safe" encryption scheme. Let's go over what we did. We first created a type synonym called `Alphabet` and defined constants for lowercase letters, uppercase letters, and digits to make it clear what data we are talking about. Then, we created functions to determine whether a character (`Char`) belongs to such an `Alphabet`. Using these definitions, we constructed a function to do the actual rotation of characters in an `Alphabet` and implemented the Caesar cipher.

Exercise: Frequency analysis on strings

ROT13 and Caesar's cipher are not a safe way to "encrypt" a message. This can be easily shown by frequency analysis. In the English language, some letters are simply more common than others (e.g., e is much more common than other letters). Write a function that counts the occurrences of a character within a `String`:

```
count :: Char -> String -> Int
```

Then, use this function to perform a frequency analysis on plain text and an "encrypted" text. To do this, you apply the counting function to every letter in the alphabets we have defined earlier. Is there a way of writing a best-guess decryption scheme for the Caesars cipher?

We defined our own type synonym for alphabets to make our code a bit more clear. We used ranges of characters to define alphabets for lowercase and uppercase letters as well as digits. Based on these definitions, we created helper functions that specify whether a character is part of one of these alphabets. Additionally, we constructed a function to determine the index of a character within an alphabet as well as a function providing a rotation of characters within an alphabet given a certain offset. We combined these functions to construct a function that can rotate an arbitrary character by determining which alphabet it belongs to and how it should thus be rotated. Using `map`, we then constructed the Caesar's cipher from this function as well as the ROT13 function.

Summary

- Every Haskell expression that evaluates to a value has an associated type expression. It is common and good practice to explicitly notate them.
- The `type` keyword can be used to create type synonyms, which are used to make type more expressive and explanatory of the functionality provided.
- We use `:type`, `:info`, and `:reload` commands in GHCi (or `:t`, `:i`, and `:r` as shorthand) to gather information about functions and values as well as reload all loaded modules in GHCi.
- Every named binary function can be written in infix notation by surrounding the function names with `.
- Pattern matching is a way of deconstructing the structure of our data types and providing proper function definitions for different patterns.
- When defining recursive functions, we assume recursive results to be correct, since the whole function definition is correct if every recursive step is correct.
- Guards provide a concise method of providing case distinctions on Boolean predicates. Thus, they are prime substitutes for if-then-else constructs.
- The `map` function is used to apply a function to every element of a list, in order.
- Parametric polymorphism is used to provide general functions that can be used on a variety of types.

Every line counts 3

This chapter covers

- Facilitating side effects and input/output within Haskell
- Using side-effect-free, pure code within impure code
- Interacting with the operating systems environment
- Incorporating a command line argument parser into our programs

In the previous chapter, we learned how to construct algorithms to transform strings and explored the basics of programming in Haskell; however, we were only able to test our functionality in GHCi. Now, we want to turn our attention to writing our first real program, which can be invoked from the command line.

When working on the command line or writing automated scripts on Unix-like systems, pipelines of multiple programs are often used for achieving certain tasks, like searching or transforming data. To facilitate interprocess communication easily, streams of texts are used to pass messages from one process to another. This is usually done with the pipe symbol |. This idea is illustrated by figure 3.1.

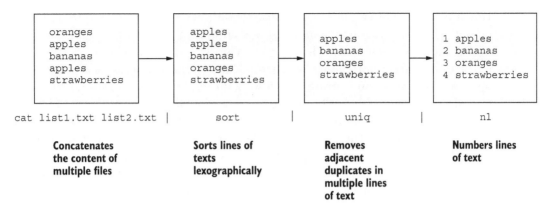

```
oranges              apples                apples              1 apples
apples               apples                bananas             2 bananas
bananas              bananas               oranges             3 oranges
apples               oranges               strawberries        4 strawberries
strawberries         strawberries
```

cat list1.txt list2.txt | sort | uniq | nl

Concatenates   **Sorts lines of**   **Removes**   **Numbers lines**
the content of   **texts**   **adjacent**   **of text**
multiple files   **lexographically**   **duplicates in**
                                                  multiple lines
                                                  of text

Figure 3.1   An example of how to transform data using pipes with shell commands

For this to work, there are many tools in the UNIX space that perform basic tasks that, when combined in a pipeline, perform a bigger action. One of these tools is nl, which is short for *number lines*. Its job is rather simple: print a file and number each line. Essentially, it creates listings for arbitrary text. Here is an example:

```
shell $ nl testFile.txt
     1  Lorem ipsum dolor sit amet, consectetur adipiscing elit. Maecenas a
     2  mattis nisi, eleifend auctor erat. Vivamus nisl sapien, suscipit non
     3  gravida sed, mattis a velit. Fusce non iaculis urna, a volutpat leo.
     4  Ut non mauris vel massa tincidunt mattis. Sed eu viverra lectus.
     5  Donec pulvinar justo quis condimentum suscipit. Donec vel odio eu
     6  odio maximus consequat at at tellus. Ut placerat suscipit vulputate.
     7  Donec eu eleifend massa, et aliquet ipsum.

     8  Mauris eget massa a tellus tristique consequat. Nunc tempus sit amet
     9  est sit amet malesuada. Curabitur ultrices in leo vitae tristique.
    10  Suspendisse potenti. Nam dui risus, gravida eu scelerisque sit amet,
    11  tincidunt id neque. In sit amet purus gravida, venenatis lectus sit
    12  amet, gravida massa. In iaculis commodo massa, in viverra est mollis
    13  et. Nunc vehicula felis a vestibulum egestas. Phasellus eu libero sed
    14  odio facilisis feugiat id quis velit. Proin a ex dapibus, lacinia dui
    15  at, vehicula ipsum.
```

This tool can be used in a variety of ways. For example, number the lines of a file, search for certain strings in that output, and then cut off the strings and keep the line numbers. The results are the line numbers that contain the searched string. This can be used to find references in source code. As another example, create a list of data entries, which are then sorted using some predicate, and then number the lines. This will result in a listing that shows you an order of the elements with their index.

Why not get our feet wet early by rewriting this little tool for ourselves in Haskell? While it can be cozy to stay with pure functions and simple definitions, it is much more beneficial for us, as programmers, to tackle the interesting problem of performing *input and output* within a language famous for its pure programming paradigm.

How are side-effect-free functions compatible with side effects produced by input and output? That's a question we want to ask and answer rather early in our journey!

Of course, we treat this as a learning exercise. The nl tool is feature packed, offering many options for formatting, which we will not copy. However, it lacks some useful options, like reverse numbering, which we want to add. So let's take our first steps toward writing real programs by writing our own tool for numbering lines of files!

This chapter starts by introducing the *do notation* and discussing how to perform input and output in Haskell. Then, we will learn how to integrate the syntax and functions we learned about in the second chapter within this new notation. After learning how to interact with the operating systems environment, we will start constructing a basis for our tool, which we will complete in chapter 4, by writing a simple example application.

3.1 *Talking to the outside*

The first obvious challenge we face has something to do with Haskell's pure functional design. Our functions are not allowed to produce side effects or any interactions with the environment outside of these functions. A function's result can *only* be dependent on its arguments and nothing else. Thus, we are not allowed to read files or talk to the operating system's environment in our functions. But how can Haskell programs then have this (rather trivial) functionality? The answer is found in a special type: IO.

In the last chapter, we saw that the main "function" in our program isn't a real function but of type IO (). Typically, this is called an IO *action*. These actions can be invoked and have to return some value. In the case of the main action, we do not return anything meaningful but the value (), which is the only value for the () type. This type is called *unit*, and it acts as a stand-in when you want to return nothing.

3.1.1 *Simple actions for input and output*

Let's look at some more examples of IO actions:

```
getLine :: IO String

putStrLn :: String -> IO ()
```

Here, we see actions that perform input and output with the environment outside of our program. getLine reads a single string terminated with a newline character from the stdin handle, which typically is text entered on the command line. Its type, thus, is IO String, since it is an IO action that will return a String value. putStrLn prints a string to the stdout, the output stream of the program, and it adds a newline to the end of it. Its type reveals that putStrLn is not an IO action but a function evaluating to an IO action. IO actions can be understood as a description of an interaction with the environment. However, this interaction does not necessarily take place just because they exist. For that to happen, they have to be evaluated.

Let's look at how to use these actions. In the following listing, we see a full program that reads some string from the user and prints it back to them.

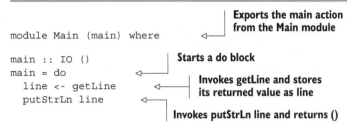

Listing 3.1 A simple program that reads a line from the user and prints it

The syntax we see here is much different from the syntax we have seen so far. This syntax is called do *notation*. It is started with the keyword do and signifies the start of an IO action. It is in this do *block* that we can invoke other IO actions. We are only allowed to do it here, since evaluating an IO action in pure functions is (typically) not possible. Using the left arrow (<-), we specify that the action should be evaluated when this point in the program is reached and assign the returned value from an IO action to a variable name. It is this evaluation that turns the description of an interaction into its realization. The invocation of getLine in listing 3.1 serves as an example. The last statement in our do block determines the type for our whole IO action. Since putStrLn line is of type IO (), the types check out!

NOTE The do notation is not just used for IO actions. It is syntactic sugar used for any kind of *monad*. However, this detail is omitted for now and explored in later chapters.

Something of note in this notation is that it looks and feels much like *imperative programming*, since the actions are being invoked from top to bottom. However, this notation should not be confused with it; we are still writing functional programs. This notation is used to *compose* actions, since they can be used to represent arbitrarily complex behavior. Some examples include

- Printing text to the screen
- Sending data over network interfaces
- Constructing and showing a GUI to the user

In fact, *any program is an IO action*, since our program's entry point (main) is of type IO (). It is, thus, also (typically) not possible to "escape" an IO action, in the sense that we could specify the evaluation of an action within pure code. When a value is returned from an IO action, it has to be handled in another IO action.

3.1.2 Simulating a loop

Let us practice this new syntax by writing a simple IO action that interactively numbers lines entered by the user, an interactive version of nl if you will. Let's start simply by reading a line and printing `1. ` in front of it:

```
interactiveLines :: IO ()
interactiveLines = do
```

```
line <- getLine
putStrLn ("1. " ++ line)
```

However, this will only print the index once. We need to repeat the process and simultaneously increment the line number. How do we achieve this? First, in Haskell, we do not have loops and our data is immutable, so we cannot make the action loop and increment a counter like we would in other languages. To achieve a "loop," we can call the action again:

```
interactiveLines :: IO ()
interactiveLines = do
  line <- getLine
  putStrLn ("1. " ++ line)
  interactiveLines
```

But how can we increment the counter? So far, every line will simply be the first line. What we need to do is to parametrize the action by an argument. Thus, we create a *function* that takes the counter as an argument and *evaluates to an* IO *action*:

```
interactiveLines :: Int -> IO ()
interactiveLines counter = do
  line <- getLine
  putStrLn (show counter ++ ". " ++ line)
  interactiveLines (counter + 1)
```

We can transform any number into a string with the show function and use it here to convert our counter. Before entering the recursive call, we increment the counter to display the next index.

> **NOTE** The show function can be used to transform a large number of values into strings. In chapter 5, we will learn how those types can be identified when talking about *type classes*.

It is important to understand that this is possible because we have constructed a function that evaluates to an IO action. Of course, this function changes the result based on its arguments. So for each new counter value, we essentially call a *new* action. Calling just interactiveLines within the do block is not enough, since it is *not* an IO action, due to the missing parameter. In short, the type Int -> IO () is not an IO action!

3.1.3 *Breaking out of a recursive action*

Now that we have found a way of looping, we have to find a way of escaping this loop. An easy stopping condition could be to stop counting and exit the loop once an input of the user is empty. This can be achieved using the null function that checks if a list is empty and an if-then-else. For now, we can assume the null function to be of type String -> Bool. However, we need to determine what to do if the list is empty. When we are in a do block of an IO action, our last expression needs to be an IO action itself.

This means that in the case of an if-then-else, we need to return an IO action in both cases. Of course, if the input isn't empty, we can simply call our action recursively, but what do we do in case the input was empty? We need to find a way of producing an IO action type of IO () which does not perform anything. For this purpose, we can use a very helpful function, called return:

```
return :: a -> IO a
```

It can be used to wrap a value into an IO action (a simply means that any type can be used here). However, you should not think of this return as actually returning from the action, since that is not what is happening. By definition, the returned value from an action is the last action to be evaluated in it!

```
myAction :: IO Int
myAction = do
  return 1
  return 2
  return 3
```

This action will always return 3! That's because it can be read like so:

```
myAction :: IO Int
myAction = do
  _ <- return 1
  _ <- return 2
  return 3
```

By using _ <-, we simply discard the returned value. That's generally what we do with actions of type IO (), since we are not interested in a value with no information.

In our interactiveLines example, we can use this return function to construct an IO action for our else case. In the case that the input is not empty, however, we perform two IO actions. But just writing two IO actions underneath each other is not an IO action. It's, thus, important to put them in their own do block, since that defines an action. This is shown in the following listing.

Listing 3.2   An IO action that repeats user input with an incrementing counter

```
                                        Reads a line from the user input

interactiveLines :: Int -> IO ()             Checks if the line is empty
interactiveLines counter = do
  line <- getLine            ◄              Returns an IO action that does nothing
  if null line           ◄
    then return ()               ◄              Starts a new do block,
    else do                         ◄            thus defining a new action
      putStrLn (show counter ++ ". " ++ line)   ◄    Prints the user input
      interactiveLines (counter + 1)      ◄          with a counter value

                                        Recursively performs the current action
                                        again with an incremented counter
```

Here, we have constructed our first prototype for the program we want to write—a simple demonstration of IO actions. Using a multiline input in GHCi (using :{ and :}), we can test our action:

```
ghci> :{
ghci| ...
ghci| :}
ghci> interactiveLines 1
Hello
1. Hello
IO
2. IO
Action
3. Action

ghci>
```

We can observe that after entering a line, it is printed, except for the empty line. Using IO actions in GHCi behaves a bit differently from a normal program. Remember that GHCi evaluates the entered statements. So simply typing a statement of some IO type will evaluate it:

```
ghci> getLine
Hello
"Hello"
```

When the IO action returns a value (which is not unit), that value is printed to the screen.

3.2 *Pure functions inside of actions*

Now that we have a first prototype for our program, we need to think about how to structure it. What parts of the program can live in pure function code, and which parts produce side-effects?

> **NOTE** To reiterate, side effects are interactions with the environment outside a function from within that function. In this chapter, we are mostly concerned with interfacing with the operating system. However, this could also include some mutable state or shared resources for multithreading.

Our program will need to read two distinct things from the operating system. First, since we are constructing a command line tool, we need to provide a way for the user to configure its behavior using command line arguments. Second, the program needs to read file contents from some file that is specified with said arguments. These functionalities, as well as the output we want to perform in the end, will require us to produce side effects, so they will have to be achieved in IO actions. However, providing a numbering for a bunch of lines read from a file can be achieved with pure code.

3.2.1 Reading and modifying user input

This should raise the question of how we can use this pure functional code within the IO actions. Of course, there are multiple ways of doing so. As we have seen, we can pass arguments into functions that evaluate an IO action. Nothing is stopping us from transforming these arguments using pure functions! Let's say we want to write a program that reads a line and prints the uppercase version of it. This is similar to the program we have seen in listing 3.1 but with a simple modification to the line variable before printing. To transform a single character to its uppercase equivalent, we can use the toUpper function from the Data.Char module. However, just transforming a single character won't do. What we need is a transformation for every single character in our string, and as you might remember from the first chapter, we have a very nice candidate for that: the map function! By using toUpper in conjunction with map, we can create a function that puts a string into uppercase. Now, we can incorporate this into our simple program from before. The resulting program will use this uppercase transformation before printing the string to the screen. This is shown in the following listing.

> **Listing 3.3   A program that reads a line from the user and prints its uppercase representation**

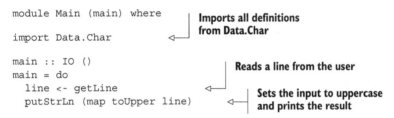

This program highlights how we can use *pure* code, free of side effects, in real programs. The side effects are being handled by the usage of our actions, which then call our pure code. While functions like map and toUpper are completely free of side effects, the IO actions have *handled side effects*, which are not directly exposed to the rest of our code. This idea is illustrated in figure 3.2. Of course, the exception handling within Haskell is a bit more involved than that, but it is a good starting point to think of IO actions as an environment that manages side effects for us.

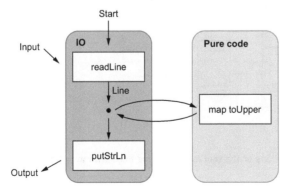

Figure 3.2   The interaction of side effects, actions, and pure code

In general, we should always think about how to decrease the amount of impure code (e.g., using actions) and increase the amount of pure code in our programs. Why? It makes it much easier to reason about and test the code. A function that is not allowed to use side effects can neatly be tested with unit or property testing, since setting up a fitting test environment is not necessary. Thus, it is good to only use IO actions when they are absolutely necessary. Otherwise, pure code should be used.

3.2.2   *Data flow between pure and impure code*

Now that we know how to use our pure code within actions, we can start to think about our nl tool in a bit more detail. What kind of components and functionalities does this tool need to have, which of these parts are pure, and which of them are impure? Working with lines of a file and even arguments is pure, since we only have to transform strings or perform case distinctions on them. So numbering, filtering, and formatting strings is pure code. However, everything that deals with resources outside of our program, such as arguments and files, will have to be done with side effects, so actions need to be used for them:

- Pure (functions)
  - Parsing arguments
  - Numbering, filtering, and formatting lines
- Impure (actions)
  - Reading arguments
  - Reading file
  - Printing to screen

We can already think about how these different tasks can be composed. A diagram showing the different components of our tool and the data flow between them is shown in figure 3.3.

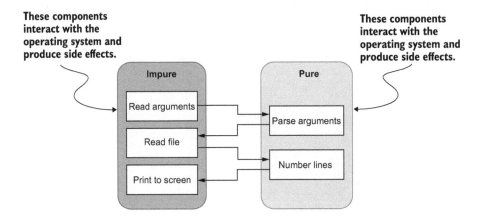

Figure 3.3   The components and actions of the tool for numbering lines with data flow represented as arrows

The reason we make such a strict distinction for these components is not really a technical one. In truth, after compilation, all of these components will have morphed into one, yet while we write them, it is good to keep in mind if and how side effects affect our program's semantics. Speaking of side effects, let us start taking care of our first side effect and read arguments from the command line!

3.3   *Reading from the environment*

An essential part of any program is communicating with the environment. Programs that are run on a modern operating system usually have access to command line arguments and the system's environment variables. Haskell provides us with a module that deals with exactly these things, called `System.Environment`. It provides us with a few functions that can be used to get information from our program environment, namely the arguments (`getArgs`), program name (`getProgName`), and a value in the environment associated with a certain key (`lookupEnv`). For our tool, we are exclusively interested in the arguments.

3.3.1   *Parsing command line arguments*

`getArgs` is an `IO` action that returns a list of strings (its type is `IO [String]`), which will retrieve a full list of command line arguments. So reading the arguments couldn't be simpler. The hard part is parsing the arguments, since they typically follow a certain schema. To keep this schema simple, we will start by letting it only contain a single file name. So a call to our program should look something like `nl <filename>`. If no argument was given, we provide the user with a help text. If at least one argument was given, we interpret the first argument as the filename and ignore the rest.

If you haven't started a new stack project, now would be a good time! Just like before, we can navigate to a desired location and start a new project called `lnums` by invoking `stack`:

```
stack new lnums
```

This time, we are not going to ignore Main.hs, but we will start by implementing our argument parsing in this file. For our simplified example, our program needs to check if any arguments have been given—and more specifically, if there is exactly one value in the list returned from `getArgs`. We can achieve this with a pure function using pattern matching. We can specify a pattern that matches if a list contains a single element by providing a list pattern with a single element in it: `[x]`. This single element is then identified by the name we use in the pattern (x in this example). This is equivalent to using a pattern in the form of `x : []`. A simple sketch for parsing this filename argument could look like the following listing.

Listing 3.4   Simple argument-parsing function

```
parseArguments :: [String] -> FilePath
parseArguments [filePath] = filePath
parseArguments _ = undefined
```

> **Evaluates to a file path if the input list has exactly one element**

> **Throws an exception if the input has any other structure**

Here, we use the `FilePath` type (which is a type synonym for `String`) to make it clear that this function evaluates to a file path. When one type is the synonym of another, we can use them interchangeably, so this `String` becomes a `FilePath`. In this example, we can also see the usage of a wildcard pattern `_`. This pattern always matches, since it is equivalent to using a simple name. In the case of the wildcard, however, the input is not tied to any identifier, so it's discarded.

> **NOTE**   Using a wildcard pattern as the last pattern in pattern matching always makes it exhaustive, since it will always match.

However, this code, of course, is unusable, since it will make our program crash once the user gives us an incorrect input. We should be a bit more polite and, instead of crashing, maybe give the user a hint about what they did wrong. This should make us think: How do we handle errors? How can we evaluate to a pure value that also represents an error? The answer comes to us in a new type, called `Maybe`!

3.3.2   *Encoding errors with Maybe*

`Maybe` is a type used for representing the possibility of a missing value, so a value of this type either is a value or simply nothing. Just like lists, it is parametrized by some type, so like a `[Int]` (a list of `Int`), `Maybe Int` also exists. The definition for `Maybe` is given thusly:

```
data Maybe a = Just a | Nothing
```

This syntax is new to us, and we will see it quite often in this book. The `data` keyword is used to define *algebraic data types* (ADTs) using *constructors*. Here, we define the `Maybe` type with a single free type variable a. A `Maybe` value is either built by the `Just` constructor in conjunction with a value of a polymorphic type or the simple constructor `Nothing`, which holds no further information. When we encounter a `Maybe` of some type, we can be sure that it is either one of the constructors. This enables us to write pure functions that can fail *without* critically failing. The result simply becomes `Nothing`.

> **NOTE**   `Maybe` is not just used for functions that fail; it can also be used to signify optional function arguments. However, it is most often found to signify an optional result value.

This type is already provided by Haskell, so we can modify our function from listing 3.4 to arrive at the definition from listing 3.5. Instead of failing using `undefined`, we can now evaluate to `Nothing` value! Of course, the type now changes to a `Maybe`

FilePath, since we are not just evaluating to a file path but the Maybe type that might contain a FilePath. In case we have a file path, we wrap it in the Just constructor.

Listing 3.5 A simple argument-parsing function with Maybe

```
parseArguments :: [String] -> Maybe FilePath                    Encodes the result with
parseArguments [filePath] = Just filePath    ◁──┘              the Just constructor
parseArguments _ = Nothing                   ◁──┐  Encodes the failed parsing
                                                 │  with the Nothing constructor
```

This function now doesn't crash our program anymore, since we can encode a fault condition as a type. But how will we work with this value? Luckily, we already know our answer: *pattern matching*! Just like with lists, we can match the specific constructors of our Maybe type. This makes it possible to extract the value of the Just constructor. Since we cannot extract a value from Nothing, we have to provide a default value. This leads us to the definition of the function in listing 3.6. Note the type signature for this function. The type a is a free type variable, meaning a could be any type, but all occurrences of a need to have the same type. So if you want to use this function with a Maybe Int value, you will have to provide an Int for the first argument.

Listing 3.6 A function to extract a value from a Maybe using a default

```
fromMaybe :: a -> Maybe a -> a              Extracts the value that was
fromMaybe _ (Just v) = v     ◁──┘          wrapped in a Just constructor
fromMaybe v Nothing = v      ◁──┐  Uses the default value if the
                                 │  Maybe value was Nothing
```

This function can be used to "break out" of a Maybe. This is helpful if we want to chain computations that result in a Maybe because they have the potential to fail. In that case, we can recognize that failure (by using pattern matching) and easily change our control flow or fall back to default values. Here, we see fromMaybe in action:

```
ghci> fromMaybe 0 (Just 100 :: Maybe Int)
100
ghci> fromMaybe 0 (Nothing :: Maybe Int)
0
```

Luckily, we do not have to implement these functions ourselves! The Data.Maybe module provides us with most functions we could hope for. Table 3.1 provides an overview of some of them.

Table 3.1 Common functions used in conjunction with the Maybe type

Name	Type	Description
maybe	b -> (a -> b) -> Maybe a -> b	This function takes a default value, a function, and a Maybe. If the Maybe is Nothing, the default value is being returned; otherwise, the function is being applied to the value in the Just constructor and returns the result of that function call.

Table 3.1 Common functions used in conjunction with the `Maybe` type *(continued)*

Name	Type	Description
`fromMaybe`	`a -> Maybe a -> a`	This function takes a default value and a maybe as arguments. If the `Maybe` is a `Nothing`, the default value is returned; otherwise, the wrapped value from the `Just` constructor is returned.
`catMaybes`	`[Maybe a] -> [a]`	This function takes a list of `Maybe` values as an argument and returns a list of all unwrapped `Just` values. All `Nothing` values are ignored.
`mapMaybe`	`(a -> Maybe b) -> [a] -> [b]`	This function takes a function that receives a value and returns a `Maybe` of potentially different type as its first argument and a list of values as its second. The returned list is a mapping of the function to the second argument, where all `Nothing` results are simply discarded. Its definition is equivalent to `mapMaybe f xs = catMaybes (map f xs)`.

The `Maybe` type constantly creeps up in the standard library as well as many external libraries, since it is a prime candidate to encode missing values or failing computations. An example would be the `elemIndex` function from the `Data.List` module, which either returns the index of an element wrapped in `Just` in a list or `Nothing` if the element is not present in that list.

> **Exercise: A safe function for indexing**
>
> In chapter 2, we constructed a poor man's version of a function to get the index of an element in a list. This function was `indexOf` of type `Char -> [Char] -> Int`, which crashed our program when the element was not present in the list. Rewrite it to use `Maybe` to encode this. The type should change to `Char -> [Char] -> Maybe Int`.

3.4   *Example: Reading and printing a command line argument*

Now, we can use our newly built `fromMaybe` function to print a helpful text if the user forgets to supply a file path. We can use the `maybe` function to choose the correct action to take based on the given file path. If it is missing, we choose an action that prints a help text. Otherwise, we construct an action from the file path that arose from the argument parsing. The code for this idea is presented in the following listing. This program simply prints the given argument if there is one and prints a help text otherwise.

Listing 3.7   A program that prints its only argument or a help text if no argument is provided

```
module Main (main) where

import System.Environment
```

```
printHelpText :: String -> IO ()
printHelpText msg = do                              │  Retrieves the name the
  putStrLn (msg ++ "\n")                            │  program was called with
  progName <- getProgName                        ←┘
  putStrLn ("Usage: " ++ progName ++ " <filename>")  ←─┤  Prints usage
                                                          information

parseArguments :: [String] -> Maybe FilePath
parseArguments [filePath] = Just filePath          │  Parses the filename argument
parseArguments _ = Nothing

main :: IO ()                                      │  Retrieves the arguments the
main = do                                          │  program was called with
  cliArgs <- getArgs                            ←┘
  let mFilePath = parseArguments cliArgs            │  Evaluates to an IO action, which will be
  maybe                                          ←┘  executed based on the parsing result
    (printHelpText "Missing filename")          ←┐
    (\filePath -> putStrLn filePath)            ←┤  Prints the help text if
    mFilePath                                        the parsing failed

                                                     Prints the filename argument
                                                   │ if parsing was successful
```

This code combines the elements we have seen so far. It reads the arguments from the environment; parses them; and, based on that result, either prints a help text or the filename that was given.

> **NOTE**   When using local variables of some `Maybe` type, it is common to prefix its variable name with a lowercase m. For example, you can read `mFilePath` as *a* `Maybe` *that might contain a file path.*

This example is a demonstration of how we can use the `Maybe` type to provide a pure method of error handling and change our control flow accordingly. What might come as a surprise is that the *actions* we perform can be a function result themselves. We see this clearly in the usage of the `maybe` function. Based on the value of our parsing result, it evaluates to different actions. So the pure `maybe` function decides what kind of actions our program performs with the environment. It is important to understand this early on when programming with Haskell. It's not just functions that are values; actions are as well.

3.4.1   The let keyword

In our example, we also see a new keyword, called `let`. This keyword allows us to create definitions, or `let` *bindings*, within our actions, much like variables can be defined in other languages. Its most basic usage looks something like this:

```
let <identifier> = <expr>
```

This might look something like this in action:

```
let x = 1 + 1
```

But please, don't let this syntax fool you. We are not creating mutable variables. You will need to treat the identifiers you create with this binding as immutable data or constants.

> **NOTE** It is also possible to use `let` bindings to create functions by naming arguments after the identifier: `let functionName arg1 arg2 arg3 = ....` This can allow you to use arguments from the outer functions in the definition of the inner functions.

This is helpful when trying to make nested expressions a bit clearer or to use the same expression multiple times. We can demonstrate this in our example program from before:

```
main = do
  line <- getLine
  putStrLn (map toUpper line)
```

The expression `map toUpper line` can be bound to a new identifier before it is used.

```
main = do
  line <- getLine
  let upperCaseLine = map toUpper line
  putStrLn upperCaseLine
```

The `let` keyword can also be used outside of actions in our normal function definitions, since they can be part of an expression:

```
ghci> let x = 1 + 1 in x + 1 :: Int
3
```

Here, we define a binding of the expression `1 + 1` to the identifier `x`, which we declare to be of type `Int`. In expressions, the `let` keyword is closed by the `in` keyword to signify the expressions for which the binding should hold.

3.4.2 *Running the program with stack*

Now, we want to test the behavior of the code in listing 3.7 by building an executable and running it. We do this with `stack run`; however, passing arguments to the program needs some special attention:

```
stack run <arguments for stack> -- <arguments for the program>
```

When we want to pass arguments to our executable, we have to precede all arguments we want to write down with a single `--`. Let's test the implementation, first with no arguments:

```
shell $ stack run
Missing file name

Usage: lnums-exe <file name>
```

We see our help text! The program name that was read from the environment was lnums-exe. In this case, *lnums* was the project name. stack automatically adds the *exe* suffix to the executable's name. Now, let's try this with an argument:

```
shell $ stack run -- Testpath
Testpath
```

It correctly parses the argument and prints it. So now, we have implemented the basis for an argument parser, which we can extend once the need arises.

Now, we have constructed the basis for our program. We can read and parse arguments and act accordingly. This is a big part of our impure code. Next, we should start thinking about how to read from the filesystem and how to number the lines in this file, which we will do in the next chapter.

Summary

- IO actions are used to perform interactions with the operating system environment, like input/output with the filesystem or network.
- Haskell's runtime system takes care of the evaluation of IO actions; we as programmers only need to specify their sequence.
- We use the do notation to specify a sequence of actions and how their resulting values are passed to other actions and functions.
- We can simulate a loop using recursive calls to functions.
- return is used to wrap a value into an IO action, but it does not signify the "return" from an action.
- When using if-then-else with actions, we need to make sure the *then* and *else* branches both evaluate to an action of the same type.
- The expressions passed to actions can be built from pure functions, allowing us to use pure code within impure code.
- Maybe is an *algebraic data type* used to return a value when the possibility of errors arises in a function and can be used to avoid the usage of undefined.
- The let keyword is used to bind definitions within actions to a certain identifier.

Line numbering tool

This chapter covers

- Reading files from the filesystem
- Parameterizing the behavior of higher-order functions by using function arguments
- Using algebraic data structures to encode possible options
- Bundling code as an executable

In the last chapter, we laid the groundwork for a tool that is able to number lines from a given file. We have learned how we can read arguments from the user. So now, we can start thinking about how to read from a file and how to get the individual lines of the file's content.

This chapter starts by providing a discussion on reading files and transforming the read contents. Following this, we will write a general function whose control and data flow are influenced by functions given as arguments. Then, we will learn how to encode options with algebraic data structures and finish the chapter by completing our tool from the last chapter.

4.1   Reading files and transforming their content

So we need some IO action to perform this task. Haskell provides rudimentary functionality around working with files with two actions:

```
readFile :: FilePath -> IO String

writeFile :: FilePath -> String -> IO ()
```

readFile, as the name suggests, reads the contents from a file and returns it as a single string. writeFile receives a string and writes it to a file on the filesystem, creating the file if it doesn't already exist. Again, here we see the logic behind using type synonyms like the one for FilePath. Just from the name of the type, it is clear what the argument refers to in both of these functions. If it was a simple string, this might not be so evident. Just from the type name, we can infer a lot about these functions.

We will use readFile to construct an action that returns the lines of a file. To do this, we need to scan the file contents and break it up based on the newline character \n, which signals a new line. Luckily, Haskell provides us with a function that can do exactly that: lines!

```
ghci> :t lines
lines :: String -> [String]
ghci> lines "Hello\nWorld\n"
["Hello","World"]
```

As you can see, it splits a string into individual lines and even gets rid of the newlines for us. This function has an inverse function, called unlines, which nearly does the exact opposite:

```
ghci> :t unlines
unlines :: [String] -> String
ghci> unlines ["Hello", "World"]
"Hello\nWorld\n"
ghci> unlines (lines "Hello\nWorld")
"Hello\nWorld\n"
```

unlines will always add a newline after each word; however, lines ignores a missing newline at the end of its argument.

In addition to these functions, there exist the functions words and unwords that split (or unsplit) a string based on whitespaces. All of these functions can be found in the Data.String module; however, we do not have to import them, since they are being exported through the Prelude, the module that is always imported.

> **NOTE** The Prelude re-exports the most important functions from different modules. For example, the readFile and writeFile functions originally stem from the System.IO module. We do not have to import this module just because the Prelude is always imported. This can be disabled with a compiler flag or pragma within the code, but in most cases, using it is fine.

So now, we can write an action that uses `readFile` and `lines` to read the lines from a file. We have to read the contents and then return the result from the `lines` function. This is shown in the following listing.

> **Listing 4.1 An action for reading individual lines from a file**

```
readLines :: FilePath -> IO [String]        Reads the whole file
readLines filePath = do                       contents from the file at
  contents <- readFile filePath     <——       the specified file path
  return (lines contents)     <——┐
                                  └── Returns the individual lines of the
                                      file contents, split at every newline
```

It's important to note that this action will fail with an exception if the file doesn't exist. This is fine for us, since the error message will tell the user what they did wrong, so we are not interested in handling this failure.

After creating a file called `testFile.txt` in the same directory as our project, we can fill it with content and test our action. In my case, my file contained the following contents:

```
Hello
dear
reader!
```

After this is done, we can start the REPL (using `stack repl`) and test our action:

```
ghci> readLines "testFile.txt"
["Hello","dear","reader!"]
```

Nice! Now, we can start giving these lines some numbers!

4.1.1 Writing a pure library

We can now turn our attention to the `Lib` module in our project. Since the code for numbering lines is rather generic, we should keep it in the library module, since that is what it is. Since we have taken care of the many *impure* aspects of our program, we can now turn our attention to the *pure* code, which should be slightly more familiar to us.

First, let's examine the features we want to support. We want to support numbering every line or only numbering lines when they satisfy some predicate, like being non-empty or containing some substring, so we need a function that can provide us with a possibility of mapping numbers to lines. Also, we want to support different formatting for our line numbers, and to support something like left- or right-aligned line numbers, we first need to collect them all to compute the length needed for padding.

Let's start by thinking about how to represent such a mapping from number to line as a data type. We know that we need to support mapping an arbitrary amount of numbers to lines. We also know that the order of our mapping is important, since we need to know in which order to print them. Lists almost provide us with everything we need, since they can grow to an arbitrary length and have a deterministic order, but how do we represent a mapping in a list? The answer comes to us in the form of *associative lists*. These lists contain elements that represent single mappings from one value to another. How can such a mapping be represented? The easiest way is the *tuple*, since it combines two types in one.

A possible type for our numberings could be

```
type NumberedLines = [(Int, String)]
```

With this type, we can represent an association between line numbers and lines.

> **NOTE**   Associative lists are extremely versatile and can be used to construct a large number of mappings. However, many of the algorithms we can construct for them are rather pricey when it comes to their run time complexity, since most often, we have to search through the whole list to find a key. If performance isn't a big concern, however, associative lists are a very nice data structure!

This would look something like this:

```
[(1, "First Line"), (2, "Second Line"), (3, "Third Line")]
```

However, this is unsuitable for our feature set because we want to leave open the possibility that we *only number certain lines*. This means that some of the lines do not have a line number! So we need to represent the possibility of a line having no line number in the type. Fortunately, we have already seen a type that can represent a *missing* value: the Maybe type! Let us represent the line numbers this way:

```
type NumberedLine = (Maybe Int, String)
type NumberedLines = [NumberedLine]
```

A single numbered line consists of an optional number and the string of the line. All numbered lines are then a list of these mappings.

> **NOTE**   Here, we see that Maybe is not just used to catch errors but to encode *optional* values. Many languages feature types equivalent to Haskell's Maybe, often called Option or similar.

Now that we have a type for our numbers, we can start thinking about what functions we have to construct for our program. We need some function that can produce line numbers. However, this function needs to be parametrized such that it can skip certain lines in its numbering. Furthermore, we need an option that controls when to increment the line numbers, since there is a fundamental difference between when we count and when we number lines. We already know that we want an option that lets us skip empty lines; however, do we still count them? As we can see from figure 4.1, there is a difference in how we handle this. Preferably, this should be configurable by the user!

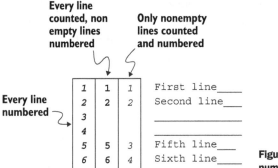

Figure 4.1   **Different ways to number empty lines**

As we have learned in the last chapter, *higher-order functions* receive other functions as arguments. These function can effectively parametrize their behavior. Since we need complex rules for ignoring and numbering lines, this seems like a good opportunity to construct a higher-order function that receives predicates on when to increment and when to number a line.

4.1.2   *Hiding auxiliary arguments*

Let's start by writing a function that numbers every single line without any predicates and then slowly evolve that function. First, let's think of the type. We receive some list of strings as our inputs (the individual lines) and have to produce the NumberedLines from before, but how will we manage the counter for our lines? Do we want to expose this as an argument? Ideally, we don't, since we want to start counting at 1. However, if we want to construct this function recursively, we need a way of passing the incremented counter to the recursive call. What we need is a *hidden* function within our accessible function. We can achieve this by creating a local function definition *inside* our function. We can use a let binding for this, which can be seen in the sketch in the following listing.

Listing 4.2   Function structure with a locally defined function

```
numberAllLines :: [String] -> NumberedLines
numberAllLines lines =
  let go :: Int -> [String] -> NumberedLines
      go counter lines = ...
  in go 1 lines
```
Creates a local function definition using a let binding

Calls the locally defined function

This is a bit different from the let we have seen so far! That's because let behaves differently when used in conjunction with do notation. When used in pure functions, the let keyword is used to create local definitions (that may reference each other) and makes these definitions available using the in keyword. This is illustrated in figure 4.2. The order in which our definitions are made is irrelevant.

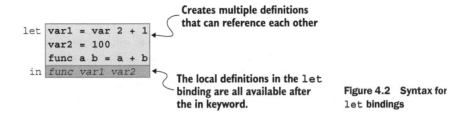

Figure 4.2   Syntax for `let` bindings

So we can use this `let` binding to create another function with a different type signature, which we then call inside our function! This function can have more (or completely different) arguments from our original function. When defining our outer function in terms of the inner function definition, we can use any (fixed or variable) arguments. This way, we can hide default parameters for recursive functions, like with the `counter` variable in the following example.

> **NOTE** When creating locally defined functions to extend the type signature by some special arguments, it's sometimes hard to find a fitting name for them. Often, they are simply called `go` or `aux`, as in *auxiliary*. This signifies that these functions are used as part of a bigger definition.

It is this counter variable that we can now recursively increment. Each recursive step will provide a new *associative mapping* for our line numberings, increment the `counter`, and start another recursive step if there are lines left to number. We are constructing a new list recursively by defining our result as the concatenation of our newly created mapping, which consists of a tuple of a `Maybe` value and the line along with the recursive result from the function with an incremented counter. This is shown in the following listing.

Listing 4.3   A function that numbers every line in order

The type signature for a locally defined function

Returns an empty list when the input list is empty and acts as the stopping condition for the recursion

```
numberAllLines :: [String] -> NumberedLines
numberAllLines lines =
  let go :: Int -> [String] -> NumberedLines
      go _ [] = []
      go counter (x : xs) = (Just counter, x) : go (counter + 1) xs
  in go 1 lines
```

Calls the helper function with a fixed argument for the counter argument

Creates a new mapping with the current line and recursively builds the rest of the numbered lines

In this example, we can observe that in its first pattern, the `go` function uses the wildcard `_` as its first argument. Why is that? Since this argument is not needed at this point (there is nothing to number), we can omit an identifier for this argument. It is generally a good idea to do this for arguments we do not need.

Exercise: Lines and words

The functions `lines`, `unlines`, `words`, and `unwords` are very helpful utilities when working with strings. Implement these functions yourself using recursive definitions! Remember that `strings` are just lists of chars, so you can pattern match them and can create definitions with more parameters inside your functions using a `let` binding. Use the pattern matches with guards to construct these functions.

So now, we have a function that can number all lines we pass to it. We can test this in GHCi:

```
ghci> numberAllLines ["Hello", "", "World"]
[(Just 1,"Hello"),(Just 2,""),(Just 3,"World")]
```

4.2   *Parametrized behavior in higher-order functions*

Let us tackle the problem of detecting empty lines next. We want to give the user the option to disable line numbering for them, but that means we have to detect them first. Of course, if a line is empty (contains no characters), we can consider it to be empty. However, what if the line contains control characters (which cannot be printed) or whitespaces? In that case, we should also consider the line empty. What we need is a predicate that decides whether we consider a string empty. In other words, it needs to be a function that returns a Boolean. To check if a string contains control characters or whitespaces, we can use helpful functions from the `Data.Char` module: `isPrint`, which identifies printable characters, and `isSeparator`, which identifies whitespaces and other Unicode separator characters:

```
ghci> import Data.Char
ghci> isPrint 'a'
True
ghci> isPrint '\n'
False
ghci> isSeparator ' '
True
ghci> isSeparator 'a'
False
```

We can use these functions to build a predicate that detects empty, nonprintable strings. To do this, we can use the `all` function, which checks if a predicate is true for every element in a list:

```
ghci> all (\x -> x == 1) [1,1,1 :: Int]
True
ghci> all (\x -> x == 1) [1,1,2 :: Int]
False
```

We can use this to construct a function that returns `True` if a string is either empty or only contains nonprintable characters or separators. This function is shown in the following listing.

Listing 4.4   A predicate that checks if a string contains at least one printable character

```
isEmpty :: String -> Bool
isEmpty str =
  null str
    || all (\s -> not (isPrint s) || isSeparator s) str
```

> **Returns True if the string is empty**

> **Returns True if the string only contains nonprintable characters or separators**

This function now lets us test strings for emptiness:

```
ghci> isEmpty "Test"
False
ghci> isEmpty "    "
True
ghci> isEmpty "\n  "
True
ghci> isEmpty "A   "
False
```

Additionally, we can define the dual of this function, which checks if a string is not empty:

```
isNotEmpty :: String -> Bool
isNotEmpty str = not (isEmpty str)
```

Now, we can start modifying our numbering function. Since we want to introduce control flow changes based on predicates on strings, we already know the type of our new function arguments: `String -> Bool`. We need to introduce two predicates, one for deciding whether we should skip incrementing the counter and one for skipping the numbering of a line. Our function signature should look something like this:

```
numberLines :: (String -> Bool) -> (String -> Bool) -> [String]
⮡ -> NumberedLines
numberLines shouldIncr shouldNumber text = ...
```

We renamed our function, since it is now a general function for numbering lines. The predicates can now be used in our function definition! We can use if-then-else in a `let` binding within the `go` function to either number lines, increment the counter, or do neither. This code is shown in the following listing.

Listing 4.5   Generalized higher-order function for numbering lines

```
numberLines :: (String -> Bool) -> (String -> Bool) -> [String] ->
⮡ NumberedLines
numberLines shouldIncr shouldNumber text =
  let go :: Int -> [String] -> NumberedLines
      go _ [] = []
      go counter (x : xs) =
```

> **A type signature for a locally defined function**

> **Returns an empty list when the input list is empty and acts as the stopping condition for the recursion**

```
let mNumbering = if shouldNumber x then Just counter else Nothing
    newCounter = if shouldIncr x then counter + 1 else counter
  in (mNumbering, x) : go newCounter xs
in go 1 text
```

Calls the helper function with a fixed argument for the counter argument

A recursive call with newly created variables

Increments the counter if the predicate for the incrementing evaluates to True

Numbers the current line if the predicate for the numbering evaluates to True

The predicates can influence the counting and numbering behavior, so from this function, we can now build other variants! Let's build our `numberAllLines` function.

4.2.1 *Partial function application*

To do this, we need functions that always return `True`, since we always want to count and number the lines. We could write the function like so:

```
(\_ -> True)
```

This function will simply ignore its input and return `True`. But why stop there? We could make this a bit more general and write a function that will always return some constant and ignore its second argument:

```
const :: a -> b -> a
const x = (\_ -> x)
```

Now, an expression like `const True` is equivalent to what we had before. Notice the type signature. We are using two free type variables. By choosing the second argument to be of type `b`, we are specifying that it can be different from the first argument. We can rewrite this function by pulling the ignored argument into the list of arguments:

```
const :: a -> b -> a
const x _ = x
```

Here, we arrive at a general function that generates a constant, unary function! Well, fortunately, this function already exists in Haskell! We can now construct our `numberAllLines` function using the `numberLines` function from listing 4.5 in conjunction with `const`:

```
numberAllLines :: [String] -> NumberedLines
numberAllLines text = numberLines (const True) (const True) text
```

What might seem strange in this function definition is the expression `const True`. Isn't that a binary function? How can we only supply a single argument? This little trick is called *partial function application*. In Haskell (and many other functional languages, for that matter), you do not need to provide a function with all the arguments it desires. If arguments are missing, the expression will evaluate to another function that still desires the missing arguments!

When we have an expression like (\x -> f x), we can perform a *eta reduction*. This reduction will reduce the expression down to f. This has rather significant implications for our syntax! A repeated eta reduction can work for functions with many arguments! This makes it possible to write extremely concise function definitions. But why does this work in the case of const? Let's examine this more closely. Suppose we have an expression like this:

```
const True
```

Remember the previous definition const x = (_ -> x). When we now replace x with the given value (True) we end up with

```
(\_ -> True)
```

So this evaluates to a unary function that returns the constant value True, but what is the type of this function? Well, we easily deduce that from the type of the const function being a -> b -> a. Since the first argument given is True, we know that a has to be of type Bool. So the final type is

```
b -> Bool
```

This simple function can take an argument of arbitrary type, with b being a free type variable, and it returns a Boolean. This makes sense, since the argument is simply ignored.

We can even perform this eta reduction on the numberAllLines function again:

```
numberAllLines :: [String] -> NumberedLines
numberAllLines = numberLines (const True) (const True)
```

We again determine if this checks out just from the types. Since numberLines is of type (String -> Bool) -> (String -> Bool) -> [String] -> NumberedLines and const True is of type b -> Bool, we can substitute b with String and find that the type signature of numberLines (const True) (const True) must be [String] -> Numbered-Lines, which is exactly the type we need!

> **TIP** Eta reductions are a very neat way of writing more concise function definitions. They are featured heavily in most Haskell code you will come across. While it is absolutely not necessary to use these reductions, it's a good idea to get familiar with this technique so that you have an easier time reading other people's code!

Now, we can check if our numberAllLines function does what it should:

```
numberAllLines ["Hello", "", "World", "!"]
[(Just 1,"Hello"),(Just 2,""),(Just 3,"World"),(Just 4,"!")]
```

Indeed, all lines are numbered! But we didn't generalize this function just so we could number all lines. Let's start ignoring some of them!

Exercise: Using eta reductions

The project from the previous chapter was implemented without using *eta reductions*, to make the syntax slightly more digestible. Now that we know how these reductions work, check the source code for the project, and see if you can perform any reductions!

First, we will write a function that still increments the counter for every line but doesn't number empty lines. Again, we can use the predicates from our generalized `numberLines` function to do that. Keep the two predicates from this function in mind. The first argument should be a constant `True`, since we always want to increment, but the second argument has to be a predicate for empty lines we created previously. We *only* want to number *nonempty* lines. Luckily, we created a predicate for that:

```
numberNonEmptyLines :: [String] -> NumberedLines
numberNonEmptyLines = numberLines (const True) isNotEmpty
```

Again, we are using eta reduction to avoid writing down the argument of type `[String]`. Let's test this definition:

```
ghci> numberNonEmptyLines ["Hello", "", "World", "!"]
[(Just 1,"Hello"),(Nothing,""),(Just 3,"World"),(Just 4,"!")]
```

We always increment the counter, but we do not number empty lines. Let's also create a version that doesn't increment the counter for empty lines. How do we do that? Easy. We can use `isNotEmpty` as the predicate for both arguments!

```
numberAndIncrementNonEmptyLines :: [String] -> NumberedLines
numberAndIncrementNonEmptyLines = numberLines isNotEmpty isNotEmpty
```

Let's test this definition too:

```
ghci> numberAndIncrementNonEmptyLines ["Hello", "", "World", "!"]
[(Just 1,"Hello"),(Nothing,""),(Just 2,"World"),(Just 3,"!")]
```

And there we have it! From the general definition in listing 4.5, we have built three functions that differ greatly in their functionality. This is summarized in the following listing.

Listing 4.6 **Three variants for functions that number lines based on different conditions**

```
numberAllLines :: [String] -> NumberedLines
numberAllLines = numberLines (const True) (const True)      ⟵┤ Numbers
                                                               │ every line
```

```
numberNonEmptyLines :: [String] -> NumberedLines
numberNonEmptyLines =
  numberLines (const True) isNotEmpty
```

Numbers every nonempty line, while incrementing the counter even on empty lines

```
numberAndIncrementNonEmptyLines :: [String] -> NumberedLines
numberAndIncrementNonEmptyLines =
  numberLines isNotEmpty isNotEmpty
```

Numbers every nonempty line, only incrementing the counter on empty lines

From these definitions, it's clear to see how easy it is to further extend these functions! We just need to write simple Boolean predicates for strings, and we can freely decide when and when not to number lines or increment the line counter.

4.3 Algebraic data structures as an encoding of possibilities

Now that we have a function for numbering lines, we only have to print them. One last challenge we have to overcome is padding the line numbers either to the right or to the left. Again, we want to take a general approach here. Since we already know that we either have to pad to the right or the left, we can imagine writing a function that is parametrized and either performs a left or right padding based on some option. But what should such an option look like?

4.3.1 Sum types or tagged unions

To do this, let us revisit the `data` keyword we started looking at in our discussion on the `Maybe` type. We learned that it can be used to define new data types with their constructors. An important feature of these constructors is their ability to be pattern matched. This makes it easy to use such a data type to create a simple *sum type*, which lets us express different variants for our padding. A *sum type* (sometimes called a *tagged union*) is a data type that consists of a finite amount of constructors of fixed types but only a single one at a time. These types are associated with a name (this is where the *tag* in *tagged union* comes from). When we want to represent the different kinds of padding for a string, we can think of the tags to mark whether we want to pad on the left or right.

Listing 4.7 Simple type for distinguishing left from right padding

```
data PadMode = PadLeft | PadRight
```

This type is shown in listing 4.7. You can read it as `PadMode` *is either a* `PadLeft` *or* `PadRight`. Our pad function can pattern match on this type to switch the way it pads a string. Just like types created with the `type` keyword, types that are created by the `data` keyword also have to be added to the export list. As this type has *constructors* associated with it (`PadLeft` and `PadRight`), we also need to export them. We can do so by adding `PadMode (..)` to the export list.

So how do we pad a string? Well, if a string is shorter than a specified length, spaces are being appended (or prepended, based on the `PadMode`, of course) such that the resulting string's length equals the desired length. We can use the `replicate` function for this:

```
ghci> :t replicate
replicate :: Int -> a -> [a]
ghci> replicate 10 ' '
"          "
```

This function takes an integer and some value of arbitrary type and evaluates to a list that contains this value as many times as the first argument specifies. But what about a negative argument?

```
ghci> replicate (-1) 'a'
""
```

It turns out that `replicate` has a clever implementation. Of course, a list of negative size does not exist, so it's simply an empty list. This is important, since it means we can use it to compute the padding for a string, regardless of where we add the padding to the string. It can be computed by

```
replicate (<desired length> - <actual length>) ' '
```

Using a `let` binding again, we can quickly come up with a function that computes the difference between desired and actual length and computes the necessary padding:

```
pad :: Int -> String -> String
pad n str =
  let diff = n - length str          ◁—  Computes the difference between desired and actual length
      padding = replicate diff ' '    ◁—  Computes the required padding for the input string
  in ...
```

But wait, we forgot about the `PadMode`! Where should be put this argument? A good answer would be using it as the first argument. Why? Think about partial function application again. If we use the mode first, we can simply pass the mode as an argument to this function and receive another function that performs the padding with the specified mode! We will see this shortly.

Let's ask another question: Where should we do the pattern matching? So far, we have only seen pattern matching within the arguments of a function, but in this case, this is not helpful, since we want to use our definitions from the `let` binding but not repeat them. That's why we can use yet another syntax to create a pattern matching within our function as a simple expression, using the `case` and `of` keywords. They look like this:

```
case <expression 1> of          ◁—  Starts the pattern matching on <expression 1>
  <pattern 1> -> <expression 2>  ◁—  If <pattern 1> matches, the result of this expression is the result from evaluating <expression 2>.
  <pattern 2> -> <expression 3>  ◁—  The same as above with <pattern 2> and <expression 3>
  ...
```

The patterns work just like we have already seen with pattern matching. We can use this syntax to match our `PadMode`, which we want to add to the `pad` function that uses our data type from listing 4.7. This makes us arrive at the function definition, shown in the following listing, that can change its behavior based on the `PadMode` argument.

Listing 4.8 A generalized function to perform either left or right padding

```
data PadMode = PadLeft | PadRight          ⟵─┐  Defines a data type that specifies
                                              │  whether to pad to the right or left

pad :: PadMode -> Int -> String -> String
pad mode n str =                           ──┐  Computes the difference between
  let diff = n - length str         ⟵────────┘  desired and actual length
      padding = replicate diff ' '  ⟵───────────┐  Computes the required padding
  in case mode of                   ⟵──────┐    │  for the input string
      PadLeft -> padding ++ str     ⟵────┐  │
      PadRight -> str ++ padding    ⟵──┐ │  │  Starts a pattern matching on
                                       │ │     the mode argument

                Performs right padding  │ │
                if mode is PadRight      │ Performs left padding if mode is PadLeft
```

And here, we have a neat function to perform some padding! After adding all the new functions to the module's export list, we can try it out:

```
ghci> pad PadLeft 10 "Pad me!"
"    Pad me!"
ghci> pad PadRight 10 "Pad me!"
"Pad me!    "
```

4.3.2 *Don't repeat yourself*

We can now create more specific functions from this very general function by using the partial function application again. This is shown in listing 4.9. Why is this a good way of going about writing our code? First of all, we don't have to repeat ourselves, which is always a good goal to have when programming. Also, imagine if we wanted to create an additional `PadCenter` mode that performs padding on the left and right to center the string. In that case, we would simply extend the data type and add another pattern in our pattern matching. We could still use the other definitions in the functions. This saves time, since you don't have to re-implement the same things over and over again. While it might seem contrived for this (rather simple) example, it can be a real time-saver to implement more complex functions like this. There is yet another advantage of having this additional `mode` parameter. Let's say we want to construct a function that uses the `pad` function (which we want to do) where the padding is not predetermined. How do you parametrize it? Sure, we could use a function as an argument that performs the padding, but it's much more clear to provide the `Pad-mode`. From that, it's immediately clear what the argument is used for.

Listing 4.9   Functions for left and right padding based on a generalized padding function

```
padLeft :: Int -> String -> String
padLeft = pad PadLeft
```
◁— **Defines a function that performs left padding from the general pad function**

```
padRight :: Int -> String -> String
padRight = pad PadRight
```
◁— **Defines a function that performs right padding from the general pad function**

Now that we can pad numbers the only thing left to do is to transform our Numbered-Lines into something we can print!

Exercise: Padding the center

We discussed how we could extend the data type and function in listing 4.8 to create a center padding, meaning the input string is being padded such that it appears in the middle of the result string. Do this! To perform division on integers, you can use the div function.

4.3.3   *The zip function*

To transform the NumberedLines we create with our numberLines function, we need another function that transforms this synonym for an associative list into something we can print more easily, more specifically a list of strings would be quite nice. For this, we need to collect all line numbers, figure out the maximum length, pad the numbers accordingly, and prepend these line numbers to the lines. So far so good; however, we are dealing with a list of tuples. We need to take this list apart to get to the individual line numbers and then again combine them afterward!

First, let's discuss what we did before and (once again) generalize it! Our function numberLines uses Boolean predicates to generate a list of tuples (of type (Maybe Int, String)) from simple strings. How can we do that generally? Assuming we have two lists we want to combine into a list of tuples, Haskell provides a nice function for that, called zip, of type [a] -> [b] -> [(a, b)]. Just as clasps combine with a zipper when fastened, the zip function takes two lists and combines them element-wise into tuples, stopping at the shortest of the two lists. This is visualized in figure 4.3. Let's look at some examples:

```
ghci> zip [1,2,3] ["Hello", "World", "!"] :: [(Int, String)]
[(1,"Hello"),(2,"World"),(3,"!")]
ghci> zip [1..10] ['a'..'z'] :: [(Int, Char)]
[(1,'a'),(2,'b'),(3,'c'),(4,'d'),(5,'e'),(6,'f'),(7,'g'),(8,'h'),(9,'i'),
➥ (10,'j')]
ghci> zip [1..10] [] :: [(Int, Int)]
[]
```

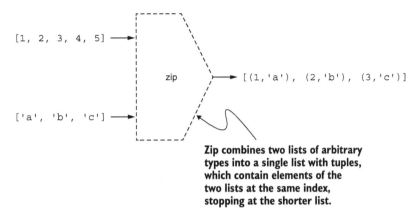

Zip combines two lists of arbitrary types into a single list with tuples, which contain elements of the two lists at the same index, stopping at the shorter list.

Figure 4.3 The interaction of side effects, actions, and pure code

The `zip` function has a quasi-inverse function called `unzip`. Just like `zip` was used to close a zipper, `unzip` opens it up again!

```
ghci> unzip [(1,'a'), (2,'b'), (3,'c')] :: ([Int], String)
([1,2,3],"abc")
ghci> unzip (zip [1..5] ['a'..'c'] :: ([Int], String))
([1,2,3],"abc")
```

However, as we can see from this example, `unzip` is not a real inverse of the `zip` function, since `zip` might drop elements (from the longer list, if one exists). These functions are very helpful when working with associative lists, since they provide a pure and safe way of constructing and deconstructing associative lists. This makes them good candidates for taking apart our `NumberedLines`, since this type is just a synonym for `[(Maybe Int, String)]`! While we could reinvent the wheel by writing a specific recursive function for deconstructing our list, this is not only error prone, but it also causes us to produce a lot of functions that, in essence, all do the same. By using functions that provide some basic functionality, we can avoid repeating ourselves and keep our function definitions easier to read!

Now, to figure out the maximum line number, we need to take all line numbers, compute their string representation (using `show`), take the length of these strings, and find their maximum. This can be done rather succinctly, using the `maximum` function, which already exists in Haskell, in conjunction with `map`:

```
ghci> xs = [1..1000000] :: [Int]
ghci> maximum (map length (map show xs))
7
```

The inner `map` transforms the list of numeric values into values of type `String`. The outer `map` computes the length of each string value, and `maximum` computes the maximum value of the whole list the outer `map` produced!

Using this to compute the maximum length of our line numbers, we can produce a function to compute the padding for our line numbers. But how do we then combine these numbers with our actual lines? We cannot use `zip`, since we want to coalesce these values into single values of type `String`. What we need is a general `zip` that allows us to control how these elements are being combined, and once again, Haskell provides us with such a function called `zipWith`!

```
ghci> :t zipWith
zipWith :: (a -> b -> c) -> [a] -> [b] -> [c]
ghci> zipWith (+) [1..10] [1..3] :: [Int]
[2,4,6]
ghci> zipWith (\x y -> (show x) ++ ": " ++ y) [1,2,3 :: Int]
➥ ["One", "Two", "Three"] :: [String]
["1: One","2: Two","3: Three"]
```

`zipWith` is another prime example of a higher-order function, since we can completely modify its behavior just by supplying a function of our choosing! As you might have guessed from the name, the function acts *exactly* like `zip` but calls its supplied function on the elements instead of creating tuples.

Exercise: The zipWith function

Just like `map`, `zip` is a typical, bread-and-butter function that any Haskell developer should know by heart. To get most familiar with it, implement this function using a recursive algorithm! Then, extend the function to create `zipWith`. Bonus question: Can you use `zipWith` to implement `zip`?

4.3.4   *Working with missing values*

The last peculiarity we have to take care of is this: our line numbers are not of a numeric type but of `Maybe Int`! Thus, the techniques we have described don't work, sadly. So where is the problem? Our problem is that within a `map` on our line numbers, we would always need to check if we encountered a `Just` or `Nothing` constructor. For this reason, we have learned about the `maybe` function. With this, we can quickly construct a `map` function, which can transform the list of `Maybe Int` into `String`:

```
ghci> ys = [Just 1, Just 2, Nothing, Just 4] :: [Maybe Int]
ghci> map (maybe "" show) ys
["1","2","","4"]
```

Here, we are using partial function application again, to make the definition a bit shorter. With all of these functions in our toolbox, we are able to write a function that creates nice, human-readable `String` representations of our `NumberedLines`. This is shown in the following listing.

Listing 4.10 A function for transforming numbered lines into human-readable strings

```
prettyNumberedLines :: PadMode -> NumberedLines -> [String]
prettyNumberedLines mode lineNums =
  let (numbers, text) = unzip lineNums
      numberStrings = map (maybe "" show) numbers
      maxLength = maximum (map length numberStrings)
      paddedNumbers = map (pad mode maxLength) numberStrings
  in zipWith (\n l -> n ++ " " ++ l) paddedNumbers text
```

Takes the list of
tuples apart into
a tuple of lists

Combines the padded line numbers with the actual lines

Casts all line numbers into strings and pads them to the maximum length

Computes the maximum length of all line numbers

Transforms line numbers into a string representation
and missing values (Nothing) to empty strings

Here, we see how each definition in our `let` binding is a part of the whole function definition. Each bound value is a puzzle piece that is only put together in the final definition to form the whole picture. This also neatly shows us which different computations are needed to perform the whole operation. Taking apart the `NumberedLines` type, numbering the strings, finding the maximum length of all numbered strings, and padding the numbers are the individual steps we need to take to finally put everything together into nicely readable strings. When you create your own functions that tackle a more complex problem, it is always a good idea to break the problem down into smaller tasks. This divide-and-conquer method works nicely with the `let` syntax!

NOTE The function prefix `pretty` is usually used for functions that transform some data into *human-readable* form.

This function also serves as a nice example of the *declarative programming style*. We define a few intermediate results, which can reference each other. Only the final expression creates the final definition for the whole function. This style of programming makes no assumptions about the order in which these definitions are used to compute the actual values. This is something we will explore more in later chapters.

4.3.5 *Printing a list of values with mapM*

Now, we have taken care of almost all parts of our program. The last thing we have to take care of is printing all the pretty numbered lines to the screen. What we need is a way of printing every string in our list of pretty lines. This reminds us of `map`, which already does something similar: evaluate a *pure* function for each element in a list. However, now, we want to perform an *action* on every element of a list. Our `map` function, thus, will not work, since it can evaluate to an action but not perform it. Luckily, there are other functions.

Haskell provides us with two functions that provide the same functionality as map in the context of actions. These are called mapM and mapM_, each taking a unary function that produces actions as an argument and evaluating to an action of a list of elements. The function given as an argument is being evaluated for every element, and the actions are being performed *in order*. This is exactly what we can use with putStrLn and our list of String values. But which one should we choose? Let's examine these functions:

```
ghci> mapM putStrLn ["Hello", "World", "!"]
Hello
World
!
[(),(),()]
ghci> mapM_ putStrLn ["Hello", "World", "!"]
Hello
World
!
```

Well, that is strange. Somehow, mapM prints the strings and then returns [(),(),()] (a list of unit), while mapM_ doesn't seem to return anything. Technically, it returns () (which GHCi is simply hiding from us). What is the difference between these two? mapM acts just like map. The returned values from the actions replace the input values from the original list. Since putStrLn returns a unit, each of the evaluations resolves to (), which is being collected in the list. mapM_ is a special variant of mapM, specifically dealing with actions for which we are not interested in the output. As previously discussed, unit holds no information. This means we can simply discard it, which is what mapM_ does, ignoring the output and simply returning a single unit.

Exercise: A monadic map
For the sake of simplicity, we can assume the types for the two map functions to look like this:

```
mapM :: (a -> IO b) -> [a] -> IO [b]

mapM_ :: (a -> IO b) -> [a] -> IO ()
```

Write these functions yourself! First, closely analyze how our pure map function was built, and then take a look at the interactiveLines example from the beginning of this chapter. You can write mapM and mapM_ the same way!

Since we are just interested in printing our list of strings, the mapM_ function is fine for our use case. We can very easily use it to print our line numbers!

4.4 From library to executable

Now, we can put everything together! We can modify our existing code from the last chapter to now read the lines from the file specified by the user, number them, create a *pretty* version of the numbered lines, and then print them to the screen, as in the following listing.

Listing 4.11 The main action for providing the basic functionality of the line-numbering tool

```
main :: IO ()
main = do
  cliArgs <- getArgs                              ← Reads arguments the
  let mFilePath = parseArguments cliArgs            program was called with
  maybe                                           ← Parses the filename argument
    (printHelpText "Missing filename")
    ( \filePath -> do                             ← Prints a help text if not exactly
        fileLines <- readLines filePath             one argument was given
        let numbered = numberAllLines fileLines   ← Reads the lines
            prettyNumbered = prettyNumberedLines   ← from a file
  PadLeft numbered                                ← Numbers every single
        mapM_ putStrLn prettyNumbered             ← line from the file
    )
    mFilePath
```

Prints each line numbering to the screen

Creates a human-readable representation of the line numberings

After putting everything together, we can finally test our program! We can start numbering some lines now! Let's look at an example:

```
shell $ stack run -- testFile.txt
 1 Lorem ipsum dolor sit amet, consectetur adipiscing elit. Maecenas a
 2 mattis nisi, eleifend auctor erat. Vivamus nisl sapien, suscipit non
 3 gravida sed, mattis a velit. Fusce non iaculis urna, a volutpat leo.
 4 Ut non mauris vel massa tincidunt mattis. Sed eu viverra lectus.
 5 Donec pulvinar justo quis condimentum suscipit. Donec vel odio eu
 6 odio maximus consequat at at tellus. Ut placerat suscipit vulputate.
 7 Donec eu eleifend massa, et aliquet ipsum.
 8
 9 Mauris eget massa a tellus tristique consequat. Nunc tempus sit amet
10 est sit amet malesuada. Curabitur ultrices in leo vitae tristique.
11 Suspendisse potenti. Nam dui risus, gravida eu scelerisque sit amet,
12 tincidunt id neque. In sit amet purus gravida, venenatis lectus sit
13 amet, gravida massa. In iaculis commodo massa, in viverra est mollis
14 et. Nunc vehicula felis a vestibulum egestas. Phasellus eu libero sed
15 odio facilisis feugiat id quis velit. Proin a ex dapibus, lacinia dui
16 at, vehicula ipsum.
```

Here, we nicely see how the PadLeft causes the line numbers to be right aligned. The tool does about what we expect it to do. So the last thing on our bucket list is adding more options.

4.4.1   *Encoding and parsing command line options*

Finally, we want to add more options to our program. For our simple application, we want to support the following three arguments:

- `--reverse`—Reverses the numbering
- `--skip-empty`—Skips numbering empty lines
- `--left-align`—Uses left-aligned line numbers

To represent this in our program, we can use an algebraic data type. We can see this in listing 4.12. Something new to us, which we will explore more in the next chapter, is the keyword `deriving`. For now, we will not get into detail; however, we need this to check the equality on this data type.

Listing 4.12   Data type used for representing options for the line number program

```
data LineNumberOption
  = ReverseNumbering           Represents --reverse
  | SkipEmptyLines             Represents --skip-empty
  | LeftAlign                  Represents --left-align
  deriving (Eq)                Derives the Eq type class for this type
```

From this data type, we can construct a function that parses single options into this type. We use `Maybe` again to signify that parsing might fail. We can see this function in the following listing.

Listing 4.13   Function to parse normal strings into the new data type for options

```
lnOptionFromString :: String -> Maybe LineNumberOption
lnOptionFromString "--reverse"    = Just ReverseNumbering       Parses a fitting string
lnOptionFromString "--skip-empty" = Just SkipEmptyLines         into the respective
lnOptionFromString "--left-align" = Just LeftAlign              constructor
lnOptionFromString _ = Nothing        Fails the parsing by returning Nothing
```

Let's assume the order in which options in conjunction with the filename can appear is fixed: options first, filename last. This makes parsing a bit easier. To extend our parsing function, we can use the `reverse` function to first reverse the list of arguments. Since we know the filename is last, it has to be the first element in the reversed list, which makes using our `x:xs` pattern very handy! When parsing the rest of the arguments, we can use `mapMaybe` (of type `(a -> Maybe b) -> [a] -> [b]`) from the `Data.Maybe` module to perform the `lnOptionFromString` function for parsing on it. Remember that `mapMaybe` will simply ignore all `Nothing` values (meaning all arguments that fail to parse will simply be ignored). Putting that together, we can now return a filepath and a list of options for our program. This is shown in the following listing.

Listing 4.14   Function to parse a list of command line arguments

```
import Data.Maybe

...

parseArguments :: [String] -> (Maybe FilePath, [LineNumberOption])
parseArguments args = case reverse args of
  [] -> (Nothing, [])
  (filename : options) ->
    ( Just filename,
      mapMaybe lnOptionFromString options
    )
```

Performs a pattern matching on the reversed list of arguments

Returns no filename and no options for an empty list of arguments

Returns a filename if it exists

Parses the optional arguments without failing or checking for duplicates

---

Finally, we can incorporate this into our `main` action from listing 4.11. To make it simple for us, we need to take a step back and think of how to change the *control flow* of our program. This control flow is mostly decided by the functions we use. When we want to change control flow based on some variables (like our options, in this case), we can simply switch out the functions we are using. In Haskell, functions are values. This means we can pass them as arguments (like we do with higher-order functions) and assign them to variables. Instead of passing options to our functions, why not simply switch out functions based on options? Here is an example:

```
let numberFunction =
      if SkipEmptyLines `elem` options
        then numberNonEmptyLines
        else numberAllLines
```

Checks if the SkipEmptyLines option is part of a list of options

Chooses the correct function based on the option

Here, we assume `options` is of type `[LineNumberOption]` and it represents the options from the result of the function from listing 4.14. As we can see, we "store" one of two functions in the variable `numberFunction`. More precisely, we change the definition of the `numberFunction` identifier based on the evaluation of a Boolean expression. We can use this to now incorporate our options into our `main` action, which is illustrated in listing 4.15. An execution of this program might look like this:

```
shell $ stack run -- --skip-empty --left-align --reverse testFile.txt
16 Lorem ipsum dolor sit amet, consectetur adipiscing elit. Maecenas a
15 mattis nisi, eleifend auctor erat. Vivamus nisl sapien, suscipit non
14 gravida sed, mattis a velit. Fusce non iaculis urna, a volutpat leo.
13 Ut non mauris vel massa tincidunt mattis. Sed eu viverra lectus.
12 Donec pulvinar justo quis condimentum suscipit. Donec vel odio eu
11 odio maximus consequat at at tellus. Ut placerat suscipit vulputate.
10 Donec eu eleifend massa, et aliquet ipsum.

8  Mauris eget massa a tellus tristique consequat. Nunc tempus sit amet
7  est sit amet malesuada. Curabitur ultrices in leo vitae tristique.
6  Suspendisse potenti. Nam dui risus, gravida eu scelerisque sit amet,
```

```
5  tincidunt id neque. In sit amet purus gravida, venenatis lectus sit
4  amet, gravida massa. In iaculis commodo massa, in viverra est mollis
3  et. Nunc vehicula felis a vestibulum egestas. Phasellus eu libero sed
2  odio facilisis feugiat id quis velit. Proin a ex dapibus, lacinia dui
1  at, vehicula ipsum.
```

4.4.2   An overview of the project

Let's review our program! The full `Main` module for our project is shown in listing 4.15, while the `Lib` module is shown in listing 4.17.

> **Listing 4.15   Header, datatypes, and utility functions in the main module**

```haskell
module Main (main) where

import Data.Maybe
import Lib                          ⟵ Imports needed modules
import System.Environment              for our definitions


data LineNumberOption           ⟵── Defines a data type
  = ReverseNumbering                  representing command
  | SkipEmptyLines                    line arguments
  | LeftAlign
  deriving (Eq)
                                                    Defines a function
                                                    for parsing single
                                                    command line
lnOptionFromString :: String -> Maybe LineNumberOption  ⟵ arguments
lnOptionFromString "--reverse" = Just ReverseNumbering
lnOptionFromString "--skip-empty" = Just SkipEmptyLines
lnOptionFromString "--left-align" = Just LeftAlign
lnOptionFromString _ = Nothing
                                         Defines a function providing
                                         help text for the user
printHelpText :: String -> IO ()    ⟵┘
printHelpText msg = do
  putStrLn (msg ++ "\n")                   Returns the name the
  progName <- getProgName        ⟵         program was called by
  putStrLn ("Usage: " ++ progName ++ " <options> <filename>")
  putStrLn "\n"
  putStrLn " Options:"
  putStrLn "    --reverse      - Reverse the numbering"
  putStrLn "    --skip-empty   - Skip numbering empty lines"
  putStrLn "    --left-align   - Use left-aligned line numbers"

parseArguments :: [String] -> (Maybe FilePath, [LineNumberOption])
parseArguments args = case reverse args of    ⟵
  [] -> (Nothing, [])                             Defines a function for
  (filename : options) ->                         parsing the filename and
    ( Just filename,                              options from the command
      mapMaybe lnOptionFromString options         line arguments
    )
```

The program starts by reading command line arguments and parsing them. The last argument is being interpreted as a filename, while the rest of the arguments are treated as optional arguments. If no filename could be extracted from the command line arguments, a help text will be printed; otherwise, the lines from a file are read. The options are used to change the program's behavior by switching definitions for the function applications.

The application creates line numberings, transforms them into human-readable form, and then prints them to the user, after which the program exits. This is shown in the following listing.

Listing 4.16 The main module for the line-numbering tool

```
readLines :: FilePath -> IO [String]          ◁          Reads the contents of
readLines filePath = do                                   a file and splits it up
  contents <- readFile filePath                           into single lines
  return (lines contents)


main :: IO ()
main = do                              Reads arguments the
  cliArgs <- getArgs          ◁        program was called with              Prints either the normal
                                                                            line numberings or the
  let (mFilePath, options) = parseArguments cliArgs     ◁                   reversed numberings
                                                                            based on the --reverse
      numberFunction =                      ◁                               option
        if SkipEmptyLines `elem` options
          then numberNonEmptyLines          Parses arguments and extracts
          else numberAllLines               the filename of the desired file
                                            as well as additional options
      padMode =                       ◁
        if LeftAlign `elem` options     Chooses a fitting function to
          then PadRight                 perform the numbering based
          else PadLeft                  on the --skip-empty option

                                              Chooses the correct pad mode
      go filePath = do                        based on the --left-align option
        fileLines <- readLines filePath     ◁
        let numbered = numberFunction fileLines     ◁     Reads the file contents
            prettyNumbered = prettyNumberedLines            and splits it up into lines
➡ padMode numbered
            revNumbered = numberFunction                                       ◁
➡ (reverse fileLines)                                                          |
            revPretty = reverse (prettyNumberedLines padMode revNumbered)      |
        mapM_                                                      Reverses the lines
          putStrLn                                                before numbering
          ( if ReverseNumbering `elem` options     ◁             and after creating
              then revPretty                                      the human-
              else prettyNumbered                    Prints either the normal      readable form
          )                                          line numberings or the
  maybe                                              reversed numberings based     Numbers the lines
    (printHelpText "Missing filename")     ◁         on the --reverse option       with the chosen
    go          ◁                                                                  numbering function
    mFilePath          Evaluates the normal          Prints a help                 and transforms it
                       numbering control             text if no                    into human-
                       flow if a filename            filename was                  readable form
                       was given                     given
```

The `main` function defines the appropriate function to perform the program's main utility. Whether the function is being run depends on the existence of a file path from the argument parsing.

> **Exercise: More options**
>
> As you might have realized, we didn't use the `numberAndIncrementNonEmptyLines` function, which not only caused empty lines to remain unnumbered but also didn't increment the line counter for them. Also, our argument parsing is rather crude. We don't check for invalid arguments and also don't feature a `--help` option for displaying the help text. Add these options to the program!
>
> Furthermore, we can think of many further options and functionalities for our little tool. For example, we could add an option to not even print empty lines or to only increment the counter on new paragraphs. The options are nearly endless! If you need inspiration, you can look at the options of GNU's `nl` tool. Get creative!

The library module consists of data type definitions for line numberings and utility functions to create these line numberings. The export list of the module should look like this:

```
module Lib
  ( NumberedLine,
    NumberedLines,
    isEmpty,
    isNotEmpty,
    numberLines,
    numberAllLines,
    numberNonEmptyLines,
    numberAndIncrementNonEmptyLines,
    prettyNumberedLines,
    PadMode (..),
    pad,
    padLeft,
    padRight,
  )
where
```

The definitions relating to numbered lines are shown in the following listing.

Listing 4.17   Header, datatypes, and utility functions in the library module

```
import Data.Char          ←——— Imports the Data.Char module

type NumberedLine = (Maybe Int, String)     ←┐ Defines types for
                                             │ line numberings
type NumberedLines = [NumberedLine]         ←┘

isEmpty :: String -> Bool      ←┐ Defines functions that can be used as Boolean
isEmpty str =                   │ predicates to decide whether a string is empty
```

```
    null str
      || all (\s -> not (isPrint s) || isSeparator s) str

isNotEmpty :: String -> Bool          <─┐  Defines functions that can be used as Boolean
isNotEmpty str = not (isEmpty str)      └─ predicates to decide whether a string is empty
```

Also contained are functions to create `NumberedLines` values from lists of strings, shown in the following listing. They are the interface we use to interact with our module.

Listing 4.18   Functions to create numbered lines from a list of strings

```
numberLines :: (String -> Bool) -> (String -> Bool) -> [String] ->
⇒ NumberedLines
numberLines shouldIncr shouldNumber text =       <──┐  Defines a function for
  let go :: Int -> [String] -> NumberedLines            numbering lines using two
      go _ [] = []                                       predicates for incrementing
        go counter (x : xs) =                  <──┐     the line counter and showing
          let mNumbering = if shouldNumber x then       the numbering
⇒ Just counter else Nothing              <──┐  Locally defines a recursive
              newCounter = if shouldIncr x then      help function
⇒ counter + 1 else counter               <──┐
          in (mNumbering, x) : go newCounter xs       Computes the line number as well as
    in go 1 text                                      the next number in the recursive step
                                                      based on the Boolean predicates

numberAllLines :: [String] -> NumberedLines          <──┐
numberAllLines = numberLines (const True) (const True)     Defines specific
                                                            functions for
                                                            creating line
numberNonEmptyLines :: [String] -> NumberedLines     <──┐  numberings
numberNonEmptyLines = numberLines (const True) isNotEmpty   based on the more
                                                            general definition
numberAndIncrementNonEmptyLines :: [String] -> NumberedLines  <──┘
numberAndIncrementNonEmptyLines = numberLines isNotEmpty isNotEmpty
```

Finally, we have functions that transform numbered lines into human-readable form. This part of the module is shown in the following listing. Note how we could potentially reuse this code in other programs too! That's why we implemented it as a library module.

Listing 4.19   Functions to create pretty numbered lines for output

```
                                   Defines a function for
                               transforming line numberings        Splits the line
                                 into human readable form           numberings
prettyNumberedLines :: PadMode -> NumberedLines -> [String]         into numbers
prettyNumberedLines mode lineNums =              <──┐               and lines
  let (numbers, text) = unzip lineNums           <──┘
      numberStrings = map (maybe "" show) numbers    <──┐  Converts line
      maxLength = maximum (map length numberStrings)  <──┤  numbers to
                                                         strings
                  Computes the maximum length     <──┘
                   of all line number strings
```

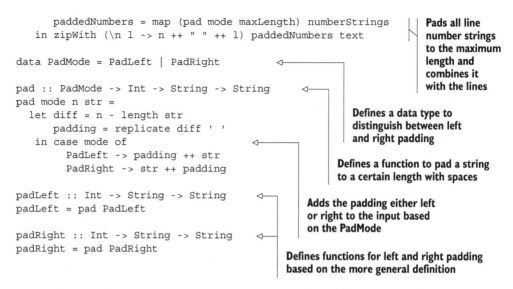

```
        paddedNumbers = map (pad mode maxLength) numberStrings
    in zipWith (\n l -> n ++ " " ++ l) paddedNumbers text

data PadMode = PadLeft | PadRight

pad :: PadMode -> Int -> String -> String
pad mode n str =
  let diff = n - length str
      padding = replicate diff ' '
   in case mode of
        PadLeft -> padding ++ str
        PadRight -> str ++ padding

padLeft :: Int -> String -> String
padLeft = pad PadLeft

padRight :: Int -> String -> String
padRight = pad PadRight
```

Pads all line number strings to the maximum length and combines it with the lines

Defines a data type to distinguish between left and right padding

Defines a function to pad a string to a certain length with spaces

Adds the padding either left or right to the input based on the PadMode

Defines functions for left and right padding based on the more general definition

It's important to understand how we encapsulate *pure code* in our library module and incorporate it into our *impure code* in our executable module. We are effectively mixing purity with impurity but keep our most-important functions, which provide our main functionality, free of any side effects!

Summary

- `readFile` and `writeFile` are used to read and write files on the filesystem.
- Functions can receive other functions as arguments that can influence the control and data flow.
- `let` can be used to define auxiliary functions within our function definitions, which can be used to hide extra arguments, needed for recursive calls, from the outer function.
- *Eta reductions* can be used to purposely leave out parameters from a function to create more concise definitions.
- *Partial function application* lets us create functions from functions by not providing all arguments the function desires.
- `data` is used to define *algebraic data types*, which are *sum types* used to model types with distinguishable values.
- `zip` and `zipWith` are used to combine two lists element-wise.
- We can use `mapM` with actions just like we used `map` with pure functions. `mapM_` is a special version that ignores the output of the actions.

Words and graphs

Our last project was a minimal clone of a popular UNIX tool. Serious business! But life is more than just writing industry-grade utilities for all of our terminal line numbering needs. Let's have some fun. And how do people usually have fun? By playing games of course!

A fun little game to play is the *word ladder game*, which makes the players build chains of words that can be found by transforming single letters within them. The game has many variants, and we will focus on a pretty complex one. But why play games when we could have the computer play for us?

Writing an artificial intelligence, even for a children's game, isn't always a cakewalk. This project will make us think about clever usage of data structures to implement the solution for a search problem. While it might seem simple on the surface, we will see that there can be pitfalls, even in child's play.

This chapter begins with a discussion on modeling graphs with Haskell types and how to create our own modules. We then explore the basics of type classes, discussing what they are, what they do, and how to use them. Then, we create a special data type for maps, using associative lists and module export lists to properly ensure invariants for our data type. By using maps, we create a data type for graphs and a lookup table for permutations of words from a list.

5.1   *Building a graph*

The ladder game is a fun exercise, requiring players (any number can participate) to dig deep into their knowledge of vocabulary. The game has several rules variants; we'll start by looking at the simplest variant, and then we'll move on to discussing how artificial intelligence could be developed for the game.

The players start with two words of the same length. One of these can be thought of as the start and the other as the end. The task is to find a chain of other words that link the starting word to the ending word, where each adjacent pair of words differs by a single letter. That means that a player starts with a word, changes a single letter to arrive at a new word, and continues these transformations until forming a complete chain, from start to end. If multiple players are playing the game, the player with the shortest chain wins. Here is an example: cat → sat → sag → dag → dog.

This is a fun game but for a computer, it's a rather trivial exercise, as we will see soon enough. In fact, it is a classic example of a *search problem*. To find a solution, we need to search a domain (a bunch of words) for a path from one element to another. This kind of problem creeps up in many applications:

- Navigation systems
- Databases
- Network routers
- Sudoku solvers

By solving the word ladder game, we learn a skill that is transferable to any of these other disciplines. To a computer, searching is the same, no matter what we are searching for. The difference comes in how a solution is modeled. For us, words are connected due to certain rules in our game, but in a navigation system, paths are given by map data. Once this abstraction layer is removed, the problems become identical.

For this problem not to be too simple, we will make things a bit more complicated: we will not only allow the player to change a single letter but to also add a completely new letter, remove a letter, and also reorder the letters arbitrarily. This modification to the game makes it much more interesting, since it is now possible to find paths between words of different lengths. With these rules, a solution can be found for the words *find* and *solution* (e.g., find → fins → ions → loins → tonsil → lotions → solution). A step-by-step solution is shown in figure 5.1.

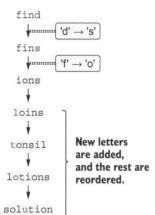

New letters are added, and the rest are reordered.

Figure 5.1   **A solution for *find* and *solution* in the modified ladder game**

Not only does this modification allow us to find more creative solutions, but it makes the problem a bit harder to solve computationally. When solving this problem, we need to start thinking about performance and clever ways to minimize unnecessary work.

5.1.1   *Polymorphic types*

Now, we can start thinking about how to build artificial intelligence for this kind of game. We assume that our intelligence somehow has a complete list of all English words. If it wants to find a valid chain, it needs to find a path from one word to the other with a valid transformation. For this, we can assume all words to be arranged in a graph, where an edge between two words is present if and only if we can reach one word from the other in a single step, a single word being a node in the graph. Such a graph is shown in figure 5.2 for a few words. As we can see, one can find a chain from *cat* to *dog* by finding a path within this graph.

We immediately see that multiple paths go from *cat* to *dog*. One solution would be cat → hat → heat → heal → held → dole → does → dogs → dog. However, this is not the shortest solution! A shorter one, for example, would be cat → cats → tags → goat → got → dog. Our artificial intelligence must be capable of finding the shortest solution in such a *ladder graph*, as we will call it.

We can quickly map out what our program should do:

1   Read a start and end word from the user.
2   Build a ladder graph from a dictionary.
3   Search for the shortest path in the ladder graph from one word to the other.

Luckily, the topic of finding such shortest paths has already been extensively studied in computer science, so that shouldn't be a problem. What *is* a problem is that we first need to compute such a ladder graph to find a solution. This should make us think: How can we represent a *graph* in Haskell?

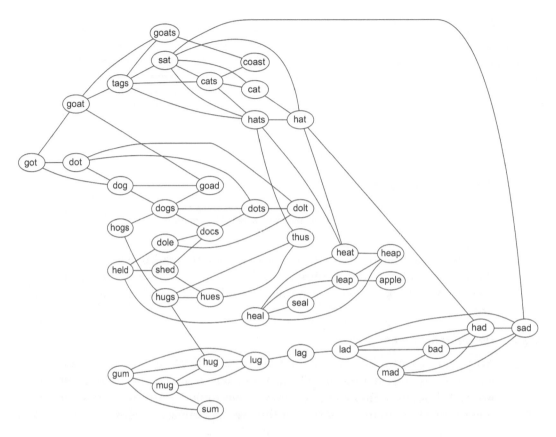

Figure 5.2   A ladder graph for a selection of English words

Let's review what graphs are. Graphs consist of *nodes* and *edges*, the last of which connect these nodes. Edges can be directed (so a path can only be constructed from one node to the other but not the other way around) or undirected. Additionally, edges can have costs, but we can ignore these for our problem. We treat every edge in the path the same: a single edge representing a single step in the ladder game. This gives us many possibilities to represent the concept as a Haskell type. First of all, what kind of elements do we want to store in our graphs? What *type* will the elements have? We could choose a fixed type but there is no need to do that. In general, the type for elements in a graph is ambiguous, so we will keep it a *polymorphic* type:

```
type Graph a = ...
```

This will enable us to be more flexible with the types we can use in our graphs, but how is a graph modeled? Since we are dealing with an undirected graph and edges have no cost, we are only interested in storing the information that two nodes are connected. This is possible by using an *adjacency list*. Such a list contains all pairs of nodes that are connected. In the previous chapter, we have already encountered a type that can represent such a data structure: the associative list!

```
type Graph a = [(a,a)]
```

Two nodes have an edge if and only if a tuple containing them is present in the list. While this type is really simple, it comes with a few drawbacks concerning performance. In the worst case, checking if an edge exists as well as gathering all children of a given node forces us to scan the whole list. The same is true for inserting a new edge into the list, since we have to check for duplicates. This is unacceptable for larger graphs, and since we want to be capable of handling whole dictionaries, this won't do. For an efficient traversal, we need a data structure that allows for fast indexing. Depending on the underlying implementation, an *adjacency map* might be a much better solution:

```
type DiGraph a = [(a, [a])]
```

This type maps a node to a list of nodes, and thus, multiple edges are implied but only in one direction! Therefore, this type is named `DiGraph`, to imply that it is directed. An example showing how this map corresponds to a graph structure is shown in figure 5.3.

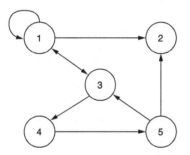

Adjacency map	
1	1,2,3
2	
3	1,4
4	5
5	2,3

Figure 5.3 Example of a graph built from an adjacency map

Sadly, this type has a downside if we want to represent undirected graphs. Adding a single undirected edge requires us to add two elements in our map. In the case of a simple undirected graph with two nodes that are connected, the value would look like `[(1, [2]), (2, [1])]` for nodes 1 and 2.

For now, let's start with this type, since a directed graph is fine for our search problem (as we will see later). We want to create not only this type but also a collection of functions that we can use to work with this type. For this, we want to bundle all of this functionality in its own module! Let's start by creating a new project! We will call this `ladder`.

5.1.2   *Introducing a new module*

After creating a new project with `stack new ladder`, we will now create a new file in our src directory, which will be our new module for our graph type. Let's call the file Graph.hs. This shall be our module for all graph-related definitions:

```
module Graph where
```

Remember that it's important for the module name to align with the name of the file.

> **NOTE**   Additionally, modules can be bundled in subdirectories in our source directories. In the case that the module is contained in a path like Foo/Bar/Module.hs, the name needs to reflect this like so: `Foo.Bar.Module`. The subdirectory names are usually capitalized.

Now, we can start thinking about the functions we want to implement. First, let us focus on building the graph. How would we add a single node to the graph? Is it as simple as adding an associative tuple to a list? Not quite, since we have to make sure that the same key is not appearing twice in our list. Remember that an associative list acts like a map. In our case, we are mapping nodes to other nodes, to which they are connected. So first, we need to implement a function that looks for the key in our map and then use it in our insertion function. This function is shown in the following listing.

Listing 5.1   Function for checking if a key is present in an associative list

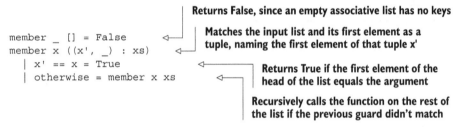

```
member _ [] = False
member x ((x', _) : xs)
  | x' == x = True
  | otherwise = member x xs
```

Returns False, since an empty associative list has no keys

Matches the input list and its first element as a tuple, naming the first element of that tuple x'

Returns True if the first element of the head of the list equals the argument

Recursively calls the function on the rest of the list if the previous guard didn't match

---

In this function's second pattern, we can see an example of pattern matching of a tuple inside of a list. The first element of the tuple (which, itself, is the first element in the list) is named `x'`, while the second element is ignored.

The type expression for this function has been intentionally omitted to make us think about how this type should look. We want to define a function for general associative lists (to use the definition for our graph type later). This leads us to conclude that the type of the associative list and the searched element need to be polymorphic:

```
member :: a -> [(a, b)] -> Bool
```

This expression seems to make sense. The keys and searched element need to be of the same type, while the second elements in the tuples can be of any other type. However, if we try to assign this type to the function and compile our code (e.g., with `stack repl`), we get an error!

```
...
   • No instance for (Eq a) arising from a use of '=='
     Possible fix:
       add (Eq a) to the context of
         the type signature for:
           member :: forall a b. a -> [(a, b)] -> Bool
...
```

What is that about? The error comes from the usage of the (==) function. We assume the type of the keys to be freely polymorphic, but how can we be sure that the type the function is used with has values that can be compared? How do we generally know which types have comparable values?

> **NOTE**   Operators in Haskell like == or && are functions, and we can use them just like any other! The compiler interprets them in an infix notation, but they can be referred to like other functions by wrapping the operator in parenthesis, as in (==). This makes it possible to use them in higher-order functions (e.g., zipWith (==) [1,2,3] [1,1,3] evaluates to [True,False,True]).

To understand this conundrum, we must quickly enter the topic of *type classes*. What are they?

5.1.3   *The Eq type class and type constraints*

Let's start the discussion by asking a simple question: What properties do types have? Types themselves are just names for a collection of values (or even no values, in rare cases). But simply because a value is of a certain type does not mean we necessarily know what kinds of operations we can perform on it. In most languages, some operations are implied for certain types, like the equality operator == in C or Java, which is defined for primitive data types. However, in Haskell, we are more explicit with defining the operations for types. This is done with *type classes*; these contain signatures of functions (or values, as functions themselves are also values) that need to be defined for an *instance* of this class. We can check this with GHCi like so:

```
ghci> :info Eq
type Eq :: * -> Constraint
class Eq a where
  (==) :: a -> a -> Bool
  (/=) :: a -> a -> Bool
  {-# MINIMAL (==) | (/=) #-}
```

This output tells us that the Eq type class defines two methods: one for equality (==) and one for inequality (/=). From the type signature of the equality operator (a -> a -> Bool), we can also immediately surmise that we are only allowed to compare values of the *same type* for which an *instance* of this type class exists. Thus, for example, we cannot compare an Int with a Float!

   An instance for a type of this class only needs to provide an implementation of one of them, indicated by the MINIMAL pragma. The missing method is simply inferred by negating the result of the given method. Thus, when we define equality (or inequality) for a type, we automatically gain the inverse functionality too!

The existing instances in our scope are also listed in the same output as this signature. Here are some of them:

```
instance Eq Bool
instance Eq Char
instance Eq Integer
instance Eq Int
instance Eq Float
```

There we have our familiar types, which we have already worked with. Each of these instances defines how to check the equality of values of their respective types. Furthermore, we see

```
instance Eq a => Eq (Maybe a)
instance Eq a => Eq [a]
```

Certain instances have *type constraints* as preconditions. These two examples tell us that if an arbitrary type a has an instance of the Eq type class, so does Maybe a and [a] for this type. This means Maybe Float and [Int] can also be compared!

> **WARNING** The vocabulary for type classes has some overlap with object-oriented programming. However, these concepts should never be confused! Type classes cannot be instantiated into objects, and methods do not behave like class methods, since their implementation can vary from type to type. Type classes relate more to interfaces in the object-oriented context than classes.

There exist many more type classes, and we will see a few of them in due time, but for now, let us focus on finding a type expression for our member function. When we want to specify that the type of the element we are searching for needs to be comparable for equality, it needs to have an instance of the Eq type class. We can achieve this by adding a *type constraint* to our type expression:

```
member :: Eq a => a -> [(a, b)] -> Bool
```

The constraint specifies which properties have to hold for the polymorphic types we use. Note that when explicitly naming the types (e.g., using Int), we do not need to add a constraint, since it is already known which instances this type has. Also, note how the methods of the type class implicitly come with their own type constraint:

```
ghci> :type (==)
(==) :: Eq a => a -> a -> Bool
```

If we want to use (==), the polymorphic type needs to have an instance of the Eq type class. This is why we get a compilation error otherwise!

NOTE In previous chapters, we have sometimes purposefully omitted type expressions to make it possible to compile some of our functions. We did this so that Haskell would figure out the constraints itself. Type inference is powerful enough to do so, at least in most cases.

5.1.4 The flip function

Now that we have finished our excursion, we can finally implement the function adding a new node to our graph. To make the naming clearer, we define a new function, `hasNode`, which is just an alias for `member` with its arguments flipped. The function for adding a new node to a graph now simply checks if a node is already present, and if not, it adds it with no outgoing edges. The code for this is presented in the following listing.

Listing 5.2 Function for checking if a key is present in an associative list

```
member :: Eq a => a -> [(a, b)] -> Bool
member _ [] = False
member x ((x', _) : xs)
  | x' == x = True
  | otherwise = member x xs

hasNode :: Eq a => DiGraph a -> a -> Bool
hasNode = flip member

addNode :: Eq a => DiGraph a -> a -> DiGraph a
addNode graph node
  | graph `hasNode` node = graph
  | otherwise = (node, []) : graph
```

Defines a function for checking if a key is present in an associative list

Defines a function for checking if a node is present in a directed graph

Flips the arguments of member to produce a definition for hasNode

Returns the unchanged graph if it already contains the node that should be added

Returns the graph with the added node if it doesn't already exist in the graph

---

Notice the order of arguments for our functions. `hasNode` intentionally has the graph as its first argument, such that it can be written in infix notation. To flip these arguments, we use a function called `flip`:

```
flip :: (a -> b -> c) -> b -> a -> c
```

This function takes a binary function and produces a function with the arguments flipped! Notice how `a` and `b` are the arguments for the function, and by using partial function application, using `flip` with a single binary function will result in a new function of type `b -> a -> c`.

Exercise: The lookup function

The `Data.List` module (as well as the always imported `Prelude`) already provides a function for looking up keys in an associative list, called `lookup`. Rewrite the `member` function by using it.

Taking a look at the type expressions, we see that we have to add `Eq` in the constraint for every function. That's because we want to use other functions (like `(==)`) with the same constraint inside their definitions. We need to make sure the types of our function arguments satisfy all constraints for their corresponding definitions. If we did not add the `Eq` constraint, we would specify that we could use arbitrary types, even those that cannot be checked for equality, inside a function that checks for equality, which isn't possible.

> **TIP**   Sometimes, you come across functions that feature some type class you have never seen before in their type constraint. I find that the quickest way to get a feel for the class—which methods and instances it has—is using GHCi to inspect the class. You can do so with `:i <name of the class>`.

Now that we know how to use type classes, we can tackle the greater problem of building our graph. We should think about which functions we could add to our module that will aid us in working with associative lists.

5.2   *Encapsulating Implementations*

When building our graph, we want to add a new function called `addEdge`, which adds a single edge between two nodes of our graph. To do this, we need to check whether the starting node is already present in the graph. Either we have to add this node to the graph with a new list of edges that only contains the ending node or the node already exists and we have to modify the list of edges. However, we need to *alter* the map somehow. To make things easier, we want to create a new function that performs arbitrary alterations to our map. Ideally, it should be capable of adding new elements, deleting them, and modifying values with a certain key. A good idea would be to use a higher-order function that receives a function argument controlling what should happen with our data structure.

This function needs to receive the information on whether a value for a given key already exists and then pass on the information of whether this value should be modified or removed to our higher-order function. Both steps can be completed using the `Maybe` type. To get a better understanding, we can look at the implementation in the following listing.

Listing 5.3   The function to modify an associative list

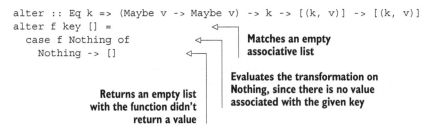

```
alter :: Eq k => (Maybe v -> Maybe v) -> k -> [(k, v)] -> [(k, v)]
alter f key [] =
  case f Nothing of
    Nothing -> []
```

Matches an empty
associative list

Evaluates the transformation on
Nothing, since there is no value
associated with the given key

Returns an empty list
with the function didn't
return a value

```
        Just value -> [(key, value)]            ◄┐ ┌─── Returns an associative list with the key and the
alter f key ((key', value') : xs)              ◄─┘ │     value returned from the transformation function
    | key == key' =                            ◄───┘   Matches a list with at least one element
        case f (Just value') of                ◄────       Matches if the key in the list head
            Nothing -> xs                       ◄───┐       equals the given key for the function
            Just value -> (key, value) : xs     ◄──┐│    Evaluates the transformation with the
    | otherwise =                                  ││    value associated with the given key
        (key', value') : alter f key xs        ◄─┐ ││
                                                 │ │└── Returns the list without the mapping for the
                                                 │ │    given key if the transformation returns Nothing
         Recursively, continues searching        │ │
         for the key, re-adding the matched       │   Returns an associative list with the key and the
         mapping to the recursive result              value returned from the transformation function
```

The function f controls the functionality. It receives a Nothing if a value for a given key does not exist and a Just value with the value from the map if it does exist. This function then either returns a Nothing—indicating that if the value exists for the key, it should be removed—or a Just—containing some value that should serve as the updated value in the map.

In the case of an empty list, the given key is missing, so there is no value associated with it. In this case, we provide the function f a Nothing and either keep the list empty or add a new mapping to the list. In the case of a nonempty list, we recursively search for the correct mapping, and once we have found it again, we check the result of the function. Nothing means that we delete the mapping, while a value wrapped in the Just constructor lets us add the updated mapping to the map. To make the types and values a bit clearer, we call the free type variables k and v, as in *key* and *value.*

> **NOTE** We can observe that we never really "modify" the associative list in the alter function. The function itself builds a completely new list, which contains the modifications we want. The list itself is simply *immutable.* This is the *pure* aspect of Haskell and generally how we deal with problems of state.

5.2.1 Adding and removing entries

Let us quickly take a look at how this function can be used to delete, update, and add mappings in our list. We can test it with this simple associative list:

```
ghci> myAssocList = [(1,1), (2,2), (3,3)] :: [(Int, Int)]
```

Removing works by providing a Nothing from our function given as an argument. When we always return Nothing (by using \x -> Nothing or const Nothing), we can use the function to delete any mapping for a given key:

```
ghci> alter (const Nothing) 1 myAssocList
[(2,2),(3,3)]
```

A new value is added by returning the `Just` constructor with some value we want to add for a certain key:

```
ghci> alter (const (Just 4)) 4 myAssocList
[(1,1),(2,2),(3,3),(4,4)]
```

We can also use this function to update values only if they already exist in the mapping. We can use the `maybe` function to either provide `Nothing` if the argument of the function was `Nothing` or update the value with a `Just` value:

```
ghci> alter (maybe Nothing (const (Just 0))) 1 myAssocList
[(1,0),(2,2),(3,3)]
ghci> alter (maybe Nothing (const (Just 0))) 4 myAssocList
[(1,1),(2,2),(3,3)]
```

If we do not explicitly check whether the value is already present in the associative list, we will add it automatically if it doesn't already exist. This is a powerful function, from which we can build many different helpful utilities for our associative list.

> ### Exercise: Another alter implementation
> In section 3.3.2, we learned about the `maybe` function, to work with `Maybe` values. However, in our implementation of `alter`, we have resorted to manual pattern matching. Rewrite the function to use `maybe` instead!

Before we add all of these functions into helper functions, we want to put a better structure into our code. Clearly, we are not defining functions for graphs but general associative lists. So let us define a new module for our code!

5.2.2   *Using export lists to hide constructors*

To more cleanly bundle our functionalities, we add a new module to our code, called `AssocMap`, in our src directory, and move the `member` and `alter` functions. We will put this module in a subdirectory of src, which we call `Data`. We do this to signify that the module we are creating is used to define the type and functions of a data type. Our project looks like this after we are done:

```
ladder
├── CHANGELOG.md
├── LICENSE
├── README.md
├── Setup.hs
├── app
│   └── Main.hs
├── package.yaml
├── src
│   ├── Data
│   │   └── AssocMap.hs
```

```
|     ├── Graph.hs
|     └── Lib.hs
├── stack.yaml
├── stack.yaml.lock
├── test
|     └── Spec.hs
└── test.cabal
```

The purpose of this new structure is not just to separate code for our graphs and associative lists but also to ensure invariants in our code. For our map, we need to make sure that each key only appears once. Ideally, we only want to perform modifications to this map in its own module. Otherwise, we cannot make sure other developers using our type also ensure that this invariant is satisfied. They could construct a value like this:

```
badAssocMap = [(1,1), (1,2)] :: [(Int, Int)]
```

Now, `alter` and `member` don't work anymore. Thus, we want to somehow hide the fact that this type is just a list. To achieve this, we give it a new type with its own constructor:

```
data AssocMap k v = AssocMap [(k, v)]
```

This type is fairly special because it only consists of a single constructor, which, in turn, only has a single field. In this case, we can use another keyword to define the type, called `newtype`:

```
newtype AssocMap k v = AssocMap [(k, v)]
```

There are technical reasons why we should use `newtype` instead of `data`. For a more detailed explanation of the differences and subtleties associated with this keyword, please check appendix B.

> **NOTE** It is possible (and mostly standard practice) to name the constructor in a `newtype` definition the same as the type itself. It's not mandatory to do so, and you can always choose a different name for the constructor if you like, but in larger projects, it makes it much clearer which value is associated with which type!

So how do we hide the constructor of this type from the outside? The answer comes to us in the form of the modules *export list*. Using this, we can control what is exported from the module and what is kept unknown. If we want to export a type without its constructors, we simply write down the name of the type. It looks something like this:

```
module Data.AssocMap
  ( AssocMap,
    member,
    alter,
  )
where
```

Here, we export the type `AssocMap` and the functions `member` and `alter`. However, we do not export the constructor for the `AssocMap` type. If we wanted to export the constructor as well, we could write `AssocMap (..)`, to export all constructors of this type.

A problem we have now is that our functions were not written for our `AssocMap` type but for simple lists of tuples. We need to rewrite them! We have two options:

1 Add the new constructor to every expression that deals with associative lists.
2 Construct a wrapper for each function for the new type using the old functions on lists.

The first option is, arguably, more canonical, since we want to define functions for this type. However, the second option allows us to construct functions for the type from any function on lists of tuples! We will, thus, choose the second option because it also makes the code easier to read.

This is also a good opportunity to get used to yet another neat, little piece of Haskell syntax: the `where` keyword. We can define internal definitions within functions using the `where` keyword just like we do with the `let` keyword, *except* the definition comes *after* it has been used. This is visualized in figure 5.4.

```
f x y = 1 + z
  where
    z = x + y
```

The definitions in the `where` clause are valid for the expression preceeding it.

Figure 5.4   The `where` clause

The export list, new type, and alterations to our functions are shown in the following listing.

Listing 5.4   The module structure for `AssocMap`

```
module Data.AssocMap
  ( AssocMap,
    member,
    alter,
  )
where

newtype AssocMap k v = AssocMap [(k, v)]

member :: Eq k => k -> AssocMap k v -> Bool
member key (AssocMap xs) = member' key xs
  where
    member' :: Eq k => k -> [(k, v)] -> Bool
    member' _ [] = False
    member' x ((x', _) : xs)
      | x' == x = True
      | otherwise = member' x xs

alter :: Eq k => (Maybe v -> Maybe v) -> k -> AssocMap k v -> AssocMap k v
alter f key (AssocMap xs) = AssocMap (alter' f key xs)
```

Exports the type AssocMap but not its constructor

Exports functions declared in the module

Defines a new type for the map built from an associative list

Creates local definitions that can be used in the expression above the where keyword

Unwraps and rewraps the associative list into our new type and uses our original functions on it

```
  where
    alter' :: Eq k => (Maybe v -> Maybe v) -> k -> [(k, v)] -> [(k, v)]
    alter' f key [] =
      case f Nothing of
        Nothing -> []
        Just value -> [(key, value)]
    alter' f key ((key', value') : xs)
      | key == key' =
        case f (Just value') of
          Nothing -> xs
          Just value -> (key, value) : xs
      | otherwise =
        (key', value') : alter' f key xs
```

Creates local definitions that can be used in the expression above the where keyword

Now, we have properly encapsulated our type and functions from the outside world! Sadly, we have now made our type unusable. Why? Here is a question: How can we create a new list? Remember, we do not have the constructor for building this type, meaning we have no way of constructing a value of any `AssocMap k v` type! How can we circumvent that?

While we could provide a function that transforms an associative list into an `AssocMap`, a simpler solution is to provide a value for an empty map and functions to add and delete new mappings. Luckily, we have our `alter` function to make this a breeze to implement! The new functions are shown in the following listing.

Listing 5.5 Definitions for an empty map and a deletion and insertion function

```
empty :: AssocMap k v
empty = AssocMap []
```
Defines an empty map

```
delete :: Eq k => k -> AssocMap k v -> AssocMap k v
delete = alter (const Nothing)
```
Defines a function that removes a key and value from the map

```
insert :: Eq k => k -> v -> AssocMap k v -> AssocMap k v
insert key value = alter (const (Just value)) key
```
Defines a function that inserts or updates a value associated with a key in a map

We must not forget to add the new definitions to our export list:

```
module Data.AssocMap
  ( AssocMap,
    empty,
    member,
    alter,
    delete,
    insert,
  )
where
```

Now, we can try it out! Let's load the project in GHCi and check it out:

```
ghci> insert 'a' "Hello" (insert 'b' "World" empty)

<interactive>:70:1: error:
    • No instance for (Show (AssocMap Char String))
        arising from a use of 'print'
    • In a stmt of an interactive GHCi command: print it
```

Whoops! Seems like we are missing a type class again.

5.2.3   *The Show type class*

The Show type class is used to provide the show function, which transforms a Haskell type into a String. It is this function that GHCi uses to display the value it evaluates, but our type doesn't feature an instance of said class.

> **WARNING**   The show function is not meant to provide human-readable representations of Haskell values! The Show type class is the dual to the Read type class, which provides automatically generated parsers for Haskell values. For most types, Show can simply be automatically derived.

Luckily, we can automatically infer it! Certain type classes (Eq and Show are two of them) can be automatically derived to behave sensibly. To derive a type class for a type, we use the deriving keyword:

```
newtype AssocMap k v = AssocMap [(k, v)]
  deriving (Show)
```

Derived instances for Show will produce String values that look pretty much like the values that would also be written down in code. Note that this only works when using types within our map that, in turn, have instances for the Show type class.

After this little alteration to our type, we can finally test our functions:

```
ghci> insert 'a' "World" (insert 'b' "Hello" empty)
AssocMap [('b',"World"),('a',"Hello")]
ghci> delete 'a' (insert 'a' "Delete me!" empty)
AssocMap []
```

As a little aside, we can also derive an instance for Eq! In that case, equality (==) is defined by *structural equivalence*. Two values of a type are equal if their constructors and, in turn, their fields are equivalent. Here are some examples:

```
ghci> data X = A | B Int | C Int Int deriving Eq
ghci> A == A
True
ghci> B 1 == B 2
False
ghci> B 1 == B 1
True
ghci> B 1 == C 1 2
False
```

```
ghci> C 1 2 == C 2 2
False
ghci> C 1 2 == C 1 2
True
```

Now, we define functions for looking up values associated with their key. After all, that is the purpose of a map. For the `lookup` function, we use the same method as we used previously: wrapping a function that works on lists into our new function. Additionally, we define a function that also provides a default in case the key is not present. This will save us some headaches later. The code for these functions can be found in listing 5.6.

We are creating a function called `lookup`, which might clash with the `lookup` function that is imported from the `Prelude` automatically. To circumvent this problem, we can hide the `lookup` function with the following import statement:

```
import Prelude hiding (lookup)
```

> **NOTE** In the case where we do not want to hide the function from the import (because we actually want to use it), we have to prefix the occurrences of these functions with the module name. In our case, that would have looked like `Prelude.lookup` and `Data.AssocMap.lookup`.

Listing 5.6   Definitions for lookup functions on maps built from associated lists

```
lookup :: (Eq k) => k -> AssocMap k v -> Maybe v        Matches an AssocMap value
lookup key (AssocMap xs) = lookup' key xs    <──────    and performs a lookup on
  where                                                 the list contained within it
    lookup' _ [] = Nothing               <──────        Returns Nothing if the list is empty
    lookup' key ((key', value) : xs)
      | key == key' = Just value                Recursively searches for the key in the associative
      | otherwise = lookup' key xs              list and returns a Just value if the key was found

findWithDefault :: (Eq k) => v -> k -> AssocMap k v -> v
findWithDefault defaultValue key map =
  case lookup key map of                    Returns the default value if
    Nothing -> defaultValue      <──────    the lookup was unsuccessful
    Just value -> value         <──────  Returns the found value from the lookup
```

Wonderful! We have completed a module for maps built from associative lists. Through close inspection, we have ensured that the functions inside our module don't violate the invariant that each key can only appear once and that the map cannot be "corrupted" from outside the module, since the constructor is not exported from it. Thus, pattern matching or constructing new maps without our functions is impossible. Now, we can implement our graph based on our new definition of a map.

5.3   *Using and reusing code*

In our `Graph` module, we can import our new map data type, but remember that it exports a function called `lookup`, which will clash with the `lookup` from the `Prelude`. This is a problem for us, and it only gets worse in bigger projects, where a module might import hundreds of other modules.

5.3.1   *Qualified imports*

An elegant way to combat our `lookup` problem is using *qualified imports*. Such an import looks like this:

```
import qualified Data.AssocMap as M
```

This imports `Data.AssocMap` and gives it the name `M`, since we don't want to write the whole name each time. The keyword `qualified` forces us to refer to functions and definitions from this module by prefixing their names with the name of the module. This means we cannot just use a definition like `alter`; we have to refer to the function like by the module name: `M.alter`. Since every import comes with its unique name, we avoid name clashes and also make it clearer in which context certain definitions stand!

Now, let's use these imports to write definitions for our directed graph. First, we define the type and define an empty graph:

```
type DiGraph a = M.AssocMap a [a]

empty :: DiGraph a
empty = M.empty
```

Now, we need to provide the following functionalities:

- Adding an edge to a graph
- Adding multiple edges to a graph
- Retrieving all the connected nodes of a node

An edge can be added by altering our map. If the entry doesn't already exist, we add the node with a single connected node. Otherwise, we will add the child node to the pre-existing nodes the original node is connected to. The only thing we have to look out for is ensuring the list of connected nodes doesn't contain any duplicates. We can do that by dropping all duplicates, and luckily, there exists a function that does that in the `Data.List` module, called `nub`!

```
ghci> import qualified Data.List as L
ghci> L.nub [1,1,1,2,3,4,1,1,1,2,3,4] :: [Int]
[1,2,3,4]
```

Now, we can construct the function for adding an edge. If the node doesn't exist in the graph, it is added. Otherwise, the list of connected nodes is extended by the new connected node, and duplicates are removed. Adding more than one edge doesn't seem complicated at all. We just have to add a list of edges to the graph calling the function for each edge that should be added. Additionally, we want to define a function that transforms an associative list of nodes and lists of nodes into a graph, which is similar in its implementation to the function adding multiple edges. Retrieving all connected nodes from a node is a simple lookup in our map! If a node cannot be found, we simply return an empty list, since there are no connected nodes to a missing node! These functions are shown in the following listing.

> **Listing 5.7 Functions for adding edges to a directed graph and retrieving connected nodes**

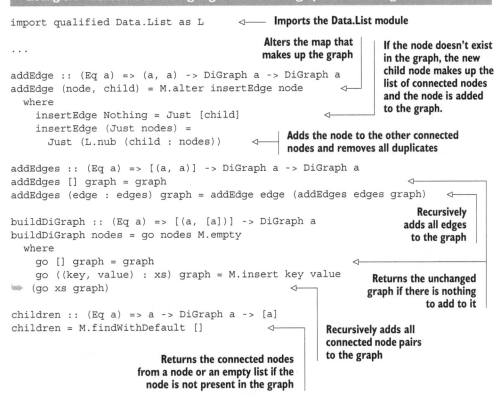

```
import qualified Data.List as L        ⟵── Imports the Data.List module

...

addEdge :: (Eq a) => (a, a) -> DiGraph a -> DiGraph a
addEdge (node, child) = M.alter insertEdge node   ⟵
  where
    insertEdge Nothing = Just [child]          ⟵
    insertEdge (Just nodes) =
      Just (L.nub (child : nodes))     ⟵

addEdges :: (Eq a) => [(a, a)] -> DiGraph a -> DiGraph a
addEdges [] graph = graph
addEdges (edge : edges) graph = addEdge edge (addEdges edges graph)    ⟵  ⟵

buildDiGraph :: (Eq a) => [(a, [a])] -> DiGraph a
buildDiGraph nodes = go nodes M.empty
  where
    go [] graph = graph
    go ((key, value) : xs) graph = M.insert key value
      (go xs graph)                    ⟵

children :: (Eq a) => a -> DiGraph a -> [a]
children = M.findWithDefault []        ⟵
```

Alters the map that makes up the graph

If the node doesn't exist in the graph, the new child node makes up the list of connected nodes and the node is added to the graph.

Adds the node to the other connected nodes and removes all duplicates

Recursively adds all edges to the graph

Returns the unchanged graph if there is nothing to add to it

Recursively adds all connected node pairs to the graph

Returns the connected nodes from a node or an empty list if the node is not present in the graph

We now have a few functions under our belt to work with directed graphs. Let's look at some of them in action:

```
ghci> import Graph
ghci> g = addEdges [(1,1), (1,2), (3,2), (3,1)] Graph.empty
ghci> children 3 g :: [Int]
[2,1]
ghci> children 2 g :: [Int]
[]
ghci> children 2 (addEdge (2,1) g) :: [Int]
[1]
```

An advantage of our implementation is that it is completely independent of the underlying implementation of the map. We could replace our `AssocMap` type with some other type as long as this type has compatible functions associated with it.

Exercise: Generalizing functions

When taking a good look at the graph functions, we can see that the implementations of `addEdges` and `buildDiGraph` are eerily similar. Try to generalize these two functions, providing a higher order function that works with lists in a similar structure, and apply this function to the two definitions. Additionally, we have not provided functions for deleting nodes and edges from a graph. Implement these functions yourself!

Now, we can confidently say we've learned how to build a graph. Armed with this knowledge, let's finally put together the ladder graph!

5.3.2 *Building maps for permutations*

To recap, the ladder graph contains all the words in a given dictionary and contains edges between all words that can be reached with a single step in the ladder game. A step constitutes a combination of any of the following transformations:

- Adding a letter to the word
- Removing a letter from the word
- Arbitrarily reordering all letters in the word

The transformation needs to result in a word, which, in turn, is present in the dictionary the word ladder game is based on. This presents us with a computational challenge! For each possible word, we have to search the whole dictionary. Since we can arbitrarily reorder words, the number of words to check from a given word is of factorial time complexity. This is a problem for larger words.

It could be of great help if we had some kind of cache or filter that could quickly tell us which permutations are valid and which aren't. Ideally, we do not want to compute the permutations of a word at all, but how do we achieve this? Let's say we want to scan the dictionary once with the goal of storing each word's permutations. What properties do these permutations have in common? They all consist of the same letters! So when we sort them, they are identical. We can scan through the dictionary to create a map of words and their permutations by sorting each word to create a key and then store the word in a list associated with the key. If we do this for every word, we have created a map associating words with their valid permutations in the dictionary!

We can start implementing this idea of *permutation maps* in a new module, which we will call `PermutationMap`. The type is a map from a string (the sorted representation of the permutations) to its valid permutations:

```
type PermutationMap = M.AssocMap String [String]
```

The operations on this map are identical to `AssocMap`, but we need to make sure that whenever we operate on the key, we sort it. We can do so using the `sort` function from the `Data.List` module. Again, we are using qualified imports for the `Data.AssocMap` module; the `Data.List` module; and, additionally, the `Data.Maybe` module. However, from the `Data.Maybe`, we only want to import a single function, which we do with an *import list*. This type of list acts like an export list, limiting the definitions being imported. The code for this module is shown in the following listing.

Listing 5.8   The module for permutation maps

```
module PermutationMap
  ( PermutationMap,
    empty,
    member,
    alter,
    delete,
    insert,
    lookup,
    findWithDefault,
    createPermutationMap,
  )
where

import qualified Data.AssocMap as M
import qualified Data.List as L
import Data.Maybe (fromMaybe)
import Prelude hiding (lookup)

type PermutationMap = M.AssocMap String [String]

empty :: PermutationMap
empty = M.empty

member :: String -> PermutationMap -> Bool
member key = M.member (L.sort key)

alter ::
  ( Maybe [String] ->
    Maybe [String]
  ) ->
  String ->
  PermutationMap ->
  PermutationMap
alter f key = M.alter f (L.sort key)

delete :: String -> PermutationMap -> PermutationMap
delete key = M.delete (L.sort key)

insert :: String -> [String] -> PermutationMap -> PermutationMap
insert key = M.insert (L.sort key)

lookup :: String -> PermutationMap -> Maybe [String]
lookup key = M.lookup (L.sort key)
```

Imports modules as qualified imports and a single function from the Data.Maybe module

Imports the Prelude module without the lookup function to avoid name conflicts

Defines the PermutationMap type to be an alias of the AssocMap type

Defines the empty permutation map

Wraps a general function from the AssocMap to be used for permutation maps by sorting the key before accessing the map

```
findWithDefault :: [String] -> String -> PermutationMap -> [String]
findWithDefault defaultValue key map =
  fromMaybe defaultValue (PermutationMap.lookup key map)
```
◁——┐ **Provides a lookup**
      with a default value

In essence, the `PermutationMap` type is just a specialized version of `AssocMap`, and thanks to our polymorphic implementation, we are free to use concrete types. Also, just like our `Graph`, the `PermutationMap` type is completely independent of the implementation of the map!

Exercise: Sorting strings

Have a look at the type expression for the `sort` function. Why can we use this function on `String` values? Why is it possible for us to use our polymorphic functions from `AssocMap` in our new module? Try to figure out why the types are compatible by inspecting the types using GHCi (`:type` and `:info`).

Next, we want to construct a function that takes a list of words and builds a permutation map from it. To accomplish this, we can assume all words to be lowercase. Each word needs to be added to the map. We expect there will be multiple words that share the same key (since that is how we find all permutations for a word), so we have to add the words by adding them to the list the key is pointing to. The code that achieves this is shown in the following listing.

Listing 5.9   The function to construct a permutation map from a list of strings

```
createPermutationMap :: [String] -> PermutationMap
createPermutationMap = go empty
  where
    go permMap [] = permMap
    go permMap (x : xs) = go (insertPermutation x permMap) xs

    insertPermutation word = alter (insertList word) word

    insertList word Nothing = Just [word]
    insertList word (Just words) = Just (word : words)
```

Calls the auxiliary function
go with an empty map

Defines an auxiliary
function for adding
each word to the map

Alters the map, using
the word as the key
and a function to add
the word to the
values that might
already be present

Defines a function to either create a list with a
single word if the key is missing in the map or,
otherwise, add the word to the existing list

This implementation is very similar to our `addEdges` function from listing 5.7, but this time, we do not separate the functions. Instead, we keep all necessary definitions as local definitions, using `where`. We can also obverse the mechanism of the `go` function seems familiar. Truthfully, there exists a function that has this exact behavior, but we will wait for chapter 8 to introduce it!

5.3.3 Creating a permutation map from a dictionary

Now, we can test our new function:

```
ghci> words =  ["traces", "reacts", "crates", "caster", "tool", "loot",
⇒ "cat"]
ghci> pm = createPermutationMap words
ghci> pm
AssocMap [("acerst",["caster","crates","reacts","traces"]),("loot",
⇒ "loot","tool"]),("act",["cat"])]
ghci> PermutationMap.lookup "tool" pm
Just ["loot","tool"]
ghci> PermutationMap.lookup "reacts" pm
Just ["caster","crates","reacts","traces"]
```

We see how each of the words appears in association with its sorted word. After building the map, we can quickly retrieve all permutations that have been present in the
original word list. Instead of computing all permutations for a word and checking
each one, we perform a simple lookup in our map!

5.4 Parameterizing transformations

Now that we have something that is computationally manageable, we can start building our ladder graph. For this purpose, we create yet another module, called `Ladder`,
containing each function that is unique to our use case. First, we define a type for lists
of words:

```
type Dictionary = [String]
```

We do this so that we can distinguish the usage of the dictionary from regular lists of
strings. We assume they contain words, which use only lowercase letters. Now, we can
write an `IO` action that reads a file with words and parses it as a dictionary. We already
know how to split the lines of a file, but we need to filter the dictionary entries such
that they only contain lowercase letters. We can do so using the `filter` function from
the `Data.List` module. This function receives a function of type `a -> Bool`, which acts
as a Boolean predicate on the elements of the list. Only the elements for which this
predicate returns `True` are returned. Here is an example:

```
ghci> filter (\x -> x <= 5) [1..10]
[1,2,3,4,5]
ghci> filter even [1..10]
[2,4,6,8,10]
```

Using this function, we can filter strings to only contain lowercase letters by checking
if each character is part of the lowercase Latin alphabet:

```
ghci> filter (\x -> x `elem` ['a'..'z']) "hello world."
"helloworld"
```

This helps us filter away any other characters. Additionally, we need to remove any duplicates, which we can do using the `nub` function. The code to achieve this is shown in the following listing. We also create qualified imports for the `Data.List`, `Graph`, and `PermutationMap` modules.

Listing 5.10 An `IO` action that reads a dictionary from a file path

```
module Ladder
  ( Dictionary,
    readDictionary,
  )
where

import qualified Data.List as L
import qualified Graph as G
import qualified PermutationMap as PM

type Dictionary = [String]

readDictionary :: FilePath -> IO Dictionary
readDictionary filepath = do
  dictionaryContent <- readFile filepath
  let
    lines = L.lines dictionaryContent
    words = L.map (L.filter (`L.elem` ['a' .. 'z'])) lines
  return (L.nub words)
```

Reads the contents from a file

Splits the file contents into a list of strings representing the individual lines

Filters each line to only contain lowercase letters

Returns the filtered words without duplicates

Here, we also see how we can use the infix notation for a function (`L.elems`, in this case) and eta reduction to get rid of a lambda abstraction.

Now, we want to use the words from the dictionary to produce the ladder graph. For this, we need to compute all possible changes for the word (i.e., adding letters, removing letters, and modifying a letter) and use the permutation map, which we build from the dictionary itself to compute all re-orderings of newly formed words. We can use the `buildDiGraph` function by building a list of nodes and their respective edges by computing all valid new words for each word in the dictionary. Assuming we already have a function `computeCandidates` that returns all possible candidates for a given word, the finished function is shown in the following listing.

Listing 5.11 The function to build a ladder graph from a dictionary

Builds a directed graph from the words in the dictionary and their related words in the ladder game

```
mkLadderGraph :: Dictionary -> G.DiGraph String
mkLadderGraph dict = G.buildDiGraph nodes
    where
      map = PM.createPermutationMap dict
      nodes =
        L.map (\w -> (w, computeCandidates map w)) dict
```

Builds a permutation map from the dictionary

Maps each word to itself and its related words in the ladder game

However, we do not already have the `computeCandidates` function, which we should take care of! Given a word, we first need to add an arbitrary letter to it and then use the permutation map to get all its valid permutations. This makes our job slightly easier because it does not matter where we add the new word. How can we add new letters to a string? One possibility is using the `map` function:

```
ghci> map (\x -> x : "word") ['a' .. 'z']
["aword","bword","cword","dword","eword","fword","gword","hword","iword",
 "jword","kword","lword","mword","nword","oword","pword","qword","rword",
 "sword","tword","uword","vword","wword","xword","yword","zword"]
```

Removing a letter is equally possible to do with a map, since we can go through the word itself to remove each letter from the word, using the `delete` function from the `Data.List` module. Note that this function only removes the first occurrence of the element to be deleted:

```
ghci> map (\x -> delete x "word") "word"
["ord","wrd","wod","wor"]
```

Again, we are not concerned with which letter gets removed, since our permutation map will sort the words on lookup anyway! To compute the words for which we switch a single letter out, we now have to combine both operations. That's because we do not want to add a letter we have just removed from the word. However, this might become slightly cumbersome to write down, which is why we will make use of another syntax for lists: list comprehensions.

5.4.1 *List comprehensions*

List comprehensions allow us to write down definitions for lists in a very simple manner. A list comprehension has two parts: the left-hand side specifies how elements of a list are built, and the right-hand side contains so-called generators and guards.

Here are some examples:

```
ghci> [ x + 1 | x <- [1..10] ] :: [Int]
[2,3,4,5,6,7,8,9,10,11]
ghci> [ x + 1 | x <- [1..10], x <= 5 ] :: [Int]
[2,3,4,5,6]
```

As we can see, the left-hand side is evaluated for each element from the generator that matches the guard! Using multiple generators will cause the left-hand side to be evaluated for the Cartesian product of elements from the generators:

```
ghci> [ (x, y) | x <- [1,2], y <- ['a', 'b', 'c']] :: [(Int, Char)]
[(1,'a'),(1,'b'),(1,'c'),(2,'a'),(2,'b'),(2,'c')]
```

We can use these comprehensions to construct our modifications for our words. For a given `word`, we can compute the possible new words like so:

```
added = [x : word | x <- ['a' .. 'z']]
removed = [delete x word | x <- word]
modified =
  [x : delete y word | x <- ['a' .. 'z'], y <- word, x /= y]
```

Here, we can observe how list comprehensions can be used to combine the functionalities of map and filter. Additionally, they give us a way to combine lists with the Cartesian product. This also scales to as many dimensions as we like, since we can use any number of generators! This way of writing definitions for lists often allows us to keep our definitions a bit shorter and, arguably, easier to read. However, this is mostly personal preference.

> **NOTE** List comprehensions can also be used for pattern matching. A failing pattern match in a generator counts as a skipped value. This way, you could define the catMaybes function like so: catMaybes xs = [x | Just x <- xs]. Any value that does not match Just x will simply be discarded.

Now, we can finish up our function by using the definitions we have just come up with. Additionally, we can remove all the duplicates from the sorted words to keep the number of lookups in our map small. Also, in the end result, we should remove the original word from the list, since a step in the ladder game should change the word. The full source code for this function is provided in the following listing.

Listing 5.12 Function to compute valid candidates for the game's next step

```
computeCandidates :: PM.PermutationMap -> String -> [String]   ◁ Sorts all possible
computeCandidates map word =                                        candidates and
  let candidates = modified ++ removed ++ added ++ [word]           removes duplicates
      uniques = L.nub [L.sort w | w <- candidates]       ◁─────── from them
      perms = L.concatMap (\x ->
⟹ PM.findWithDefault [] x map) uniques    ◁──── Computes the valid permutations
  in L.delete word perms                   ◁──── for each possible candidate
  where
    added = [x : word | x <- ['a' .. 'z']]   ◁──── Removes the original word
    removed = [L.delete x word | x <- word]  ◁──── from the valid candidates
    modified =
      [x : L.delete y word |                  Computes strings that have a single
⟹ x <- ['a' .. 'z'], y <- word, x /= y]  ◁── letter added to the original word
```

Computes strings that have
a single letter exchanged
for another one

Computes strings that have
a single letter removed
from the original word

A function here we have not yet seen is concatMap. What does it do? This function is closely related to the concat function, which simply takes a list of lists and *flattens* them, creating a single list that contains all the elements of the previous lists by concatenating them. concatMap is just a combination of map followed by a concat. This is helpful for situations where the result of the map function is a list, but you want to combine all elements in those lists to a single list. Since this is rather common, this function is already pre-defined:

```
ghci> concat [[1,2,3], [4,5,6]] :: [Int]
[1,2,3,4,5,6]
ghci> concat ["Hello", " ", "World"] :: String
"Hello World"
ghci> concatMap (\x -> [1..x]) [1..5] :: [Int]
[1,1,2,1,2,3,1,2,3,4,1,2,3,4,5]
```

Now, we can construct the ladder graph for a given dictionary! Let's look at a small example:

```
ghci> mkLadderGraph ["cat", "cats", "act", "dog"]
AssocMap [("dog",[]),("act",["cat","cats"]),("cats",["act","cat"]),
➡ ("cat",["act","cats"])]
```

Here, we supply the function with a dictionary of four words. We can see that the words *cat*, *cats*, and *act* are all reachable within one step from each other, while *dog* cannot be reached by any node and has no neighbors in the graph. Now that we can construct the structure to search for a solution, we can tackle the challenge at the heart of our artificial intelligence: the search problem!

Summary

- Algebraic data types can contain free type variables, which can be used to make a data structure contain arbitrary types.
- Module names have to align with the path of the file in the project.
- The Eq type class is used to provide functions ((==) and (/=)) for comparing values for equality.
- The flip function is used to flip the arguments of a binary function.
- Higher-order functions can change their behavior completely based on the received function argument.
- We can exclude the constructors of a type in the export list of a module to make it impossible to create values of that type outside of the module.
- The Show type class features the show function, which is used to transform Haskell values into strings.
- Qualified imports are used to force us to use the name of a module (or its alias) when using definitions from it.
- List comprehensions feature a special syntax to filter, map, and combine lists.

Solving the ladder game 6

This chapter covers

- Writing complex algorithms with multiple helper functions
- The intricacies of type variables and their scoping
- Profiling the performance of our application and adding external dependencies to the project

In the last chapter, we covered the ladder game and discussed how to implement a data structure that can represent graph structures. Furthermore, we can construct a graph that represents all possible outcomes of our game.

Now, we want to turn our attention to solving the problem of computing a solution within this graph. We can achieve this goal using a search algorithm that will guarantee we always find the shortest possible solution to our game.

This chapter begins by discussing how to implement a breadth-first search algorithm for our ladder game AI. Then, type variables are discussed, and language extensions are introduced. The chapter closes with a discussion on profiling of our project and how to improve its performance.

6.1   Constructing a breadth-first search

Knowing we can construct a ladder graph from a given dictionary, the only computational complex task we need to perform is to search in it. An additional requirement for our algorithm is that it needs to find the shortest path to produce an optimal word ladder. Our graph is special, in that it has uniform edge cost, since none of them are weighed. In this case, we are guaranteed to find the shortest path with a *breadth-first search*!

6.1.1   Overview of the algorithm

Let's think about the graph. When searching for a path, we start at a certain node. From there, we need to visit every neighbor and then repeat this process for each neighbor of each new node we have not previously visited. When performing such a search, we create an ordering of *layers* of nodes. Such an ordering is shown in figure 6.1.

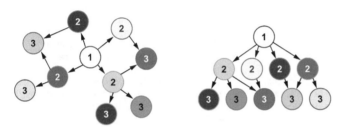

Figure 6.1   A breadth-first ordering of nodes in a graph

To construct a *breadth-first* search, we have to simultaneously update a frontier of new nodes we are visiting. We cannot just perform a recursive search for every node, since this would be a *depth-first* search, where we forgo searching in every neighbor node of a given node and instead immediately continue searching at the first neighboring node we find. Thus, when searching, we have to keep track of the nodes we are currently visiting and update them accordingly in each step. This is shown in figure 6.2.

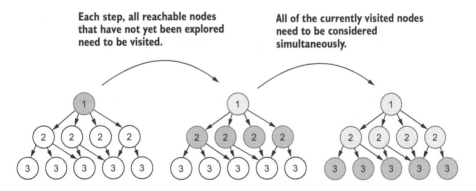

Figure 6.2   An example of a breadth-first search

Not only do we have to search for the existence of a path, but we also need to identify which nodes are part of it to solve the word ladder game. To achieve this, we have to keep a history of our searched nodes and keep track of predecessors of nodes while we are searching them. To do that, we must ensure we never visit a node twice, since every node must have a single predecessor; otherwise, we would need to search the whole graph again to find the actual path we found in the first place. To combat this, we can delete every node we have seen from the graph while we are searching in it. Is this OK for our purposes? The answer is yes! It is impossible for the shortest path from one node to the other to visit a node twice. The nodes that connect the two visits of the same node could be removed to produce a shorter path that still connects the starting node to the end node. The creation of this *predecessor graph* is shown in figure 6.3.

We start the search at the first node, deleting it from the graph, since we have visited it.

In the next step, we remember the predecessor of node 2 and 3 and delete them from the graph.

Just like before, the predecessors for the new nodes are saved, and the new nodes are deleted from the graph. This also removes the edge from node 5 to 4.

In the last step, we find our end node. The predecessors of the new nodes are saved. Note how 5 is not a predecessor of 4, even though in the original graph, they have been connected. We are only interested in the direct predecessors of nodes when starting the search at node 1. All other predecessors are irrelevant, since they will always result in a longer path than the one we have found!

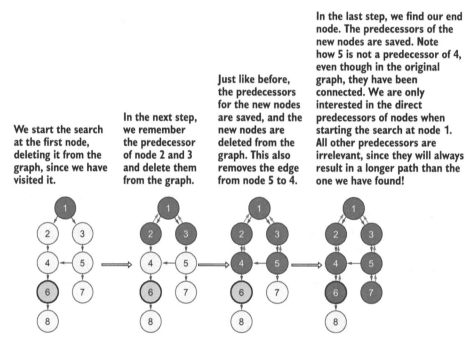

Figure 6.3   An example of a search on a graph (searching from 1 to 6) and the predecessors being built in every step

Let us recap. Our search algorithm will need to perform the following actions:

1   Start with the graph and a starting node as the initial frontier.
2   Collect all neighboring nodes for each node in the frontier.
3   Delete the current frontier from the graph.
4   Store each node in the frontier as predecessors for their respective neighboring nodes.

5 Check if the target node is part of the neighboring nodes.

   a If yes, the search is over and the predecessors can be backtracked to find the path.

   b If no, continue the search (step 2), using the neighboring nodes as the new frontier.

To delete multiple nodes at once, we need to introduce a new function that does that for us. Similar to previous implementations, we call `delete` from our `AssocMap` module recursively for each element that should be deleted from the graph. The code for this is shown in the following listing.

Listing 6.1   The function to delete multiple nodes from a graph

```
deleteNodes :: Eq a => [a] -> DiGraph a -> DiGraph a
deleteNodes [] graph = graph
deleteNodes (x : xs) graph = M.delete x (deleteNodes xs graph)
```

Returns the graph when no nodes should be deleted

Removes a single node from the graph and recursively removes the rest

---

From our description of the search algorithm, it's clear that we need to handle some kind of state. We need to keep track of our frontier but also our graph to search on (since we are deleting nodes from it) and our predecessors.

6.1.2   Keeping track of search state

Luckily, we already have a type that can be used for this purpose: our `DiGraph` type. We can, thus, represent our search state as its own type that contains the frontier as a list of elements, our graph, and another graph we use to keep track of the predecessors:

```
type SearchState a = ([a], DiGraph a, DiGraph a)
```

Additionally, we define a type for the result of a search. It is either unsuccessful or successful, returning the predecessors we could find. It is assumed that the predecessor graph will then make it possible to backtrack a solution.

```
data SearchResult a = Unsuccessful | Successful (DiGraph a)
```

In our actual search, we have to perform two tasks:

1 Perform the actual search, and update the state accordingly.

2 Backtrack the predecessors to get the searched path.

The general skeleton for our function might look like this:

```
bfsSearch :: Eq a => DiGraph a -> a -> a -> Maybe [a]
bfsSearch graph start end
  | start == end = Just [start]
  | otherwise =
    case bfsSearch' ([start], graph, empty) of
```

```
Successful preds -> Just (findSolution preds)
Unsuccessful -> Nothing
```

Our function is supposed to search for a path in a graph that connects the start and end nodes. We return a `Maybe` of the path, since the search can be unsuccessful—in which case, we, of course, return `Nothing`. We now concentrate on implementing `bfs-Search'`. This function is meant to work with the search state and return a result telling us if the search was successful as well as the predecessors. The current frontier from the graph can be deleted using with the newly created `deleteNodes` function. When collecting all connected nodes (or child nodes) from each node in the current frontier, we have to make sure to filter them based on their membership of our now updated graph with deleted nodes, since we do not want to add nodes to the frontier that are not part of our graph anymore. To add all of these new nodes as predecessors, we construct a new help function, which adds a list of tuples of nodes and their connected nodes in reverse to a graph, thus adding edges to a graph that signify which node precedes which in the search. These functions (meant to be used as local definitions in our `bfsSearch` function) are shown in the following listing.

Listing 6.2 Auxiliary functions to perform a breadth-first search

```
addMultiplePredecessors :: Eq a => [(a, [a])] -> DiGraph a -> DiGraph a
addMultiplePredecessors [] g = g
addMultiplePredecessors ((n, ch) : xs) g =          Calls the auxiliary function on each
  addMultiplePredecessors xs (go n ch g)            pair of nodes and connected nodes
  where
    go n [] g = g                                   Adds each connected node
    go n (x : xs) g = go n xs (addEdge (x, n) g)    as a predecessor of the
                                                    original node recursively

bfsSearch' :: Eq a => SearchState a -> SearchResult a
bfsSearch' ([], _, preds) = Unsuccessful           Returns a negative
bfsSearch' (frontier, g, preds) =                  result if the frontier is
  let g' = deleteNodes frontier g       Deletes the nodes    empty, since the search
      ch =                              from the frontier    was unsuccessful
        L.map                           from the graph
          (\n -> (n, L.filter (`M.member` g')
  (children n g)))                                  Creates pairs of nodes
        frontier                                    from the frontier and their
      frontier' = L.concatMap snd ch                connected nodes, which
      preds' = addMultiplePredecessors ch preds     are members of our
  in if end `L.elem` frontier'                      modified searching graph
      then Successful preds'
      else bfsSearch' (frontier', g', preds')       Concatenates the lists of
                                                    connected nodes, creating
    Searches                                        the new frontier
    recursively with       Returns a positive
    the new frontier,      result with the          Adds predecessors to the
    graph, and             predecessor graph        current nodes in the frontier
    predecessor            if the target node
    graph                  has been found           Checks if the target node has
                                                    been found in the new frontier
```

6.1.3 *Finding the solution by backtracking*

The last puzzle piece is the backtracking algorithm to find the solution from the predecessor graph. We know that the nodes in this graph all only have a single predecessor, except for the start node, which is the only node containing no predecessor. This allows us to recursively backtrack from the end to the start node. We can stop our search, once no more predecessors can be found. The code for this algorithm is shown in the following listing. Note that the auxiliary function performing the search produces a solution in the reverse order. Also, for this algorithm to work, a solution must exist and the assumptions we have made about the predecessor graph must hold!

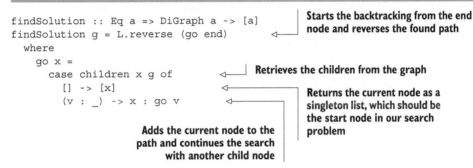

Listing 6.3   Our backtracking algorithm to find a path in a predecessor graph

```
findSolution :: Eq a => DiGraph a -> [a]          Starts the backtracking from the end
findSolution g = L.reverse (go end)               node and reverses the found path
  where
    go x =
      case children x g of                Retrieves the children from the graph
        [] -> [x]                         Returns the current node as a
        (v : _) -> x : go v               singleton list, which should be
                                          the start node in our search
              Adds the current node to the    problem
              path and continues the search
              with another child node
```

Now, we can put everything together! After adding the definitions from listing 6.2 and listing 6.3 to our code skeleton with a `where` clause, we arrive at the final definition for our search algorithm! However, this will not compile, and instead, we get an error:

```
• Couldn't match expected type 'a1' with actual type 'a'
  'a1' is a rigid type variable bound by
    the type signature for:
      findSolution :: forall a1. Eq a1 => DiGraph a1 -> [a1]
    at .../ladder/src/Graph.hs:...
  'a' is a rigid type variable bound by
    the type signature for:
      bfsSearch :: forall a. Eq a => DiGraph a -> a -> a -> Maybe [a]
    at .../ladder/src/Graph.hs:...
```

For some reason, the types of `bfsSearch` and `findSolution` don't seem to match up—but why? Aren't they both polymorphic? Both even have the same type constraint and name, so the types should be compatible.

6.2 *Type variable scoping*

This error might be confusing, and to understand we have to cover some theoretical ground. Simply put, this kind of error is caused by the way Haskell treats type variables and their scoping.

6.2.1   *Universal quantification*

To better understand this error, let us take a look at type expressions once more. Something that Haskell hides from us is that a type expression like this doesn't exist:

```
const :: a -> b -> a
```

Haskell sees this type a bit differently:

```
const :: forall a b. a -> b -> a
```

This is called *universal quantification* and is performed implicitly to the outermost level of all type signatures that contain free type variables by default. The `forall` brings new type variables into the scope for the declaration of the function to use. To the outside of the function declaration, this can be thought of as a promise: for all types that may replace a and b, the declaration holds. It's easy to see that this promise holds when we play around with the function:

```
ghci> const (1 :: Int) ("Hello" :: String)
1
ghci> const (True :: Bool) (3.1415 :: Float)
True
ghci> const (() :: ()) ((\x -> x) :: (a -> a))
()
```

We can replace a and b with arbitrary types and still get a result. While this is a promise to the outside of the function declaration, it is, however, a restriction to the definitions inside it. That makes sense, since the concrete type is not chosen by the function declaration but by the callee of the function! Inside the function declaration, the types are fixed (sometimes called *rigid* in error messages).

```
f :: a -> a
f x = y
 where y = x
```

The type in this example will be implicitly changed to `forall a. a -> a`; thus, the type variable a is introduced as well as fixed for the declaration. It will be inferred that x is of type a, and since y = x, y also must be of type a. The types are correct. But what if we add a type expression to x, declaring it as type a?

```
f :: a -> a
f x = y
 where y = (x :: a)
```

This will raise the same error again. But why? After adding the implicit universal quantification, it looks like this:

```
f :: forall a. a -> a
f x = y
 where y = (x :: forall a. a)
```

The `forall a. a -> a` restricts the variable `a` to be *arbitrary but fixed* for the function's declaration. This also extends to the declarations in the `where` clause! However, `forall a. a` of x makes the promise that this can be of any arbitrary type. This promise is made to the rest of the definition of the function and, ultimately, causes the types to be incompatible! x cannot be of a fixed and arbitrary type at the same time! When checking these properties, the compiler does not take the names of types into account!

6.2.2 Language extensions

This exact problem comes up when constructing our search function. Luckily, we can tell Haskell to perform a *lexical scoping* of type variables, meaning when a type variable is introduced by `forall`, it can be reused in the types of a functions declaration and still refer to the same type. We can enable this behavior by using a so-called *language extension*. These extensions allow us to change the behavior of the Haskell compiler, either on a global scale (by using compiler flags) or on a per-file basis. The language extension we are interested in is called `ScopedTypeVariables`. We can enable this by adding the following line to the beginning of our module:

```
{-# LANGUAGE ScopedTypeVariables #-}

module Graph (...) where
```

This now allows us to *explicitly* use `forall` in our type definitions and changes its behavior. `forall` now introduces lexically scoped type variables! This enables us to construct the function from before by explicitly quantifying the type variable in the outermost type signature. This is shown in the following listing.

> **Listing 6.4 Example of using a lexically scoped type variable**
>
> ```
> f :: forall a. a -> a          ⟵  Introduces the type variable a to be
> f x = y                             used in the functions declaration
>   where y = (x :: a)           ⟵  References the introduced type variable and
>                                    may not be universally quantified again
> ```

A nice side effect is that constraints on the type are *carried* to other definitions, so we only have to apply type constraint on the outermost type signature! Also note that function definitions without explicit usage of `forall` still behave the same as before.

> **IMPORTANT** The usage of `forall` is overloaded and has different meanings, depending on the language extension being used. In addition to `ScopedType-Variables`, there also exist `RankNTypes` and `ExistentialQuantification`, which have a profound effect on how the type system works. In general, the explicit `forall` should only be used when it is needed! `ScopedTypeVariables`, however, is relatively safe and enabled globally in many projects.

6.2.3   *Using lexically scoped type variables*

After modifying the types for our search function, we arrive at a complete (and compiling) definition for our search algorithm! The full source code is shown in the following listing. Take note of the explicit forall in the outermost type signature and how the type constraint Eq a only appears in this signature, since the type variable a is now available in the whole function declaration.

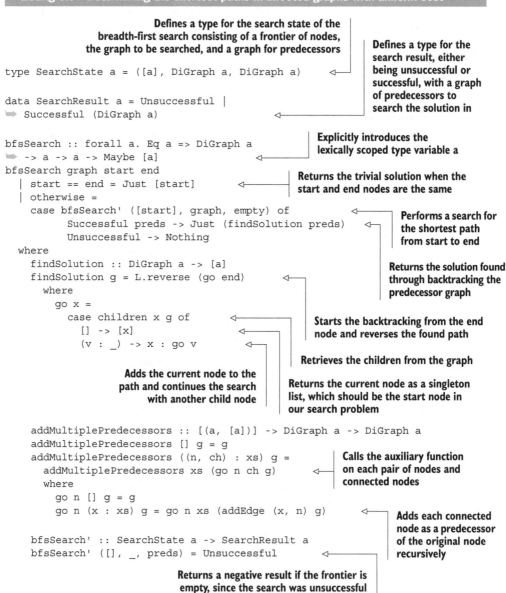

Listing 6.5   Determining the shortest paths in directed graphs with uniform cost

Defines a type for the search state of the breadth-first search consisting of a frontier of nodes, the graph to be searched, and a graph for predecessors

Defines a type for the search result, either being unsuccessful or successful, with a graph of predecessors to search the solution in

```
type SearchState a = ([a], DiGraph a, DiGraph a)

data SearchResult a = Unsuccessful |
➡ Successful (DiGraph a)

bfsSearch :: forall a. Eq a => DiGraph a
➡ -> a -> a -> Maybe [a]
bfsSearch graph start end
  | start == end = Just [start]
  | otherwise =
    case bfsSearch' ([start], graph, empty) of
        Successful preds -> Just (findSolution preds)
        Unsuccessful -> Nothing
  where
    findSolution :: DiGraph a -> [a]
    findSolution g = L.reverse (go end)
      where
        go x =
          case children x g of
            [] -> [x]
            (v : _) -> x : go v
```

Explicitly introduces the lexically scoped type variable a

Returns the trivial solution when the start and end nodes are the same

Performs a search for the shortest path from start to end

Returns the solution found through backtracking the predecessor graph

Starts the backtracking from the end node and reverses the found path

Retrieves the children from the graph

Adds the current node to the path and continues the search with another child node

Returns the current node as a singleton list, which should be the start node in our search problem

```
addMultiplePredecessors :: [(a, [a])] -> DiGraph a -> DiGraph a
addMultiplePredecessors [] g = g
addMultiplePredecessors ((n, ch) : xs) g =
  addMultiplePredecessors xs (go n ch g)
  where
    go n [] g = g
    go n (x : xs) g = go n xs (addEdge (x, n) g)

bfsSearch' :: SearchState a -> SearchResult a
bfsSearch' ([], _, preds) = Unsuccessful
```

Calls the auxiliary function on each pair of nodes and connected nodes

Adds each connected node as a predecessor of the original node recursively

Returns a negative result if the frontier is empty, since the search was unsuccessful

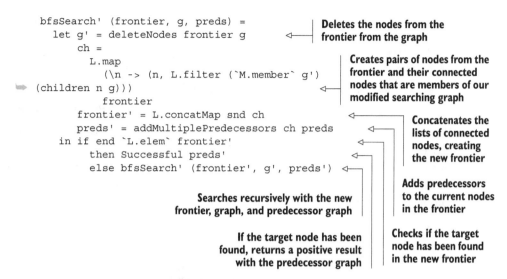

```
bfsSearch' (frontier, g, preds) =
    let g' = deleteNodes frontier g            ←─┤  Deletes the nodes from the
        ch =                                       frontier from the graph
            L.map
                (\n -> (n, L.filter (`M.member` g')       Creates pairs of nodes from the
    (children n g)))                            ←─       frontier and their connected
                frontier                                 nodes that are members of our
        frontier' = L.concatMap snd ch    ←─             modified searching graph
        preds' = addMultiplePredecessors ch preds  ←─        Concatenates the
    in if end `L.elem` frontier'           ←─                lists of connected
        then Successful preds'         ←─                    nodes, creating
        else bfsSearch' (frontier', g', preds')  ←─          the new frontier
```

Searches recursively with the new
frontier, graph, and predecessor graph

Adds predecessors
to the current nodes
in the frontier

If the target node has been
found, returns a positive result
with the predecessor graph

Checks if the target
node has been found
in the new frontier

We have constructed a breadth-first search algorithm for our direct graph, finding the shortest path by keeping track of the visited nodes, the modified graph, and the previously found predecessor. A predecessor graph is built from the visited nodes, which is then used to find the actual solution via backtracking.

Exercise: More search algorithms

To search for the shortest path in a graph, we have used *breadth-first search*; however, there are other algorithms for searching as well. If we just want to find *any* path and are not interested in its length, the *depth-first search* might be suitable. Also, the bidirectional breadth-first search serves as a performance improvement to the ordinary breadth-first search by performing two searches, coming from both sides at the same time, where one searches from start to end and the other searches from end to start. Once the two searches meet, a solution has been found. Implement both of these search algorithms! (Note, however, that the bidirectional breadth-first search algorithm is tricky to implement!)

Now, we are capable of building the ladder graph and can also find the shortest path within it. Now, we have all the pieces we need to build our program!

6.3 *Improving performance with hashmaps*

Building a function for solving the word ladder game is rather simple. We just need a dictionary and a start and end word! We can simply build the ladder graph with the mkLadderGraph function and search for a solution with our search algorithm! The code as it appears in the Ladder module is shown in the following listing.

Listing 6.6   A function for searching for the optimal solution to the ladder game

```
ladderSolve :: Dictionary -> String -> String -> Maybe [String]
ladderSolve dict start end =
  let g = mkLadderGraph dict          Generates the ladder graph
  in G.bfsSearch g start end          from the dictionary

                                      Performs a search in the generated graph
```

We can keep the `Main` module of our program rather simple. Just like in our last chapter, we provide a help text if the number of arguments doesn't match our expectations. Otherwise, we simply build the dictionary with the `readDictionary` action and solve it with the aforementioned `ladderSolve` function. We then print the solution and its length. The full code for the module is shown in the following listing.

Listing 6.7   The `Main` module for the word ladder solver

```
module Main (main) where
                                    Imports all definitions
import Ladder                       from the Ladder module
import System.Environment
                                         Defines an action for
printHelpText :: String -> IO ()         printing a help text
printHelpText msg = do
  putStrLn (msg ++ "\n")
  progName <- getProgName
  putStrLn ("Usage: " ++ progName ++ " <filename> <start> <end>")

main :: IO ()                    Reads arguments that were
main = do                        supplied to the program
  args <- getArgs
  case args of                            Matches if there exist
    [dictFile, start, end] -> do          exactly three arguments
      dict <- readDictionary dictFile
      case ladderSolve dict start end of         Reads the dictionary from
        Nothing -> putStrLn "No solution"        the provided file path
        Just sol -> do
          print sol                      Performs the search for
          putStrLn ("Length: " ++ show (length sol))   the shortest path and
    _ -> printHelpText "Wrong number of arguments!"     reports the result
```

The `print` action is just a combination of `show` and `putStrLn`, printing a value to stdout. This application can now be tested!

For this, the code repository has two dictionary files already prepared: `small_dictionary.txt`, containing 200 words, and `large_dictionary.txt`, containing 58,110 words. In our projects directory, we can now call the program like so:

```
shell $ stack run -- path/to/small_dictionary.txt cat flower
["cat","oat","lot","volt","love","vowel","lower","flower"]
Length: 8
shell $ stack run -- path/to/small_dictionary.txt dog book
["dog","dot","lot","tool","look","book"]
Length: 6
```

That looks good! So why not test it with the larger dictionary? Well, sadly, we are unable to observe the program functionality in all its glory because at least on my machine, it doesn't seem to produce a result. It simply takes too long. We should improve this somehow.

6.3.1 Analyzing performance with profiling

Before deciding what we want to improve, we should first analyze which operation takes so long. For this, we want to profile our program. We can do so by first compiling the program with `stack`, using the `--profile` flag. This will set a few options in GHC that will enable profiling of the application while running. We can then set the run-time option for basic time and memory profiling using `+RTS -p -RTS`. `+RTS` and `-RTS` are used to start and end supplying arguments to the Haskell run-time system, instead of a normal application. The full invocation of the program looks like this:

```
shell $ stack run --profile -- \
           path/to/small_dictionary.txt dog book +RTS -p -RTS
```

After the program has finished, a file will be created, which, in our case, is called ladder-exe.prof. This file contains profiling information and looks like this:

```
Mon Jul 25 16:22 2022 Time and Allocation Profiling Report  (Final)

        ladder-exe +RTS -N -p -RTS path/to/small_dictionary.txt dog book

        total time  =       0.03 secs   (100 ticks @ 1000 us, 8 processors)
        total alloc = 46,192,080 bytes  (excludes profiling overheads)

COST CENTRE                   MODULE        SRC
        ⮕ %time %alloc

lookup.lookup'                Data.AssocMap  src/Data/AssocMap.hs:(54,5)-(5
  ⮕ 7,34)   54.0    0.1
computeCandidates.uniques     Ladder         src/Ladder.hs:19:7-50
          ⮕ 21.0   26.9
member.member'                Data.AssocMap  src/Data/AssocMap.hs:(24,5)-(2
  ⮕ 7,32)   14.0    0.0
alter.alter'                  Data.AssocMap  src/Data/AssocMap.hs:(33,5)-(4
  ⮕ 3,40)    5.0   44.7
lookup                        PermutationMap src/PermutationMap.hs:31:1-34
          ⮕  3.0   12.3
readDictionary                Ladder         src/Ladder.hs:(10,1)-(14,22)
          ⮕  2.0    0.2
computeCandidates.perms       Ladder         src/Ladder.hs:20:7-69
          ⮕  0.0    1.7
computeCandidates.modified    Ladder         src/Ladder.hs:(25,5)-(26,58)
          ⮕  0.0    7.1
computeCandidates.canditates Ladder          src/Ladder.hs:18:7-57
          ⮕  0.0    2.5
```

This is a brief overview of our program's *cost centers*, which mostly consist of our functions. This tells us how much time was spent in each function and how much memory was allocated. From this, we can see that a lot of time is used in our `lookup` function in our `AssocMap` module. More than half of the run time is occupied by this function! This makes sense, since we are constantly looking up values in our graph, which is just an `AssocMap`. So if we want to speed up our program execution, we have to optimize it!

This is the question: What is wrong with this function? It is a simple lookup in the associative list that makes up our map. In the worst case, it has to traverse the whole list on each lookup! It makes sense that a larger dictionary would result in a larger graph, which would result in more time spent looking up values. Sadly, this is simply the slow reality that we face when using associative lists. This downside is inherent in their design. What we need to do is to completely replace it with something faster.

6.3.2   *Adding project dependencies*

A great candidate would be a *hash map*, which is known for its fast accessing times. However, this time, we are not going through the work of building our own hash map. We will simply use one that is already available! For this, we need to add the dependencies `unordered-containers` and `hashable` to our project. For this, we edit our package.yml file to contain these dependencies. The relevant part of the file should look something like this:

```
dependencies:
- base >= 4.7 && < 5
- unordered-containers
- hashable
```

This will automatically make `stack` take care of downloading and building the dependencies with our project. Now, we can substitute our `Data.AssocMap` module with `Data.HashMap.Lazy`. Additionally, in the `Graph` and `PermutationMap` modules, we need to change our types to use `M.HashMap` instead of `M.AssocMap`. For a value to be a key in a `HashMap`, it needs to have an instance of the `Hashable` type class. So we need to change our type signature in the `Graph` module to include `Hashable a` in its type constraints. This class provides a hash method that is used in the `HashMap` and can be imported from the `Data.Hashable` module.

> **NOTE**   It's not a coincidence that switching out `AssocMap` with `HashMap` is so easy, since we have essentially implemented the same functions as those present in the hash map module. If you understood how the functions work for the `AssocMap`, you now also know how the `HashMap` module works!

After compiling and running the program again, we will be able to handle even the large dictionary! Another look at the cost centers, by running the program with profiling enabled, shows us something very interesting:

```
computeCandidates.uniques     Ladder                src/Ladder.hs:19:7-50
                       ⮕ 67.4    34.7
readDictionary                Ladder                src/Ladder.hs:(10,1)-(
⮕ 14,22)                       4.7     0.2
```

```
liftHashWithSalt.step        Data.Hashable.Class    src/Data/Hashable/Clas
⮡ s.hs:656:9-46             4.7    7.2
liftHashWithSalt             Data.Hashable.Class    src/Data/Hashable/Clas
⮡ s.hs:(653,5)-(656,46)     4.7    0.0
lookup#                      Data.HashMap.Internal  Data/HashMap/Internal.
⮡ hs:597:1-82               2.3    1.3
insert'.go                   Data.HashMap.Internal  Data/HashMap/Internal.
⮡ hs:(759,5)-(788,76)       2.3    1.1
```

Our lookup has become so fast that computing the unique candidates for lookup in the permutation map seems to be a major time sink! Luckily, we can simply get rid of it, since we only added it to minimize the number of lookups we have to perform in the permutation map. Now that the map implementation is so fast, that is no longer necessary. Yet another performance improvement! After profiling the application some more, but this time, with a large dictionary, we get another surprising result:

```
readDictionary               Ladder                 src/Ladder.hs:(10,1)-(14
⮡ ,22)                      95.7    5.5
readDictionary.words         Ladder                 src/Ladder.hs:13:7-60
                        ⮡   1.3    6.0
alter                        PermutationMap         src/PermutationMap.hs:22
⮡ :1-36                     0.4   18.5
readDictionary.lines         Ladder                 src/Ladder.hs:12:7-39
                        ⮡   0.4   14.5
insert'.go                   Data.HashMap.Internal  Data/HashMap/Internal.hs
⮡ :(759,5)-(788,76)        0.3    5.8
```

We spend the most time simply reading the file! That's great news, since that tells us that our algorithm is relatively optimized. However, there is a way to improve even the reading of the file. So far, we have been happily using a performance killer without even knowing. The culprit is called `String`. The problem lies in the construction of strings, which are single `Char` values in a list. This list has two major problems:

- It lives on the heap; therefore, memory access is rather slow
- It is implemented as a linked list, which is bad for cache locality

When performance is of utmost importance, the `String` type must be avoided. Suitable replacements are the `Text` type from the `text` package or the `ByteString` from the `bytestring` package. Both provide a more performant, packed representation of strings. Their disadvantage is that we cannot use our usual list functions on them, making them slightly less portable. We will not cover in detail how to replace our `String` usage with anything faster because the performance improvement is marginal. However, inquisitive readers are free to check the code repository for the optimized version of this project!

IMPORTANT   When designing programs for performance, switching out types should be your *last resort*. The right choice of algorithms and data structures is much more important than technical details.

6.3.3   *Lazy evaluation*

We will close our discussion on performance by looking a bit more closely at how evaluation works in Haskell. Much different from other languages, Haskell is a language with *lazy evaluation*. This means that expressions do not immediately get evaluated but only if their evaluation is *forced*. Let's look at the following as an example:

```
ghci> :{
ghci| const :: a -> b -> a
ghci| const x _ = x
ghci| :}
ghci> x = (1000 :: Int)^(100000000 :: Int)
ghci> y = 0 :: Int
ghci> const x y
0
```

The const function has two arguments, and the second of which is completely discarded. What happens in the evaluation we perform? The expression const 0 1000^100000000 is reduced to 0, since const x _ is reduced to x. The second argument, which is a huge number that should take a long time to calculate, is simply discarded and, thus, not evaluated! You can check appendix B for more details on this.

Our algorithm exploits this lazy evaluation, too! We are not constructing the whole graph before searching for a solution; we are building the graph as we are searching! Only the necessary graph elements are being evaluated. However, this only works if all of our data structures are *lazy*. Lists and types we define ourselves are lazy by default. When improving our performance using hash maps, we specifically imported the lazy version of HashMap, which doesn't force the evaluation of values.

> **NOTE** While it might seem that *lazy evaluation* is generally preferred to its counterpart *strict evaluation*, this isn't the case. Certain algorithms, like the search algorithm in this chapter, benefit from laziness, while others see a stark performance decrease. Laziness also can lead to unexpected memory usage, which is why some developers ban it from their projects entirely with the help of language extensions, such as StrictData.

Let us recap what we have achieved by completing this project. We have created an artificial intelligence that, given a dictionary of words, is capable of finding the shortest solution to a modified version of the word ladder game. We did so by implementing an algorithm that can create a graph that represents the possible solutions for the game, and by searching this graph, we find the solution. To do so, we have implemented our own version of a map using associative lists and we have bundled the functionality of this type into its own module for reusability. Based on this implementation, we have created another map type that is used to quickly retrieve valid permutations of a given word to make our program viable. The graph was modeled as an adjacency map, using our custom map implementation. We have used a breadth-first search to find the shortest path. After testing and profiling the program, we have improved its performance by switching out the map built from associative lists to hash maps.

Now, we are ready to enter the next word ladder world championship! ... If such a thing exists.

Summary

- Free type variables are implicitly universally quantified.
- Universally quantified variables are a promise to the outside of a declaration that any variable fitting certain constraints can be used with the declaration.
- The callee of a function decides what concrete types are going to be used for an expression with universally quantified variables.
- Language extensions can be used to change the default behavior of the language and are enabled with the `{-# LANGUAGE ... #-}` pragma.
- We can enable profiling in a stack project by invoking `stack` with the `--profile` flag.
- Using `+RTS` and `-RTS`, we can add run-time system options to a Haskell application when running it.
- External dependencies can be added to our stack projects by adding the package names to the `dependencies` section of the `package.yml` file.
- Lazy evaluation means that expressions are only evaluated once their result is needed.

Working with CSV files 7

This chapter covers

- Haskell's record syntax and how to use it
- Using *smart constructors* to safely create data structures satisfying some property
- Creating instances for type classes
- Defining your own type classes with default implementations

In the last chapter, we tackled a search problem and wrote some powerful artificial intelligence for a children's game. In this chapter, however, we want to take care of earnest business, and nothing screams business like spreadsheets! Don't worry, we will not deal with any data directly. As programmers, we obviously want to automate such tasks, and the easiest way for us to deal with data in spreadsheet form is using comma-separated values (CSV) files.

In this chapter, we will cover how to parse such files, extract meaningful data from them, and work effectively with structured data. We will learn how to generalize the appending and slicing of data as well as how to bring type classes into the mix to help us write our program.

This chapter will begin with an introduction to CSV files and how to model them using Haskell's record syntax. We will learn how to encode errors using the `Either` type. We will cover using the dollar operator and certain language extensions to simplify our syntax. Following this, we will create our own type classes to generalize the use case for our data types. All the while, we will learn about the type classes `Semigroup` and `Monoid`, what they represent, and what they are used for.

7.1 Modeling CSV data

In this chapter, we want to tackle working with CSV files from the command line. While these files are not too hard to parse for a human, they can be very cumbersome to work with once they become large. This often requires us to default to some tool with a graphical user interface to wrangle the data. We can do better! Our tool will have many capabilities to display and convert this tabular data. The features include the following:

- Reading CSV files and printing them in as an ASCII table, offering support for files with and without a header
- Appending two CSV files
- Filtering rows in the table by a search term
- Potentially cutting the table to a specific range of columns
- Counting nonempty rows per column and seeing the result in the printed table
- Alternatively, writing the result from our transformation to a file in the CSV format

As a small example, let us see what it would look like if our program (which we will call `csview`) were to read a file, search for a string, and slice some of the columns:

```
shell $ head -n 4 cities.csv
"LatD","LatM","LatS","NS","LonD","LonM","LonS","EW","City","State"
   41,    5,   59, "N",    80,   39,    0, "W", "Youngstown", OH
   42,   52,   48, "N",    97,   23,   23, "W", "Yankton", SD
   46,   35,   59, "N",   120,   30,   36, "W", "Yakima", WA
shell $ csview --in=cities.csv --with-header --search=Ya --slice="8,10"
-------------------
| City    | State |
+---------+-------+
| Yankton | SD    |
| Yakima  | WA    |
-------------------
```

Before we can even start constructing such a tool, we'll have to get an understanding of this file format.

CSV files are simple text files containing lines of *data records*. These records contain values that are separated by commas, so a CSV file contains lines of comma-separated values. Additionally, the first line can (optionally) be considered to be a header, giving a title to the columns. Sounds easy enough, doesn't it?

Sadly, even though the file format is somewhat set in stone (the proposed specification for it is given by RFC 4180), seemingly every implementation uses its own rules for constructing CSV files. Some common constraints associated with CSV files include that they

- Are plain text using a common character encoding (UTF-8, ASCII, etc.)
- Contain one record per line delimited by line breaks
- Divide a record into fields using the same delimiter throughout the file (which does not have to be a comma)
- Have the same number of fields for each record
- May contain an optional header line
- May use quoting in fields using double quotes

A tool meant to inspect and analyze the data in such files must, therefore, have some options to deal with the multitude of different ways to parse its contents. Let's discuss the goals of our application and what it should do. We want an application that reads CSV files and prints them in a tabular form. Additionally, we want to search for values and compute statistics on the data. The workflow will look something like this:

1 Read arguments and infer parsing options and requested functionality.
2 Parse the CSV file into a data structure.
3 Perform a search and/or compute statistics on the data.
4 Write the data back to a file.
5 Optionally, print the information back in human-readable form.

Before we worry about reading arguments from the command line, we should first define how to represent CSV files in our program and then talk about parsing!

7.1.1 Record syntax

We start, as always, by creating a new project with `stack new csview`. As we have discussed, CSV files contain text. In this project, we want to diverge from working with the `String` type and use a more common way to work with text in Haskell: the `Text` type, which is a better performing, packed representation of strings of characters. To use this type, we first have to incorporate the *text* package into our project. We edit the dependencies section in our package.yaml file to include this package. While we are at it, we can also change the name of our executable and remove the `-exe` suffix. Later, we want to install this application locally on our machine, so a better name might be in order!

```
dependencies:
- base >= 4.7 && < 5
- text
...
executables:
  csview:
    main:              Main.hs
    ...
```

The `Text` data type can be imported from the `Data.Text` module, which contains a large number of functions working with text, since we cannot use the functions from `Data.List` anymore. To perform conversions from `String` to `Text` and back, we can use the `pack` and `unpack` functions:

```
ghci> import Data.Text
ghci> myString = "Hello Text"
ghci> :t pack myString
pack myString :: Text
ghci> :t unpack (pack myString)
unpack (pack myString) :: String
```

The module contains many functions that replace the functionalities we normally get from the `Data.List` module, like `null` or `length`. For the sake of brevity, we leave reading some of the module's documentation (found at https://mng.bz/1a8n) to get a better feel for the data type to the reader.

Now, we are all set to think about modeling CSV files in our program. Since CSV files generally are not typed, the values in them can be considered text, no matter what the content is. However, later, we assume CSV files to contain either numeric or textual information so that we can later construct algorithms, like searching for strings and summing numbers. The columns as well as the optional header in such a file can be represented by simple lists. Thus, we could create a type like so:

```
type Column = [Text]

type Csv = (Maybe [Text], [Column])
```

In this type, the first element of the tuple is the optional (represented by `Maybe`) header, and the second element represents the columns of our file, with each column being a list of fields. Based on this definition, we can define functions to retrieve values from it:

```
header :: Csv -> Maybe [Text]
header = fst

columns :: Csv -> [Column]
columns = snd
```

We previously saw `snd` in chapter 6. To recap, `fst` retrieves the first element of a tuple and `snd` retrieves the second element of the tuple. These definitions seem good, but we can do better. We are facing a few problems here:

- The type is a type synonym, so we cannot hide its construction through the modules export list.
- Every time we extend the type, we need to change the functions accessing its elements or construct more of them.
- Without a comment in the code, it's not clear what the fields in the tuple represent.

Luckily, we can get around these problems by using Haskell's *record syntax*. It enables us to give names to the fields of data constructors. Let's look at the syntax in action by defining the type properly this time, also deriving an instance for Show in the process. That code for the type and a new module, called Csv.Types, is shown in the following listing.

Listing 7.1 A data type for CSV file contents using the record syntax

```
module Csv.Types where                      Imports Data.Text qualified
                                             and gives it the alias T
import qualified Data.Text as T

type Column = [T.Text]                       Defines the Csv type with
                                             a single constructor
data Csv = Csv
  { csvHeader :: Maybe [T.Text],             Defines two fields for
    csvColumns :: [Column]                   the Csv constructor
  }
  deriving (Show)                            Derives the Show instance
                                             for the new type
```

We create a qualified import for Data.Text, since it features many functions whose names will clash with the Prelude import. As we can see, the record syntax lets us identify fields of data constructors by name! This has an additional effect: the names of fields serve as functions that retrieve said field from the data type. These are called *field selectors*:

```
ghci> :{
ghci| data Record = Record
ghci|   { field1 :: Int,
ghci|     field2 :: String
ghci|   }
ghci| :}
ghci> :t field1
field1 :: Record -> Int
ghci> :t field2
field2 :: Record -> String
ghci> field1 (Record {field1 = 1, field2 = ""})
1
```

This means that if we were to extend this data type by a new field, we would automatically add a new function for retrieving that field! Also, our type is now bundled with a minimal version of documentation, since the names signify the purpose of the fields. Finally, since we now have a constructor for our type, we can exclude it from the module's export (similarly to how we did it in chapter 5 for our AssocMap type) to ensure values cannot be constructed with invalid data.

> **NOTE** Since the field names create functions, the names of these functions can clash. When using records with the same field names, we have to be very careful while importing them into modules. It is standard practice to prefix the field names with some identifying abbreviation (e.g., the acronym of the type name, using csvHeader or csv_header instead of header).

When constructing values with the record syntax, we can explicitly name fields and their values like in the previous example or we can simply write down the values as fields for the constructor in the same order as the fields we want to fill:

```
ghci> data Record = Record {field1 :: Int, field2 :: String} deriving Show
ghci> Record {field1 = 100, field2 = "Hello"}
Record {field1 = 100, field2 = "Hello"}
ghci> Record 100 "Hello"
Record {field1 = 100, field2 = "Hello"}
```

When fields are only partially supplied, we see a similar behavior as with the constructors for algebraic data types we already know. They are partially applied and evaluated to a function that evaluates the record type once all missing fields are supplied:

```
ghci> :t Record
Record :: Int -> String -> Record
ghci> :t Record 100
Record 100 :: String -> Record
```

It is important to note that constructing the data type with unnamed fields and named fields at the same time is not supported:

```
ghci> Record 100 {field2 = "Hello"}

<interactive>:25:8: error:
    • Couldn't match expected type 'Int' with actual type 'Record'
    • In the first argument of 'Record', namely
        '100 {field2 = "Hello"}'
      In the expression: Record 100 {field2 = "Hello"}
      In an equation for 'it': it = Record 100 {field2 = "Hello"}
```

Records can also be modified by explicitly naming fields and specifying a value for them for an existing record:

```
ghci> :{
ghci| f :: Record -> Record
ghci| f rec = rec {field1 = 0}
ghci| :}
ghci> f (Record 100 "Hello")
Record {field1 = 0, field2 = "Hello"}
```

Something we do not explicitly cover here is that the record syntax can be used in conjunction with multiple constructors, using different fields for each of them. However, it works analogously to records with a single constructor with the added problem of partial field selectors, which are covered in chapter 10 and should generally be avoided.

7.1.2 *Encoding errors with Either*

As we hinted at toward the start of the chapter, we later want to work with our Csv type, searching for text in it or computing sums. To do this, we have to differentiate between values in our table that represent text and those that represent numbers. We can achieve this using a new type that encodes our data fields, as shown in the following listing.

Listing 7.2   A data type for fields in a CSV table

```
data DataField
  = IntValue Int          ◄──── Defines a constructor for Int values
  | TextValue T.Text      ◄──── Defines a constructor
  | NullValue             ◄────   for Text values
  deriving (Eq, Show)           Defines a constructor for empty values
```

A Csv table is filled not by arbitrary data but by DataField values. The final version of our Csv type is shown in the following listing.

Listing 7.3   A data type for CSV tables

```
type Column = [DataField]     ◄──── Defines a Column to be a
                                     list of DataField values
data Csv = Csv
  { csvHeader :: Maybe [T.Text],   ◄──── Defines a record field
    csvColumns :: [Column]                for the header
  }                            ◄────
  deriving (Show)                    Defines a record field for
                                     the columns
```

This enables us to freely contain text and numeric values in our tables, even mixing the values within a column.

Next, we want to take a look at the constructors for our Csv type and how we can make sure only sensible data is constructed with them.

7.2   *Smart constructors*

Sometimes, we want to specify properties for our types that cannot be ensured by the type system itself. In our case, the number of fields in the header needs to equal the number of columns, and each column also needs to have the same number of elements. In chapter 5, when working with the AssocMap type, we outright disallowed constructing values of said type directly and only made it possible through certain functions we exported. For the CSV case, however, we would like to allow this, but we want to have some kind of error checking. This ensures that we don't have to check the invariants for this type in each function that deals with it. This brings us to the topic of *smart constructors.*

7.2.1   *Ensuring a property at the time of construction*

We can ensure these properties by only allowing Csv values to be built by a dedicated function that checks the arguments for their validity. It is common for this function to simply crash the program if something goes wrong, and while we will do this too, we also want a *safe* version. What should that function look like?

```
mkCsv :: Maybe [T.Text] -> [Column] -> ???
```

`Maybe Csv` seems to be a sensible choice, but it would be rude to just fail silently without letting the user of this function know what went wrong. We would like to have a type that either returns a specific error or the actual `Csv` value. A type for that might look like this:

```
data ErrorOrCsv a = Error String | Value Csv
```

Luckily, there already exists a similar type with this capability, called `Either`!

```
data Either a b = Left a | Right b
```

This type can be used in a variety of ways, but it is most often used to encode the possibility of errors. In this case, `Right` encodes a correct value and `Left` an error value. Thus, if we would like to either have an error message or a value, we could encode it like this:

```
type ErrorOrValue a = Either String a
```

It is this type that we can use for our function! We can quickly check if the length of the header matches the number of columns in the input. Additionally, we have to check that every column has the same length. We can do so by using the `nubBy` function from the `Data.List` module. It has the same functionality as `nub` but receives a binary function as a predicate that determines when two values in the list are equal. If the result from this function has a length less than or equal to 1, we know that all columns have the same number of elements. This is shown in the following listing.

Listing 7.4 A function to safely construct a CSV value

```
mkCsv :: Maybe [T.Text] -> [Column] -> Either String Csv    Returns an error message
mkCsv mHeader columns                                        for an incorrect header size
  | not headerSizeCorrect =                         ◄─┘
      Left "Size of header row does not fit number of columns"   Returns an error
  | not columnSizesCorrect =                              ◄──┤    message for incorrect
      Left "The columns do not have equal sizes"                 column sizes
  | otherwise = Right Csv
    {csvHeader=mHeader, csvColumns=columns}  ◄─┤ Returns a CSV value with   Checks
  where                                          the arguments as fields    if the
    headerSizeCorrect =                                                      header's
      M.maybe True (\h -> L.length h == L.length columns) mHeader  ◄──       size is
    columnSizesCorrect =                                                     equal to the
      L.length (L.nubBy (\x y -> length x == length y) columns) <= 1         amount of
                                                                             columns
                                              Checks if all columns
                                              have the same size
```

Here, we assume `M` is a qualified import of `Data.Maybe`. For the rest of this book, we will assume a few qualified imports for our code. `T` stands for `Data.Text`, `L` for `Data.List`, `M` for `Data.Maybe`, and `E` for `Data.Either`.

7.2.2 *Providing an unsafe alternative*

Returning to the code, this function can be considered "safe," since it does not crash our program if some or all of the arguments are invalid. Just like with the `Maybe`, we encode the possibility for errors in a type. However, this function requires us to pattern match the type each time we use the function, even if we already have made sure the invariants are satisfied. To make our life easier, we create the "unsafe" version of this function, which simply crashes if the arguments are not what we expect them to be.

> **NOTE**   In some code bases, the "safe" function bears a special prefix in the name, while the "unsafe" function does not. In our case, we give unsafe functions a name like `unsafeName` to signify the grave danger associated with using them.

To achieve this, we use the `error` function, which raises an exception:

```
ghci> :t error
error :: GHC.Stack.Types.HasCallStack => [Char] -> a
ghci> error "Oh no!"
*** Exception: Oh no!
CallStack (from HasCallStack):
  error, called at <interactive>:... in interactive:Ghci1
```

Just like the `Maybe` type features its own `Data.Maybe` module and `maybe` function to quickly work with it, so does `Either`:

```
ghci> import Data.Either
ghci> :t either
either :: (a -> c) -> (b -> c) -> Either a b -> c
```

The `either` function receives two functions, one for the `Left` and one for the `Right` case, to ultimately produce a value of some common type. In our case, we can construct `unsafeMkCsv` by using the `error` function for the `Left` case and the `id` function for the `Right` case, which simply returns its argument. The resulting one-liner is shown in the following listing.

> **Listing 7.5   An unsafe function that crashes if the arguments for a CSV value are invalid**

```
unsafeMkCsv :: Maybe [T.Text] -> [Column] -> Csv
unsafeMkCsv header columns =
  E.either error id (mkCsv header columns)
```
Either raises an exception after getting a failing result from safeMkCsv or returns its result

This function can only produce a correct result of type `Csv` or crash the program.

> **WARNING**   The `error` function should only be used to signify a serious programming error that cannot be recovered from. Don't use it liberally, as it is meant to crash your program.

Now, we can test our smart constructors:

```
ghci> :set -XOverloadedStrings
ghci> int x = IntValue x
ghci> mkCsv (Just ["First", "Second"]) [[int 1, int 2], [int 3, int 4]]
Right (Csv {csvHeader = Just ["First","Second"], csvColumns =
```

```
⇨  [[IntValue 1,IntValue 2],[IntValue 3,IntValue 4]]})
ghci> mkCsv (Just ["First", "Second"]) [[int 1, int 2], [int 3]]
Left "The columns do not have equal sizes"
ghci> mkCsv (Just ["First"]) [[int 1, int 2], [int 3, int 4]]
Left "Size of header row does not fit number of columns"
ghci> unsafeMkCsv Nothing [[int 1, int 2], [int 3]]
*** Exception: The columns do not have equal sizes
```

But which constructor should we use? `unsafeMkCsv` inherently has the problem of producing an exception that (if it isn't caught) crashes the program. If we want to stay on the safe side, we should use `mkCsv`. `unsafeMkCsv` is only helpful when we already know that nothing can go wrong because we have checked it at some other point.

As you can also see from the previous example, we can use our usual way of writing down `String` values to declare a `Text` value. We will see why that is in a bit. First, we have to take care of some syntactic sugar.

7.2.3 *The dollar sign operator*

The `unsafeMkCsv` function features a pattern of code that we see quite often. A function is supplied with a few arguments, whereas the last argument is an expression itself:

```
E.either error id (mkCsv header columns)
```

This can become rather cumbersome when the last expression becomes larger. Luckily, we can use a new operator we have not seen so far: the `$`. What this operator lacks in complexity, it more than makes up for in elegance and simplicity. Its full definition is shown in the following listing.

> **Listing 7.6   Haskell's dollar operator**

```
($) :: (a -> b) -> a -> b
($) f x = f x
```

The `$` operator simply applies a function to a value! It can be used to nicely write a function application without needing to use parentheses on its last argument:

```
ghci> either (+1) (*2) (Right 100) :: Int
200
ghci> either (+1) (*2) $ Right 100 :: Int
200
```

This is very helpful when arguments become large terms:

```
someFunc ... =
  someOtherFunc ... $
    anotherFunc ... $
      yetAnotherFunc ... $
        andYetAnotherFunc ...
```

However, that isn't the full story:

```
ghci> :i ($)
($) :: (a -> b) -> a -> b
infixr 0 $
```

When getting some more information on this operator, we see a peculiar note: `infixr 0 $`. This tells us that this operator is written in an *infix* style with *right associativity* (given by the r after infix) with an additional *precedence* of 0. Right associativity means if there are multiple operators with the same precedence, the operations are grouped from the right. The precedence of 0 specifies that other operators take precedence over $ (except they also have a precedence of 0). Why is this helpful?

```
ghci> :i (++)
(++) :: [a] -> [a] -> [a]
infixr 5 ++
ghci> map (*10) [1..5] ++ [6..10] :: [Int]
[10,20,30,40,50,6,7,8,9,10]
ghci> map (*10) $ [1..5] ++ [6..10] :: [Int]
[10,20,30,40,50,60,70,80,90,100]
```

Here, we see that since the append operator (++) has precedence of 5, it *binds stronger* than $. Thus, its evaluation is done before the result is passed to the call of the map function in this example.

> **NOTE** The $ is ubiquitous in Haskell code. That's why it is important to get familiar with its intricacies and usage. However, using it is certainly not a must. If you feel more comfortable using parentheses, you should stick with them.

We will encounter this operator many more times over the course of this book. If it seems confusing, just remember that you can rewrite the terms with parentheses at any time.

Now, we can construct CSV values and give a safe interface to the outside that guarantees no faulty values are being produced!

7.3   *Using type classes*

Next, we want to construct functions to better work with our CSV tables, namely functions that determine the number of columns and rows. Working with the record syntax can become somewhat complicated, so we want to take a look at a few language extensions that make working with it a bit easier. The default way of working with records forces us to write down the fields we want to access and give them a name:

```
f Csv {csvHeader=h, csvColumns=c} = ...
```

We are allowed to omit fields we don't need:

```
f Csv {csvColumns=c} = ...
```

But what if we don't care to give a field a new name?

```
f Csv {csvColumns=csvColumns} = ...
```

It would make sense to avoid giving this field a superfluous name. Using the `Named-FieldPuns` language extension, we can do this:

```
f Csv {csvColumns} = ...
```

This still requires us to list all the fields we want to use. This becomes unwieldy once we use a record with a large number of fields. However, we can use the `RecordWild-Cards` language extension to make *all* fields available with their name:

```
f Csv {..} = ...
```

Now, we can quickly access fields from a record without having to write them down! This lets us construct our functions to compute the numbers of rows and columns. To do this, we can assume all columns have the same number of elements (since that's the invariant for our type). So computing the number of rows from the columns is trivial. Determining the number of columns requires us to either take the number of header elements or (if it's `Nothing`) the number of columns. We can do this easily with the `maybe` function. This is shown in the following listing.

> **Listing 7.7 Functions to compute the number of rows and columns in a CSV file**

```
numberOfRows :: Csv -> Int
numberOfRows Csv {..} =            ◁──── Extracts all fields from the CSV record and
  case csvColumns of                      makes them available in the rest of the function
    [] -> 0                        ◁──── Returns 0, since there are no rows if there are no columns
    (x : _) -> length x            ◁──── Returns the length of the first column

numberOfColumns :: Csv -> Int
numberOfColumns Csv {..} = length csvColumns   ◁── Returns the size of the header if it
                                                    exists or the number of columns
```

Now that we have several functions to build and describe our CSV tables, we want to think about transforming them. We want to be able to combine CSV tables, cut them up, and compute statistics on them. Let's start with combining CSV tables!

7.3.1 Semigroup and Monoid

When combining two CSV tables, we want to consider adding two completely different tables, meaning their number of rows could be different and one might have a header while the other does not. This is shown in figure 7.1.

To rectify this situation, we have to fill values with empty values. We can simply leave headers as an empty string, and we can use `NullValue` to fill the table for data fields. Our function will combine the headers by checking if one of the values has a header. If not, the new value also won't have a header. Otherwise, any missing header is replaced by a list of empty strings of fitting length. The columns are appended by filling the shorter columns with empty cells (`NullValue`). This code is shown in listing 7.8.

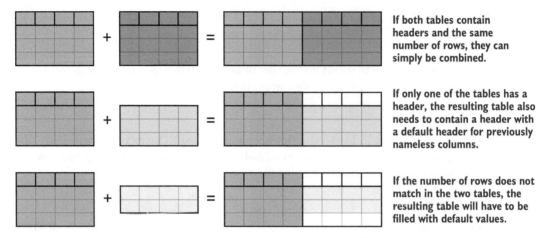

Figure 7.1   Different scenarios when appending two tables of data

If both tables contain headers and the same number of rows, they can simply be combined.

If only one of the tables has a header, the resulting table also needs to contain a header with a default header for previously nameless columns.

If the number of rows does not match in the two tables, the resulting table will have to be filled with default values.

Listing 7.8   A function to append two CSV values

Specifies that an instance for the HasDefault class for the type variable of Csv values to be appended must exist with a type constraint

Sets the appended header to Nothing if none of the values to be appended have a header

```
appendCsv :: Csv -> Csv -> Csv
appendCsv a b =
  Csv
    { csvHeader =
        if M.isNothing (csvHeader a) && M.isNothing (csvHeader b)
          then Nothing
          else Just $ header' a ++ header' b,
      csvColumns = appendColumns (csvColumns a) (csvColumns b)
    }
  where
    header' csv =
      M.fromMaybe
        (L.replicate (numberOfColumns csv) "")
        (csvHeader csv)

    appendColumns colsA colsB =
      map (\cols -> cols ++ fillA) colsA
        ++ map (\cols -> cols ++ fillB) colsB
      where
        fillA = replicate (numberOfRows b - numberOfRows a) NullValue
        fillB = replicate (numberOfRows a - numberOfRows b) NullValue
```

Combines the headers, which are filled with empty strings if missing

Computes the header of the Csv value or returns a list of empty strings the size of the number of columns if missing

Appends columns by appending default values to the shorter columns

We can immediately see that this algorithm only works because we assume all columns to have the same size. Otherwise, we would need to check the maximum column size and fill all columns to that size.

Exercise: Joining CSVs

appendCsv fills the table with empty cells when the sizes of the two CSV files do not match. Alternatively, we could have simply cut off rows from the shorter CSV file. Implement this alternative append operation!

Observe how these strategies are somewhat similar to an *outer* and *inner joins* we find in databases. However, we are not joining CSV files on a certain value or predicate but blindly appending columns. Write functions that perform joins on the Csv type. This function should receive some Boolean predicate as an argument that decides whether rows should be joined or not.

We can observe another property of this function. When we want to append three Csv values, we can do it like so: appendCsv a (appendCsv b c). However, order is not necessarily important. We could also do it like this: appendCsv (appendCsv a b) c. This property, called *associativity*, is a fundamental mathematical concept. It allows us to disregard the order of operations. This property is so important that Haskell has its own type class dedicated to types that feature such an associative operation: Semigroup.

The most important operation of this type class is <>, which is the binary, associative operation of this type. By convention, it should be an associative function, meaning that a <> (b <> c) == (a <> b) <> c holds for all values a, b, and c of that type. However, the compiler doesn't check or prove this property. You have to make sure the property is correct on your own.

For the compilation of results, it is only important to add them in the correct order, so any a <> b in the term that evaluates the end result cannot be changed to b <> a.

An extension of the Semigroup type class is the Monoid type class, as shown in the following listing.

Listing 7.9 Class signature for Monoid

```
class Semigroup a => Monoid a where      Defines the neutral element for mappend
  mempty :: a
  mappend :: a -> a -> a                  Defines an associative operation for the type
  mconcat :: [a] -> a
  {-# MINIMAL mempty #-}        Defines a function that applies mappend to all
                                values of a list, condensing them into a single value
```

mappend is the same function as <>, and by default, its definition is mappend = (<>). However, Monoid also features a constant, called mempty, which is the *neutral element* with respect to mappend, meaning the properties mappend mempty a == a and mappend a mempty == a hold. mconcat looks very suspiciously like our combine function from earlier. Let's look at Monoid in action:

```
ghci> [1,2,3] <> mempty <> [4,5,6] :: [Int]
[1,2,3,4,5,6]
ghci> mconcat [[1,2,3], mempty, [4,5,6]] :: [Int]
[1,2,3,4,5,6]
```

Well, doesn't that look familiar? Lists have an instance for `Semigroup` and `Monoid`:

```
instance Semigroup [a] where
  (<>) = (++)

instance Monoid [a] where
  mempty = []
  mconcat xss = [x | xs <- xss, x <- xs]
```

That also means we can work with `Strings` in that fashion!

```
ghci> "Hello" <> " " <> "World" :: String
"Hello World"
ghci> mconcat ["Hello", " ", "World"] :: String
"Hello World"
```

However, there exist types for which we can't define `Semigroup` or `Monoid`, since there exist *multiple* associative functions! `Int` is a great example, where we could use the addition *and* multiplication for our definition. However, there exists no canonical choice. That's why there exist the `Sum` and `Product` types, which wrap an `Int` and choose the appropriate function for their instances of the type classes.

> **WARNING** While currently, `mappend` can be implemented differently from `<>`, that should never be the case in your implementation. In the future, `mappend` might be completely removed from this type class and replaced with `<>`.

Now that we understand these type classes, why not implement instances for these two? The binary, associative function of `Semigroup` is already given by `appendCsv`. The only puzzle piece we need is the `mempty` value, a neutral value for `appendCsv`. Which `Csv` value does not change another value after it has been appended? Only an empty `Csv` value of course! By *empty*, we mean a `Csv` with no header and no columns. It's also important that our `appendCsv` has a type constraint, which also needs to be satisfied by the class instance. The code for this is shown in the following listing.

Listing 7.10 Instances for `Semigroup` and `Monoid` for the `Csv` type

```
instance Semigroup Csv where
  (<>) = appendCsv                                        ◁── Defines the associative, binary
                                                                function to be appendCsv

                                                                              Defines an
                                                                              empty Csv value
instance Monoid Csv where
  mempty = Csv {csvHeader = Nothing, csvColumns = []}     ◁──
```

We can now also use the `mconcat` function to concatenate a list of `Csv` values!

> **Exercise: Typeclass laws**
> Our definition for the instances of `Csv` is correct, but how can we be certain? For that, we need to take a look at the `appendCsv` function; specifically, we need to check how data gets appended. Why is our definition of `mempty` correct? Try to determine why the law for these type classes holds!

Combining multiple CSV tables is fine, but what about cutting them up? For this, we want to generalize a way of cutting up data structures.

7.3.2   *The IsString type class*

As we have seen, we can combine `String` values using the methods from `Semigroup` and `Monoid`. It turns out this also works for `Text` values:

```
ghci> import Data.Text
ghci> pack "Some text" :: Text
"Some text"
ghci> pack "Hello" <> pack " " <> pack "World" :: Text
"Hello World"
```

To do this more easily, we will take a look at another type class, called `IsString`. Using this class, we can write down values of type `Text`, just like `String` values:

```
ghci> :set -XOverloadedStrings
ghci> "Some text" :: Text
"Some text"
ghci> "Hello" <> " " <> "World" :: Text
"Hello World"
```

With this extension, we can use the typical syntax for string literals to write down values for all types for which an instance of `IsString` exists. That is true for `String` *and* `Text`! This is why you often see string values being appended by `<>` instead of `++` in many code bases.

But how does this work? When the `OverloadedStrings` extension is enabled, we can write down values as strings that are later converted to the actual type with the `fromString` method from the `IsString` type class:

```
class IsString a where
    fromString :: String -> a
```

So we can write down all types for which an instance for `IsString` (from the `Data .String` module) is defined. Conveniently, `Text` features an instance for said class. Other types, like `ByteString`, also can be used with this extension.

> **NOTE** Like `OverloadedStrings` and `IsString`, there also exist the `Overloaded-Lists` extension and the `IsList` type class, which enable us to write down lists and transform them into other types. This is very useful when defining data types that are similar to lists but have an otherwise unwieldy syntax to write them down.

Because this extension doesn't hurt anyone and is extremely useful when building a project with these types, we want to globally enable this extension. We can do so in the package.yaml file in our project. There, we can add a list of default extensions, containing all extensions that are enabled. While we are at it, we can also add the aforementioned `RecordWildCards` and `NamedFieldPuns` extensions, since they are also universally useful:

```
default-extensions:
  - OverloadedStrings
  - RecordWildCards
  - NamedFieldPuns
```

This will enable these extensions for each module in our project (excluding external libraries).

> **NOTE** Haskell supports setting a specific language "edition" that enables a large number of language extensions considered safe to always enable. You can find them here: https://mng.bz/2gwm.

Now that we have experience with using type classes, we turn our attention to writing our own!

7.4 *Creating a new type class*

When a type class like `Semigroup` can be used to combine data, a type class may come in handy when defining how data gets cut up. Practically, we want to extract parts of our table to work with them as new tables. This can be extended to other data structures, such as lists. To this end, we ask ourselves a question: Can we generalize cutting up data structures?

In pursuit of this goal, we begin by creating a new module called `Data.Sliceable` in a new src/Data directory. This module will contain all the necessary code for sliceable data. We want to create a new type class inside this module, which defines the operations necessary to separate parts of data structures.

When slicing data, we want to select a certain range within the data structure. We will assume it is indexable. Then, we can define the range simply by specifying two indices. The value is partitioned into three parts; however, only the middle part will be of particular interest to us.

7.4.1 *A type class for slicing data structures*

We can now think of the methods we want to expose through our type class. A `slice` method, which lets us cut out a part of a data structure based on two indices, is an essential one. However, since partitioning gives us the slice we are interested in for free, we should also have a `slicePartition` method. Furthermore, we can already implement the `slice` method from the `slicePartition` method! The implementation of such a class is shown in the following listing.

Listing 7.11 Class definition for sliceable data

```
class Sliceable a where
  slice :: Int -> Int -> a -> a        ◁── Declares a slice method that returns
                                           some partial slice of the data
```

```
slice idx1 idx2 xs =
  let (_, s, _) = slicePartition idx1 idx2 xs
  in s
slicePartition :: Int -> Int -> a -> (a, a, a)
```

◁─┐ **Provides a default implementation
    for the slice method**

◁─┐ **Declares a slicePartition
    method that splits some
    data into three parts**

Since this class introduces a general concept, we can put it in a module called `Data`
`.Sliceable`. `Sliceable` is the name of our class, and a is the type variable we are now
defining type expressions for. This type variable is lexically scoped within the class, so if a
type contains the variable a, it relates to the type a later instance of this class will be created for. The class then defines two methods, called `slice` and `slicePartition`.

In this code, we can also see how to add defaulting behavior to a method. In a
class, the declared methods are known to other definitions. The implementation we
define for `slice` is the default implementation that is automatically inferred when it is
not explicitly defined in the instance.

NOTE Default implementations of methods can be overwritten. This is helpful when we can find a more performant implementation for a specific type.

When loading the new module and retrieving information on our type class using
GHCi, we see the following:

```
ghci> import Data.Sliceable
ghci> :i Sliceable
type Sliceable :: * -> Constraint
class Sliceable a where
  slice :: Int -> Int -> a -> a
  slicePartition :: Int -> Int -> a -> (a, a, a)
  {-# MINIMAL slicePartition #-}
```

Just like with many other classes, we see a minimal definition that just contains our
`slicePartition` method, since `slice` can be inferred from it! We can now construct an
instance for lists by using the `take` and `drop` functions, which either take a certain number of elements from a list and return it or drop a certain number of elements from a
list and return the rest. A *slice* of a list from one index to another is a list that contains
the elements starting from the first index on the original list and ending at the second
index, not including the element in that index. This leaves us with a list whose length is
the difference of both indices. This code is shown in the following listing.

Listing 7.12 An instance of the `Sliceable` type class for lists

```
instance Sliceable [a] where
  slicePartition idx1 idx2 xs =
    ( take idx1 xs,
      take (idx2 - idx1) $ drop idx1 xs,
      drop idx2 xs
    )
```

**Defines the slicePartition function that
partitions the list into three parts**

**Defines the first part of the list
as the elements before the slice**

Defines the slice itself

**Defines the first part of the
list as the elements after the slice**

This definition now automatically yields the slice function!

```
ghci> import Data.Sliceable
ghci> slicePartition 2 8 [0..9] :: ([Int], [Int], [Int])
([0,1],[2,3,4,5,6,7],[8,9])
ghci> slice 2 8 [0..9] :: [Int]
[2,3,4,5,6,7]
```

Furthermore, we can find another instance for this class for `Maybe`. If the type within this `Maybe` is sliceable, then we can slice a `Maybe` of this type. Either the partitioned pieces are put in a `Just` or every partition is a `Nothing`. The instance is defined in the following listing.

Listing 7.13   An instance of the `Sliceable` type class for `Maybe`

```
instance Sliceable a => Sliceable (Maybe a) where      ⟵  Defines instances for every
  slicePartition idx1 idx2 Nothing =                        Maybe, where its type
    (Nothing, Nothing, Nothing)                   ⟵        parameter also has an
  slicePartition idx1 idx2 (Just xs) =                      instance of Sliceable
    let (hd, s, tl) = slicePartition idx1 idx2 xs  ⟵
    in (Just hd, Just s, Just tl)           ⟵
```

Defines instances for every Maybe, where its type parameter also has an instance of Sliceable

Returns every partition as Nothing if the input was Nothing

Calls slicePartition on the Just value

Wraps the result from slicePartition into Just constructors

Just like functions, type classes can have type constraints. We use this in the code of listing 7.13 to specify that the values wrapped inside a `Maybe` have to be sliceable to provide an implementation for the concrete `Maybe` type. Therefore, we can use the `slicePartition` given to us by the instance of `Sliceable a` in our definition of the class instance for `Sliceable (Maybe a)`.

Now, we can use `slice` on any `Maybe a` for which a has an instance of `Sliceable`:

```
ghci> slicePartition 2 8 $ (Just [0..9] :: Maybe [Int])
(Just [0,1],Just [2,3,4,5,6,7],Just [8,9])
ghci> slice 2 8 $ (Just [0..9] :: Maybe [Int])
Just [2,3,4,5,6,7]
ghci> slice 2 8 $ (Nothing :: Maybe [Int])
Nothing
```

Both instances are important for our `Csv` type, since it essentially consists of a `Maybe` of a list and a list of lists. When slicing CSV tables, we cut the table column-wise and create new values from those slices. This is illustrated in figure 7.2.

A `Csv` can be sliced by slicing the header and columns separately. The instances we already have created can be used for this! The code is shown in listing 7.14.

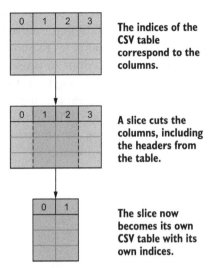

The indices of the
CSV table
correspond to the
columns.

A slice cuts the
columns, including
the headers from
the table.

The slice now
becomes its own
CSV table with its
own indices.

Figure 7.2   Slicing CSV tables

Listing 7.14   An instance of the `Sliceable` type class for CSV tables

```
instance Sliceable Csv where
  slicePartition idx1 idx2 Csv {..} =
    let (headerHd, headerSpl, headerTl) =
          slicePartition idx1 idx2 csvHeader
        (columHd, columnSpl, columnTl) =
          slicePartition idx1 idx2 csvColumns
    in ( Csv {csvHeader = headerHd, csvHeader = columHd},
         Csv {csvHeader = headerSpl, csvHeader = columnSpl},
         Csv {csvHeader = headerTl, csvHeader = columnTl}
    )
```

Slices the header using the implementation for Maybe

Slices the columns using the implementation for lists

Wraps the partitions into Csv constructors

Using this, we can slice arbitrary `Csv` values!

Exercise: Mapping slices

`slicePartition` can be used to write even more functions, since it breaks up a value into smaller parts that can be used independently of each other. One function could be `sliceMap`, which maps a function over the slice but not the other parts and then appends these parts again. Write that function completely polymorphically. You will need a second type class in your type constraint.

Similarly, write a `sliceDelete` function that deletes a slice from some value. This will also require you to think about type classes.

7.4.2   Re-exporting modules

With some functionality for our application now implemented, we should begin to consider the project structure and which definitions to import into which other modules.

In Haskell, importing modules into other modules is a nice way to share code, but it comes with problems. Name conflicts, and (even worse) cyclical imports can make it hard to get projects to compile. To avoid these pitfalls, it's a good idea to bundle modules working with the same concepts for convenient re-export done in single files. In our project, we will bundle CSV functionality into a subdirectory called Csv, which will contain modules to work with the `Csv` type. In this directory, we can first define a `Types` module that will export all the necessary types; `Csv` is one of these types. Next, would be the `Conversion` module, which is used for defining transformations and data conversions for our tool. Our directory structure will look like this:

```
src
├── Csv
│      ├── Conversion.hs
│      └── Types.hs
└── Data
        └── Sliceable.hs
```

Now, we want to add a `Csv` module on the top level to expose the modules from the Csv subdirectory. We can do so using the modules export list by referencing the module with the `module` keyword, as shown in the following listing.

Listing 7.15   A re-export of modules

```
module Csv
   ( module Csv.Conversion,        ◄──┐  Re-exports the imported
     module Csv.Types,                 │  modules from the Csv module
   )
where

                                    ┌── Imports modules into
import Csv.Conversion      ◄────────┘   the Csv module
import Csv.Types
```

This will enable us to only import a single module and get all the definitions we need, without worrying about cyclical imports. This module can also be the home for code that requires definitions from multiple modules.

It is now time to test our functions. Before we can do so, we need to get CSV tables into our program. For this reason, we want to explore parsing CSV files in the next chapter.

Summary

- Records can be used to model complex data with automatically generated accessing functions.
- The `Either` type can be used to encode errors in a program, giving us the possibility to produce an error value, like an error message.
- Smart constructors are functions used to build a value as well as check properties on those values.

- `RecordWildCards` and `NamedFieldPuns` can be activated to make working with records easier.
- `Semigroup` and `Monoid` are type classes that specify an associative function on a type.
- By using type classes, we can generalize behavior to a variety of types and create more general code with them.
- Module re-exports can be used to bundle multiple module exports with a single module.

A tool for CSV

8

This chapter covers

- Parsing numerical values from text
- Defining and using foldings on data structures
- Using the `Functor` type class and its functionality to deal with errors
- Creating a simple command-line parsing interface

In the last chapter, we started building the backbone for an application that can work with CSV files. This chapter is concerned with finishing the project and providing functionality for parsing and printing our `Csv` data type.

The chapter will continue where we left off by showcasing very important concepts, such as the `Functor` type class and folding, to make you familiar with core functional programming concepts. We close the chapter by bringing all of these newly learned skills together in a short program, putting our library to use. Finally, we will also install the created binary to our computer locally.

8.1 Parsing data

Next, we want to give our program a way of reading and parsing CSV files. For this, we need to write functions that can read the file contents of such a file, parse delimiters and fields, and write them to a data structure.

Parsing CSV files is a difficult topic, since every application seemingly treats these files differently, especially when it comes to the choice of delimiters and newline characters. Headers are also optional in CSV files, but there is no reliable way of determining whether a CSV file has a header or not. Thus, we should provide options for parsing them. We can model these options with types. This is shown in the following listing.

Listing 8.1 Options for CSV file parsing

```
data Separators = Separators              ◁──┐  Defines a data type for
  { sepLineSeparator :: Char,                 │  separators containing a
    sepFieldSeparator :: Char                 │  line and field separator
  }
  deriving (Eq, Show)

data HeaderOption = WithHeader | WithoutHeader    ◁──┤  Defines an option
  deriving (Eq, Show)                                  │  for headers

data CsvParseOptions = CsvParseOptions    ◁──┐  Defines a combination of
  { cpoSeparators :: Separators,               │  options for parsing
    cpoHeaderOption :: HeaderOption
  }
  deriving (Eq, Show)

defaultSeparators :: Separators
defaultSeparators =
  Separators
    { sepLineSeparator = '\n',         ◁──┐  Defines default separators to use the
      sepFieldSeparator = ','               │  newline character as the line separator
    }                                       │  and a comma as the field separator

defaultOptions :: CsvParseOptions
defaultOptions =
  CsvParseOptions
    { cpoSeparators = defaultSeparators,    ◁──┤  Defines the default options
      cpoHeaderOption = WithoutHeader          │  for parsing CSV files
    }
```

These options can live in a new `Csv.Parsing` module, which we can also reexport in the `Csv` module. Later, we can set these options through the command line. As a sensible default, we will assume files to not contain a header and have fields separated by commas.

When thinking about the parsing rules, we need to make some assumptions and rules about how we treat CSV files. As mentioned in the beginning, we consider CSV files to

- Contain one record per line, delimited by line breaks
- Divide a record into fields using the same delimiter throughout the file
- Have the same number of fields for each record
- Possibly contain an optional header line

Additionally, we will *skip empty lines* and not consider them to be malformed. However, we will completely disregard quoted fields and escaped double quotes that could end up in quoted fields, since it makes the task at hand a bit too complicated for learning purposes.

Nevertheless, we want our parser to be somewhat descriptive when parsing fails. By that, we mean that the parser should be able to indicate to us that two rows contain different numbers of fields. While that is already possible through our smart constructors, we also want to get information on the line number where parsing failed.

For this, we need to first split a text into individual lines, then split these lines into fields and check if the length matches up. First, let's worry about splitting a Text into lines and fields. Luckily for us, Data.Text already provides functions for splitting, namely split, which splits a Text on a Boolean predicate and splitOn, splitting on a specific substring:

```
ghci> import qualified Data.Text as T
ghci> :t T.split
T.split :: (Char -> Bool) -> T.Text -> [T.Text]
ghci> :t T.splitOn
T.splitOn :: T.Text -> T.Text -> [T.Text]
ghci> T.split (== '\n') "a\nb\nc"
["a","b","c"]
ghci> T.splitOn "\n" "a\nb\nc"
["a","b","c"]
```

So splitting Text values into lines and splitting these lines into fields can be achieved with splitOn using the separators from our CsvParseOptions type. Next, we should take care of how to parse arbitrary text into meaningful data.

8.1.1 *Parsing numeric values*

When parsing, the only type we work with is Text. Ultimately, we would like to transform the Text from the parsed CSV table into something we can work with, like designated numeric and text values (i.e., into DataField values). For this, we want to be able to transform Text into this type.

For the conversion to Int, we can use readMaybe from the Text.Read module. This function can parse values with an instance of the Read type class from String to their respective value and return a Nothing if this conversion fails:

```
ghci> import Text.Read
ghci> :t readMaybe
readMaybe :: Read a => String -> Maybe a
ghci> readMaybe "100" :: Maybe Int
```

```
Just 100
ghci> readMaybe "abc" :: Maybe Int
Nothing
```

This can be used to write a function that transforms `Text` to `DataField` values. Additionally, we will provide a function to turn a `DataField` back to `Text`. The code for this is presented in the following listing.

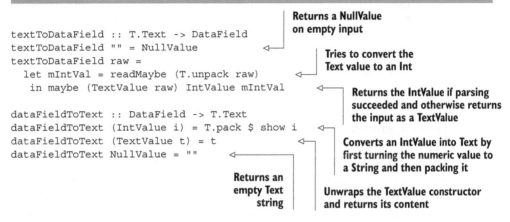

Listing 8.2 Functions for converting a `DataField` to and from `Text`

```
textToDataField :: T.Text -> DataField
textToDataField "" = NullValue                          ◁──  Returns a NullValue
textToDataField raw =                                         on empty input
  let mIntVal = readMaybe (T.unpack raw)    ◁──  Tries to convert the
  in maybe (TextValue raw) IntValue mIntVal              Text value to an Int
                                            ◁──  Returns the IntValue if parsing
                                                 succeeded and otherwise returns
dataFieldToText :: DataField -> T.Text               the input as a TextValue
dataFieldToText (IntValue i) = T.pack $ show i  ◁──
dataFieldToText (TextValue t) = t           ◁──  Converts an IntValue into Text by
dataFieldToText NullValue = ""    ◁──            first turning the numeric value to
                                                 a String and then packing it
                    Returns an
                    empty Text          Unwraps the TextValue constructor
                    string              and returns its content
```

Notice how the type inference is able to determine that the polymorphic `readMaybe` needs to return a `Maybe Int`. That is due to the usage of `IntValue` with a correctly parsed value.

8.2 *Folding data structures*

To perform validation on the parsed file contents, we have to check that each line has the same number of fields. Let us deal with checking the single lines for correct lengths first. After splitting the file into lines, we are presented with a list of them to check. Of course, we know how to tackle this problem using recursion and pattern matching, but let's take a step back. We have encountered this problem countless times before. Our strategy for traversing a data structure like a list and computing some result from it was laid out like this:

- Recursively enumerate every element of the data structure.
- Keep some state in an accumulator argument.
- Compute a new accumulator on each step, given an element from the data structure and the accumulator from the previous step.
- Once the data structure is empty (the final recursion step has been reached), simply return the accumulator.

This is a powerful strategy—so powerful, in fact, that it is used almost universally in functional programming because it essentially replaces the need for loops. This concept is

well known as *folding*. Before we go into what folding can do, lets explain the concept
with a more playful example.

8.2.1   *The concept of folding*

Imagine you have a trail in front of you. That trail is littered with hard candies of different flavors just lying on the floor (in their wrapper of course). How would we model that? Maybe with a list:

```
data Candy
  = Lemon
  | Apple
  | Coffee
  | Caramel
  deriving (Eq, Show)

type CandyTrail = [Candy]
```

Now, imagine you want to walk down this trail, and with each hard candy you find, you will make a choice about what to do with it. Picking up the candies means you are holding them in your hand, and the next time to come across one, you can make a decision on what to do next based on the candies you are holding and the one you found. This also means that you obviously start with an empty hand, and once you are at the end of the trail, you are only left with what is in your hand. This can be presented like this:

```
walkOnTrail :: (a -> Candy -> a) -> a -> CandyTrail -> a
walkOnTrail _ hand [] = hand
walkOnTrail f hand (x : xs) = walkOnTrail f (f hand x) xs
```

With this higher-order function, you can now perform several actions. For example, you can collect only fruity candies, or you can collect only the last five of them, since only so many can fit into the palm of your hand:

```
isFruity :: Candy -> Bool
isFruity c = c == Lemon || c == Apple

collectFruits :: CandyTrail -> [Candy]
collectFruits =
  walkOnTrail
    ( \hand c ->
        if isFruity c
          then hand ++ [c]
          else hand
    )
    []

collectLastFive :: CandyTrail -> [Candy]
collectLastFive =
  walkOnTrail
    ( \hand c ->
```

```
        if length hand == 5
          then tail hand ++ [c]
          else hand ++ [c]
    )
    []
```

Now, imagine that the candy trail is just a simple list (or, more generally, any data structure that can be traversed similarly to a list). Generalizing walkOnTrail makes us arrive at the definition for a *left fold*. The definition for this fold on lists is shown in the following listing.

Listing 8.3 A left fold function on lists

```
foldLeft :: (b -> a -> b) -> b -> [a] -> b
foldLeft _ z [] = z                           ←  Returns the accumulator
foldLeft f z (x : xs) = foldLeft f (f z x) xs     on an empty list
```
                                              ← Recursively folds the rest
                                                of the list with a newly
                                                computed accumulator

This is called a *left fold* because elements are being reduced from left to right. Alternatively, it's possible to create a *right fold* by first traversing the list and then applying the function. This is shown in the following listing.

Listing 8.4 A right fold function on lists

```
foldRight :: (a -> b -> b) -> b -> [a] -> b
foldRight _ z [] = z                           ←  Returns the accumulator
foldRight f z (x : xs) = f x $ foldRight f z xs   on an empty list
```
                                              ← Applies the function to the
                                                head and the recursively
                                                folded tail of the list

Folding is such a general concept that it has its own type class: Foldable. The class provides a right fold called foldr as well as many other convenience functions, such as null, length, elem, sum, maximum, and minimum. The minimal definition, however, only requires the foldr function to be implemented, since all other functions can be inferred from just foldr!

Exercise: The power of foldables

Take a look at the Foldable type class again. First, try to implement the convenience functions found in it by just using foldr. You can implement these functions for lists only. After you've done that, take a look at this type for a simple binary tree and implement an instance for Foldable for it. What is a left/right fold in relation to trees?

```
data Tree a = Leaf a | Node (Tree a) a (Tree a)
```

Folding is easiest to imagine when talking about lists and other linear structures, since the elements are laid out in an order that can be reduced from left to right or the other way around. `Data.List` and `Data.Text` both provide `foldl` and `foldr` implementations for lists and `Text`, respectively. However, folding can be defined for many other data structures.

> **NOTE** Folding is present in other non-functional programming languages too, such as `reduce` in Python and Java and `accumulate` in C++.

While the terms *left* and *right* fold seem to imply that elements are being evaluated either from left to right or right to left, this is not true. Both folding functions evaluate from left to right. The difference is that `foldl` *associates* the accumulating function from the left, while `foldr` does so from the right. When we fold over a data structure, what we are essentially doing is building a term over the elements of that structure with some function. Since we are lazy, that term is not evaluated until we haven't forced its evaluation somehow. We can imagine the expressions to look like the following example:

```
ghci> foldl (\a d -> "(" <> a <> "+" <> show d <> ")") "0" [1..9 :: Int]
"(((((((((0+1)+2)+3)+4)+5)+6)+7)+8)+9)"
ghci> foldr (\d a -> "(" <> show d <> "+" <> a <> ")") "0" [1..9 :: Int]
"(1+(2+(3+(4+(5+(6+(7+(8+(9+0)))))))))"
```

Here, we can see the left associativity of `foldl` and the right associativity of `foldr`. Using folding, we essentially build a new expression from a data structure. This is illustrated in figure 8.1.

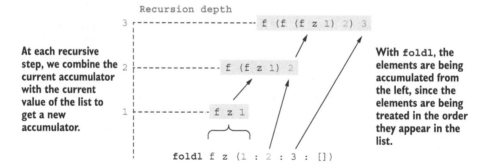

Figure 8.1   An example of how an expression gets built from a fold

The laziness of Haskell can have some unexpected consequences, which are discussed in appendix B. In short, it can lead to catastrophic memory inefficiencies. To combat these effects with laziness, strict versions of folds are sometimes featured. In our `Data.List` and `Data.Text` modules, they are called `foldl'`.

> **NOTE** The general rule holds: if the accumulating function is lazy (more specifically, not strict in the second argument), one should use `foldr`, and if not, `foldl'` is preferred.

Additionally, cases exist where we don't want to provide a "starting value" for the accumulator in a fold and use the first element of our data structure instead. For this variant of a fold, many modules provide a fold function suffixed with a 1 (e.g., foldl1 to indicate that the data structure to work on needs to have at least a single element).

> **WARNING** Functions like foldl1 are partial and throw an exception if the argument does not have at least one element.

When examining the implementations we have done in the past projects, we realize that we could have used folding in a whole host of other functions in the projects we have seen so far. Chapter 5 even featured an exercise on generalizing a recursive pattern in the functions addEdges and buildDiGraph. The solution to this exercise is to implement a fold that performs an action meant for a single element on a list of elements!

8.2.2   *A structure for parsing*

Now that we know what folds are and how to work with them, we can use it to validate the lines from the CSV file. To do that, we have to traverse the lines in order, splitting them into fields and then validating their length, all while keeping track of the line number we are in. Of course, adding line numbers to a bunch of lines is child's play for anybody who has read chapter 3. Using zip to add numbers to a list and filter to get rid of empty lines is simple to do. Our parsing function, which we will call parseCsv, receives options of type CsvParseOptions and the raw file contents of type Text as arguments and returns either a Csv or an error message. This result can be encoded with an Either.

To check for the correct number of fields, we take a look at the first line and later verify that all other lines have the same amount of fields. The function performing parsing is shown in the following listing.

Listing 8.5   A left fold function on lists

```
parseCsv ::
  CsvParseOptions ->
  T.Text ->
  Either String Csv
parseCsv options raw = case lines of
  [] -> mkCsv Nothing []
  ((_, firstLine) : rest) ->
    let expectedLength = length $ splitFields firstLine
    in case cpoHeaderOption options of
         WithHeader ->
           let headerFields = splitFields firstLine
           in unsafeKkCsv (Just headerFields)
                 <$> parseColumns expectedLength rest
         WithoutHeader ->
```

Returns an empty Csv if no lines exist

Determines the expected length of a row in the table to be the number of fields in the first line of the file, regardless of whether it represents the header or not

Creates a Csv with header from a positive (Right) result returned from parseRows

```
                     unsafeMkCsv Nothing <$>
⇨  parseColumns expectedLength lines
   where
     lines :: [(Int, T.Text)]
     lines =
       L.filter (\(_, t) -> not $ T.null t) $
         L.zip [1 ..] $
           T.split
             (== (sepLineSeparator $ cpoSeparators options))
             raw

     splitFields :: T.Text -> [T.Text]
     splitFields = L.map T.strip . T.splitOn separator
       where
         separator :: T.Text
         separator =
           T.singleton $
             sepFieldSeparator (cpoSeparators options)


   parseColumns ::
     Int ->
     [(Int, T.Text)] ->
     Either String [[DataField]]
     ...
```

Creates a headerless Csv from a positive (Right) result returned from parseRows

Filters nonempty lines

Incrementally combines every line with a line number

Splits the raw file contents into lines using the line separator from the parsing options

Implements the parseColumns function (omitted)

In this function, we are using the `<$>` operator (which is the operator form of the `fmap` function) to pass a `Left` from `parseRows` to our own return value. To better understand what this operator and the `fmap` function do, we have to take a look at the `Functor` type class.

8.2.3 *The Functor type class*

Where does `fmap` come from? Its name is somewhat strange. GHCi can tell us something about it:

```
ghci> :t fmap
fmap :: Functor f => (a -> b) -> f a -> f b
ghci> :i fmap
type Functor :: (* -> *) -> Constraint
class Functor f where
  fmap :: (a -> b) -> f a -> f b
```

The `fmap` function stems from a type class called `Functor`. Its type is eerily similar to the type of `map` for lists:

```
ghci> :t map
map :: (a -> b) -> [a] -> [b]
ghci> :t fmap
fmap :: Functor f => (a -> b) -> f a -> f b
```

So what is the purpose of `Functor`? It allows us to define types that can be mapped. Mostly, these are containers that contain mappable values. More specifically, these types contain free type variables that can be mapped. Something we have yet not seen in type expression is a type like f a, with f being the type of the functor and a being its type variable. What type could replace f? Maybe could, for example, since it contains a free type variable. Lists are another candidate! Both of these types feature an instance of the Functor type class. We have already seen fmap for Maybe, which was nothing special. fmap for lists is even more boring: it is simply map!

However, let's return to the discussion of types with type variables. Not every type has this property. (e.g., Int). This means we cannot instantiate Functor for Int. We can see that in GHCi's output:

```
ghci> :i fmap
type Functor :: (* -> *) -> Constraint
```

Here, we see the Functor types *kind*. A kind is to types what a type is to values. Just like values have a certain type, types have a certain kind. The usual kinds you come across in day-to-day programming are easy to read:

- * (read as *type*) is a *monomorphic type*, like Int, Maybe String, or Maybe [Bool].
- * -> * is a type that takes a parameter.
  - By extension, a type that takes two parameters is denoted like * -> * -> *, which can be read like * -> (* -> *) (a type that takes a parameter and evaluates to a type that takes another parameter).
- Constraint is a type used as a constraint e.g. in class constraints.

Now, we understand how to read (* -> *) -> Constraint. It's a type that takes another type, which takes a type as a parameter and becomes a Constraint. Let's explore kinds a bit more with the :kind command in GHCi (which can be shortened to :k):

```
ghci> :kind Int
Int :: *
ghci> :kind []
[] :: * -> *
ghci> :kind [Int]
[Int] :: *
ghci> :kind Functor []
Functor [] :: Constraint
```

This is also an important distinction. Int is a type, and [] is a parametrized type. Conversely, Functor [] is not a type but a Constraint; thus, we cannot use it to define new data types!

```
ghci> newtype MyFun = MyFun (Functor [])

<interactive>...: error:
    • Expected a type, but 'Functor []' has kind 'Constraint'
    • In the type '(Functor [])'
      In the definition of data constructor 'MyFun'
      In the newtype declaration for 'MyFun'
```

When thinking about which types we can instantiate, looking at the kind of `Functor`
(`* -> *`) is crucial! We can only instantiate type classes with types of this kind. This
is in contrast to `Semigroup`, `Monoid`, and our `Sliceable`, which are of the `* ->
Constraint` kind.

8.2.4   *Using folding for parsing*

Now, we can take care of `parseColumns`, which is going to split lines into fields and validate the number of fields in each row. Additionally, we want to transform the parsed
rows into columns we can use in our `Csv`. As we have discussed, a fold might be the
correct solution for this function. The fold goes through each line in order, transforms it into fields, and validates its expected length, returning either a `Left` with an
appropriate error message or a `Right` on success. In our fold, we have to check if we
have previously found an error and return it; otherwise, we continue adding up
parsed rows. Transforming the rows into columns can be done by "rotating" our
result. A list of rows becomes a list of columns by flipping the two dimensions that
make up this list. This can be done using the `transpose` function from the `Data.List`
module, which performs this operation:

```
ghci> import Data.List (transpose)
ghci> transpose [[1,2,3], [4,5,6]] :: [[Int]]
[[1,4],[2,5],[3,6]]
```

Again, we can use `fmap` to propagate the error state outwards. The code for this function is shown in the following listing.

Listing 8.6   The function to parse lines of text into columns in a CSV table

```
parseColumns ::
  Int ->
  [(Int, T.Text)] ->
  Either String [[DataField]]
parseColumns expectedLength lines =
  let textColumns =
        L.transpose                                    ◁── Transposes a
          <$> L.foldl' parseRow (Right []) lines        │   Right result
    in fmap (L.map (L.map textToDataField)) textColumns ◁── Folds the parseRow
  where                                                     function over the
    parseRow ::                                             lines with an empty
      Either String [[T.Text]] ->                           starting value
      (Int, T.Text) ->
      Either String [[T.Text]]      ┌─ Returns a Left value if a
    parseRow mRows (lNum, line) =   │  previous value was Left and
      E.either                   ◁──┘  otherwise processes the row
        Left
        ( \rows ->                          ┌─ Splits the row into fields
            let fields = splitFields line ◁──┘
              in if length fields /= expectedLength  ┌─ Returns a Left with an error
                then                             ◁───┤  message if the row does not have
                  Left $                              │  the expected amount of fields
```

```
          "Number of fields in line "
            <> show lNum
            <> " does not match"
            <> " expected length of "
            <> show expectedLength
            <> "! Actual length is "
            <> show (length fields)
            <> "!"
      else Right $ rows ++ [fields]
)
mRows
```

Returns a Right and adds the fields to the already parsed rows

Putting all the functionality we have already built together gives us the `parseCsv` function, which can parse `Csv` values from simple `Text`! For convenience, we can create two functions that wrap different options with the `parseCsv` function, one parsing with default options and the other parsing with default options and the optional header. For this, we need to update the `defaultOptions` we created earlier. We can do so by specifying a new value in the record in curly braces after the identifier of the record. The code for this is shown in the following listing.

Listing 8.7   Helper functions for parsing CSV tables

```
parseWithHeader :: T.Text -> Either String Csv
parseWithHeader =
  parseCsv (defaultOptions
  {cpoHeaderOption = WithHeader})

parseWithoutHeader :: T.Text -> Either String Csv
parseWithoutHeader = parseCsv defaultOptions
```

Parses a CSV file with default separators and a header

Parses a CSV file with default separators and no header

Now, we can go about starting to parse some files! The code repository for this chapter features a few CSV files we can use for testing our new functionalities!

```
ghci> file <- readFile "cities.csv"
ghci> fileText = T.pack file
ghci> Right csv = parseWithHeader fileText
ghci> csvHeader csv
Just ["LatD","LatM","LatS","NS","LonD","LonM","LonS","EW","City","State"]
ghci> numberOfRows csv
128
```

We have come quite far and can parse and validate files, but we can only *interpret* the values in those files as `Text`. This won't do for more complex tasks. Next, we want to focus on mapping these `Text` values to something we can work with better.

8.3   Printing a CSV

Our tool wouldn't be complete without the possibility of outputting our CSV tables to the terminal or a file. For this, we want to create a module called `Csv.Print` that will contain all the necessary functionality for printing and writing. First, let's tackle how to convert a `Csv` into the CSV file format and write it to the filesystem.

For this, we want to convert the columns of the `Csv` into rows, using `transpose`. From there on out, we have to convert the `DataField` values into `Text` and combine the fields within our rows by using `intercalate` from the `Data.Text` module. It combines each element of a list of `Text` values with some `Text` connecting each adjacent pair. We can use this to separate fields by commas and lines by a newline! After this comes the question of how to write a `Text` to a file. The `Data.Text.IO` module provides functions like `readFile` and `writeFile` to work with `Text` instead of `String` directly! The code providing functions for writing a `Csv` to a file is shown in the following listing. The `Data.Text.IO` module is imported as `TIO`.

Listing 8.8   Functions to write CSV values to files

```
toFileContent :: Csv -> [T.Text]
toFileContent Csv {..} =
  let rows = L.map (L.map dataFieldToText)
     $ L.transpose csvColumns
    in L.map (T.intercalate ",") $
         M.maybe rows (: rows) csvHeader

writeCsv :: FilePath -> Csv -> IO ()
writeCsv path = TIO.writeFile path .
    T.intercalate "\n" . toFileContent
```

- Converts CSV rows to a list of text
- Separates the columns with commas
- Adds the header to the rows if present
- Transforms a Csv into CSV file format and writes it to a file path

In this definition, we see yet another new operator: a simple dot (.). This operator is the *function composition*. Simply put, it receives two functions as arguments, first applying the second one and then the first one. Its definition is pretty simple:

```
ghci> (.) f g x = f (g x)
ghci> f = (+1) . (*3)
ghci> f 10
31
```

It allows us to quickly chain together functionalities while still using partial function application. This keeps the definitions short. Additionally, this operator even can be used to compose functions that are stored within data structures:

```
ghci> f = foldl (flip (.)) id
ghci> f [(+1), (*100), (/50)] 1
4.0
```

Since the function composition shown here is sometimes hard to wrap one's head around, we want to quickly delve a bit deeper into an explanation. In *functional* programming, *functions* are first-class objects, which allows us to treat functions as values. We can pass them to other functions, receive them from other functions, give them a name, put them into data structures, and compute new functions from functions. Often, an emphasis is placed on the *composition* of functions. In truth, all we do when programming declaratively is compose functions, since we do not define a sequence of operations, like in an imperative language, but we describe how the results of some functions are passed to other functions. Whether we do that with let bindings or by using the dot and dollar operators is irrelevant. This is essentially what we see in the preceding code example, where we compute the final IO action to write our Csv to a file from a bunch of other functions. Whether we explicitly write that down or do it by folding is not important.

Observe how the RecordWildCards language extension and operators ($ and .) come together nicely in our code. Haskell (and functional programming, in general) is *all about composition* of functions, and here, we have a prime example of composition of different functionalities that come together to build something much greater than the sum of their parts!

Finally, we want to tackle *pretty printing*, the art of displaying information in human-readable form. Of course, this matter is highly subjective. This is why we want to use this part of the chapter largely as an exercise. While we will discuss the structure of our architecture, the actual implementation will be left to you, the reader.

Let's discuss how the *interface* for pretty printing should look. A problem we face is that Csv is parametric. It could contain any type, even ones that cannot be printed. So we should restrict pretty printing to types that at least can be transformed into Text. Additionally, in our printing, we would like to print summaries per column. This is not explicitly modeled in our Csv type. To model this additional constraint and to better differentiate between normal values and values that can be pretty printed, we define a new type, which is shown in the following listing.

Listing 8.9   Functions to write Csv values to files

```haskell
data PrettyCsv = PrettyCsv
  { pcHeader :: Maybe [T.Text],
    pcColumns :: [[T.Text]],
    pcSummaries :: Maybe [T.Text]
  }
  deriving (Eq, Show)
```

- Defines a field for the pretty printed header
- Defines a field for the pretty printed columns
- Defines a field for the optional summaries for each column

Notice how we use the abbreviation of the type (pc) as a prefix for the fields to avoid any conflicts with the field names of our Csv type. Using the new type, we can transform our Csv type into a PrettyCsv type, which we can then use to add summaries and create some pretty output for users to marvel at. However, beauty is subjective, so I do not want to set a certain standard for it in stone. It is *your* task now to write algorithms for pretty printing! For this, you can use the template code shown in the following listing.

Listing 8.10   Functions to write Csv values to files

```haskell
fromCsv :: Csv -> PrettyCsv
fromCsv = ...
```

- Transforms a Csv into a PrettyCsv

```
withSummaries ::
  PrettyCsv ->
  [T.Text] ->
  Either String PrettyCsv
withSummaries = ...
```

> Safely adds summaries to a PrettyCsv, overwriting any existing summaries and checking if the number of summaries is consistent with the amount columns

```
pretty :: PrettyCsv -> String
pretty = T.unpack . prettyText
```

```
prettyText :: PrettyCsv -> T.Text
prettyText = ...
```

> Transforms a PrettyCsv into a human-readable Text

The source code for this project contains possible implementations for these functions, but feel encouraged to try implementing this yourself!

8.3.1   *Operations on CSVs*

So far, we have implemented a few useful operations on CSV tables and a way to show them to the screen with additional summaries. Now, it's time to fill these summaries for columns with something meaningful. For this, we would like to *fold* our Csv values on a per-column basis to coalesce all values in a column into one *summary*.

We can do so by mapping over each column and folding them separately. This is shown in the following listing.

Listing 8.11   Folding on CSV tables, coalescing each column into a value

> Maps a fold over each column and returns the result

```
foldCsv :: (DataField -> b -> b) -> b -> Csv -> [b]
foldCsv f z (Csv {csvColumns}) = map (foldr f z) csvColumns
```

Sadly, we cannot use this fold to create an instance of Foldable Csv, since the kind of Csv is * instead of * -> *.

Another operation useful for working with this data is a search operation on the rows of the table. Similar to the filter function for lists, we can define a filter function for Csv. For this, we need to transpose the columns to rows, filter them, and then transpose them back. This is shown in the following listing.

Listing 8.12   A function to filter CSV tables

> Extracts the columns from the Csv argument

```
filterCsv :: (DataField -> Bool) -> Csv -> Csv
filterCsv p csv@(Csv {csvColumns}) =
  let rows = L.transpose csvColumns
      filtered = L.filter (any p) rows
  in csv {csvColumns = L.transpose filtered}
```

> Transposes the columns into rows

> Filters the rows based on if the predicate matches for any value

> Builds the filtered Csv from the filtered rows

any is a function for lists that returns `True` if a given predicate is valid for any of the list's elements. In our code, we accept all rows for which at least one of the fields is valid based on the predicate.

In this definition, we see yet another syntactical trick Haskell has up its sleeve. The @ is known as a *pattern binding*; it binds a part of a pattern to a name. In our function, the second argument, which is pattern matched, is bound to the name `csv`; thus, the "unmatched" value becomes accessible in the functions definition as well as the `csv-Columns` field.

Now that we have constructed two very general functions, we can define more specific functionalities. On `Csv` values, we can count all nonempty values, since empty values are denoted with a `NullValue`, using `foldCsv`. Similarly, we can count the exact number of occurrences of a specific `DataField`. Finally, we want to define a filter that matches if an entry of the `Csv` *contains* a certain `Text`. For this to work, the polymorphic type of the CSV needs to have an instance of `ToText`. The implementations of these functions are found in the following listing.

Listing 8.13   Operations on CSV tables based on folding and filtering

```haskell
countNonEmpty :: Csv -> [Int]
countNonEmpty = foldCsv f 0
  where
    f NullValue acc = acc
    f _ acc = acc + 1

countOccurences :: DataField -> Csv -> [Int]
countOccurences df =
  foldCsv (\x acc -> if x == df then acc + 1 else acc) 0

searchText :: T.Text -> Csv -> Csv
searchText t = filterCsv (\f -> dataFieldToText f `contains` t)
  where
    contains = flip T.isInfixOf
```

Counts all nonempty values by folding over each column and incrementing the accumulator each time a value is not a NullValue

Counts the number of fields in a column equal to some specified field

Filters fields that contain some specified Text

These functions now serve as a basis for our CSV operations! We can put all of them into a new module, called `Csv.Operations` and, again, re-export this module from the `Csv` module.

Exercise: Summaries and filters

Of course, there exist a variety of other possible summaries and filters that only wait to be implemented! For example, we could create a summary that counts how often a specific `Text` occurs in a column or how often some numerical value was higher or lower than some specified amount.

For the adventurous, you might want to try out the regex package and implement a filter on `Csv` based on regular expressions. It will require you to read up on the package's documentation (https://hackage.haskell.org/package/regex)!

8.4   *A simple command-line parser*

In this project, we have implemented a large number of functionalities to work with CSV files. We can parse them, slice them, put them together, map them, and write them to a file or print them to the terminal. However, so far, we only have this loose functionality with no real usage behind it. Now, we will take a look at transforming our code into a real tool.

For this, we will again take a look at parsing arguments from the command line; however, this time, we want to use our newfound skills to write little parsers, to tell us if certain keys have been set or not.

First, we need to wrap the getArgs function from System.Environment somehow to return Text instead of String. Let's look at its type again:

```
getArgs :: IO [String]
```

Here, we see that we need to map over the list returned from this IO action and pack all String elements into Text. While we already know how to use the do notation to achieve this, there exists an easier way: IO has an instance of Functor! This means we can map the internal type and value of an IO action by using fmap and <$>. In this case, we want to map a function into the IO that packs the list of String. The code for this looks like this:

```
getArguments :: IO [T.Text]
getArguments = map T.pack <$> getArgs
```

The result from getArgs is being mapped with T.pack. Remember that the <$> operator is the infix version of fmap. It makes map T.pack operate directly on the arguments. However, it is clear that this means that the result is, in itself, IO when looking at the type of fmap. This is a general rule. When operating with fmap on lists, the result stays a list, and if we are working with Maybe, it will remain Maybe.

From this, we can create even more IO actions we can use to parse our arguments. The implementation of these functions will be left to the reader, even though the project repository will contain the full source code for them. Here, we want to discuss how the arguments should be structured and formatted.

All arguments for our program should start with --. Anything that is not a Boolean flag but contains data should be formatted like this: --argument-name=value, where value can be of some specified form. The following types of arguments shall exist:

- Bool—Set to True if the argument is set and False otherwise (e.g., --argument-name)
- Char—Represents the entered Char but only if it was a single char (e.g., --argument-name=, but not --argument-name=abc)
- Text—Represents the entered Text in the value
- Interval—An interval represented as Int separated by a single comma (e.g., --argument-name=1,5)

The appropriate functions that should reside in their own module are

```
getBool :: T.Text -> IO Bool
```

```
getChar :: T.Text -> IO (Maybe Char)
```

```
getText :: T.Text -> IO (Maybe T.Text)
```

```
getInterval :: T.Text -> IO (Maybe (Int, Int))
```

In our examples, these functions are implemented in a module called `Util.Arguments`, which will be addressed in code in its qualified name, `Args`. Again, it is your turn to implement these functions (or just copy them from the code repository if you feel lazy). It helps to write a helper that reads general values from the arguments, since they all should have the form `--key=value`.

> **NOTE** Of course, most people do not implement their own argument parsers, since many libraries already exist for this purpose. One of them is `optparse-applicative`, which you could alternatively use for this project. We will cover this library in later chapters.

8.4.1 *Supporting flags and complicated arguments*

With argument parsing done, we can think about how to bring together all the different functionalities we have constructed so far. For this, we want to use our argument utilities to define the behavior of the parser, how to transform the data, and how to print or write it. We want to be able to support the following arguments:

- `--in=<path>`—Uses the CSV file at `<path>` as the main input
- `--append=<path>`—Uses the CSV file at `<path>` as an additional input that is being appended to the right side of the data coming from the main input
- `--field-separator=<char>`—Specifies the field separator for CSV parsing of both the main input and additional input file
- `--with-header`—Makes the parser look for headers in both main input file and additional input file
- `--slice=<x>,<y>`—Will slice the resulting CSV at the specified indices
- `--search=<term>`—Will filter the CSV for rows that contain the searched term
- `--count-non-empty`—Adds summaries to the pretty output of how many non-empty fields are in each column
- `--no-pretty`—Will disable the output of the pretty version of the CSV, which is enabled by default
- `--out=<path>`—Specifies the path to write the resulting CSV (after all transformations are done), printing the contents to `stdout` if the path is -

Since we want to have multiple arguments that read a CSV file and also use additional flags in parsing, we want to bundle the functionalities for reading a file in its own `IO` action. It creates the parsing options based on the arguments given and parses accordingly. The code for this action is shown in the following listing.

Listing 8.14   Action to read a file with the parsing options specified by the arguments

```
parseInFile :: T.Text -> IO (Either String (Csv.Csv T.Text))
parseInFile key = do
  mInFile <- Args.getText key
  mFieldSep <- Args.getChar "field-separator"
  hasHeader <- Args.getBool "with-header"

  let separators =
        Csv.defaultSeparators
          { Csv.fieldSeparator =
              M.fromMaybe
                (Csv.fieldSeparator Csv.defaultSeparators)
                mFieldSep
          }
      headerOpt =
        if hasHeader
          then Csv.WithHeader
          else Csv.WithoutHeader
      parseOpts =
        Csv.CsvParseOptions
          { Csv.separators = separators,
            Csv.headerOption = headerOpt
          }

  case mInFile of
    Just inFile -> do
      contents <- TIO.readFile $ T.unpack inFile
      return $ Csv.parseCsv parseOpts contents
    _ -> return $ Left "argument not set"
```

Reads path and parsing options from the command-line arguments

Sets the field separator if overwritten by the command-line argument and otherwise uses the default

Sets the appropriate header based on the command-line argument (using no header being the default)

Reads the input file as Text

Parses and returns the file contents

Returns a generic error if the specified argument for supplying the file path does not exist

After this function has been constructed, we can think about how to write our `main` action. It's clear that we first have to check whether the `in` argument was set. If not, we can simply print an error message and end the program:

```
main :: IO ()
main = do
  mCsv <- parseInFile "in"
  case mCsv of
    Left _ -> putStrLn "no input file given (do so with --in=...)"
    Right csv -> do
      ...
```

The next step will be more challenging. We have to perform transformations on our parsed `Csv`. How should we go about doing that? While we could check every single argument and then perform transformations based on them, there is an arguably nicer way of doing things. Since functions are just values, we can, of course, work with them just like any other data. This also means that we can collect them (by putting them into a list) and compute new values (or functions in this case) from them. This is our strategy going forward, where we will map the results from the argument lookup to operations, which will then be combined into a single transformation operation that can be called for the Csv value in question. The code for this is shown in the following listing.

Listing 8.15   Reading optional arguments and deriving behavior from them

```
...
Right csv -> do
  mAppend <- eitherToMaybe <$> parseInFile "append"          Performs a lookup on the
  mSliceInterval <- Args.getInterval "slice"                 arguments resulting in
  mSearch <- Args.getText "search"                           Maybe values

  let mAppendOp = fmap (flip (<>)) mAppend                    Maps the Maybe values
      mSliceOp = fmap (uncurry slice) mSliceInterval          of the arguments to
      mSearchOp = fmap Csv.searchText mSearch                 functions within Maybe
      transformOp =
        foldl                                          <---   Composes the functions in
          (\t mOp -> (M.fromMaybe id mOp) . t)                order, defaulting to id if a
          id                                                  function does not exist
          [mAppendOp, mSliceOp, mSearchOp]
      dataCsv = Csv.toDataCsv $ transformOp csv        <---   Applies the composed
...                                                           function to the input
                                                              Csv and converts it
eitherToMaybe :: Either b a -> Maybe a                        into a DataCsv
eitherToMaybe (Left _) = Nothing
eitherToMaybe (Right x) = Just x
```

The uncurry function used here takes a binary function and creates a unary function receiving a tuple of both arguments producing the same result. Its dual is the curry function. We use uncurry here to get the slice function to accept the interval tuple inside mSliceInterval.

> **NOTE** The name curry stems from the concept of *currying*. This tells us that any function with multiple arguments can be rewritten to a sequence of unary functions. You might remember the example from the second chapter, where we explored how to construct a binary function with two anonymous, unary functions (f = \x → \y → ...). This is the exact concept that lets us rewrite any function with a finite number of arguments as a sequence of unary functions. It was popularized by mathematician Haskell Curry, who this concept and the programming language we are learning in this book are named after!

In our program, we are now at a point where we have exposed functionality through command-line arguments and now only have to worry about presenting our data to the outside world. We want to allow the user to either write the CSV table to a file or print the file contents to stdout for further data manipulation. Alternatively, the user should get some pretty representation of the data. Luckily, we don't have to learn any new fancy features to achieve that. It's down to some pattern matching and a little

help from a function that presents us a syntactically nice way to optionally perform an
IO action:

```
when :: Bool -> IO () -> IO ()
when True act = act
when False _ = return ()

unless :: Bool -> IO () -> IO ()
unless b = when (not b)
```

Using unless, we can write down a larger expression without having to wrap it into a
case or if. The code for this is shown in the following listing.

Listing 8.16   Reading optional arguments and deriving behavior from them

Reads an argument from the command line

Prints the file content representation of the CSV table to stdout

```
mOut <- Args.getText "out"
case mOut of
  Just "-" -> TIO.putStrLn $ Csv.toFileContent dataCsv
  Just fp -> Csv.writeCsv (T.unpack fp) dataCsv
  _ -> do
    countNonEmpty <- Args.getBool "count-non-empty"
    let mSummary =
          if countNonEmpty
            then Just $ Csv.countNonEmpty dataCsv
            else Nothing
    noPrettyOut <- Args.getBool "no-pretty"
    unless noPrettyOut $
      TIO.putStrLn $
        Csv.prettyText $
          maybe
            id
            (flip Csv.withSummaries)
            mSummary
            (Csv.fromCsv dataCsv)
```

Writes the CSV table to a file

Computes an optional summary from the count-non-empty argument

Aborts if the no-pretty argument was set

Prints the pretty representation of the CSV table

Either keeps the CSV table unaltered if no summary was computed or adds it to the pretty representation

---

This concludes our implementation. We have constructed a library that can parse CSV
files into a data model with which we can build algorithms. We have introduced general concepts for working with data, such as the Semigroup and Monoid type classes
and even introduced our own to slice data and to handle conversion from and to
Text. Then, we exposed the functionalities to the outside world and made them accessible and configurable.

Exercise: A multitude of options

Now, it is your turn. We have created the baseline for a tool that can read, manipulate, and write CSV files, but we have not unlocked its full potential. Extend the program by implementing more filters, search strategies, or ways of creating outputs
from the CSV. Here are some ideas to get you started:

- Joins on CSV tables
- Filters on numeric values (> n and < n)
- Uses configurable formatting for file output
- Specifies more than one file for input and append
- Finds and replaces strings on rows
- Exports CSV tables to SQL CREATE statements
- Offers support for more data types, such as floating-point numbers or Boolean values
- Uses delimiter *sniffing*, meaning the program infers which delimiters are likely used in the file

The more adventurous can try to implement some additional features that will require a bit more work:

- Conversion of CSV files to and from JSON files
  - For this, have a look at the aeson package.
- An interactive mode with a terminal user interface for exploring larger CSV tables
  - Have a look at the brick package, which helps you to construct user interfaces on the command line.
  - It features a Table type that can be used to print tables to the screen.

Finally, we want to *install* our tool on our computer! This step is optional, of course, but well worth it, when we construct useful software. By running stack install, our program gets built and installed to a local directory. After putting the path to this directory in the PATH variable of your environment, you can use the program! In our case, csview is an executable we can now use for all our CSV exploration needs!

Summary

- readMaybe from the Text.Read module can be used to safely parse numeric values.
- Folding is used to reduce complex data down to a single value.
- foldl associates its function from the left, while foldr does so from the right.
- Functors are used to map data contained in a type.
- Kinds are to types what types are to values.
- (<$>) is the infix version of fmap.
- The (.) operator is used to compose functions for which (.) f g x = f (g x) holds.

Quick checks and random tests

This chapter covers

- Working with random values
- Building a small property testing framework
- Using the popular testing framework QuickCheck
- Tailoring random value generators for special test cases
- Equipping software projects with test suites

The previous chapters have dealt with writing Haskell code for various applications. Something we have neglected to ask is this: Is the code we wrote even correct? Does it do the right things? Are our algorithms producing the correct results? In software engineering, this question is often answered by *testing*, which is what we want to explore in this chapter. To get familiar with testing, we cover the popular testing library *QuickCheck* and explore property testing in the context of Haskell, learning how to formalize correctness properties for pure functional code.

This chapter will start by introducing the concept of *property testing*, after which we will implement our own testing framework. In the meantime, we will learn about how to work with random values within Haskell. Then, QuickCheck is introduced. The chapter covers how to write properties, use the `Arbitrary` type class, and modify testing behavior to our liking. The chapter will close by showing how to incorporate QuickCheck test suites into Stack projects.

9.1 *How to test*

Testing can be done on different levels. While *integration testing* looks at the interplay of different software components and *system testing* checks if requirements on the finished system are met, *unit testing* focuses more on smaller code "units," whose behavior is individually tested. This allows us to write self-contained tests that verify the correct functionality of smaller, individual components. This is graphically laid out in figure 9.1.

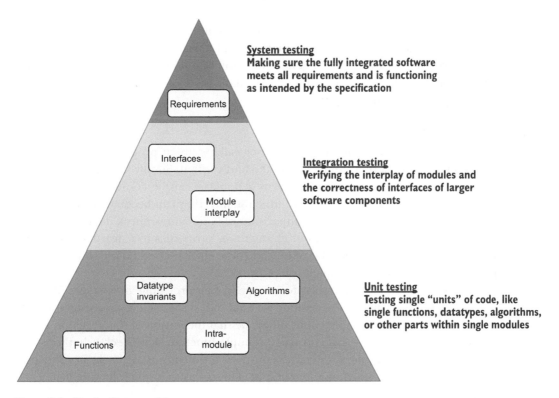

Figure 9.1 The testing pyramid

The validity of integration and system tests is dependent upon the correctness already hinted at by unit tests. If we cannot be sure that the smallest components of our system work as intended, there is no use in testing the software from the outside. Thus, the trust that we try to gain in our software by using tests is dependent on the thoroughness of the self-contained tests on the deepest level. In this chapter, we want to focus on unit testing and constructing these tests for single functions.

However, this raises the question of *how* we can test code. A simple way of writing tests is example based, meaning we specify certain inputs for our code and test if running it produces a predetermined result. While this is a simple way of testing, it comes with many drawbacks:

- Each test input has to be handcrafted.
- Test coverage correlates with the amount of test cases written.
- Edge cases for testing have to be manually specified (and might be forgotten).

This is error prone. If we were able to think of a complete test set, each time we write code, we would not need to specify tests anyway. In the end, we simply write test cases for functionality we already know works fine (especially if the designer of the test also implemented the tested functionality). In that way, tests are insurance against regressions. What we rarely do is *discover* errors while testing.

This is where *property testing* comes into play. When we formalize the correct functionality as a mathematical property that should be true for an input and an output, we can test our code by randomly generating inputs and simply checking this property on each of them. This way, we have a higher chance of spotting errors, since we do not have to specify the testing input.

9.1.1   *Property testing*

First, let us think about what we mean when talking about properties. A *property* is a characteristic of data that can be computed and verified. Simply speaking, a function that receives some argument and returns a Boolean can be considered a property. When using them for testing software functionality, they can become arbitrarily complex. We can make rather simple comparisons of basic values, check if data adheres to some rule set, or use a combination of any other properties to construct a new one. Equality-based testing, where the output of some code is checked on equality with a predefined value, is a very simple form of property.

Let's start exploring this testing technique by first providing an example. We start with a new project using `stack`. Assume we want to test some kind of sorting function. A property for such a function could simply be that the output of that function always has to be a sorted list. We can construct a simple function that checks whether some list is sorted (in ascending order) and construct a function that checks if a function produces a sorted list based on some output. This is shown in the following listing.

Listing 9.1   Predicates on the sortedness of lists

```
sorted :: Ord a => [a] -> Bool
sorted [] = True
sorted [_] = True
sorted (x : y : xs) = x <= y && sorted (y : xs)

sorts :: Ord a => ([a] -> [a]) -> [a] -> Bool
sorts f input = sorted $ f input
```

Returns True if the list consists of less than two elements

Checks if the first two elements are sorted and recursively tests if the tail of that list is also sorted

Returns True if a given function on a given input produces a sorted output

Now, we can use the `sorts` property to test functions on some inputs. `sorted` is a property, while `sorts` tests the `sorted` property function on a given input. Let's test the sort function from `Data.List` with it.

```
ghci> import Data.List (sort)
ghci> sort `sorts` [5,4,3,2,1 :: Int]
True
ghci> sort `sorts` [1,3,2,5,4 :: Int]
True
ghci> sort `sorts` ([] :: [Int])
True
```

This seems to work well! However, for constructing a test suite, we are not interested in writing down such test cases ourselves. We want to randomize the input, but randomness will require us to leave the world of pure functions and create something else.

9.1.2 Generating random values

Since property testing is a randomized testing technique, we will now spend a great amount of time dealing with the generation of random inputs. It is important to not only support a wide variety of types for which random generators exist but to support their modification as well. Building new generators for complex data types should be simple, and a good framework needs to facilitate this.

For now, we are interested in creating random lists for our property test on `sort`. Random values are something we haven't yet touched and also somewhat special in a language like Haskell, simply because random generators need to keep track of a state to compute new random numbers. In languages with side effects, random values are simple to implement (using some globally managed state), but in Haskell, this is somewhat different. A function's output is *only* determined by its input!

So how do random values work? To get a feel for it, we want to first examine a little example. Suppose we want to create a function that generates a random value. We know that we have to input some random state for it to return the random value; however, a new random state needs to be returned afterward. Otherwise, the same random state will be used for successive function calls. If the state gets modified by a pure function (e.g., to perform a pseudo-random transformation), we can use the new state afterward. When repeatedly looping back the state into the function, we can create a sequence of random values. This is shown in the following listing.

Listing 9.2 **Functions to explicitly work with random state**

```
newtype RandomState = RandomState Int          ← Defines a type for random
   deriving (Eq, Show)                              state as a single Int

randomInt :: RandomState -> (Int, RandomState)
randomInt (RandomState rs) = (newRs, RandomState newRs)    ← Returns a random
                                                              value and a new
                                                              random state
```

```
  where
    newRs = (1103515245 * rs + 12345) `mod` (2 ^ 31)    ◄─── Computes a new
                                                             random state
randomIntList :: RandomState -> Int -> [Int]
randomIntList rs n
  | n <= 0 = []                                         ┐  Recursively builds a list
  | otherwise =                                         │  of random values from
    let (v, rs') = randomInt rs                         │  a set random state
     in v : randomIntList rs' (n - 1)                   ┘
```

The `randomInt` function uses a *linear congruential generator* to compute new pseudo-random values. By repeatedly feeding the state into this function, we can create a stream of random values. This is what `randomIntList` uses to create a list of random integers:

```
ghci> randomIntList (RandomState 100) 5
[829870797,1533044610,1478614675,1357823696,413847241]
```

While this is one way of generating random numbers, it isn't general enough. We need to be able to describe random values that are outside of the realm of numbers. Also, we do not have to implement any of this ourselves as it already exists. We can use an assortment of functions from the `System.Random` module to get random values of different types.

To use this module, we need to add `random` to the dependencies in our package.yaml. Its dependency section should look something like this:

```
dependencies:
- random >= 1.2.1.1
```

The `System.Random` module provides us with a plethora of functions, types, and type classes to generate random values. However, parts of it are deprecated and should not be used. The most modern approach (at the time of writing) can be found in the `System.Random.Stateful` module. It provides access to many different types of random generators and ways of interacting with them, but we will only deal with `StdGen`, which is a typical pseudo-random generator.

9.1.3 *Random and Uniform*

Using `StdGen` is very similar to the `RandomState` we previously created:

```
ghci> import System.Random
ghci> import System.Random.Stateful
ghci> g = mkStdGen 100
ghci> g
StdGen {unStdGen = SMGen 16626775891238333538 2532601429470541125}
ghci> random g :: (Int, StdGen)
(9216477508314497915,StdGen {unStdGen = SMGen 712633246999323047
⮕ 2532601429470541125})
```

As we can see, we can create a `StdGen` with a seed (`100`, in this case) and use the `random` function to generate a tuple of a random number and the modified `StdGen`. `random` is one of four important functions for creating random values from a generator:

- `random :: (Random a, RandomGen g) => g -> (a, g)`
- `randomR :: (Random a, RandomGen g) => (a, a) -> g -> (a, g)`
- `uniform :: (Uniform a, RandomGen g) => g -> (a, g)`
- `uniformR :: (UniformRange a, RandomGen g) => (a, a) -> g -> (a, g)`

While `random` generates random values where the distribution of possible values of a type is *not known*, `uniform` generates uniformly distributed random values for a given type. This is why the type classes in the constraints for both functions differ. Both functions also have a ranged equivalent, suffixed with `R`, which generates random values in a given range.

Since both `Random` and `Uniform` have many instances for different values, we can use this to write polymorphic random functions. We don't have to write them specifically for `Int` values or numeric values in general. This way, we can generalize our list for random values. Furthermore, we can use our generator to produce a random length for our random list (with an upper bound, so it stays manageable). This is shown in the following listing.

Listing 9.3   Functions to produce random lists of random sizes

```
randomListN :: (Random a) => StdGen -> Int -> ([a], StdGen)
randomListN gen n
  | n <= 0 = ([], gen)
  | otherwise =
    let (v, gen') = random gen                    ◁   Generates a random value
        (xs, gen'') = randomListN gen' (n - 1)    ◁   and modifies the generator
    in (v : xs, gen'')                                Recursively builds a
                                                      list of random values

randomList :: (Random a) => StdGen -> Int -> ([a], StdGen)
randomList gen maxVal = randomListN gen' n     ◁   Generates a random
  where                                            list of random size with
    (n, gen') = uniformR (0, maxVal) gen    ◁     the modified generator

                                                   Generates a random
                                                   integer between 0 and the
randomList' :: (Random a) => StdGen -> ([a], StdGen)   specified maximum value
randomList' = flip randomList 100    ◁             and modifies the generator

                                              Returns a random list of a
                                              size between 0 and 100
```

Just like before with `RandomState`, we advance the modified generator to recursive function calls to produce new random values. In the end, we return the modified generator, so it can be used further; however, it is somewhat cumbersome to always pass and return these generators. What we might want to do is typical for most programming languages: use a global random value generator.

9.1.4   *Using a global random value generator*

Stateful global values seem impossible in a language like Haskell, but luckily, `System.Random` provides us with this functionality. The simplified signatures for the two actions we are interested in are

- `getStdGen :: IO StdGen`
- `setStdGen :: StdGen -> IO ()`

They allow access and set a global `StdGen` in `IO` actions. The global `StdGen` also comes pre-initialized on program start-up. However, there is a pitfall waiting for us here!

```
ghci> g <- getStdGen
ghci> g
StdGen {unStdGen = SMGen 9118772029923285118 15072976524409580889}
ghci> random g :: (Int, StdGen)
(7972809293454871112,StdGen {unStdGen = SMGen 5745004480623314391
➡ 15072976524409580889})
ghci> getStdGen
StdGen {unStdGen = SMGen 9118772029923285118
➡ 15072976524409580889}
```

`getStdGen` does not return a reference to the global generator but a copy. So when we modify it, we have to make sure to write the modified generator back to the global state.

> **NOTE**   Global resources can be implemented in `IO` actions with the help of `IORef`, as is the case with `getStdGen` and `setStdGen`. These are mutable references that can be used to read, store, and modify globally accessible data (in the case that `IORef` is global). However, the implementation is not safe for concurrent usage, so its usage is not recommended and is only shown for demonstration purposes. Instead, one should use `applyAtomicGen` and `globalStdGen`, as will be done later in this chapter.

Using the global generator, we can write an `IO` action that does *not* need a `StdGen` as an argument and stands on its own by first retrieving the global generator, applying the `randomList'` function, and then writing back the modified generator before returning the random list. The code for this is shown in the following listing.

Listing 9.4   An `IO` action that generates random lists

```
randomListIO :: (Random a) => IO [a]        Retrieves the global StdGen
randomListIO = do
  g <- getStdGen                            Generates a random list
  let (xs, g') = randomList' g              and a modified StdGen
  setStdGen g'
  return xs
```

Stores the modified StdGen as the global generator

Returns the random list

Now, we can use this action to generate random values of different types without having to worry about supplying or initializing the random generator:

```
ghci> randomListIO :: IO [Bool]
[True,False,True,True,True,True,True,False,False,False,True,True,True,
 True,False,False,True,True,False,False,False,True,False,False,False,
 True,False,False,True,True,False,False,False,True,True,False,True,
 True,True,False,True,True,True,False,False,False,True,True,False,
 False,True,False,False,False,False,False,False,False,False,False,
 False,False,False,False,False,False,True,False,True,False,False,True,
 True,True,True,False,True,True,False,False,False,True,True,False,
 False,True,False]
ghci> randomListIO :: IO [Int]
[3691255068706279388,-2800187626527368700,3917553492683069837,
 4227660806806667542,3268527085094962027,-5741538607687626546,
 2150401921944371087,-94788782940232908,-7272037394668750655,
 6615906112287910112,-7876828434837980022,-3967934342698301492,
 -8761894913785559922,3300716267348171691,2746716191340705260,
 501540442220827077,7580997570714960595,4369396272232835442,
 4464186059485273848,-1170916352399186521,-9175236237513240717,
 -3497815391797361407,-8229136869197540017,7239141001949992062,
 6119772250924788401,-4616451576842552626,-3121301812412732082,
 181124167447568155,1914103012390535081]
```

The code we have written, however, uses deprecated functions that should not be used in case of concurrency. While many tutorials online and older sources will teach them, `System.Random.Stateful` offers a new interface that is significantly safer to use. For this, we have to use the type `AtomicGenM` and `globalStdGen`, which, fortunately, has the type `AtomicGenM StdGen`. To use a function like `random` with it, we can use the `applyAtomicGen` function:

```
ghci> applyAtomicGen random globalStdGen :: IO Int
-8749052575918541620
ghci> applyAtomicGen (uniformR (0, 100)) globalStdGen :: IO Float
60.164364
ghci> applyAtomicGen randomList' globalStdGen :: IO [Bool]
[True,False,False,True,True,False,False,False,True,True,True,True,True,
 False,True,False,False,False,False,True,True,True,False,True,True,
 False,False,False,True,False,False,True,False,True,True,False,True,
 True,True,False,False,False,False,True,True,True,False,False,False,
 True,False,False,False,True,False,False,True,True,True]
```

This function essentially performs the same action as we did with `randomListIO`. It reads the global generator, performs the generation while modifying it, and writes it back to the global reference. However, it does so *atomically*, hence the name. This means that using this generator is safe in the context of concurrency. Since `globalStdGen` is a constant, we can write a little convenience function to more easily generate random values. This function is shown in the following listing.

Listing 9.5   An `IO` action that applies a function to the global pseudo-random generator

```
applyGlobalStdGen :: (StdGen -> (a, StdGen)) -> IO a
applyGlobalStdGen f = applyAtomicGen f globalStdGen        ◄─────────
```
Applies a function mapping a StdGen to a value and a new StdGen to the global StdGen of the program and returns the generated random value

Now, we can easily (and safely) generate random values in `IO` actions, which enables us to write a simple property test.

9.1.5   A basic property test

The last part of constructing our property test is putting all the pieces together into an `IO` action that generates a certain number of test cases and tests a given function on them, printing the input in the case of a found counter-example. This is shown in the following listing.

Listing 9.6   An example property test that checks if a function correctly sorts its input

```
propertyTestSorts :: ([Int] -> [Int]) -> Int -> IO ()
propertyTestSorts f n
  | n <= 0 = putStrLn "Tests successful!"              ◄─────────
  | otherwise = do
    xs <- applyGlobalStdGen randomList'                ◄─────────
    if f `sorts` xs                                    ◄─────────
      then propertyTestSorts f $ n - 1                 ◄─────────
      else putStrLn $ "Test failed on: " <> show xs    ◄─────────
```
Prints a success message if there are no cases to test left

Creates a random list

Checks if the function correctly sorts the random list

Prints the failing test case in case the test did not succeed

Runs the rest of the test cases if the test was successful

We can generalize the notion of a property test completely by making the function to test, the predicate that tests the function, and the `IO` action that generates the random value an argument. The code for this is shown in the following listing.

Listing 9.7   A generic property testing action

Prints a success message if there are no cases to test left

```
propertyTest :: Show a => (a -> b) -> (b -> Bool) -> IO a -> Int -> IO ()
propertyTest fun predicate random n
  | n <= 0 = putStrLn "Tests successful!"                  ◄─────────
  | otherwise = do
    testCase <- random                                     ◄─────────
    if predicate $ fun testCase                            ◄─────────
      then propertyTest fun predicate random $ n - 1       ◄─────────
      else putStrLn $ "Test failed on: " <>
➡ show testCase    ◄─────────
```
Prints the failing test case in case the test did not succeed

Runs the rest of the test cases if the test was successful

Creates a random value with the given random value generator

Checks if the function behaves correctly with the random value, according to a given predicate

Here, we arrive at a very general and usable definition of a very general wrapper we can use to construct all kinds of property tests. Let's make the trivial assumption that the sort function, indeed, sorts and the id doesn't:

```
ghci> propertyTest sort sorted (applyGlobalStdGen randomList' ::
➥ IO [Int]) 100
Tests successful!
ghci> propertyTest id sorted (applyGlobalStdGen randomList' ::
➥ IO [Int]) 100
Test failed on: [8872,9320,331,9174,7295,7971,7136,4134,7692,1235,8030,
➥ 3595,9078,4121,2722,23,3092,998,1005,2172,795,8495,1960,7359,7353,
➥ 16,3706,4893,6819,3984,7179,8933,8109,951,6330,542,4480,2864,2411,
➥ 2531,8971,2380,4653,1649,224,3466,5091,1834,5436,2803,7251,445,2795,
➥ 8274,7546,3241,3971,3624,955,6299,7857,1152,5028,2899,686,355,6695,
➥ 7098,6713]
```

Now that we have a very basic idea of how a property test is implemented, let's discuss some problems with our approach:

1 We have to construct a dedicated random value generator for each data type we want to test.
2 Each random value generator needs to be explicitly defined and referenced when performing the test.
3 The test doesn't allow for preconditions for the input data that must hold before the test can be done.
4 The test doesn't have a result indicating success or failure.

Astute readers might quickly see the solution for the first problem: a type class! The second problem can be addressed by providing random value generators that are *composable*, meaning that we have some way of taking existing generators and creating new ones from them. Let's focus on that.

9.1.6 *Defining postconditions for random values*

The System.Random module provides us with the Random type class that can be used with the StdGen we have already seen to generate random values:

```
ghci> applyGlobalStdGen random :: IO Int
-7583503057972408353
ghci> applyGlobalStdGen random :: IO Bool
False
ghci> applyGlobalStdGen random :: IO Double
0.5396729243902469
```

Haskell will automatically use the correct implementation of it, depending on the type we want to test. This is an example of *return-type polymorphism*. The correct implementation is chosen based on the type that is expected *at the call site*. The caller of the function can choose the type! While many other languages feature parametric polymorphism, the choice of type often happens at the creation of the value, not at the consumption of it.

The `Random` type class already features many instances for basic types. However, there are none for lists. Additionally, the type class does not allow us to easily compose generators (e.g., by providing preconditions for the generated values). To solve these problems, we want to wrap generic `IO` actions into a new type that signifies that the result is randomly generated. We do this by creating a `newtype`, where the only field is an `IO` action. We can then rewrite a more generic version of our previous `randomListIO` function. This is shown in the following listing.

Listing 9.8   Type and smart constructors for random value generators

```
newtype RandomIO a = RandomIO {runRandomIO :: IO a}    ◁───
```
> **Defines a type with a single field that encapsulates an IO action**

```
one :: Random a => RandomIO a
one = RandomIO $ applyGlobalStdGen random           ◁───
```
> **Creates a RandomIO by using the global StdGen to produce a random value of some type**

```
some :: Random a => RandomIO [a]
some = RandomIO $ do
  n <- applyGlobalStdGen $ uniformR (0, 100)
  replicateIO n $ runRandomIO one
```
> **Generates a list of random size, using one to produce random elements**

The type is called `RandomIO`, since it encapsulates an `IO` action capable of producing random values. `one` and `some` are smart constructors that build `RandomIO` values for types that have an instance of the `Random` type class. `replicateIO` is a function that replicates an `IO` action a specified number of times and aggregates the results in a list. The code for it is shown in the following listing.

Listing 9.9   Aggregate function to replicate an `IO` action

```
replicateIO :: Int -> IO a -> IO [a]
replicateIO n act
  | n <= 0 = return []                   ◁───
  | otherwise = do
    x <- act                             ◁───
    xs <- replicateIO (n - 1) act        ◁───
    return $ x : xs                      ◁───
```
> **Returns an empty list if the specified size is zero or negative**
> **Calls the action**
> **Recursively replicates the action**
> **Prepends the action's result with the recursively replicated results and returns the final list**

Now, the `RandomIO` can be embedded into any `IO` action by accessing the `runRandomIO` field and then simply calling the `IO` action like that:

```
ghci> runRandomIO one :: IO Float
0.12762898
ghci> runRandomIO some :: IO [Bool]
[True,True,True,True,False,False,False,False,False,False,False,True,False,
➥ True,False,False,True,False,True,True,True,True,False,True,False,
➥ False,True,False,True,False,True]
```

Again, using return-type polymorphism, we can use `RandomIO` to generate values of varying types. However, for testing purposes, we may want to specify what kinds of values should be generated more precisely.

> **NOTE** When actions or computations get wrapped into a `newtype`, the field in the new constructor often has such a run prefix. Since the record contains only a single field, the action can be wrapped using the constructor alone (without specifying the field). Generally, this makes the code a bit easier to read.

For this purpose, we can write a function that modifies an existing `RandomIO` by filtering values that we do not want to see generated. This way, we can compose our smart constructors with functions that specify how the random value should look. For this, create a function that reruns the random generator indefinitely until some predicate has been met. Using this, we can already form new generators for nonnegative and nonempty values. This is shown in the following listing.

Listing 9.10   A function to modify the output of a random value generator

```haskell
suchThat :: RandomIO a -> (a -> Bool) -> RandomIO a
suchThat rand pred = RandomIO $ do
  val <- runRandomIO rand
  if pred val
    then return val
    else runRandomIO $ suchThat rand pred

nonNegative :: (Num a, Ord a, Random a) => RandomIO a
nonNegative = one `suchThat` (> 0)

nonEmpty :: Random a => RandomIO [a]
nonEmpty = some `suchThat` (not . null)
```

- Encapsulates the following IO action with the RandomIO constructor
- Runs the provided RandomIO to generate a random value
- Returns the value if it satisfies the given property and otherwise retries the action
- Reruns a RandomIO until a nonnegative number was generated
- Reruns a RandomIO until a nonempty list was generated

`suchThat` is a good example of how we unwrap a `RandomIO` to use it in an `IO` action and then put it back into the `RandomIO` by wrapping the whole `do` block with the constructor. Using this, we can create a generator for human-readable `String` values. Sadly, the default instance of `Random Char` produces many characters that we cannot print. Thus, we can use `isAscii` and `isControl` from `Data.Char` to check if the characters within the string are printable and nicely human readable. Using the `all` function, we can check that this predicate holds for all elements of the `string`. However, running this generator presents us with a problem:

```
ghci> import Data.Char
ghci> asciiString = some `suchThat`
⇒ all (\c -> isAscii c && not (isControl c))
ghci> runRandomIO asciiString
```

```
""
ghci> runRandomIO asciiString
""
ghci> runRandomIO asciiString
""
```

What's going on here? As it turns out, the predicate we have given is so specific that it is more likely to produce just an empty list than a list with correct values. That's because the `Char` values are still generated at random. Just one wrong `Char` makes us retry the whole generation!

Exercise: A functor for random values

`suchThat` acts more or less like a filter on our random generator. What we have not yet built is an equivalent to the `map` function for our random values. To keep things as general as possible, we might want to implement an instance for the `Functor` type class for `RandomIO`, where `fmap` applies some function to the random value. Implement this instance!

Luckily, there is a way to fix this by first creating a generator for human-readable `Char` values and then using this generator to build a `asciiString` generator from it. For this, we restrict ourselves to ASCII characters. Normal (nonextended) characters are either human-readable or control characters, so it is enough to filter them away when additionally checking if a character is ASCII. To build a `String` from a `Char` generator, we create a function that acts just like `some` but uses a generator that is passed as an argument instead of `randomIO`. This is shown in the following listing. Additionally, we can create a generator for `String` values just containing letters this way.

Listing 9.11 Generators for for random ASCII characters and strings

```
asciiChar :: RandomIO Char
asciiChar = one `suchThat`
➥  (\c -> isAscii c && not (isControl c))
```
◁ **Defines a random generator for printable ASCII characters by requiring a generated Char to be within ASCII range and disallow control characters**

```
letterChar :: RandomIO Char
letterChar = asciiChar `suchThat` isLetter
```
◁ **Defines a random generator for letter characters by restricting the generator for ASCII characters even more**

```
manyOf :: RandomIO a -> RandomIO [a]
manyOf rio = RandomIO $ do
  n <- applyGlobalStdGen $ uniformR (0, 100)
  replicateIO n (runRandomIO rio)
```
Generates a random list from a given RandomIO

```
asciiString :: RandomIO String
asciiString = manyOf asciiChar

letterString :: RandomIO String
letterString = manyOf letterChar
```
◁ **Defines random generators for String values that only contain certain characters by composing other generators with manyOf**

Now, we can produce random String values for our testing purposes!

```
ghci> runRandomIO asciiString
"N:=P!RVyo7O{=QU6"
ghci> runRandomIO asciiString
"&q~,=Dm:"
ghci> runRandomIO letterString
"EdgcdiBHQcwIJAkCKlhemiaUWBMeNxrHOkWigRuktokfMyxXzYklFBO"
ghci> runRandomIO letterString
"uEETBtLDCIneVmHFNvICxPLuEwSoSnj"
```

We are now able to modify our `propertyTest` function to not only use our `RandomIO` as a generator but also simplify the function to only use a single predicate that returns a `Bool` to determine the correctness of a test. This will allow us to test more complex cases, where we want to observe the correctness of some more general computation instead of just observing the output of some function. The finished function is shown in the following listing.

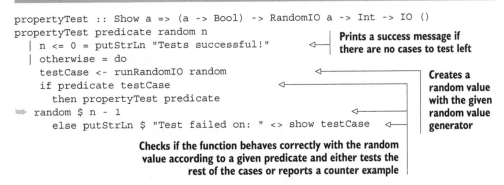

Listing 9.12 **An action for property testing using custom random value generators**

```
propertyTest :: Show a => (a -> Bool) -> RandomIO a -> Int -> IO ()
propertyTest predicate random n
  | n <= 0 = putStrLn "Tests successful!"        ← Prints a success message if
  | otherwise = do                                 there are no cases to test left
    testCase <- runRandomIO random               ← Creates a
    if predicate testCase                        ←  random value
      then propertyTest predicate                   with the given
      random $ n - 1                             ←  random value
        else putStrLn $ "Test failed on: " <> show testCase  ← generator
```

Checks if the function behaves correctly with the random value according to a given predicate and either tests the rest of the cases or reports a counter example

Now that we have successfully constructed random generators and helpers to construct and modify them, we can finally dip our toes into using the `propertyTest` function to test some code we have previously written and see how we will fare.

Exercise: Efficient ASCII strings

The way we have defined `letterString` is highly inefficient. Instead of randomly choosing from a set of wanted `Char` values, we choose from a huge set, which we then filter by invalidating elements we do not want to see. To make it a bit more efficient as well as more general, write a function that receives a nonempty list of elements and randomly chooses one. Then, use this function to build new ASCII and letter generators that are faster this time:

```
elements :: [a] -> RandomIO a
elements [] = error "elements cannot work with an empty list!"
elements xs = ...
```

9.2   *Randomized testing*

After our extensive study of random value generators, we can now think a bit more about how to *properly* deal with *properties*. This specifically means that we need to figure out how to write properties that give us safety on the correctness of our program.

Before we can start, we should structure our project. For this, we put all the testing code we have created so far into a module called `Test.SimpleCheck`. This will serve as our framework for testing. After this is done, we can start to copy the code for our Caesar's cipher project from chapter 2 into our source code, and we can start to write tests on it.

What kind of property should we test on our code? Of course, this is highly dependent on the specification of the software. In our case, we just want to make sure that our core assumptions about the code hold. One assumption we have made was that applying the ROT13 cipher twice will yield the original value. Thus, ROT13 is symmetrical. This can be expressed in our test framework. The property of the function is that for any input s, it must hold that `s == rot13 (rot13 s)`. This can be simply expressed through a function, which we can plug into our `propertyTest` function! This is shown in the following listing.

Listing 9.13   A property test for the symmetry of the ROT13 function

```
propRot13Symmetrical :: IO ()          Tests that applying rot13 twice on a
propRot13Symmetrical =                 value leaves the value unchanged
  propertyTest
    (\s -> s == rot13 (rot13 s))   ←┐  Uses the generator for
    asciiString                  ←─┘  ASCII strings for the test
    100            ←───────────────┘  Specifies there must be 100 test cases
```

The choice of the random value generator for this property matters! In chapter 2, we said that the symmetrical property holds for *letters*. However, in this test, we are testing a more general case. Not just letters are being evaluated but all human-readable ASCII characters. Therefore, this test not only tests if `rot13` is symmetrical but also if this symmetric property is robust with regard to the `Char` values in the input. Luckily, we build `rot13` this way, and thus, the test is successful!

```
ghci> propRot13Symmetrical
Tests successful!
```

The test we have just seen is somewhat of a *specification test*. It is part of our specification that ROT13 is symmetrical. This property ensures that the finished function `rot13` implements this specification correctly. Now, we can happily refactor `rot13` and all the underlying machinery that makes it possible without having to worry about breaking the specification. If we did something wrong, the test will hopefully tell us!

NOTE   It's a good idea to give property tests in your code a special name. In some code bases, such functions are prefixed with `prop` or even `prop_` (even though using an underscore in identifiers is frowned upon by some linters). When the code base contains property tests as well as example-based unit tests, you can sometimes see functions with a `test` or `test_` prefix for the latter case.

We can add more tests that more thoroughly test the helper functions we have built. Of course, for this project, writing a test suite is more than overkill, but it is a good opportunity to get familiar with this testing technique. For this, we want to inspect some helper functions more closely and see if we can verify their functionality.

First, let's investigate the `alphabetRot` function. It served the purpose of rotating a `Char` through an alphabet. A property that must then hold is that after rotation, the new `Char` that was returned from the function needs to be an element of the original alphabet. This is something we can test and verify! However, the input to this function is a bit more complex than what we have previously seen. This function receives an `Alphabet` (which was a type alias for `String`), an `Int`, and a `Char`, which needs to be an element of the first argument. As we can already see, we do not have a generator ready that would supply that. However, we can create a new one just for this test, which will create a nonempty alphabet and specifically choose the `Char` argument to be an element from that created alphabet. The code for this is shown in the following listing.

Listing 9.14   A property test for the closedness of the alphabet rotation function

```
propAlphabetRotClosed :: IO ()                          Runs the property test
propAlphabetRotClosed = propertyTest prop gen 100       with 100 test cases
  where
    prop (alphabet, n, c) =                 Defines the test's property to
      let c' = alphabetRot alphabet n c     check if a rotated character is
      in c' `elem` alphabet                 still in the same alphabet

    gen = RandomIO $ do                          Generates a nonempty
      alphabet <-                                alphabet, consisting of
        runRandomIO $                            ASCII characters
          asciiString `suchThat` (not . null)
      n <- runRandomIO $ elements [-100 .. 100]     Chooses a random value
      c <- runRandomIO $ elements alphabet          from -100 to 100
      return (L.nub alphabet, n, c)
                                               Chooses a random value from
                   Removes duplicates from     the generated alphabet
                   the alphabet and returns
                   the generated values
```

In this test, the generator does all the heavy lifting to provide a sensible foundation for the test. Before passing the arguments to the test, the generator filters duplicates from the alphabet, since we can assume them to not contain any element twice. The `Char` argument must be specifically chosen *randomly* from the random alphabet. This means that even if the same random alphabet is being generated twice, there is a good chance that another `Char` was chosen from it.

9.2.1   *The benefit of referential transparency*

We want to take a short gander into some theoretical discussion on *why* property testing is effective in Haskell specifically. So far, we have exploited a very important aspect of the language to make our tests useful: Haskell is *pure*. This means that the functions we write are inherently free of side effects. The result of a function is not changed by *anything but the input*. This means that the simple observation of input and output is enough to determine the correctness of a function, since there is no other output or behavior in the system to observe. Additionally, it is enough to design a random value generator for the function, since there is no artificial environment we have to set up for the test to be valid. The test's validity is only determined by the correct choice of random values and a correct interpretation of the property under test.

This property is also called *referential transparency*. Any referentially transparent expression (such as a function application with a pure function) can simply be replaced by the value the expression is evaluated to. The only thing we need to make sure of is that the values the expressions evaluate are what we expect them to be.

As an example, let's look at the `isMisc` function from chapter 2. It is a simple function that determines whether a char is not a letter or a digit. Additionally, we have a few other predicates in our project (`isLower`, `isUpper`, and `isDigit`) that determine whether a character is a lowercase letter, an uppercase letter, or a digit. It is implied that `isMisc` evaluates to `True` if and only if none of the other predicates evaluate to `True`. While writing our Caesar's cipher, we simply assumed this to be true. However, it can easily be tested by a property test, as is shown in the following listing.

Listing 9.15   Property test for checking predicate invariant

```
propIsMiscIsDefault :: IO ()              Tests that isMisc is true if and only if
propIsMiscIsDefault =                     no other predicate on Char is true
  propertyTest
    (\c -> isMisc c == not                Uses the generic random value
⇨  (isLower c || isUpper c || isDigit c)) ◁  generator for a single value, which
    one                               ◁      will generate Char values
    10000      ◁      Specifies there to be 10,000 test cases
```

The property under test is a simple predicate that checks the equivalence of `isMisc` with a logical term. Again, it's thanks to Haskell's pure nature that the equivalence of terms can be checked by a simple `==`. It is important to note that these terms are only *observationally equivalent*. They produce the same output for a given input, but they do have different technical behavior and a different memory footprint. However, this is fine, since in pure code, the observational equivalence is all that matters when it comes to program correctness. Our functions are only controlled by their input, and the only thing they can do is evaluate some output. Now that we have some grasp on property testing, we are ready to mature our testing methodologies by upgrading from our own little framework to a real powerhouse of testing: QuickCheck.

9.3 The QuickCheck testing framework

We started this chapter by working on our own little testing framework: SimpleCheck. However, it faces a few problems that are hard to ignore:

- Constructing random value generators is complicated and laborious.
- It is difficult to compose properties.
- There is no way to get insights into the data under test (what kind of values are being tested or how often).
- It is not possible to modify tests by giving preconditions.
- Our random value generators have a fixed behavior that cannot easily be changed.
- Failing test cases are not being minimized and can become large and hard to understand.

These problems would make our framework hard to use in the real world. However, there is a solution to all of these problems: a testing framework called *QuickCheck*. Originally developed by Koen Claessen and John Hughes in 1999 at the Chalmers University of Technology, QuickCheck has popularized the concept of property testing, and re-implementations exist in a huge variety of languages, from functional (OCaml, Clojure, Scala) to non-functional (C++, Java, TypeScript). It's design is very much like our SimpleCheck framework. It provides

- Functions for testing properties
- Combinators for composing and modifying properties
- Helper functionality for debugging testing behavior
- Types and type classes for random value generation

We now want to review this library and get a quick overview of its functionalities before we delve deep into some property testing case studies.

Before we begin, let us look at how to incorporate QuickCheck into our project. Since QuickCheck is in the Stackage repository, we can simply add it to our package.yaml file under *dependencies*. We want to add the line - `QuickCheck >= 2.0` to force the version of QuickCheck to be `2.0` or newer. When building the application or starting the REPL, `stack` will automatically resolve this dependency. The `dependencies` section should look something like this:

```
dependencies:
- base >= 4.7 && < 5
- QuickCheck >= 2.0
- random >= 1.2.1.1
```

Now that we know how to get the framework running, let's get an overview. Let's first go over the most basic concepts in QuickCheck.

9.3.1 Using Property in QuickCheck

The first one would be the most simple building block: the `quickCheck` function. It receives some property as its input and tests it for us, creating an `IO` action. Two important instances of such a property are `Bool` and QuickCheck's type `Property`. Furthermore, such a property can also be a function that returns a property! So a function that returns `Bool` (like a simple predicate) is a property.

> **NOTE**   Internally, a property must have an instance of the `Testable` type class. This class defines how to convert some type to a property. It will not be covered here, since we do not need to construct custom instances for it, but it helps to think of *property* when encountering `Testable prop` somewhere in QuickChecks's documentation.

Let's test this by verifying the symmetry of the `rot13` function, just like we did before:

```
ghci> import Test.QuickCheck
ghci> prop_rot13Symm s = s == rot13 (rot13 s)
ghci> :t prop_rot13Symm
prop_rot13Symm :: String -> Bool
ghci> quickCheck prop_rot13Symm
+++ OK, passed 100 tests.
```

QuickCheck was able to successfully test this property. It is notable that it was able to somehow *magically* create input data for our function. This is something that we will explore later. For now, let us explore the checking of properties a bit further.

> **NOTE**   QuickCheck properties are usually written with a `prop_` prefix. This way, QuickCheck can automatically run tests on all found properties in a module. Some Haskell linters disallow the usage of _ in identifiers, but we make an exception for QuickCheck properties.

What if we wanted to check an incorrect implementation with this property? What would happen?

```
ghci> symbols = upperAlphabet ++ lowerAlphabet ++ digits
ghci> rot13' = map $ (\ch -> if ch `elem` symbols then alphabetRot symbols
➥ 13 ch else ch)
ghci> prop_rot13Symm s = s == rot13' (rot13' s)
ghci> quickCheck prop_rot13Symm
*** Failed! Falsified (after 2 tests and 1 shrink):
"a"
```

In this example, we intentionally created an incorrect implementation of `rot13` and used it in the same property. Essentially, we created a bug while refactoring (while the property under test stayed the same). QuickCheck tells us that the test failed (after completing two tests, one of which was successful) and failed with the input `"a"`. This is quite similar to our old property testing function!

Another notable concept is the notion of *shrinks*. When a test case fails, Quick-Check will automatically try to make it smaller, in the sense that numeric values become smaller in value or that lists and maps have fewer elements, and so on. Of course, the shrunken value still needs to be a counterexample; otherwise, QuickCheck

will just tell us about the bigger value. We do this to arrive at a more easily understood counterexample. In our example, the problem with our property is the rotation of single characters. However, it can also be falsified by using a huge string with
a variety of characters. We see this when testing the same property with our Simple-
Check implementation:

```
ghci> propertyTest prop_rot13Symm asciiString 100
Test failed on: "JQCj_s&S>mOSLnPW5XXIqi9+*IF4WLbTW$&hW?4FTg\\:
➡  !a-vo_QfR/cy4,w2.Xg~5R0sCsX==-KPyD^Wy\\"
```

It is not necessary to ask the question of which test result is easier to debug in this case.
Another great thing about QuickCheck is that its shrinking is deterministic for many
types. Running the test multiple times will give us the same counterexample each time!

```
ghci> quickCheck prop_rot13Symm
*** Failed! Falsified (after 2 tests and 1 shrink):
"a"
ghci> quickCheck prop_rot13Symm
*** Failed! Falsified (after 5 tests and 1 shrink):
"a"
ghci> quickCheck prop_rot13Symm
*** Failed! Falsified (after 4 tests and 2 shrinks):
"a"
```

This ensures much better repeatability of tests and helps with classifying common
bugs in our functions.

Now, it's time to test something more elaborate. We can write down our property on the closedness of the `alphabetRot` function. The property is shown in the
following listing.

Listing 9.16 A QuickCheck property on the closedness of the alphabet rotation function

```
prop_alphabetRotClosed :: Alphabet -> Int -> Char -> Bool
prop_alphabetRotClosed alphabet n c =
  let c' = alphabetRot alphabet n c
  in c' `elem` alphabet
```
| **Defines the test property to check if a rotated**
| **character is still in the same alphabet**

Let us quickly check this property:

```
ghci> quickCheck prop_alphabetRotClosed
*** Failed! Falsified (after 1 test and 1 shrink):
""
0
'a'
```

There are two things of note here. First, QuickCheck can generate arguments for a function with three arguments! We can use any number of arguments in our functions, and
all of them will be independently generated. The second thing to note is that our property is wrong! But why? We see that the arguments for this property were `""` for `alphabet`,

0 for n, and `'a'` for c. The problem here is that c needs to be an element of `alphabet`, and more importantly, `alphabet` should not be empty! How do we solve this problem?

In our framework, we solved it by modifying the random value generator to only produce correct values. This is what we now have to do in QuickCheck. s

9.4 *Generating random values for testing*

Random value generation is at the heart of QuickCheck, since property testing is meaningless without it. Furthermore, the library can automatically infer the correct generators just from the types we see. How is this implemented?

The answer comes to us with the type class called `Arbitrary`:

```
ghci> :i Arbitrary
type Arbitrary :: * -> Constraint
class Arbitrary a where
  arbitrary :: Gen a
  shrink :: a -> [a]
  {-# MINIMAL arbitrary #-}
```

It defines `arbitrary`, which is used to produce random values, and `shrink`, which we will take a look at later. From the minimal definition we see that we can ignore `shrink` completely for now! So what is `arbitrary`, and what is a `Gen`?

9.4.1 *The random generator Genrandom value function*

`Gen` is very similar to our `RandomIO` type. It defines how to generate random values for a specific type. We can use the `generate` function to produce random values from a `Gen` in an `IO` action:

```
ghci> generate arbitrary :: IO Int
15
ghci> generate arbitrary :: IO [Bool]
[True,True,True,False,True,False]
ghci> generate arbitrary :: IO (Maybe Float)
Just (-9.993277)
ghci> generate arbitrary :: IO (Either String Char)
Right '.'
```

Here, we see how the generators can produce values for a variety of types. We can also define some ourselves, using a few helper functions provided by QuickCheck. Here, we will review a small selection of them:

- `choose :: Random a => (a, a) -> Gen a`—Behaves like `randomRIO` and can be used to generate numeric values in an interval
- `chooseAny :: Random a => Gen a`—Transforms the random value from a `Random` instance to a `Gen` of the same type
- `oneof :: [Gen a] -> Gen a`—Randomly chooses a generator in the given list
- `elements :: [a] -> Gen a`—Produces a generator that randomly picks an element from the given list

- `suchThat :: Gen a -> (a -> Bool) -> Gen a`—Modifies a generator to skip unwanted elements, based on a Boolean predicate
- `listOf :: Gen a -> Gen [a]`—Generates a list of random length from a generator
- `listOf1 :: Gen a -> Gen [a]`—Like `listOf` but does not generate empty lists
- `vectorOf :: Int -> Gen a -> Gen [a]`—Generates a list of random values of a given length
- `vector :: Arbitrary a => Int -> Gen [a]`—Like `vectorOf` but the generator for the list is inferred on the type level
- `shuffle :: [a] -> Gen [a]`—Produces random permutations of the given list
- `sublistOf :: [a] -> Gen [a]`—Produces random sublists of the given list

These are not all of the helper functions that QuickCheck provides but probably the most helpful. Here, we also see our old friend `suchThat`! Using these functions, we can define new generators. But what exactly does that look like?

Exercise: Generator combinators

We have already implemented `suchThat` in our SimpleCheck framework. Now, it is time to copy more of the functions from QuickCheck to get a better feel for how it computes the value it uses. Make sure the type signature is the same (just using `RandomIO` instead of `Gen`), and try to keep the performance as good as it can be.

Defining generators is very similar to defining `RandomIO`. To create them, we can use the `do` notation we are already familiar with from `IO` actions. This notation will help us recreate the generator we used for our alphabet property from before. Using `runRandomIO` is not necessary within the `do` notation of a generator. We can simply use another generator, such as `arbitrary` or `choose` and get their respective values. In the end, we return the finished value. Just like before, we need to return a tuple, since the generation of the values is dependent on each other. This is shown in the following listing.

Listing 9.17 A QuickCheck generator for test data on the alphabet rotation function

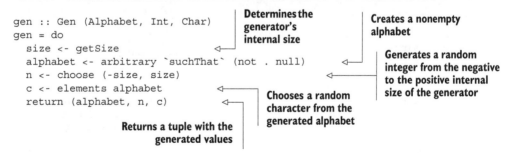

A small difference this generator has from our last one is its usage of the `getSize` generator and its usage in determining n. Generators in QuickCheck have an *internal size*. The size determines some of the parameters of the generated values. For example, the

standard generator for `Int` will produce values that have an absolute value of the internal size of that generator. The default size for generators is 30, but that can be changed with the `resize` function. Here is a quick example:

```
ghci> import Control.Monad
ghci> import Test.QuickCheck
ghci> sample = replicateM 10
ghci> sample $ generate (arbitrary :: Gen Int)
[0,-8,12,9,-9,29,-15,19,-28,-26]
ghci> sample $ generate (resize 100 $ arbitrary :: Gen Int)
[-69,-38,13,-29,40,79,-33,-59,-28,-33]
ghci> sample $ generate (resize 10000 $ arbitrary :: Gen Int)
[270,-5063,-121,-5645,-6974,9861,-1830,-5653,4493,9132]
```

This solves a problem where sometimes, we want to externally control the size of a generator for performance reasons. `listOf` is such an example, where the internal size dictates how large a list can become. The same goes for the `arbitrary` of `String`. When constructing our generators, we should respect this size and use `getSize` internally whenever we can. When calling generators inside a generator, the size propagates through, so we can happily build generators from other ones without having to worry about resizing generators internally (except if we explicitly want to do so).

> **NOTE** The `sample` function already exists in QuickCheck; however, it samples the generator with different sizes (starting from 0 and ending at 20). You can use it to quickly get insight into how the generated values look and how the behavior of the generator changes with different sizes.

Now that we have created a generator for our task, it is time to use it. When we want to run a specific generator on some property, we can use the `forAll`, which explicitly lets you set a generator for the test cases on a given property. The result of this function is again a property. This enables us to rewrite our property test on the closedness of `alphabetRot` entirely with QuickCheck's functionality. This is shown in the following listing.

Listing 9.18   Property describing closedness of the `alphabet` function

```
prop_alphabetRotClosed :: Property
prop_alphabetRotClosed =
  forAll gen prop
  where
    prop :: (Alphabet, Int, Char) -> Bool
    prop (alphabet, n, c) =
      let c' = alphabetRot alphabet n c
      in c' `elem` alphabet

    gen :: Gen (Alphabet, Int, Char)
    gen = do
      size <- getSize
      alphabet <- arbitrary `suchThat` (not . null)
```

Defines the property to be tested with the provided generator

Defines the test's property to check if a rotated character is still in the same alphabet

Returns the current internal size of the generator

Generates a random nonempty alphabet

```
n <- choose (-size, size)
c <- elements alphabet
return (L.nub alphabet, n, c)
```

Chooses a random value on a range that is based on the internal size of the generator

Removes duplicates from the alphabet and returns the generated values

Chooses a random value from the generated alphabet

This implementation should reside in a new module so that it does not conflict with our previous implementation. We can notice that while the code looks similar to what we had before, it allows for more expressive testing than it did before.

We have seen how we can create our generators, but obviously, we do not want to do this on a per-test basis. If we have custom types, we will want to create an instance for the `Arbitrary` type class to more easily compose our generators. This is something we should take a look at next.

9.4.2   Example: AssocMap

Let us think back to chapter 5, where we introduced the `AssocMap` type, our polymorphic map type. This is something we want to test next. However, for this, we need to be able to produce random values of this type. The `Arbitrary` type class is exactly for this purpose, so we want to create an instance of this type for it!

Let's recap what the type was and how it functioned. The `AssocMap` is a type that uses a list of tuples `[(k, v)]` to keep a map of *keys* and *values*. It's full type definition is shown in the following listing.

Listing 9.19   The `AssocMap` definition from chapter 5

```
newtype AssocMap k v = AssocMap [(k, v)]
  deriving (Show)
```

Each key can only occur once, so if we want to generate arbitrary values of this type, we need to respect this property. We can use the fact that `Gen` also has a `Functor` instance, so we can use `fmap` and `<$>` to modify generated values. Using this, we can generate a list of keys that has no duplicates and, based on that, create just as many values, which we then combine in our map. The code for a generator for `AssocMap` is shown in the following listing.

Listing 9.20   A QuickCheck generator for associative maps

```
import qualified Data.List as L
import Test.QuickCheck
```

Imports necessary imports

```
...

genAssocMap :: (Eq k, Arbitrary k, Arbitrary v) => Gen (AssocMap k v)
genAssocMap = do
  keys <- L.nub <$> arbitrary
```

Creates a random list of keys with duplicates removed

```
vals <- vectorOf (L.length keys) arbitrary
return $ AssocMap (L.zip keys vals)
```

Creates as many random values as there are keys

Returns the generated AssocMap by combining the generated keys and values

The constraint for this type is important. Since we want to use *arbitrary* keys and values, the types have to have an instance of the `Arbitrary` type class. Using `arbitrary` in our generator enables us to use *any* type for which an `arbitrary` generator exists within our `AssocMap` generator. We can now test this generator to see what it produces for different types:

```
ghci> generate genAssocMap :: IO (AssocMap Int Bool)
AssocMap [(0,True),(-1,False),(-23,True),(19,False),(14,False),(2,False)]
ghci> generate genAssocMap :: IO (AssocMap Int (Either Bool Int))
AssocMap [(-10,Left True),(-20,Right 19)]
ghci> generate genAssocMap :: IO (AssocMap Bool [Float])
AssocMap [(True,[7.2917347,17.285803,-12.867395,-3.3579175])]
```

Now, we have completed the first puzzle piece in writing our `Arbitrary` instance. However, the second part—the `shrink` function—should not be ignored.

9.4.3 *Shrinking test cases*

When testing and especially when falsifying a test case, we are often not interested in convoluted and overly complex counterexamples of our properties. However, if inputs for our property tests are chosen at random, eventually, we will generate large counterexamples. QuickCheck has a built-in feature called *shrinking*, which tries to minify a found counterexample. Once some input has been found for which a property test fails, the input is shrunk and rechecked to see if it still constitutes a counterexample. This is repeated until the value cannot be shrunk further without it ceasing to be a counterexample. At that point, we can be somewhat sure that we have found a minimal falsifying input. This idea is highlighted in figure 9.2.

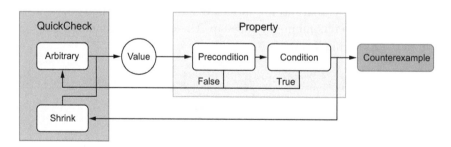

Figure 9.2   The interplay of QuickCheck, properties and shrinking

For each data type for which QuickCheck knows how to generate random data, it also knows if and how to shrink values from this type. This is due to the `Arbitrary` type class that defines a function that does the shrinking, called `shrink`. Its type signature `a -> [a]` tells us something very important about it: it is a *pure function* that generates a list of shrunk values from its input! Thus, its output is only dependent on the input, which means the function is deterministic! There is nothing random about it. This is why the counterexamples that QuickCheck generates sometimes appear to be deterministic; based on the input, we can return predetermined candidates for Quick-Check to further try. A good example is the `shrink` function on `Char`:

```
ghci> shrink 'H'
"abchABC"
ghci> shrink 'A'
"abc"
ghci> shrink 'h'
"abc"
ghci> shrink '\n'
"abcABC123 "
ghci> shrink '1'
"abcABC"
```

Here, we see how the continuous shrinking of `Char` values will at some point add `'"abc"'` into the mix. This is done purposefully, since if `'H'` is a counterexample, maybe any value of `'"abchABC"'` is too. Another important note is that `shrink` should not return its input as part of its shrunk values. Otherwise, shrinking might run into an infinite loop!

Now, how can we shrink our `AssocMap`? If we specify the key and value type to have an `Arbitrary` instance, this also means that a tuple of them and a list of tuples of them have an instance. This means that we can simply shrink the list in our `AssocMap` type, but we have to be careful. `shrink` could potentially change values, which might invalidate our invariant that no key can occur twice. So when shrinking, we have to make sure that keys only occur once. The implementation for shrinking is shown in the following listing.

Listing 9.21   A `shrink` function for associative maps

```
shrinkAssocMap ::
  (Eq k, Arbitrary k, Arbitrary v) =>
  AssocMap k v ->
  [AssocMap k v]
shrinkAssocMap (AssocMap xs) =
  L.map
    (AssocMap . L.nubBy (\(k1, _) (k2, _) -> k1 == k2))
    (shrink xs)
```

Creates new AssocMap values from the shrunk candidates by removing duplicate keys

Shrinks the values present in the given map and produces candidates based on them

---

We can test this shrinking function on an arbitrary `AssocMap`:

```
ghci> am <- generate (genAssocMap :: Gen (AssocMap Int Int))
ghci> am
AssocMap [(-26,11),(6,3),(12,-24),(-24,-4),(30,12),(-5,27),(-18,9)]
```

```
ghci> shrinkAssocMap am
[AssocMap [],AssocMap [(-24,-4),(30,12),(-5,27),(-18,9)],...
```

This will enable us to get much simpler counterexamples if we write a property that fails with `AssocMap`! To do this, the last puzzle piece is to construct the `Arbitrary (AssocMap k v)` instance using the functions we have created. The code is shown in the following listing.

Listing 9.22 An instance for the `Arbitrary` type class for associative maps

```
instance (Eq k, Arbitrary k, Arbitrary v) => Arbitrary (AssocMap k v)
   where
      arbitrary = genAssocMap       ◁——⌐  Uses genAssocMap as the
      shrink = shrinkAssocMap       ◁——┘  random value generator
                                          Uses shrinkAssocMap as the
                                          shrinking function for this type
```

This instance enables us to freely generate random values for our `AssocMap` type inside of properties. Also, our type can now be used in a larger generator to produce even more complex values.

Exercise: Properties for associated lists

Since we have implemented an instance of the `Arbitrary` type class for `AssocMap`, it is now your turn to write properties for the type that can be tested. It's important to check the basic function of this type as a map, so we need to check the following:

- A value can be looked up after it has been inserted.
- Inserting under the same key multiple times overwrites the already present value.
- Deleting a key works as intended.
- `empty` is indeed empty.
- Altering the map does not invalidate the invariant.

Implement QuickCheck properties that check this type thoroughly. If you can think of more properties to test, do so!

Now, we know the basics of QuickCheck, how to write properties and generators, and how shrinking works. Next, we will turn our attention to actually using QuickCheck and incorporating it into our projects.

9.5 *Practical usage of property testing*

So far, we have learned different concepts within QuickCheck, how properties are being tested, and how random values are being generated. We want to focus our attention now on using the library to test code and what to look out for when designing tests.

Let us start with the interactive usage of the `quickCheck` function we have seen. For this, we want to go back to the testing of sorting functions, mainly our `sorts` predicate. Let's test this with QuickCheck:

```
ghci> quickCheck $ sorts sort
+++ OK, passed 100 tests.
ghci> quickCheck $ sorts id
+++ OK, passed 100 tests.
```

Wait, what? Something is wrong. id cannot possibly sort a list! We will need to investigate.

9.5.1   *Verbosity and coverage reports*

To begin our investigation, we can use several *modifiers* that change how the property test is executed. The first one is verbose, which will give us a detailed printout of the test cases:

```
ghci> quickCheck . verbose $ sorts sort
Passed:
[]

Passed:
[()]

Passed:
[()]

Passed:
[(),()]

Passed:
[(),()]

...

+++ OK, passed 100 tests.
```

This already looks wrong. The lists under test are of the unit type! Obviously, any list that only consists of this type is trivially sorted, since the type only has a single inhabitant. What we need to do is explicitly name the type that QuickCheck should use for testing.

> **NOTE**   What happened here is so-called *type defaulting*. In certain situations, when it's not clear how a type should be resolved, GHC will automatically default to a type. Our property testing a list of elements defaulted to () as the type for those elements. This is something GHC will usually warn about.

We can do this by explicitly naming the property and giving it a type signature:

```
ghci> :{
ghci| prop_sortSorts :: [Int] -> Bool
ghci| prop_sortSorts xs = sort `sorts` xs
ghci| :}
ghci> quickCheck . verbose $ prop_sortSorts
Passed:
[]
```

```
Passed:
[]

Passed:
[]

Passed:
[]

Passed:
[0,3]

Passed:
[4,-3]

...

+++ OK, passed 100 tests.
```

The values now look good! However, since QuickCheck is only slowly increasing the size of the generator, it starts the test by testing the same trivial value multiple times: the empty list! Of course, this isn't a good test. We should get some more insights into what kind of data we are testing with. To do that, we can use the `collect` function to get a statistic on some value we would like to compute on the input. In our case, we can use it to check how many of the test cases are empty:

```
ghci> :{
ghci| prop_sortSorts :: [Int] -> Property
ghci| prop_sortSorts xs = collect (null xs) $ sort `sorts` xs
ghci| :}
ghci> quickCheck prop_sortSorts
+++ OK, passed 100 tests:
95% False
 5% True
```

Interesting! A total of 5% of our test cases seem to be empty. We could get a bit of a nicer output by using the `label` function, which lets us provide a label for the different statistics:

```
ghci> :{
ghci| prop_sortSorts :: [Int] -> Property
ghci| prop_sortSorts xs = label (if null xs then "empty" else "not empty")
➥ $ sort `sorts` xs
ghci| :}
ghci> quickCheck prop_sortSorts
+++ OK, passed 100 tests:
95% not empty
 5% empty
```

Notice how in both cases, the type signature for our property has changed from `[Int] -> Bool` to `[Int] -> Property`. That's because `collect` and `label` both produce a `Property`. Now, our question is this: How do we improve this test? Testing it on trivial cases will not do. We want to test the property on lists that have at least two elements. We could change the test case generator, but that is overkill for the solution we are searching for. It is easier done using a *precondition*. Just like we added preconditions to SimpleCheck, we also have preconditions in QuickCheck. You can add them to a property by using the ==> operator:

```
ghci> :{
ghci| prop_sortSorts :: [Int] -> Property
ghci| prop_sortSorts xs = length xs >= 2 ==> sort `sorts` xs
ghci| :}
ghci> quickCheck prop_sortSorts
+++ OK, passed 100 tests; 43 discarded.
```

This makes an interesting change in the output. QuickCheck now tells us that 43 test cases were discarded! These cases did not meet the precondition and were ignored completely. We do this primarily to improve the test coverage of our property. There is no use in testing the function with trivial inputs, since the likelihood of it finding an error is low. However, excluding them completely might not be the best option. Using a precondition is good when we want to absolutely rule out test cases because they do not reflect the specification or are not relevant to the functionality under test. Testing coverage is something else entirely.

QuickCheck is helpful enough to provide functions for exactly that. One of them is cover, which reports some information on coverage:

```
ghci> :{
ghci| prop_sortSorts :: [Int] -> Property
ghci| prop_sortSorts xs = cover 25 (length xs >= 2) "non-trivial" $
➥ sort `sorts` xs
ghci| :}
ghci> quickCheck prop_sortSorts
+++ OK, passed 100 tests (93% non-trivial).
```

cover expects three arguments: first, a number between 0 and 100 that specifies the minimum amount of passing cases that are required; then, a condition for a value to be passing; and finally, a label for passing values. cover will then collect a statistic on how many of the test cases were passing and label them accordingly.

> **NOTE** cover doesn't make a property test fail! It only *warns* if the required coverage isn't met. If you want to make the test fail, in this case, you have to wrap it with the checkCoverage function, which will turn the warning into an actual failed test.

9.5.2 *Modifying a test's parameters*

Finally, we want to again look at how we can modify QuickCheck's behavior. We have already seen how verbose makes QuickCheck more verbose; however, we can have a more profound effect on the testing behavior with other modifiers:

- `verbose :: Testable prop => prop -> Property`—Makes the property test more verbose and can be used in conjunction with `quickCheck` or as the helper function `verboseCheck`
- `verboseShrinking :: Testable prop => prop -> Property`—Includes shrinking in the output
- `noShrinking :: Testable prop => prop -> Property`—Disables shrinking for the property
- `withMaxSuccess :: Testable prop => Int -> prop -> Property`—Configures at what number of successes the test is done and accepted, with the default being 100
- `within :: Testable prop => Int -> prop -> Property`—Makes a property test fail if it wasn't completed in the specified number of microseconds

`withMaxSuccess` and `within` are especially important for testing. Sometimes, 100 test cases are not enough, and other times, we want to make sure that time-critical code is executed promptly. However, this is highly dependent on the test case. Next, we want to investigate how to incorporate all of these properties and checks into our projects.

9.5.3 *Constructing test suites*

When initializing a new project with `stack new`, Stack does a bit more than just create a structure for our library and executable. It also creates a Spec.hs file inside a subfolder called *test*. This substructure of the project is reserved for code that is supposed to test our library and executable. This test suite can be executed with `stack test`, but how does Stack know if a test failed or not? By default, this is determined with the exit code of the program that is compiled by using Spec.hs as the main module. So how can we write test suites with this?

First, we need some kind of template for constructing test suites that makes the program return a failure exit code, if the test does not succeed. A very simple template is shown in the following listing.

Listing 9.23 **A template for using a test suite with Stack**

```
module Main where

import System.Exit (exitFailure, exitSuccess)    ◁──┐ Imports the necessary
                                                     actions for exit statuses

main :: IO ()
main = do
  success <- ...
    if success          │ Uses the appropriate
      then exitSuccess  │ exit status based on the
      else exitFailure  │ success of the test
```

Now, the question is how to run the actual tests. For this, QuickCheck doesn't give us a clear structure but, again, gives us some very helpful functions. The most helpful is `quickCheckAll`. It collects all properties that are defined in a module and uses `quickCheck` on all of them. How, you might ask? It does it using the power of *Template Haskell* and the naming scheme of our properties.

Template Haskell is an extension to GHC that allows us to use metaprogramming and manipulate the abstract syntax tree of our programs directly. This can be used to automatically generate functions that otherwise would need to be manually constructed. Enumerating all properties with a `prop_` suffix and calling `quickCheck` on them is one such transformation that QuickCheck uses. This way, a module can define a bunch of properties as well as provide some way of running all tests within it (using `quickCheckAll`). In our main module, we can collect these tests from the test suites and then check their result.

For this, we want to create two new modules alongside `Spec.hs`, which will be our test suites. `SuiteOne.hs` and `SuiteTwo.hs` will contain some irrelevant properties with different modifiers and behaviors. Both also export an action called `runTests`, which uses Template Haskell to collect all properties in the module. We can then reference these suites from our main module. The code for the first test suite is shown in the following listing.

Listing 9.24 An example test suite

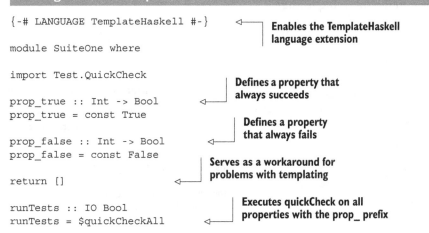

```
{-# LANGUAGE TemplateHaskell #-}      ◁──┐  Enables the TemplateHaskell
                                          │  language extension
module SuiteOne where

import Test.QuickCheck
                                      ┌── Defines a property that
                                      │   always succeeds
prop_true :: Int -> Bool        ◁────┘
prop_true = const True
                                      ┌── Defines a property
                                      │   that always fails
prop_false :: Int -> Bool       ◁────┘
prop_false = const False
                                  ┌── Serves as a workaround for
                                  │   problems with templating
return []                   ◁────┘
                                      ┌── Executes quickCheck on all
                                      │   properties with the prop_ prefix
runTests :: IO Bool
runTests = $quickCheckAll         ◁──┘
```

Note that we have to activate the `TemplateHaskell` language extension for these to work. The dollar sign before `quickCheckAll` is the special syntax used for Template Haskell. Somewhat curiously, we have a stray `return []` in our code. This is due to a bug in the templating and is the currently recommended workaround for it.

Similarly to this suite, we can implement another one, this time with more involved properties. This is shown in the following listing.

Listing 9.25 Another example test suite

```
{-# LANGUAGE TemplateHaskell #-}      ◁──┐  Enables the TemplateHaskell
                                          │  language extension
module SuiteTwo where
```

```
import Test.QuickCheck
                                          Defines a property with a
prop_addPos :: Int -> Int -> Property     modified amount of test cases
prop_addPos x y =
  withMaxSuccess 500 $
    x > 0 && y > 0 ==> x + y > 0          Defines a property that does
                                          not use shrinking and has a
prop_multZero :: Int -> Property          coverage requirement
prop_multZero x =
  noShrinking $
    cover 95 (x /= 0) "non-zero" $ x * 0 == 0
                                          Serves as a workaround for
return []                                 problems with templating

runTests :: IO Bool                       Executes quickCheck on all
runTests = $quickCheckAll                 properties with the prop_ prefix
```

Of course, the number of properties could be in the hundreds, and we would never need to write their checks down ourselves. If we want to extend the test suites, we simply write down another property, which is automatically checked the next time we run stack test. Now, we can incorporate these suites into our main module. This is shown in the following listing.

Listing 9.26   An example main module for using the example test suites with Stack

```
module Main where

import qualified SuiteOne as S1
import qualified SuiteTwo as S2          Imports the example test suites
import System.Exit (exitFailure, exitSuccess)
                                          Imports the necessary
main :: IO ()                             exit status actions
main = do
  s1success <- S1.runTests
  s2success <- S2.runTests                Runs the example test suites
  if s1success && s2success
    then exitSuccess                      Returns the appropriate exit code
    else exitFailure                      based on the success of the tests
```

runTests returns a Boolean that tells us whether the tests failed. More importantly, they also produce some output when we run the test. So the order in which we let these tests run matters. The test we want to appear first should also go first in our main IO action.

Exercise: Short-circuiting tests

In our implementation, we do not use any kind of short circuiting in our logic to prematurely end the test if a suite fails before another. We test *all* properties before deciding whether the test was successful or not. This might not be the behavior we want for development. Add an argument to the test that enables or disables a fastfail if a test suite fails.

You can pass arguments to the test by using `--test-arguments`:

```
shell $ stack test --test-arguments "--my-cool-flag"
```

It's time to finally execute our test. In my case, the Stack project is called `properties`, which is why the suite is called `properties-test`:

```
shell $ stack test
properties> test (suite: properties-test)

=== prop_true from test/SuiteOne.hs:7 ===
+++ OK, passed 100 tests.

=== prop_false from test/SuiteOne.hs:10 ===
*** Failed! Falsified (after 1 test):
0

=== prop_addPos from test/SuiteTwo.hs:7 ===
+++ OK, passed 500 tests; 1758 discarded.

=== prop_multZero from test/SuiteTwo.hs:12 ===
+++ OK, passed 100 tests (97% non-zero).


properties> Test suite properties-test failed
Test suite failure for package properties-0.1.0.0
    properties-test:  exited with: ExitFailure 1
Logs printed to console
```

This is a rather crude way of performing our tests. We could also create more suites from our package.yaml file or use a library like *Tasty*, which is used to combine Quick-Check, *SmallCheck* (yet another testing library), and manual unit tests into test suites that can be listed independently of each other. For smaller projects, however, there is no point in going that far, and our method is fine.

Exercise: Project test suites

Now that we know how to incorporate test suites into our projects, it is your turn to do so for our projects! Think of fitting properties for the various cases we have seen so far and verify that everything works as intended! There is no real right or wrong here; just get creative, create `Arbitrary` instances for our types, and see what properties you can come up with.

It is also important to mention that other testing frameworks for Haskell exist, like *Hedgehog*, which is similar to QuickCheck, and *HUnit*, which focuses more on example-based unit tests. Each framework comes with unique abilities, and depending on your project size and functionality, you might prefer one over the other.

9.5.4　*The effectiveness of testing*

Although we have already covered the benefits of Haskell's pure functions when it comes to testability, we want to conclude this chapter with a bit more discussion on this subject. Why are we writing tests for our software? What are we trying to achieve? The most obvious property of our programs we want to ensure is *correctness*. We want programs to produce results according to some specifications. For example, a prime number generator should trivially only produce prime numbers. However, we also want to make sure these properties do not change over time. After code refactoring, our software should still pass all the test suites we wrote.

This ensures confidence in our programs. We can be confident that they produce the correct results and that we can still work on the code without adding regressions. If there is any major strong suit to Haskell, it is exactly this: confidence. Static types, pure functions, and clear separation of side effects from side-effect-free programming are what make Haskell not just very test friendly but also what make these tests *effective*. Since pure functions have no side effects, they are simply *transformations* on data. Property tests on these transformations have to make sure the properties about them hold, meaning that if the data satisfies some properties going in, it has to satisfy some properties going out. In this chapter, we have seen how we implement these tests:

- We use a precondition or a specially crafted generator to ensure properties on our input data.
- The properties we want to ensure are checked on the result of the transformation.
  - Functions are tested for their correct results.
  - Data types are tested for their correct construction and invariants during transformations.
- We bundle properties in test suites to gain confidence in the interplay of our functions and data types on an intramodule or system-wide basis.

While other programming languages also enable developers to write tests, such high confidence can rarely be gained from so little testing, as we have seen in this chapter. Property tests in pure functional code are akin to *formal verification*, in the sense that they use formalized properties instead of observing the behavior of our programs. This leaves us with software that is much easier to refactor, extend, and scale. In practices like *continuous integration* and *continuous delivery*, these tests are the backbone for a successful operation and can more often than not save you and your company from doom and gloom scenarios.

Summary

- Random values in pure functions require the random value generator to be an argument and part of the returned value.
- A global random value generator can be accessed from `IO` actions using `AtomicGenM` and `globalStdGen`.

- The `Random` and `Uniform` type classes give us a variety of types for which random generation is possible.
- Property testing uses formalized characteristics and random inputs to find errors in implementations.
- Random generators should be composable to be easier to write.
- QuickCheck automates the choice of random value generators by using the type system and type classes.
- The `Arbitrary` type class does not only provide a random value generator for a type but also a function to shrink a value to a smaller or simpler one.
- QuickChecks generators use an internal size to create random values of varying complexities.
- `quickCheckAll` can be used to automatically collect properties in a module and execute checks on them.
- Property testing in purely functional code ensures formalized properties on data types, functions and modules.

Digital music box 10

This chapter covers

- Correctly dealing with numeric values and their type classes
- Working with infinite lists
- Modeling a domain-specific problem using Haskell's data types
- Building abstractions and high-level structures around low-level implementations

So far, we have been dealing with very earnest topics. Ancient encryption schemes, shortest paths, and CSV file mangling are all serious business. In this chapter, we want to be a bit more playful and let our creative spirit run free by making music! Don't worry if you have no instrument ready at hand or lack any general idea of how to compose. We will use the power of Haskell not just to serve as our own musical synthesizer but also to function as a composition tool allowing us to easily create the next musical masterpiece remembered by audiences for centuries.

Modeling real-world data inside programs is a normal activity for any programmer. This chapter will specifically teach you how to think about abstracting details and modeling a part of a system in reality (the system of western music theory) as types and values. This kind of modeling comes up every time you want to write software that incorporates some kind of business logic or concepts not directly related to software specifications or architecture. Haskell allows for highly abstract modeling, which fully omits any details that are not relevant to the use case. This is what we are trying to achieve in this chapter.

To achieve our musical dreams, we will model sound within our program, writing code that can produce it. In doing so, we will also come across some specificities regarding Haskell's numeric values and domain-specific problems that we have to take care of. With functions and types for creating sound, we will then build abstractions around them to facilitate compositions within our program without having to worry about low-level implementations. This will make us think about what the correct abstractions are and how to define transformations that take care of the heavy lifting.

10.1 Modeling sound with numbers

The most important question we have to answer is this: How does our program create sounds? What even is a sound? In the context of the real world, *sounds* are vibrations in the air that tickle our eardrums, producing a stimulus in our brain, which results in the phenomenon of *hearing*. For a computer, this is slightly more straightforward. In the case of mono audio, sound is a signal. When two channels (left and right) are required, sound consists of two signals. What is a signal? In the analog world, a signal is a value that changes over time with an arbitrarily small resolution. We can think of it as a continuous mathematic function with time as its parameter. In the digital world, we use sampling to approximate an analog signal. A sample is just a single numeric value. A sequence of these samples is a sampled signal. This is shown in figure 10.1.

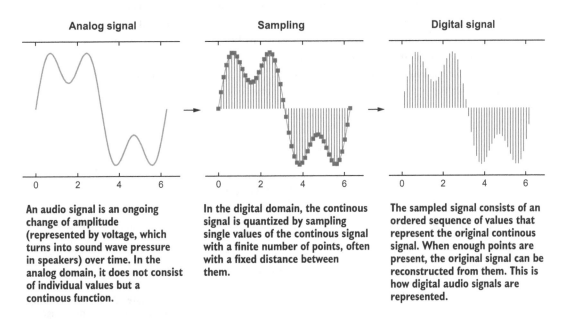

Analog signal	Sampling	Digital signal
An audio signal is an ongoing change of amplitude (represented by voltage, which turns into sound wave pressure in speakers) over time. In the analog domain, it does not consist of individual values but a continous function.	In the digital domain, the continous signal is quantized by sampling single values of the continous signal with a finite number of points, often with a fixed distance between them.	The sampled signal consists of an ordered sequence of values that represent the original continous signal. When enough points are present, the original signal can be reconstructed from them. This is how digital audio signals are represented.

Figure 10.1 Sampling of an analog signal

As we can see from this figure, we are limited in our accuracy to recreating an analog signal by the *sample rate* (how many samples per second of the signal are sampled) and *resolution* (how many bits are used to represent a single sample value). What are sensible values for these two properties? Thanks to the Nyquist–Shannon sampling theorem, we know that when we want to sample a signal with a known highest frequency, we have to use a sample rate that is at minimum double that highest frequency. For audio signals, frequencies higher than 22 kHz are not relevant, since we humans cannot hear them (and most audio gear is not able to reproduce these frequencies anyway). This is where the often-used sample rate of 44.1 kHz comes from, since it, theoretically, allows us to perfectly sample sound signals. What about resolution? It mainly affects the *signal-to-noise ratio* of our signal, meaning how much of the desired signal is coming through the background noise, which might be produced by quantization errors. For music, anything from 8 to 32 bits is used in the representation. The WAV file format, which we will be using in this chapter, often uses 16 bits in its representation.

10.1.1 *The zoo of numeric type classes*

Let us first focus on how to represent the sampled signal we have been discussing so far. A single sample is, as previously mentioned, just a numeric value. We can use a `Double` to represent it. A signal, then, is nothing but a list of these samples, a `[Double]`. This also brings us to the decision of which sample rate we want to support. While a higher sample rate of 92 kHz can help with aliasing of higher frequencies, we opt for the standard CD-quality audio, using 44.1 kHz as our sample rate.

We can also define some other types, so we can talk more easily about our subject matter. Since we have to specify frequencies and durations at some point, we can define frequencies as `Hz` as well as `Seconds` to be `Double`. Based on this, we can create our first helper functions that will tell us how many samples we need for a period of a certain frequency for a certain duration. This will become important later. The code for these types and functions is shown in the following listing.

Listing 10.1   Types and helper functions for dealing with signals

```
type Sample = Double          ◁─┐
                                 │ Defines type aliases for
type Signal = [Sample]        ◁─┤ samples, signals, Hertz,
                                 │ and seconds
type Hz = Double              ◁─┤
                                 │
type Seconds = Double         ◁─┘

sampleRate :: Double          ◁─┐ Defines a constant for the
sampleRate = 44100              │ sample rate used in the project

samplesPerPeriod :: Hz -> Int                      ┐ Computes the number of samples
samplesPerPeriod hz = round $ sampleRate / hz   ◁─┤ needed to represent a single
                                                   ┘ period of a given frequency
```

```
samplesPerSecond :: Seconds -> Int
samplesPerSecond duration = round $
➥ duration * sampleRate
```

**Computes the number of samples needed to
represent a specified amount of seconds**

Here, we see the usage of the round function. It takes a value with an instance of the
RealFrac type class and returns a value with an instance of the Integral type class.
This means we can take a Float or a Double and transform it into an Int or Integer.
We use this because the number of samples must be an integer. There can't exist half
of a sample. Both functions can be understood once we understand the simple fact
that the sample rate is the number of samples in a second. The period of a frequency
with n Hertz is exactly 1 / n. Multiplying by the sample rate gives us the number of
samples needed to fit in a single period of that frequency.

Before we continue, we want to quickly talk about the classes RealFrac and
Integral. What are they, and how are they used? As it turns out, there exists a large
zoo of type classes for numeric types, which the two aforementioned classes are part
of. We have covered Num, which defines basic operations for arithmetic; however, it
does not provide an operation for division, which is strange because we have seen two
functions to perform it:

```
ghci> :t div
div :: Integral a => a -> a -> a
ghci> :t (/)
(/) :: Fractional a => a -> a -> a
```

These functions are part of the Integral and Fractional type classes, respectively.
The Integral class features functions for computing divisions and remainders on
whole numbers, while the Fractional type class defines functions for division and
reciprocals for floating-point numbers:

```
ghci> :i Integral
type Integral :: * -> Constraint
class (Real a, Enum a) => Integral a where
  quot :: a -> a -> a
  rem :: a -> a -> a
  div :: a -> a -> a
  mod :: a -> a -> a
  quotRem :: a -> a -> (a, a)
  divMod :: a -> a -> (a, a)
  toInteger :: a -> Integer
  {-# MINIMAL quotRem, toInteger #-}
instance Integral Word
instance Integral Integer
instance Integral Int
ghci> :i Fractional
type Fractional :: * -> Constraint
class Num a => Fractional a where
  (/) :: a -> a -> a
  recip :: a -> a
  fromRational :: Rational -> a
```

```
  {-# MINIMAL fromRational, (recip | (/)) #-}
instance Fractional Float
instance Fractional Double
```

An important function in the `Integral` class is `toInteger`, which lets us freely convert types to `Integer` values. Somewhat curiously, we see more unfamiliar type classes in the constraint for `Integral`—the `Real` and `Enum` classes:

```
ghci> :i Real
type Real :: * -> Constraint
class (Num a, Ord a) => Real a where
  toRational :: a -> Rational
  {-# MINIMAL toRational #-}
ghci> :i Enum
type Enum :: * -> Constraint
class Enum a where
  succ :: a -> a
  pred :: a -> a
  toEnum :: Int -> a
  fromEnum :: a -> Int
  enumFrom :: a -> [a]
  enumFromThen :: a -> a -> [a]
  enumFromTo :: a -> a -> [a]
  enumFromThenTo :: a -> a -> a -> [a]
  {-# MINIMAL toEnum, fromEnum #-}
```

Types with an instance of the `Real` class can be converted to a `Rational`, which is a type that defines a ratio of integers and which we will look at later in the chapter.

> **NOTE** Mathematically speaking, the `Real` type class is a misnomer, since theoretically, irrational numbers, such as `pi` from the `Prelude`, are also part of the class and can be converted to a rational number using `toRational`. This is a point where theory and practice diverge.

The `Enum` class defines enumerations on types; it is used in the list syntax when we define a range. We will take a closer look at this class in chapter 15:

```
ghci> toRational (5 :: Double)
5 % 1
ghci> toRational (5.5 :: Double)
11 % 2
ghci> [1..10] :: [Int]
[1,2,3,4,5,6,7,8,9,10]
ghci> enumFromTo 1 10 :: [Int]
[1,2,3,4,5,6,7,8,9,10]
```

Now, we can take a look at `RealFrac`, which is a class that bundles functions to turn fractions into integer values:

```
ghci> :i RealFrac
type RealFrac :: * -> Constraint
class (Real a, Fractional a) => RealFrac a where
```

```
properFraction :: Integral b => a -> (b, a)
truncate :: Integral b => a -> b
round :: Integral b => a -> b
ceiling :: Integral b => a -> b
floor :: Integral b => a -> b
{-# MINIMAL properFraction #-}
```

The `round`, `ceiling`, and `floor` functions are our way to convert floating-point numbers to integers. `round` returns the nearest integer to its argument, while `ceiling` returns the least integer not less than its argument, and `floor` returns the greatest integer not greater than its argument. Another subclass of `Fractional` is `Floating`, which features several trigonometric functions, such as `sin`, `log`, and `sqrt`, to compute the sine, logarithm, and square root of numbers.

While this zoo of type classes seems complicated, we can take solace in the fact that numeric types we usually use, like `Int`, `Integer`, `Float`, and `Double`, feature instances of these type classes, when it makes sense. This allows us to convert `Int` to `Float` values, using `fromIntegral` and `Double`, to `Integer` values, using `round`:

```
ghci> fromIntegral (1 :: Int) :: Float
1.0
ghci> round (3.1415 :: Double) :: Integer
3
```

However, `Floating` has no instances for integer values. So when we want to compute the sine of an integer, we are forced to perform an explicit conversion, since implicit type coercion or casting does not exist in Haskell:

```
ghci> sin (fromIntegral (1 :: Int)) :: Double
0.8414709848078965
```

A class we will not cover is `RealFloat`, which can be used to access low-level components of floating-point numbers, since it is not relevant to our projects.

10.1.2 Creating periodic functions

Now that we have the intricacies of numeric type classes covered, we can worry about creating sound. In music, we are interested in the *timbre*, which refers to the qualitative characteristics of sounds. But before we go down a rabbit hole of overtones, we can simply take a shortcut and look how other synthesizers do it. Different sound characteristics can be achieved by using different kinds of waveforms for signals. The four most standard waveforms are shown in figure 10.2.

These waveforms show a single period in their signal. The repetition of these periods is determined by the length of the signal and the frequency we try to generate. If the time is fixed, a change in frequency will stretch or squish the signal. The `samplesPerPeriod` and `samplesPerSecond` can be used to compute how many samples we require for a period of a given frequency. Repeating these samples until the whole duration is filled will give us a tone at a certain frequency over a set amount of time.

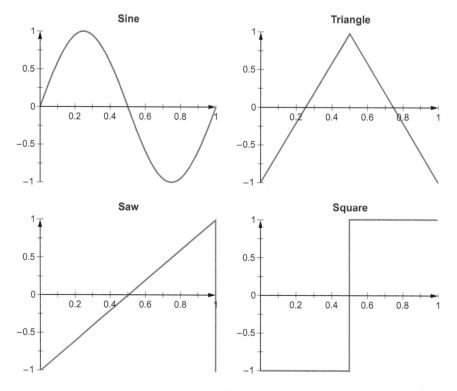

Figure 10.2   Four standard waveforms

Varying these frequencies will result in music! For our purposes, sample values range from -1 to 1. We will worry about modulating this later, when we want to control the volume of our signal. For now, we should implement the waveforms.

A wave, in our case, is just a function that receives a numerical argument between 0 and 1 and returns the sample value for the position in the waveform at that point. We can then use this parameter to "scan" through the waveform. The faster we scan (meaning the larger the distance between single time steps becomes), the shorter the period and the higher the frequency will be. Since the waveforms from figure 10.2 are just mathematical functions, we can model them in code. The sine wave can be generated with the sin function present in Prelude. The square wave is case distinction on the input parameter, resulting in -1 when the input is less than or equal to 0.5 and 1 otherwise. The sawtooth and triangle waves require a bit more thought, since we have to create slopes. The sawtooth is a slope of 2 * t for an input t offset by -1. For the triangle wave, we have to create two slopes. The first half is a sawtooth with its length exactly halved, so it can be computed as the function 4 * t - 1. In the second half, the sign of the computed value switches, since the slope needs to be mirrored. To accommodate this, we set the offset to + 3 to create values between 1 and -1. This is shown in the following listing.

Listing 10.2 Types and helper functions for dealing with signals

```
type Wave = Double -> Sample            ◁──┐  Defines a type for
                                           │  waveforms as a function
sin :: Wave
sin t = Prelude.sin $ 2 * pi * t      ◁──────  Defines a sine waveform, using
                                               the pi constant from the Prelude
sqw :: Wave
sqw t
  | t <= 0.5 = -1          │ Defines a square waveform
  | otherwise = 1          │ with a 50% duty cycle

saw :: Wave
saw t
  | t < 0 = -1            │
  | t > 1 = 1            │ Defines a sawtooth
  | otherwise = (2 * t) - 1   │ waveform

tri :: Wave
tri t
  | t < 0 = -1            │
  | t > 1 = -1           │ Defines a triangle
  | t < 0.5 = 4 * t - 1     │ waveform
  | otherwise = -4 * t + 3
```

All of these functions are only valid with inputs between 0 and 1. For values outside of this range, the functions become constant. For our purpose, it isn't important what the functions do outside of their valid input range.

We can now use the functions for computing the number of samples we need to construct a function for creating silence (which is just a signal with a constant 0 value) and a tone that will produce a certain frequency for a certain duration using one of our waveforms. For this, we compute how many samples we need to generate and enumerate them from 0 to the number of samples. Then, we divide those values modulo the number of samples needed for the period to be at the correct frequency. This creates a list of input parameters that we can then plug into whatever Wave function we want. The resulting signal is our tone. The code for this is shown in the following listing.

Listing 10.3 Functions to produce signals from waveforms

Returns a signal with the constant value 0 to match some length

Maps the wave function over the repeating values to create the desired signal

```
silence :: Seconds -> Signal
silence t = replicate (samplesPerSecond t) 0   ◁──┘

tone :: Wave -> Hz -> Seconds -> Signal
tone wave freq t = map wave periodValues        ◁─
  where
    numSamples = samplesPerPeriod freq          ◁─
    periodValues =                              ◁─
      map
        (\x -> fromIntegral (x `mod` numSamples) / fromIntegral numSamples)
        [0 .. samplesPerSecond t]
```

Computes the necessary number of samples for a single period of the wave

Creates a list containing repeating input parameters for the wave function to create a tone for the specified duration at the specified frequency

Again, we have to use `fromIntegral` to divide floating point numbers instead of integers. In this function, we manually ensure that the `wave` function is fed with repeating values for the right duration. This seems somewhat complicated, since we could just compute the wave once and then repeat it. Look out for a later exercise, where you will get the chance to implement this!

Exercise: Adjustable duty cycle oscillator

For our waveforms, we have implemented a square wave. The square wave is special, in that it is a so-called pulse wave with a 50% duty cycle, meaning the amount of time the signal is "low" is equal to the amount of time the signal is "high." Pulse waves can be defined for any duty cycle, and when they are used for music, the sound characteristics do change with the duty cycle! Implement a generic pulse waveform with an adjustable duty cycle.

Finally, we can use these functions to create real sounds! For this, we will utilize a library called *HCodecs*, which can read and write WAV files, an uncompressed audio format most audio players can play. For this library to become available to us, we add `HCodecs` and `array` to the dependencies section of our package.yml file. This library features a function called `exportFile`, which lets us write audio data to a WAV file. The dependencies section of package.yml should look like this:

```
dependencies:
- base >= 4.7 && < 5
- HCodecs >= 0.5.2
- array >= 0.5.4
```

To do this, we have to construct an `Audio` value, which is a record consisting of information on the sample rate, sample data, and channel number. To construct this value, we first have to convert our `Signal` into something the library calls `SampleData`, which internally uses *arrays* to store audio data. Arrays are present in Haskell but will not be covered in this book, which is why we will not go into depth on them. It is important for us to know that we need to add `array` to our dependencies to use them. Then, we can use the `listArray` function to construct an array from a list, which is a function receiving a tuple as an argument specifying the bounds for the array and the data from the list we are trying to convert. Here, need to make sure the tuple specifies the range from `0` to the length of the list minus 1. To convert our `Sample` type into a sample that HCodecs can understand, we can use the `fromSample` function. The full code for all of this is shown in the following listing.

Listing 10.4   Functions to write audio data to WAV files

```
import Data.Array.Unboxed (listArray)    ⟵  Imports the listArray function
                                             for unboxed arrays
import Data.Audio                         ⟵  Imports functions and types
                                             provided by the HCodecs library
```

```
import Data.Int (Int16)                    ◄──┐  Imports the Int16 type

signalToSampleData :: Signal -> SampleData Int16
signalToSampleData signal =
  listArray (0, n) $ map fromSample signal   ◄──┐  Converts a Signal to an
  where                                            array of 16-bit samples
    n = length signal - 1
```

When converting our `Signal` to `SampleData`, we need to make sure that our values are in the range between -1 and 1, which we can ensure with a function limiting our values. However, we never want to hit these values, so we should dampen the limited signal by a small factor. By using `min` and `max`, we can clamp down on the value to a threshold value. A function that achieves this is shown in the following listing.

Listing 10.5   The function to clamp the values of a signal

```
limit :: Signal -> Signal
limit = map (min threshold . max (-threshold) . (* threshold))
  where
    threshold = 0.9
```

Here, we see the composition of three operations inside the `map` function. The values being mapped are first multiplied by the threshold value before the clamping with `max` and `min` is performed.

We can now put these functions together to create an `IO` action that writes our `Signal` to a WAV file, using a type and function from the HCodecs library. The code for this is shown in the following listing.

Listing 10.6   Functions to write audio data to WAV files

```
import Util.Types
import qualified Codec.Wav         Imports functions provided
import Data.Audio                  by the HCodecs library

writeWav :: FilePath -> Signal -> IO ()
writeWav filePath signal = do
  putStrLn $
    "Writing " ++ show (length signal) ++ " samples to " ++ filePath
  let sampleData = signalToSampleData $ limit signal       ◄──
      audio =                                              ◄──
        Audio
          { Data.Audio.sampleRate = round Util.Types.sampleRate,
            channelNumber = 1,
            sampleData = sampleData
          }
  Codec.Wav.exportFile filePath audio   ◄──┤
```

Clamps the absolute value of the samples down to a threshold and converts the signal to sample data that HCodecs understands

Exports the audio data to a WAV file with a specified file path

Creates audio data that can be exported as a WAV file

We can use these functions to finally create a WAV file:

```
ghci> writeWav "4waves.wav" $ concatMap (\w -> tone w 220 5)
⇒ [Sound.Synth.sin, tri, saw, sqw]
```

This will create a file called 4waves.wav with 20 seconds of audio split up into the 4 different waveforms being played at 220 Hz for 5 seconds each. Since our signal is just a simple list, we can use functions like `(++)`, `concat`, or `concatMap` to append signals.

We can inspect our sound files with a free audio editor, like *Audacity*, to inspect the signal we have created. This is shown in figure 10.3.

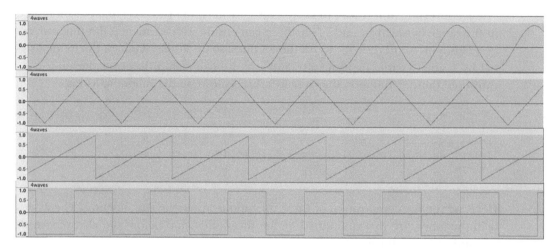

Figure 10.3   Waveforms of the exported audio file

Using an audio player (or an editor), we can also listen to the file. However, be careful: the audio is very loud and doesn't sound too pleasant at the moment.

10.2   Using infinite lists

Next, we want to give our tones a bit of contour. As you might have heard when playing around with our newly created tone generator, the sound sometimes "clicks" when a tone stops. That's because our period function can get cut off abruptly when the desired duration is reached. This is shown in figure 10.4. We need some way to contour the tone, especially the end of the signal, to get rid of this click.

Figure 10.4   Example of a sudden change in the waveform, causing a "click" in the audio

10.2.1 *Attack, decay, sustain, and release*

In most synthesizers, this is achieved with an envelope that shapes the amplitude of the signal, often tapering off the beginning and end. For our synthesizer, we want to implement the very common attack, decay, sustain and release (ADSR) envelope. This envelope lets the signal rise for a certain duration (attack), then take a certain amount of time to taper off (decay) to a fixed value (sustain), and then slowly fade out (release). Such an envelope is shown in figure 10.5, showing how an envelope can influence a signal.

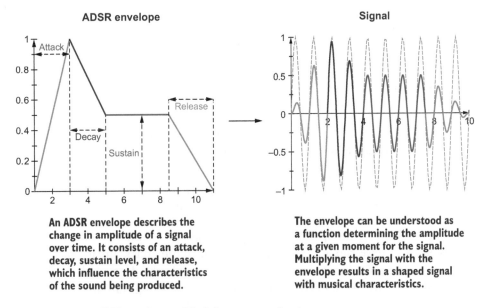

An ADSR envelope describes the change in amplitude of a signal over time. It consists of an attack, decay, sustain level, and release, which influence the characteristics of the sound being produced.

The envelope can be understood as a function determining the amplitude at a given moment for the signal. Multiplying the signal with the envelope results in a shaped signal with musical characteristics.

Figure 10.5   An ADSR envelope and its influence on a signal

This raises a new question: How can we represent an ADSR envelope? Since an envelope needs to influence the amplitude of our signal, we can understand it as a list of factors we want to multiply the signal by, as is shown in figure 10.5. So again, the solution is a simple [Double].

To represent the parameters of the envelope, we can use a record. Attack, decay, and release are all durations. Their curves are all linear, even though in other synthesizers, they don't have to be. However, the sustain is a level being held. The duration for which this level is being held is determined by the duration of the signal being modulated and the lengths of the other parameters. The code for the parameters of such an envelope is shown in the following listing.

Listing 10.7   A type to represent the parameters of an ADRS envelope

```
data ADSR = ADSR          ⟵⎯⎤   Defines a new data type for an ADSR envelope
  { attack :: Seconds,
    decay :: Seconds,            Defines types for the
    sustain :: Double,           parameters for an
    release :: Seconds           ADSR envelope
  }
  deriving (Show)         ⟵⎯⎯⎯   Derives an instance for the Show type class
```

Now, we can think about how to apply these parameters to a signal. Since we have to generate a list of factors between 0 and 1 for our samples, we can use our well-known list operations.

The linear functions we want to generate can be computed with list expressions, dividing each value by the maximum:

```
ghci> map (/ 10) [1..10] :: [Double]
[0.1,0.2,0.3,0.4,0.5,0.6,0.7,0.8,0.9,1.0]
```

This already serves as our attack curve. For the decay, we want to achieve something similar but create a linear falloff from 1 to a specified value.

```
ghci> s = 0.5 :: Double
ghci> map (\x -> (x / 10) * (1 - s) + s) [1..10] :: [Double]
[0.55,0.6,0.65,0.7,0.75,0.8,0.85,0.9,0.95,1.0]
```

When we reverse this list, we have our decay already implemented! However, we need to make sure we can add it to the attack. Since the attack already includes the maximum value 1, we do not want to have it repeated in the decay. We can fix this by starting the base list at 0 and counting up to the desired length minus 1:

```
ghci> map (\x -> (x / 10) * (1 - s) + s) [0..9] :: [Double]
[0.5,0.55,0.6,0.65,0.7,0.75,0.8,0.85,0.9,0.95]
```

Here, we have constructed a decay that tapers off to a sustained value of 0.5. Speaking of which, since the sustain is just a fixed value, we can use `replicate` to produce a list of it. However, then, we need to compute how many values we need, which should be determined by the amount of release samples that still need to be added. We could reuse the logic we used to build the attack curve to build a release curve and then modify the sustain that way. But how can we combine these curves?

10.2.2 *Building and working with infinite lists*

Thinking back to some functions we have used on lists, we can think of `zipWith`, which combines two lists with a given function, stopping at the *shorter* list. Additionally, `zipWith3` is an option that works on three instead of two lists. We can treat the attack, decay, and sustain as one list and the release curve as another list. These have to be combined with the signal. Now, we just need to build the release curve. While we could do a lot of calculations on the length of the signal and how many values we need for each part, we can simplify the process by using *infinite lists*.

Haskell's laziness has the interesting feature of allowing use to create definitions that are infinite but not infinitely evaluated. Definitions of lists can be infinitely recursive without causing problems because functions do not necessarily need to evaluate all of the (infinitely many) values:

```
ghci> ones = 1 : ones :: [Int]
ghci> take 10 ones
[1,1,1,1,1,1,1,1,1,1]
```

As long as we use functions that do not evaluate the whole list, like `take`, `takeWhile`, `(!!)`, `head`, and so on, we can happily work with these lists, even mapping, filtering, or zipping them. This also extends to other data types that we can generate infinitely, like graphs.

For lists, we can use the familiar range expressions to create infinite lists quite easily by simply omitting a maximum value. This way, it is almost trivial to generate all natural or odd numbers with very concise expressions:

```
ghci> take 10 [1..] :: [Int]
[1,2,3,4,5,6,7,8,9,10]
ghci> take 10 [1,3..] :: [Int]
[1,3,5,7,9,11,13,15,17,19]
```

> **WARNING** Infinite data structures are cool but *dangerous*. Great care should be taken to make sure that no function is called that tries to evaluate them fully. The rules we make up for ourselves for working with data sadly break down once we cannot be sure that our data is finite. Calling `length` on an infinite list will run forever and, thus, cause our program to hang indefinitely!

For our usage, we want to repeat some fixed values (1 for the beginning of the release curve and the sustain level), which can be achieved using the aptly named `repeat` function, which returns an infinite list with a single value:

```
ghci> take 10 $ repeat 1
[1,1,1,1,1,1,1,1,1,1]
```

We can use the fact that `zipWith` stops at the *shorter list* to combine infinite lists and finite lists:

```
ghci> zipWith (+) [1,2,3] (repeat 1)
[2,3,4]
```

Returning to the use case of our envelope, we can use one list that combines the attack and decay curves and then infinitely repeat the sustain level. Second, we can build the release curve the same as the attack curve and repeat 1, taking just as many elements from that curve as we need for the signal and reversing it. Multiplying these curves with the original signal will yield our desired result.

Exercise: Cycling through a list

Just like `repeat` creates an infinite list with a single value, the `cycle` function takes a list as an argument and cycles through the values of that list infinitely. In our `tone` function, we manually calculated the cycling waveform, using `mod`. Now, use `cycle` and `take` to re-implement the `tone` function, by computing the waveform once and then cycling through it.

The implementation for this envelope is shown in the following listing. The function computes and applies the curve to the signal that is given as the argument. The usage of `zipWith3` ensures the whole signal will be affected, since the sustain is infinitely long and the release is just as long as the signal is. The correctness for this function is, thus, given by construction.

Listing 10.8   A function to apply an ADSR envelope to a signal

```haskell
import Util.Types

adsr :: ADSR -> Signal -> Signal
adsr (ADSR a d s r) signal =
  zipWith3
    (\adsCurve rCurve sample ->
  adsCurve * rCurve * sample)
    (att ++ dec ++ sus)
    rel
    signal
  where
    attackSamples = fromIntegral $ samplesPerSecond a
    decaySamples = fromIntegral $ samplesPerSecond d
    releaseSamples = fromIntegral $ samplesPerSecond r

    att = map (/ attackSamples) [0.0 .. attackSamples]
    dec =
      reverse $
        map
          (\x -> ((x / decaySamples) * (1 - s)) + s)
          [0.0 .. decaySamples - 1]
    sus = repeat s
    rel =
      reverse $
        take
          (length signal)
          (map (/ releaseSamples)
  [0.0 .. releaseSamples] ++ repeat 1.0)
```

- Multiplies the combined attack, decay, and release curves by the sustain level and the signal
- Concatenates the attack and decay curves with the sustain level
- Computes the number of samples necessary for each curve
- Computes the attack curve as a linear ramp
- Computes the decay curve as a linear ramp from the sustain level to 1
- Reverses the decay curve ramp
- Generates an infinite list consisting of the sustain level
- Reverses the release curve
- Takes as many values from the release curve as there are samples in the signal
- Computes the release curve as a linear ramp from 0 to 1 and an infinite amount of 1

Now, we can apply this envelope to our tone and hear the contour for the first time:

```
ghci> params = ADSR 0.1 0.2 0.5 0.1
ghci> writeWav "adsrSignal.wav" $ adsr params (tone tri 550 1)
```

When we open the resulting file in an audio editor, we can see the contour. The linear attack curve takes 100 ms to reach its full volume. The signal is then linearly tapered off over 200 ms to the sustain level, which is half volume (0.5). The release curve then decreases the volume to 0 over 100 ms. This is shown in figure 10.6.

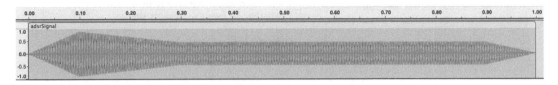

Figure 10.6   A signal with an ADSR envelope applied

With this envelope, we can shape tones more drastically. We can create "plucky" sounds by using a short attack, decay, and release and also keeping the sustain level very low. We can also create "swelling" sounds by keeping the attack and decay longer. With tone generation and contouring taken care of, we can now build our noisemakers, called oscillators, in the synthesizer world.

10.3   *Controlling synthesis*

Synthesizers have to do one job: take control signals (coming from a keyboard, an electronic signal, or a digital serial port) and produce appropriate sounds. We are also interested in taking control of our noise. We specifically want to take control over the pitch, duration, and moment in time of our generated tones to create music.

10.3.1   *Partial field selectors*

To do this, we encode events for our tone generators. An event is either a tone being played at a specific moment in time for a certain duration, at a specified frequency, or it is silence that also has a defined start and duration. We encode these events as a type with the record syntax. We can then define some helper functions that differentiate tones from silence and also compute the end of an event. The code for this is shown in the following listing.

> **Listing 10.9   A function to apply an ADSR envelope to a signal**

```
module Composition.Performance where

import Util.Types

data Event
  = Tone {freq :: Hz, start :: Seconds,
```

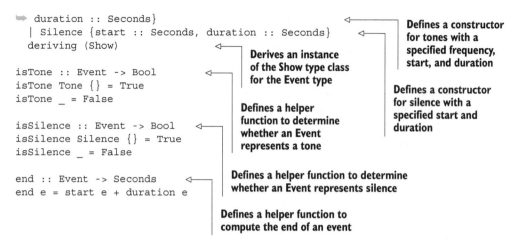

```
 ⇨  duration :: Seconds}
   | Silence {start :: Seconds, duration :: Seconds}
    deriving (Show)

isTone :: Event -> Bool
isTone Tone {} = True
isTone _ = False

isSilence :: Event -> Bool
isSilence Silence {} = True
isSilence _ = False

end :: Event -> Seconds
end e = start e + duration e
```

Defines a constructor for tones with a specified frequency, start, and duration

Derives an instance of the Show type class for the Event type

Defines a constructor for silence with a specified start and duration

Defines a helper function to determine whether an Event represents a tone

Defines a helper function to determine whether an Event represents silence

Defines a helper function to compute the end of an event

Something of note in this type is the usage of fields. As we saw in chapter 7, the record syntax will automatically create functions from the specified fields of a record that retrieve the value of that field for us. This is also the case when we have multiple constructors in our type that use the record syntax:

```
ghci> :t start
start :: Event -> Seconds
ghci> :t duration
duration :: Event -> Seconds
ghci> :t freq
freq :: Event -> Hz
```

If a field is shared by multiple constructors, the generated functions, called *field selectors*, are smart enough to still match the correct field. This is why the usage of start and duration is fine for the definition of the end function:

```
ghci> start $ Tone 0 1 2
1.0
ghci> start $ Silence 1 2
1.0
```

However, freq is special, since it doesn't occur in all constructors. This makes it a *partial field selector*:

```
ghci> freq $ Tone 440 1 2
440.0
ghci> freq $ Silence 1 2
*** Exception: No match in record selector freq
```

In essence, partial field selectors are partial functions, meaning that they are undefined for some values. This makes them dangerous to use, and great care should be taken to avoid using them.

NOTE Using the `-Wpartial-field` compile flag, GHC can automatically warn you when partial field selectors occur. It's always good to have warnings like these active in the compilation process. Sometimes, you might not want to add a partial field to your code but accidentally do so by refactoring the fields of another record, which the warning can then catch for you!

We do not want to expose partial functions. So how do we reconcile this problem? A way of dealing with this is using the `NoFieldSelectors` language extension, which disables automatically creating functions for the fields of records defined in a module. This allows us to define our functions for accessing fields:

```
{-# LANGUAGE NoFieldSelectors #-}                    ◁─┤ Enables the NoFieldSelectors
                                                        language extension

module Composition.Performance      ┤ Exports the Event type and its constructors
   ( Event (..),                   ◁─
     start,              ┤ Exports custom field selector
     end,                  functions defined at the top level
   )
where

...

data Event
   = Tone {freq :: Hz, start :: Seconds, duration :: Seconds}
   | Silence {start :: Seconds, duration :: Seconds}
   deriving (Show)

start :: Event -> Seconds        ◁─┐
start (Tone _ s _) = s              │  Defines functions to
start (Silence s _) = s             │  access fields of the
                                    │  Event record
duration :: Event -> Seconds     ◁─┘
duration (Tone _ _ d) = d
duration (Silence _ d) = d
```

Now, our module exports `start` and `duration`, which work for both constructors. However, the dangerous partial field selector is hidden.

10.3.2 A function as a type

Now that we have a definition for our events, we can worry about creating components that produce signals based on them. In our code, we want to call them `Oscillator`, due to their connection to oscillators in musical synthesizers. For the most part, these oscillators have a preselected waveform and are directly connected to some envelope for contouring. The type for our oscillators is a simple `newtype` that wraps a function `Event -> Signal` in a new type. We can then construct a function that combines a `Wave` function and `ADSR` parameters to create an oscillator that generates tones from events. The code for this is shown in the following listing.

Listing 10.10 A function for defining oscillators

```
module Sound.Synth (
  ...
) where

import Composition.Performance

...

newtype Oscillator = Osc {playEvent :: Event -> Signal}

osc :: Wave -> ADSR -> Oscillator
osc wave adsrParams = Osc oscf
  where
    oscf (Silence _ t) = silence t
    oscf (Tone f _ t) = adsr adsrParams $ tone wave f t
```

Defines a type for oscillators with a field selector for the underlying function

Wraps the created function into the Osc constructor

Creates silence for a specified amount of time

Creates a signal containing a tone held at a specified frequency for a certain amount of time and contours the signals with an ADSR envelope

As we can see, we are ignoring the start parameter of our events. That's because we don't want to worry about how signals are combined within the oscillator. In the end, our synthesizer can have multiple oscillators that play their tones, sometimes at completely different times and sometimes at overlapping times. To handle this correctly, we need to do some housekeeping later, but for now, we can start building different oscillators with their own characteristics determined by their underlying wave and ADSR parameters. In the following listing, we can see three candidates for noisemakers. You can play around with the waves and ADSR parameters to create your unique music machine.

Listing 10.11 A function for defining oscillators

```
module Sound.Synth (
  ...
) where

import Prelude hiding (sin)
import qualified Prelude

...

piano :: Oscillator
piano = osc saw $ ADSR 0.01 0.6 0.3 0.2

ocarina :: Oscillator
ocarina = osc sin $ ADSR 0.01 0.3 0.7 0.01

violin :: Oscillator
violin = osc saw $ ADSR 2 2 0.1 0.2
```

Defines a sharp oscillator with transient response and long sustain

Defines a mellow oscillator with nearly constant volume

Defines a sharp oscillator with long swelling attack and decay

```
pluck :: Oscillator
pluck = osc sqw $ ADSR 0.01 0.05 0.0 0.01
```
Defines a plucky
oscillator with no sustain

```
bass :: Oscillator
bass = osc tri $ ADSR 0.001 0.2 0.9 0.1
```
Defines a calm and loud oscillator
that can be used for deeper tones

Using the field selector of our `Oscillator` type, we can try those oscillators out for ourselves:

```
ghci> oscs = [piano, ocarina, violin, pluck, bass]
ghci> signal = concatMap (`playEvent` (Tone 440 0 1)) oscs
ghci> writeWav "oscillators.wav" signal
```

The resulting signal shows us the drastic change in sound that occurs when switching the waveform or contouring of our sound. This concludes our work on the sound generation part of our synthesizer.

Exercise: The Tremolo effect

We have created a basic set of functionalities for sound generation. Synthesizers in the real world offer a bit more flexibility in terms of sound shaping, implementing filters, and other types of envelopes. Extend our oscillator capabilities by adding possibilities for modulation, meaning that another signal (which is at a low frequency of 0–10 Hz) influences some characteristic of our oscillator over time. When we influence the amplitude of our signal, that is called a *tremolo effect*. Implement this effect to give our synthesizer a bit more depth.

With our noisemakers ready at our disposal, we can start worrying about composition, how to model and group notes, and then how to play these compositions.

10.4   Note models

When we want to create musical compositions, we need a way of classifying pitches and durations in relation to some global time measurement. This chapter shall not devolve into a boring lecture on music theory, which is why we will mostly skip those details, but the implementation of the modeling of music theory should be interesting for us.

10.4.1   A type class for pitches

First, let us tackle pitch. We already have a way of quantifying pitch for our `Oscillator` type, which was `Hz`, the frequency of the signal. However, Beethoven and Mozart did not compose with frequencies but with musical notes. What is the relation between those and what our `Oscillator` can create? That's what we will now figure out.

To establish a relation, we already know that at some point, we will need to convert notes to frequencies. For this, we can create a type class. This class is shown in the following listing.

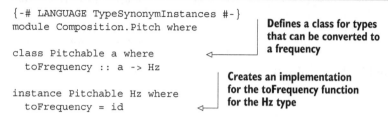

The class contains a single function that can convert a type to a frequency. The first instance for this class is already given, which is for Hz itself. Of course, frequencies can be converted to frequencies by doing … nothing at all, which is why the implementation for toFrequency is the identity function in this case.

On a keyboard (the piano kind, not the one connected to your computer), musical notes are spaced by semitones. This is shown in figure 10.7. Moving your finger from one key to the next changes the played note by a single semitone. It makes sense to create a type for these semitones, but how shall that type look?

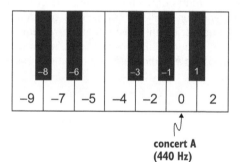

concert A
(440 Hz)

Figure 10.7   A musical keyboard with semitone distances from concert A

Most music played today revolves around the same tuning. This tuning defines concert A to be 440 Hz. When we define semitones to be the distance from concert A (in semitones), we can use the handy little formula from figure 10.8 to compute the frequency of our note.

$$f = 440\ Hz * 2^{s/12}$$

Figure 10.8   Formula to compute the frequency (f) from a given semitone distance to concert A (s) in 12-tone equal temperament

This leads us to a definition of semitones for our synthesizer. A semitone is just an Integer specifying some distance to concert A. The calculation needed to create a Pitchable Semitone instance is given in figure 10.8. The code for this is shown in the following listing.

Listing 10.13 A type for semitones

```
{-# LANGUAGE TypeSynonymInstances #-}
module Composition.Pitch where
```

←┐ **Enables the TypeSynonymInstances language extension to allow class instances for type synonyms**

```
...

type Semitone = Integer
```

←——— **Creates a type synonym for semitones**

```
instance Pitchable Semitone where
  toFrequency semitone =
    440 * (2.0 ** (fromInteger semitone / 12))
```

┐ **Computes the frequency of a given semitone distance from concert A**
←┘

Now, we can try the calculations out. It is expected that once we go up or down one octave from a specific semitone, the frequency should double or halve:

```
ghci> toFrequency (0 :: Semitone)
440.0
ghci> toFrequency (12 :: Semitone)
880.0
ghci> toFrequency (-12 :: Semitone)
220.0
ghci> toFrequency (5 :: Semitone)
587.3295358348151
ghci> toFrequency (5+12 :: Semitone) / 2
587.3295358348151
```

Now, we have our first idea about specifying tones and their pitch relations. However, Beethoven and Mozart didn't compose in semitones; they used *musical notes*. It's time we tackle this last problem.

Exercise: A test for semitones

So adding or subtracting 12 semitones from a given one should result in double or half the frequency? That sounds a lot like a formal property! Write a QuickCheck test for the frequency calculations of `Semitone`. What problem arises when constructing this test? How can we fix it?

Here is a little secret: musical notes are nothing but fancy names for semitones. *Concert A* is also called *A4*, with *A* being the name of the semitone in the octave and *4* specifying the octave. The number of octaves and semitones is limited, since human hearing is confined to a range of roughly 20 Hz to 20 kHz. Everything under 20 Hz sounds less like a pitch and more like a rhythm, and most frequencies over 20 kHz can only be picked up by our pets but not us.

Back to the topic of notes. The semitones in an octave on the keyboard are broken up into note names. Notes broken up by the interval of a semitone are also called *chromatic*. The names for these are shown in figure 10.9.

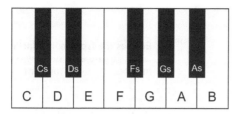

Figure 10.9   A musical keyboard with note names

How should we represent these? In theory, we could just enumerate *all* possible values as a huge sum type, like so:

```
data Chromatic
  = C0 | Cs0 | D0 | Ds0 | E0 ...
  | C1 | Cs1 | D1 ...
  ...
  | C8 | Cs8 ...
```

However, this is not just a pain to write down but also to pattern match, which is why we want to split up the information of which octave a note is in and which semitone offset it has from the base of that octave (given by the note name). So it makes sense to split up the data types for the chromatic note names and the actual chromatic notes. For the number associated with the chromatic note, it makes no sense to allow negative numbers, which is why we want to use the `Natural` type from `Numeric.Natural`. This type encodes natural numbers, meaning nonnegative integers. The code for the new data type is shown in the following listing.

Listing 10.14   Types for chromatic notes

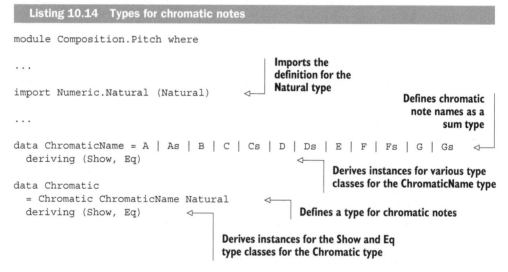

Sadly, writing down values of this type is a bit cumbersome. We can define some helper functions for each possible note name, only requiring the octave the value is in:

```
a :: Natural -> Chromatic
a = Chromatic A

as :: Natural -> Chromatic
as = Chromatic As

...

gs :: Natural -> Chromatic
gs = Chromatic Gs
```

Now, the last step is to transform these notes into frequencies. Since they are just fancy names for semitones and we already know how to compute frequencies from semitones, our final task is to convert the chromatic notes to those semitones. We know that A4 must be 0 and that a deviation from A by a single note equals a single semitone. Therefore, we can compute the semitones by adding the offset of the note within the octave by the octave number minus 4×12 (since there are 12 semitones in an octave). The offsets can simply be enumerated. We can also use this to compute the frequency, as shown in the following listing.

Listing 10.15 Conversion from chromatic notes to semitones and frequency

```
chromaticToSemitone :: Chromatic -> Semitone
chromaticToSemitone (Chromatic name oct) =
  (12 * (fromIntegral oct - 4)) + noteOffset name
  where
    noteOffset C = -9
    noteOffset Cs = -8
    noteOffset D = -7
    noteOffset Ds = -6
    noteOffset E = -5
    noteOffset F = -4
    noteOffset Fs = -3
    noteOffset G = -2
    noteOffset Gs = -1
    noteOffset A = 0
    noteOffset As = 1
    noteOffset B = 2

instance Pitchable Chromatic where
  toFrequency = toFrequency . chromaticToSemitone
```

Computes the Semitone from a chromatic note by adding the offset of the note within the octave to the semitone number of the octave

Defines the offset for the chromatic note names

Computes the frequency from a chromatic note by converting it to a Semitone value and using the toFrequency implementation of that type

Again, we can check if our property for frequencies and octaves holds for this new type:

```
ghci> toFrequency (a 4)
440.0
ghci> toFrequency (a 5)
880.0
ghci> toFrequency (a 3)
220.0
ghci> toFrequency (c 2)
65.40639132514966
```

```
ghci> toFrequency (c 3) / 2
65.40639132514966
```

With these types as our building blocks, we can create our first little melodies:

```
ghci> melody = map toFrequency [c 4, e 4, g 4, d 5, c 5  :: Chromatic]
ghci> signal = concatMap (\f -> playEvent piano $ Tone f 0 0.7) melody
ghci> writeWav "melody.wav" signal
```

This is fine and all, but it sounds somewhat monotone. All the notes are played for the same amount of time. We could vary the duration for each note, but we have no nice way of writing that down.

> **Exercise: Properties for different pitches**
> Create new QuickCheck properties for the new type by also implementing a `Arbitrary Chromatic` instance, and check if the conversion to `Semitone` as well as `Hz` is working correctly.

What we need in our composition is a way of speaking about note lengths, which we will tackle next.

10.4.2 *The Ratio type*

Musical notes are categorized by ratios. The ratios specify how much time the note occupies, as a fraction of a bar. A whole note occupies a whole bar, a half note occupies half of a bar, a quarter note occupies a quarter of a bar, and so on. Also, the ratios are always positive, since we have no notion of "negative time." So how do we represent them in our code?

While we could use `Double` or `Float` to represent the ratios, we can be much more explicit by using the `Ratio` type from `Data.Ratio`. A ratio is exactly what you would expect: a numerator and denominator. This makes it possible to represent ratios with arbitrary precision if the underlying numeric type can be infinitely large. Additionally, `Ratio` implements the `Num` type class, so we can use these ratios for calculations.

The main operator to use with `Ratio` is (`%`) to specify a rational number with a numerator and denominator:

```
ghci> import Data.Ratio
ghci> :k Ratio
Ratio :: * -> *
ghci> 1 % 2 :: Ratio Int
1 % 2
ghci> 3 % 2 + 1 % 2 :: Ratio Int
2 % 1
ghci> 4 % 5 - 2 % 10 :: Ratio Int
3 % 5
```

As we can see, the kind of `Ratio` is `* -> *`, so it is parametrized by another type. The `(%)` operator makes sure that only integral types can be used. So you can construct `Ratio Int` and `Ratio Integer` but not `Ratio Double`:

```
ghci> :t (%)
(%) :: Integral a => a -> a -> Ratio a
```

We have already seen a `Ratio` type when taking a look at the `toRational` function: the `Rational` type, which is nothing but an alias for `Ratio Integer`:

```
ghci> :i Rational
type Rational :: *
type Rational = Ratio Integer
```

For our purposes, we want to disallow negative values on a type level, so it makes sense to use `Natural`, which, luckily, also has an instance of the `Integral` type class. Using this, we can already construct many note lengths known in western music theory.

IMPORTANT While `Natural` seems like a good choice when we want to represent values with nonnegative numeric values, this isn't always the case. When a calculation with `Natural` numbers goes into negative values (which is possible because the instance `Num Natural` exists, so you can subtract them), an exception will be thrown. This can cause a program to crash at unexpected times!

The types for note lengths as well as some constants are shown in the following listing.

Listing 10.16 Conversion from chromatic notes to semitones and frequency

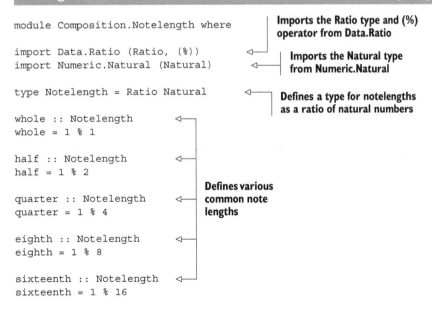

```
module Composition.Notelength where
```
Imports the Ratio type and (%) operator from Data.Ratio

```
import Data.Ratio (Ratio, (%))
import Numeric.Natural (Natural)
```
Imports the Natural type from Numeric.Natural

```
type Notelength = Ratio Natural
```
Defines a type for notelengths as a ratio of natural numbers

```
whole :: Notelength
whole = 1 % 1

half :: Notelength
half = 1 % 2

quarter :: Notelength
quarter = 1 % 4

eighth :: Notelength
eighth = 1 % 8

sixteenth :: Notelength
sixteenth = 1 % 16
```
Defines various common note lengths

However, there also exist modifiers for note lengths in western music notation. The ones we are interested in are *dotted notes* and *tuplets*. Dotted notes can be understood as an elongation of the original note. If a note is dotted, its duration is increased by half the original length. This can also be done multiple times, so a note can be dotted twice or even thrice. Tuplets are very interesting because they allow us to create irregular rhythms that fall outside of our normal ratios. They subdivide beats differently for the notes that are written down as a tuplet. They are also parametrized by some constant; three for "triplets" and five for "quintuplets" are common values. Note durations are being multiplied by two over the tuplet value, so for triplets, it's two over three, and for quintuplets, it's two over five.

While humans have some limit to the complexity of note lengths they can interpret and perform, our synthesizer is not held back by such meager biological constraints. So we will allow for arbitrary dotting and tuplets. We can implement these modifiers as simple functions shown in the following listing.

Listing 10.17   Conversion from chromatic notes to semitones and frequency

```
dots :: Natural -> Notelength -> Notelength
dots n x = x + x * (1 % 2 ^ n)

dotted :: Notelength -> Notelength
dotted = dots 1

doubleDotted :: Notelength -> Notelength
doubleDotted = dots 2

tripleDotted :: Notelength -> Notelength
tripleDotted = dots 3

tuplet :: Natural -> Notelength -> Notelength
tuplet n x = x * (2 % n)

triplet :: Notelength -> Notelength
triplet = tuplet 3

quintuplet :: Notelength -> Notelength
quintuplet = tuplet 5
```

Now, we can modify note lengths, which will enable us to create much more interesting rhythmic patterns later:

```
ghci> nl = 1 % 2 :: Notelength
ghci> dotted nl
3 % 4
ghci> triplet nl
1 % 3
```

10.4.3 *Different kinds of exponentiation*

Something of note in listing 10.17 is the usage of the (^) operator. Previously, we used (**) to compute frequencies, but now, we are using the (^) operator, even though both do exponentiation. To make things even more confusing, there is a third operator for exponentiation, which looks a bit like a happy emoticon: (^^). What's going on here? Why so many? Each of these operators has their own little quirk of implementation. First, let's gather some information on their types:

```
ghci> :t (**)
(**) :: Floating a => a -> a -> a
ghci> :t (^)
(^) :: (Num a, Integral b) => a -> b -> a
ghci> :t (^^)
(^^) :: (Fractional a, Integral b) => a -> b -> a
```

From the signatures alone, we see that (**) must be used when the exponent is a floating point number. (^) and (^^) can be used with integer exponents, but (^^) can only be used with a fractional base. Their biggest differences, however, come in their precision and which values are allowed for the exponent. (^) does not allow negative exponents. For integral exponents, (^) and (^^) are preferred when it comes to precision but not necessarily for negative exponents:

```
ghci> (1.2 :: Double) ** (5 :: Double)
2.4883199999999994
ghci> (1.2 :: Double) ^ (5 :: Int)
2.48832
ghci> (1.2 :: Double) ^^ (5 :: Int)
2.48832
ghci> (1.2 :: Double) ^ (-5 :: Int)
*** Exception: Negative exponent
ghci> (1.2 :: Double) ^^ (-5 :: Int)
0.4018775720164609
ghci> (1.2 :: Double) ** (-5 :: Double)
0.40187757201646096
```

As you can see, it gets messy quite fast, and the correct choice of operator is not always obvious. Generally speaking, we use (^) for integers, (^^) for rational values, and (**) for floating-point numbers, but exceptions still apply when negative exponents are at play.

Now that we have a good grasp on our note lengths, we have to take the last step and relate these values to our Seconds type. In western music composition, a time signature and some notion of beats per minute (BPM) are usually set. The time signature is usually concerned with how to divide and count the measures, while the BPM gives an exact measure of time. However, knowing how many beats are in a minute is not enough, since we also have to know how many beats are in a whole note.

Because we do not want to deal with time signatures, since they are irrelevant to how we will compose music (we are not composing on a sheet of paper, after all), we only want to support the notion of BPM and how many beats are in a whole note. We can compile this information in its own type, as shown in the following listing.

Listing 10.18   Types for info on tempo

```
type BPM = Double                            ⟵—  Defines the type for
                                                 BPM to be a Double

data TempoInfo = TempoInfo        ⟵—
  { beatsPerMinute :: BPM,              Defines a type that specifies how
    beatsPerWholeNote :: Double         many beats are in a minute and how
  }                                     many beats are in a whole note
```

With the `TempoInfo` type, we can finally build a bridge between the real world (the measure of minutes) and our compositions (the whole note). For this, we can determine how many beats are in a particular note length (which is a fraction of a whole note), how many seconds a beat occupies, and how many seconds a particular note length fills. The code for this is shown in the following listing.

Listing 10.19   Functions for conversion of note lengths to time

```
module Composition.Notelength where

import Util.Types (Seconds)
import Data.Ratio (Ratio, (%), denominator, numerator)

...
                                            Computes the number
                                            of seconds in a beat for
timePerBeat :: BPM -> Seconds               a specified BPM value
timePerBeat bpm = 60.0 / bpm       ⟵—

timePerNotelength :: TempoInfo -> Notelength -> Seconds
timePerNotelength
  (TempoInfo beatsPerMinute beatsPerWholeNote)
  noteLength =                                       Computes how
  let beatsForNoteLength = beatsPerWholeNote *       many beats are in the
⟹    toDouble noteLength                      ⟵—     specified note length
  in beatsForNoteLength * timePerBeat beatsPerMinute  ⟵—  Computes how many
  where                                                   seconds are in the
    toDouble :: Ratio Natural -> Double                   specified note length
    toDouble r =
      (fromInteger . toInteger $ numerator r)   ⟵—
        / (fromInteger . toInteger $ denominator r)   Converts a Ratio Natural to
                                                      a Double by converting the
                                                      numerator and denominator
                                                      to Double and manually
                                                      dividing them
```

Here, we use the `numerator` and `denominator` functions imported from `Data.Ratio` to access the numerator and denominator of `Ratio` values. To convert a `Natural` to `Double`, we first have to convert it into an `Integer`, which we then convert back to a `Double`.

With pitch and tempo now taken care of in our composition framework, we can begin adding form to our compositions by developing our own structure for the way notes and pauses relate to each other. We will explore this in the next chapter.

Summary

- The `Integral` and `Fractional` type classes define functions for divisions for integer and floating-point values.
- The `Enum` type class defines how to build enumerations of values for types and is used in the list range syntax.
- The `round`, `ceiling`, and `floor` functions from the `RealFrac` type class are used to convert floating-point numbers to integers, and `fromIntegral` can be used to convert integers to floating-point numbers.
- Lists can be created lazily to contain an infinite number of elements, which are only created once they are accessed.
- Infinite lists have to be handled carefully, as they should not be evaluated fully.
- Using the same field names in a record type with multiple constructors can lead to partial field selectors if a field is not present in all constructors.
- Using the `NoFieldSelectors` language extension, we can suppress the automatic creation of field selectors.
- The `Ratio` type defines ratios of numbers.
- When computing exponentiation, we use (`^`) for integers, (`^^`) for rational values, and (`**`) for floating-point numbers.

11
Programming
musical compositions

This chapter covers

- Constructing a polymorphic data structure that contains data from different types
- Interpreting complex data structures to compute more information
- Implementing a domain-specific language within Haskell

In the last chapter, we built the basis for a software synthesizer. We have introduced types to abstractly represent audio signals and pitch information. By using the HCodec library, we were able to write our audio data to the filesystem.

With the technical details taken care of, we now can talk about composing within our program. We obviously do not want to write down notes on a piece of paper; we want to do it directly within our program. Essentially, our compiled Haskell binary becomes the composition, packed with a synthesizer that also plays the composition! We can think of it as our own digital music box.

In this chapter, we will build this music box by designing a type for representing compositions. While doing so, we will learn how to construct heterogenous data structures, mixing values of different types in the same structure. After defining musical structures and how to interpret them, we will design our own domain-specific language for music compositions within Haskell!

11.1 *Polymorphic data structures with multiple types*

So how do we represent compositions in our program? In music, we can distinguish between notes and pauses. An instrument either plays notes or remains quiet for a certain amount of time. These notes and pauses are arranged either in a sequence or in groups.

As we can see in figure 11.1, a melody is a sequence of notes, and a chord is a group of notes, all being played at the same time. However, sequences of notes can also be in a sequence or a group. Groups can be sequenced as well. For example, multiple chords can be played in a sequence, as we can see in figure 11.2. So how can we model this?

Figure 11.1   A melody is a sequence of notes

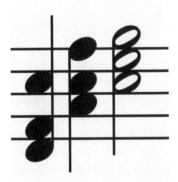

Figure 11.2   A sequence of chords which are simultaneously played notes

Our data structure needs to allow for recursion or nesting. Otherwise, we cannot allow sequences of sequences, for example. Also, we have to think about what we want to achieve. Later, we do not want to write this data type in terms of its constructors but use operators to construct notes, pauses, sequences, and groups. We want to be able to mix all of these elements by, for example, putting them all into a group that should be played simultaneously. Therefore, whatever we model should be contained in a single data type. A data type that meets all of these requirements might look like this:

```
data NoteStructure a
  = Note Notelength a
  | Pause Notelength
  | Sequence [NoteStructure a]
  | Group [NoteStructure a]
```

However, this poses a problem. In the previous chapter, we used the `Pitchable` type class to define types for which we can calculate a pitch. These types are `Hz`, `Semitone`, and `Chromatic`. For our synthesizer, it should not matter whether it is working with frequencies or chromatic notes, so it makes sense to mix these types. The `NoteStructure` type, however, is parametrized with a single type. This means we can define a `Note-Structure Hz` and `NoteStructure Chromatic` but not a `NoteStructure` that can mix both `Hz` and `Chromatic` values.

The same restriction applies to lists. We consider these data structures to be *homogeneous*, since they only contain values of the same type. If we wanted to bundle values of different types in a data structure, that would make it *heterogenous*. But is such a thing possible in Haskell?

11.1.1 *Existential quantification*

Let's review how Haskell's types work again and look at this example:

```
ghci> data D a = D a
ghci> :t [D (1 :: Int), D (2 :: Int)]
[D (1 :: Int), D (2 :: Int)] :: [D Int]
ghci> :t [D (1 :: Int), D (2 :: Float)]

<interactive>:1:19: error:
    • Couldn't match expected type 'Int' with actual type 'Float'
    • In the first argument of 'D', namely '(2 :: Float)'
      In the expression: D (2 :: Float)
      In the expression: [D (1 :: Int), D (2 :: Float)]
```

Here, we define a simple data type with a single constructor and type variable. We can define a homogenous list of type `[D Int]`, where all values must be of type `D Int`. Once we define a list that contains a `D Int` and a `D Float` value, the types clash, since `Int` is not the same as `Float`, and therefore, `D Int` is not the same type as `D Float`. Can we somehow hide the type parameter? If we were capable of hiding it, we could simply create a `[D]` list and no type errors would arise. It turns out that this is possible with the `ExistentialQuantification` language extension.

When this language extension is enabled, we can define data types that can use type variables on the *right side* of their definition without specifying them on the *left side*:

```
ghci> :set -XExistentialQuantification
ghci> data E = forall a. MkE a
```

```
ghci> :t MkE
MkE :: a -> E
ghci> :t MkE (1 :: Int)
MkE (1 :: Int) :: E
ghci> :t MkE (1 :: Float)
MkE (1 :: Float) :: E
ghci> :t [MkE (1 :: Int), MkE (2 :: Float)]
[MkE (1 :: Int), MkE (2 :: Float)] :: [E]
```

We introduce these decoupled type variables with the `forall` keyword. As we can see, the `E` type has no type variable, but its constructor is of type `a -> E`. Therefore, it can take a value of *any type* and produce a value of type `E`. This means that no matter what we put into the `MkE` constructor, we will always get the same type, and with that, we can put these values into a list to construct a *heterogenous* list.

But how do we work with such a type? How can we access the values we put into the constructor? To do this, we would need to construct a function of type `E -> a`, where `a` matches up with the `a` used in the `MkE` constructor. Sadly, this is not possible, as the `E` type does not expose this `a`. After all, that is the whole point of what we are trying to achieve. The problem we are facing is that we do not know anything about `a`. It could potentially be anything.

This can be fixed by providing a type constraint for the existentially quantified type variable:

```
ghci> data ShowData = forall a. (Show a) => ShowThis a
ghci> :{
ghci| showThis :: ShowData -> String
ghci| showThis (ShowThis x) = show x
ghci| :}
ghci> showValues = [ShowThis (1 :: Int), ShowThis ("Hi" :: String)]
ghci> :t showValues
showValues :: [ShowData]
ghci> map showThis showValues
["1","\"Hi\""]
```

In this example, we can use `show` on the values inside the `ShowThis` constructor, since the definition of the `ShowData` type makes it clear that the values inside the constructor have an instance for the `Show` type class. Hence, we know that values inside a list of `ShowData` values might be heterogenous but definitely can be used with `showThis`.

11.1.2 Using existentially quantified types

We can use this to make the `NoteStructure` accept values from different types. To do this, we first create a new type for a general description of a pitch. We will need the following extensions:

```
{-# LANGUAGE ExistentialQuantification #-}
{-# LANGUAGE StandaloneDeriving #-}
module Composition.Pitch where
```

Now, we can define a `Pitch` type, which contains values for which a `Pitchable` instance exists. Then, we define the `Pitchable Pitch` instance, which uses `toFrequency` on the value inside the `Pitch` value. The code for this is shown in the following listing.

Listing 11.1 A data type for structuring notes

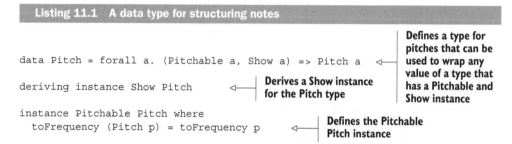

```
data Pitch = forall a. (Pitchable a, Show a) => Pitch a
```
Defines a type for pitches that can be used to wrap any value of a type that has a Pitchable and Show instance

```
deriving instance Show Pitch
```
Derives a Show instance for the Pitch type

```
instance Pitchable Pitch where
   toFrequency (Pitch p) = toFrequency p
```
Defines the Pitchable Pitch instance

We also use `Show` as a constraint, such that we can derive a `Show` instance for `Pitch`. With existentially qualified data types, we are forced to use *standalone deriving* enabled by the `StandaloneDeriving` language extension, which forces us to write down the deriving clause in a separate line from the data type definition. Now, we can use this type to wrap any `Pitchable` type and build data structures from them that can contain values from different types:

```
ghci> pitches = [Pitch (a 4), Pitch (440 :: Hz), Pitch (0 :: Semitone)]
ghci> :t pitches
pitches :: [Pitch]
ghci> pitches
[Pitch (Chromatic A 4),Pitch 440.0,Pitch 0]
ghci> map toFrequency pitches
[440.0,440.0,440.0]
```

Even though we have created a heterogenous list of pitches, we are still able to convert them to frequencies using the `toFrequency` function.

Now, we can get rid of the type variable in our `NoteStructure` type and replace it with the `Pitch` type. This is shown in the following listing.

Listing 11.2 A datatype for structuring notes

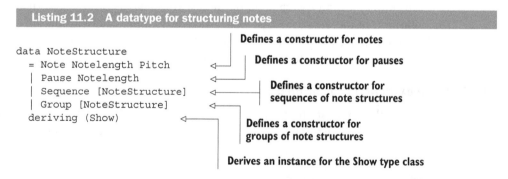

```
data NoteStructure
  = Note Notelength Pitch
  | Pause Notelength
  | Sequence [NoteStructure]
  | Group [NoteStructure]
  deriving (Show)
```
Defines a constructor for notes

Defines a constructor for pauses

Defines a constructor for sequences of note structures

Defines a constructor for groups of note structures

Derives an instance for the Show type class

With this type, we need to find a way to translate whatever is being composed with it to something we can create sounds from. We already have a type for sounds, which was our Event. Now it's time to bring a NoteStructure into multiple events. For this, we define a type for a performance, which is our way of describing multiple events:

```
module Composition.Performance where

type Performance = [Event]
```

This type must contain all events (with correct start times) such that we can plug them into our Oscillator type and hear some sweet, sweet music.

11.2 Interpreting structures

To do that, we need to parse the NoteStructure recursively, keep track of durations, and combine the elements into a list. Since we need to do that recursively, we know that the function we want to implement needs to have a Seconds argument, which is the current time at interpretation. Also, we need a TempoInfo argument to know how long a note or pause needs to be held, since the Event type only knows Seconds as a measurement of time. As a result, we not only need the Performance but also Seconds, since we recursively need some information about elapsed time. With this, parsing of sequences and groups is a fold over the elements in their respective lists. For a sequence, an element's start is determined by the already elapsed time, and the returned Seconds value is given by the end of the last produced Event. In a group, all elements start at the same time, and the returned Seconds value is given by the end of the longest Event produced. Given this information, we can put together the function shown in the following listing.

Listing 11.3 A function to convert structures of notes and pauses to playable events

```
module Composition.Performance where

...

import Composition.Note
import Composition.Notelength
import Composition.Pitch
import Data.List (foldl')

...

structureToPerformance ::
  TempoInfo ->
  Seconds ->
  NoteStructure ->
  (Seconds, Performance)
structureToPerformance tempoInfo start structure =
  case structure of
    (Note length pitch) ->
      let freq = toFrequency pitch
          duration = timePerNotelength tempoInfo length
      in (start + duration,
   [Tone {freq, start, duration}])
    (Pause length) ->
```

Determines the frequency of the pitch information given by the note

Computes the length of the note or pause from its length and given information on tempo

Returns the end of the note and a Performance with a single tone as its Event

Folds over the recursive structures in the sequence or group with the given start time as the moment in time

Returns the end of the pause and a Performance with silence as its Event

Computes the length of the note or pause from its length and given information on tempo

```
      let duration = timePerNotelength tempoInfo length
      in (start + duration,
   [Silence {start, duration}])
     (Group structs) -> foldl' f (start, []) structs
       where
         f (durAcc, perf) struct =
           let (dur, tones) =
   structureToPerformance tempoInfo start struct
           in (max dur durAcc, perf ++ tones)
     (Sequence structs) -> foldl' f (start, []) structs
       where
         f (durAcc, perf) struct =
           let (newdur, tones) = structureToPerformance tempoInfo durAcc
              struct
           in (newdur, perf ++ tones)
```

Folds over the recursive structures in the sequence or group with the given start time as the moment in time

Returns the duration of the given moment in time and adds the Event values to the accumulator in no specific order

Returns the maximum of the given moment in time and produces the end from the recursive call and adds the Event values to the accumulator in no specific order

Recursively computes the Performance and its end time from the current structure in the fold, using the current moment in time as the start of this specific Performance

Recursively computes the Performance and its end time from the given structures, using the given start time as the start of this specific Performance

This function does not put the `Event` values in the correct order given by their start time and needs a special `start` argument, which should be 0 when a `NoteStructure` is being converted for the first time. Also, it returns a tuple with some duration, which is not important to us when we just want to play those events. Thus, we can write a wrapping function that gets rid of this tuple as a return value and also sorts the values correctly. This is shown in the following listing.

Listing 11.4   Wrapper function for converting note structures into a performance

```
...
import Data.List (sortBy, foldl')
...


toPerformance :: TempoInfo -> NoteStructure -> Performance
toPerformance tempoInfo =
```

```
sortBy (\x y -> compare (start x) (start y))
  . snd
  . structureToPerformance tempoInfo 0
```

Sorts the resulting Event values in the Performance by their start time

Calls structureToPerformance with 0 as the start time

Accesses the second value in the returned tuple

With this function, we have built a bridge between our compositions, given as `Note-Structure` values and a `Performance` playable by an `Oscillator`.

Exercise: Combining silence

While our `toPerformance` function works fine, there is one possibility for improvement. Pauses always result in silence. Our `NoteStructure` type makes it possible to create a sequence of silences. Of course, these silences can be consolidated into one large silence. Write a function `Performance → Performance` that does exactly that, and then add it to the `toPerformance` function. Think about how we can test this function. Can you come up with a QuickCheck property for this function?

We have not yet implemented an `Oscillator` being able to play a whole `Performance`. This will be our last puzzle piece before we can implement a composition.

11.2.1 Mixing signals

To keep playing a `Performance` general, we want to abstract it through a simple type class. We do this to make it possible to add more possible noisemakers later. After all, oscillators are not the only thing that can produce sound. The type class is shown in the following listing.

Listing 11.5 Type class for transforming performances into a signal

```
module Sound.Sound where

import Util.Types
import Composition.Performance

class Performer p where
  play :: p -> Performance -> Signal
```

The `play` function will later be applied to the performance to construct our signal. How will that work? A problem we are dealing with here is that events can naturally overlap. The synthesizer we are creating is polyphonic, meaning it can play multiple notes at the same time. This requires us to first think about mixing multiple signals into one. For this, we want to write a function that can add signals without them clipping. *Clipping* occurs when our sample levels exceed `1` or reach a value lower than `-1`. In that case, our `limit` function will cut off the signal and cause distortion. This should be avoided. So when we add signals, we have to make sure they don't ever exceed the maximum and minimum sample value. We can achieve this by dividing the added signals by the number of added signals. Adding signals themselves is similar to a `zipWith (+)`; however, we can't stop at the shorter signal. We must include all signals from the longer signal too. But then, how can we add an arbitrary amount of signals when no `zipWithN` exists? The answer comes to us in another fold. By adding each signal, one after the other, in a fold, we can add them all up and then divide the samples by the number of signals added. This is shown in the following listing.

Listing 11.6   Function to mix multiple signals into a single signal

```
module Sound.Sound where

...
import Data.List (foldl')           Folds the signals,
...                                  adding them up
                                     and then dividing
                                     the samples by the
mix :: [Signal] -> Signal           number of signals
mix signals = (/ n) <$> foldl' addSignals [] signals
  where
    n :: Double
    n = fromIntegral $ length signals    Determines the number of signals
                                         and converts it to a Double
    addSignals :: Signal -> Signal -> Signal
    addSignals xs [] = xs
    addSignals [] ys = ys                Returns the end of the longer signal
    addSignals (x : xs) (y : ys) = (x + y) :
    addSignals xs ys              Adds the first samples of two signals
                                  together and recursively adds the rest
```

With the mixing of signals taken care of, we need to find a way to identify overlapping `Event` values so that we can group them, play them with our `Oscillator`, and then mix the signals back together. What we have created here is a method of generating polyphonic sounds, meaning multiple sounds playing at the same time. In most synthesizers, the maximum number of sounds that can be played polyphonically is limited by hardware restrictions. We can see how this concept works in figure 11.3.

Since our synthesizer is not in real time, we have the incredible advantage that we have no restrictions on how long the generation of sounds can take. Our synthesizer is infinitely polyphonic if we allow ourselves to take a long time to compute the sound!

Let's get back to those simultaneously played events. To determine whether two `Event` values overlap, we can use the `start` field selector and the `end` function to check whether the start of any of the events lies in the duration of the other one. If that is the case, the events overlap. A function that checks this is shown in listing 11.7.

When multiple notes should be played simultaneously, they need to be split and distributed to multiple oscillators, each generating the signal for a single note.

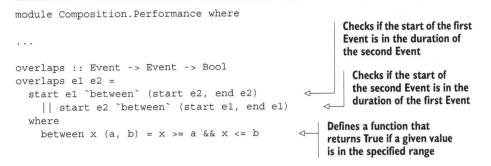

When mixing the generated signals, their combined amplitudes should not exceed the maximum level set for each of them individually. The process of adding up signals needs to make sure to lower the amplitude for the resulting signal.

Figure 11.3   The basic concept behind the generation of polyphonic audio signals

Listing 11.7   Function to check whether events overlap

```
module Composition.Performance where

...

overlaps :: Event -> Event -> Bool
overlaps e1 e2 =
  start e1 `between` (start e2, end e2)
    || start e2 `between` (start e1, end e1)
  where
    between x (a, b) = x >= a && x <= b
```

Checks if the start of the first Event is in the duration of the second Event

Checks if the start of the second Event is in the duration of the first Event

Defines a function that returns True if a given value is in the specified range

Just with the `between` helper function, we design the name of this function in a way to allows it to be written in an infix style to keep the code readable.

Exercise: Properties for sound functions

As with many functions, our `mix` and `overlaps` functions have some properties. `mix` is an especially critical function, due to the clipping problem explained earlier. Write some QuickCheck properties that check the correctness of this function.

With these functions now complete, we can tackle writing our `Performer` instance for `Oscillator`.

11.2.2 *Groups of polyphony*

When transforming a `Performance` into a `Signal`, there are a few pitfalls we do not want to fall into. First of all, the list of `Event` values is ordered. So when we fold over the list, the folding direction matters. Second, we need to group the events based on them overlapping other ones. This will create disjointed groups of events that may have nonexplicit pauses between them, meaning there could be an event that ends long before another one begins. We also need to make sure we mix the signals such that no clipping can occur; however, our `mix` function already takes care of that.

First, let us talk about grouping events. When we fold the events from left to right, we can start at the first event we come across and put it into its own group. For the next event in the `Performance`, we first have to evaluate that it does not overlap with any event in the current group. If there is no overlap, we can add it to the group. If there is overlap, we need to start a new group with the event as its member. We repeat this for all remaining events. An important property of this algorithm is that it does not change the order of events within the groups. To make the syntax readable, we want to make use of list comprehensions and the `or` function:

```
ghci> :t or
or :: Foldable t => t Bool -> Bool
ghci> :t and
and :: Foldable t => t Bool -> Bool
```

The `or` and `and` functions are pretty simple to explain: they fold a `Foldable` of Booleans and either build the disjunction or conjunction of those values. This can be used rather neatly with list comprehensions to produce a list of Booleans on the fly and then work with `or` or `and`:

```
ghci> xs = [Tone 0 0 1, Tone 0 2 1]
ghci> x1 = Tone 0 2 1
ghci> x2 = Tone 0 1.5 0.1
ghci> or [ x1 `overlaps` e | e <- xs ]
True
ghci> or [ x2 `overlaps` e | e <- xs ]
False
```

Since those expressions evaluate to a single `Bool`, we can use them as *guards* in our functions! This helps us complete a quick case distinction on a rather complex property on lists.

Now, we still have to think about how we can play those groups of events. Since they can have implicit pauses between them, we need to keep track of the time. In a recursive function, we can simply do this with an argument similar to how we achieved it in our `structureToPerformance` function. Then, we need to scan (from left to right) through the list and play the event with our `Oscillator`. If the event group was somehow wrongly ordered, we might need to go back in time and play a tone that we might already have filled with silence. In that case, there is nothing to do for us but fail with `error`. This case should never happen anyway if the rest of our implementations are correct.

After the grouping and the generation of signals from the events, the last thing we need to do is to mix all signals in terms of their constructors. Luckily, this is the simple usage of `mix`. The full code for this function is shown in the following listing.

Listing 11.8 A type class instance to perform with an oscillator

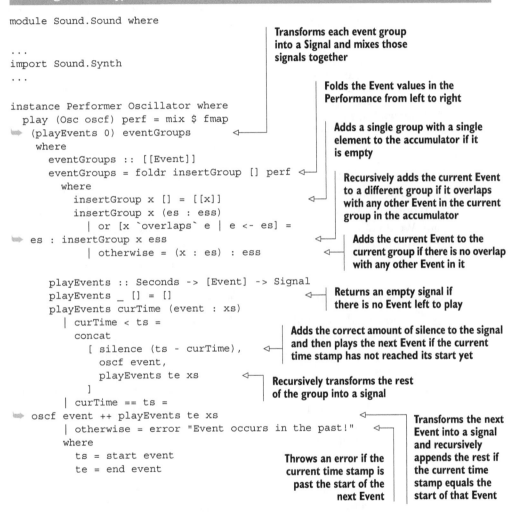

```
module Sound.Sound where

...
import Sound.Synth
...

instance Performer Oscillator where
  play (Osc oscf) perf = mix $ fmap
    (playEvents 0) eventGroups
    where
      eventGroups :: [[Event]]
      eventGroups = foldr insertGroup [] perf
        where
          insertGroup x [] = [[x]]
          insertGroup x (es : ess)
            | or [x `overlaps` e | e <- es] =
              es : insertGroup x ess
            | otherwise = (x : es) : ess

      playEvents :: Seconds -> [Event] -> Signal
      playEvents _ [] = []
      playEvents curTime (event : xs)
        | curTime < ts =
          concat
            [ silence (ts - curTime),
              oscf event,
              playEvents te xs
            ]
        | curTime == ts =
          oscf event ++ playEvents te xs
        | otherwise = error "Event occurs in the past!"
        where
          ts = start event
          te = end event
```

Transforms each event group into a Signal and mixes those signals together

Folds the Event values in the Performance from left to right

Adds a single group with a single element to the accumulator if it is empty

Recursively adds the current Event to a different group if it overlaps with any other Event in the current group in the accumulator

Adds the current Event to the current group if there is no overlap with any other Event in it

Returns an empty signal if there is no Event left to play

Adds the correct amount of silence to the signal and then plays the next Event if the current time stamp has not reached its start yet

Recursively transforms the rest of the group into a signal

Transforms the next Event into a signal and recursively appends the rest if the current time stamp equals the start of that Event

Throws an error if the current time stamp is past the start of the next Event

Notice how we create a short circuit in the `playEvents` function. If there are no events left in the group, we return an empty `Signal` because `mix` will take care of reaching the correct length.

With this function, we can finally play our `NoteStructure` values as well as our first composition:

```
ghci> melody1 = Sequence [Note whole (Pitch $ c 4), Pause half,
➥ Note whole (Pitch $ f 4)]
ghci> melody2 = Sequence [Note whole (Pitch $ f 4),
➥ Note half (Pitch $ g 4), Note whole (Pitch $ a 4)]
ghci> melody3 = Sequence [Note whole (Pitch $ f 3),
➥ Note half (Pitch $ c 3), Note whole (Pitch $ c 4)]
ghci> group = Group [melody1, melody2, melody3]
ghci> perf = toPerformance (TempoInfo 120 4) group
ghci> perf
[Tone {freq = 261.6255653005986, start = 0.0, duration = 2.0},Tone {freq
➥ = 349.2282314330039, start = 0.0, duration = 2.0},Tone {freq =
➥ 174.61411571650194, start = 0.0, duration = 2.0},Silence {start
➥ = 2.0, duration = 1.0},Tone {freq = 391.99543598174927, start
➥ = 2.0, duration = 1.0},Tone {freq = 130.8127826502993, start
➥ = 2.0, duration = 1.0},Tone {freq = 349.2282314330039, start
➥ = 3.0, duration = 2.0},Tone {freq = 440.0, start = 3.0, duration
➥ = 2.0},Tone {freq = 261.6255653005986, start = 3.0, duration = 2.0}]
ghci> signal = play piano perf
ghci> writeWav "performance.wav" signal
Writing 220500 samples to performance.wav
```

Here, we see a little motive using three melodies that are then combined into one group. The notes are played simultaneously, and the resulting signal does not clip.

Wonderful! But as we can see, writing down even such a small composition is a true pain. We do not want to write down Haskell data types. What we would like to have is an easier-to-write and understand representation of the same thing, which ideally presents as an abstraction away from the underlying data type.

11.3 *Implementing a domain-specific language*

We are now ready to finally discuss how we will compose music in our program. Clearly, we are not interested in writing down constructors manually in a huge syntax tree of unending complexity. What we would like to construct is a *domain-specific language* (DSL).

Haskell allows us to define our own operators with their own rules when it comes to how they relate to the rest of the data you specify. Additionally, it allows us to define precedences of operators to result in a clean syntax for whatever we want to represent. This makes Haskell a nice platform for developing domain-specific languages made for a specialized use case.

> **NOTE** To be completely pedantic about semantics, when a domain-specific language is directly embedded in a programming language, like in this chapter, it would rather be called an *embedded domain-specific language* (EDSL). However, we want to keep things a bit shorter and omit the extraneous distinction.

We will use this to define syntax that lets us easily compose music based on the NoteStructure type that the composer (user of the DSL) never needs to see or learn about. What we want first and foremost is to write down notes. Our current method is a bit too verbose: `Note whole (Pitch $ e 4)`. Since the constructor is a bit to verbose, we can create an operator to replace it:

```
module Composition.Note where

...

(.|) :: (Pitchable a, Show a) => a -> Notelength -> NoteStructure
(.|) p l = Note l (Pitch p)

infixr 4 .|
```

We choose `.|` as the operator, since it somewhat resembles a musical note. Our definition defines an *infix* operator by default. The first argument goes in front of the operator, and the second argument goes behind it. Replacing the constructor is important because the DSL user should not have to interface with the underlying `Notestructure` type. We explicitly only allow types with a `Pitchable` and `Show` instance, since the `Pitch` constructor requires this constraint. Again, we can see how `Note-Structure` is heterogenous, since we pass a polymorphic argument (a) to the function but that type variable is not present in the function's result!

11.3.1 *Simplifying syntax*

This new operator keeps writing notes concisely. However, the length (`whole`, `half`, etc.) values are still very verbose. To get shorter length identifiers, we can create shorter names for `Notelength` constants:

```
module Composition.Notelength where

...

wn :: Notelength
wn = whole

hn :: Notelength
hn = half

...

sn :: Notelength
sn = sixteenth
```

This simple step makes writing down notes very easy:

```
ghci> c 4 .| wn
Note (1 % 1) (Pitch (Chromatic C 4))
ghci> f 8 .| triplet sn
Note (1 % 24) (Pitch (Chromatic F 8))
ghci> (400 :: Hz) .| (100000 % 100001)
Note (100000 % 100001) (Pitch 400.0)
```

We can do the same with pauses by just creating a one-letter synonym for the `Pause` constructor:

```
p :: Notelength -> NoteStructure
p = Pause
```

That's another constructor taken care of.

11.3.2 *Custom operators for list-like data structures*

Let's investigate `Sequence` and `Group` next. In general, the user of our DSL should do the following:

1 Not care about lists
2 Not care how to combine sequences and groups
3 Easily use repetition

This means we need to completely abstract the notion of sequencing and grouping. We can make these their operators with which we can combine our notes and pauses. Regarding sequences, if two are encountered, we simply combine them into a new sequence. If only one argument of our operator is a sequence, we add the other argument to it. If none of the arguments are a sequence, we create a completely new sequence. This operator is shown in the following listing.

Listing 11.9   An infix operator to construct sequences of compositions

```
(<~>) :: NoteStructure -> NoteStructure -> NoteStructure      Adds two sequences
(<~>) (Sequence xs) (Sequence ys) = Sequence $ xs ++ ys       together
(<~>) (Sequence xs) x = Sequence $ xs ++ [x]                  Adds the other argument
(<~>) x (Sequence xs) = Sequence $ x : xs                     to a sequence
(<~>) a b = Sequence [a, b]
                                                Creates a new sequence
infixr 3 <~>                                    from the two arguments
```

This lets us sneakily avoid writing down the `Sequence` constructor *and* the list needed for it:

```
ghci> c 4 .| wn <~> e 4 .| wn <~> g 4 .| wn
Sequence [Note (1 % 1) (Pitch (Chromatic C 4)),Note (1 % 1)
➥  (Pitch (Chromatic E 4)),Note (1 % 1) (Pitch (Chromatic G 4))]
```

Funny enough, the function for groups looks very, very similar (if not completely identical). The code for it is shown in the following listing.

Listing 11.10   An infix operator to construct groups of compositions

```
(<:>) :: NoteStructure -> NoteStructure -> NoteStructure      Adds two groups
(<:>) (Group xs) (Group ys) = Group $ xs ++ ys                together
(<:>) (Group xs) x = Group $ xs ++ [x]
(<:>) x (Group xs) = Group $ x : xs                   Adds the other argument to a group
```

```
(<:>) a b = Group [a, b]          ◁───┐ Creates a new group from
                                       │ the two arguments
infixr 2 <:>
```

The similarity is not by accident of course. Since the structure of `Sequence` and `Group` are identical, it makes sense that operators for them are also identical. The only difference is in the name of the constructor, since that is what determines how the data gets interpreted later.

NOTE The DSL proposed in this chapter is, in part, inspired by the Haskore project, which features similar operators.

Now that we have the operators ready, there is one a last question to ask before we can begin. What is the result of this expression: `c 4 .| wn <~> e 4 .| wn <:> g 4 .| wn`? Here, we have a question of *operator precedence*. Should `<~>` or `<:>` have precedence? This is not an easy question to answer, since it depends on how the DSL will be used, but we will give `<~>` precedence over `<:>`. So how do we do that?

11.3.3 *Fixity declarations*

Haskell provides syntax to declare the precedence rules. We have already seen this when discussing the `$` operator in chapter 7. It begins with the keywords `infixr`, `infixl`, or `infix` to determine whether the operator is right, left, or not associative at all. This is followed by the precedence between 0 and 9. The declaration is completed by mentioning which operator we are talking about. This is called a *fixity declaration*.

In our case, we will make all operators right associative. The `(.|)` operator must take precedence over all over operators, since it isn't used for combining compositions but makes up the atomic building blocks. Then, `(<~>)` takes precedence over `(<:>)`. With the following fixity declarations, we can enforce these rules:

```
infixr 4 .|

infixr 3 <~>

infixr 2 <:>
```

We have taken care of almost all desired properties for our DSL. The last is to make repetition easier. If we want to repeat a melody or chord, we still have to copy the declarations. Of course, we can invent *new* operators that achieve repetition! These operators can replicate a given `NoteStructure` for a specified number of times and either wrap them inside a `Sequence` or `Group`. This is shown in the following listing.

Listing 11.11 Operators to repeat compositions

```
(<~|) :: NoteStructure -> Natural -> NoteStructure
(<~|) (Sequence xs) n = Sequence $ concat [xs | _ <- [1 .. n]]
(<~|) struct n = Sequence $ [struct | _ <- [1 .. n]]
```

```
(|~>) :: Natural -> NoteStructure -> NoteStructure
(|~>) = flip (<~|)

(<:|) :: NoteStructure -> Natural -> NoteStructure
(<:|) (Group xs) n = Group $ concat [xs | _ <- [1 .. n]]
(<:|) struct n = Group $ [struct | _ <- [1 .. n]]

(|:>) :: Natural -> NoteStructure -> NoteStructure
(|:>) = flip (<:|)
```

To make the syntax a bit more flexible, there is an operator with the number of repetitions on the left and the right. Since repetition should "wrap around" other compositions, the precedence of these operators should be lower than all the other operators:

```
infixr 1 <~|
```

```
infixr 1 |~>
```

```
infixr 1 <:|
```

```
infixr 1 |:>
```

Let's try out our new language:

```
ghci> c 4 .| wn <~> e 4 .| wn <:> g 4 .| wn <~| 2
Sequence [Group [Sequence [Note (1 % 1) (Pitch (Chromatic C 4)),
➡ Note (1 % 1) (Pitch (Chromatic E 4))],Note (1 % 1)
➡ (Pitch (Chromatic G 4))],Group [Sequence [Note (1 % 1)
➡ (Pitch (Chromatic C 4)),Note (1 % 1) (Pitch (Chromatic E 4))],
➡ Note (1 % 1) (Pitch (Chromatic G 4))]]
```

As we can see, the syntax has become much simpler to read and write, and it doesn't require knowledge of our data structures to construct.

> ### Exercise: Switching precedences
> We made the choice that the `(<~>)` takes precedence over `(<:>)`. However, we could have avoided this problem by creating synonyms for both operators with their precedences switched. The composer, then, wouldn't need to use parentheses but could switch to the other operator! Implement these synonyms.

There we have it: our own digital music box!

Let us recap what we have done here. First, we implemented types and functions for a domain-specific problem: musical sound generation. We have modeled properties of the real world in our program as data types and effectively modeled basic synthesizer technology. In doing so, we have created a small framework to build synthesized instruments that can easily be extended.

Exercise: Adding a sampler

Our little synthesizer is somewhat biased. Its only sound generator is the `Oscilla-tor` type, which can create chords and melodies, but it leaves much to be desired when it comes to percussion. Where is the cowbell? In electronic music, this is often fixed by using samplers, machines that can sample other audio (such as drums) and play them back in a musical arrangement. Implement such a `Sampler` type for our synthesizer framework. This will require you to get crafty. You will need to think about how to give this component access to sound files, how playing these files should be triggered, and how this all fits together with our DSL.

Second, we have modeled another domain-specific problem: music composition. We have used data types and various functions to abstract the meaning of musical compositions into something that can be controlled more easily from within our code.

Third, we have created a domain-specific language for the aforementioned subject of composition. This domain-specific language builds an abstraction around our data types and is usable even without understanding our internal implementations. It can also be extended to allow for more varied compositional techniques, like aleatoric (a fancy word for *random*) compositions. Since the language is embedded in Haskell, we can add any functionality that we implement in our framework to it.

All that is left to do is to put our synthesizer to the test and compose some music. Check the code repository for a little sample!

Summary

- The `ExistentialQuantification` extension can be used to create heterogenous data structures, hiding type parameters inside types.
- For a heterogenous type to be useful, type constraints have to be given so that it is clear what can be done with a specific value for the type.
- Data structures can serve as a description for a result, which has to be interpreted to yield it.
- Custom operators can be implemented as normal functions.
- Domain-specific languages can be implemented in Haskell by letting custom operators define a data structure, which is then interpreted.
- We can define the associativity and precedents of our defined operators by using the `infix`, `infixl`, and `infixr` fixity declarations.

Parsing pixel data

In previous chapters, we tackled the task of reading data in a certain way, be it lines of a file or more intricate formats, like CSV. For our purposes, we have created custom functions for reading this data, tailor-made to the task at hand. However, this is not what we typically do in these situations. Usually, no matter what language we are using, we would construct some kind of parser to do this. In Haskell, the development of parsers is an almost unique experience in how cleanly they compose, to build a bigger parser from simple building blocks.

In this chapter, we will write our own simplified parser library to read PNM files, a family of simple image file formats, which will not only teach us how to compose effectful actions but also how to gracefully handle any errors and failures we might run into on the way. We do this by using *applicatives* and *monads*, and we will understand how they work and why they are an essential building block in Haskell. After that, we will get to know Attoparsec, a widely used parser combinator library, which will help us to create performant parsers for image files.

The chapter will begin with defining the problem we are trying to solve. Then, we will build our own parser library to begin solving this task. Finally, we apply our learned knowledge by using an existing state-of-the-art parser library.

12.1 Writing a parser

Since the dawn of photography, we have not just been interested in capturing the real world but also in modifying our images after their creation. This does not just hold for photography but any visual art. In our modern world, photographers and artists alike are lucky, since most of their work has shifted into the digital realm, where their images are nothing but bits and bytes. Coincidentally, computers are masters at transforming and mangling these bits and bytes to create something completely new.

Furthermore, we, as programmers, have the ability to make computers do whatever we tell them to. So it's time for us to write software that is capable of transforming image data! For this, we have to make the choice of which image formats we want to support. While nowadays, there is a plethora of highly compressed and complex formats, we want to keep our image manipulation library old school by writing it for the formats of the Netpbm project.

12.1.1 Portable images from the past

In the 1980s, sharing images wasn't as straightforward as uploading them into the cloud. If you wanted to share anything, it had to be done over email, which, at the time, wasn't the best for sending binary data. If you wanted to send images, they had to be in good ol' 7-bit ASCII. To facilitate this, Jef Poskanzer invented a family of file formats that could be distributed in ASCII or binary form and are free from superfluous metadata, making them easy to parse and understand.

These formats—sometimes referred to as portable anymap format (PNM)—are the *portable pixmap format* (PPM), *portable graymap format* (PGM), and *portable bitmap format* (PBM). These can used to store color, grayscale, and color pixel data. There also exists a suite of tools to work with these formats, called *Netpbm*, which lets you transform more commonly used formats to and from these portable formats.

Let us quickly go over how these formats work. All of them contain a header, which always contains a magic number. This number specifies which kind of format is being used and if its encoding is ASCII or binary. The file extension is typically not used to determine the type of format we are working with. The header then continues with the width and height of the image. For the PPM and PGM formats, a fourth value signifies the maximum value of a single data point. Let us look at the example in the following listing.

Listing 12.1   A simple PBM file with comments in its header

```
P1  # PBM in ASCII
2 2 # 2x2 pixel size
1 0
0 1
```

As we can see, headers can contain comments signified by #. They are also always in ASCII, no matter the magic number. This example specifies a bitmap image 2 pixels in width and 2 pixels in height. The following binary data represents the value of these pixels. Scaling the resulting image up, we get the result shown in figure 12.1.

Each pixel value in the data gets mapped to an individual pixel in the finished image (with1 signifying pure black and 0 signifying white).

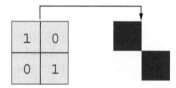

Figure 12.1   An example portable bitmap upscaled by 150%

In table 12.1, we see an overview of the file formats, their magic numbers, and the data they contain, respectively. We can see that each format has two magic numbers corresponding to the ASCII and binary versions of the format.

NOTE   The header in the PNM formats is always encoded in ASCII!

For bitmap and graymap files, a single value after the header corresponds to a single pixel in the image. However, in the pixmap format, a pixel is made up of three values, each for red, green, and blue values making up that pixel.

Table 12.1   Overview of the magic numbers for the PNM formats

| Format | Magic numbers | | Extension | Image data (for one pixel) |
	ASCII	Binary		
Portable bitmap format (PBM)	P1	P4	.pbm	0 (white) or 1 (black)
Portable graymap format (PGM)	P2	P5	.pgm	From 0 to maximum value (gray-scale), where the maximum value is given in the header
Portable pixmap format (PPM)	P3	P6	.ppm	From 0 to maximum value for each RGB channel, where the maximum value is given in the header

We can see the usage of this maximum value in the header in listing 12.2. There are also no strict rules for the elements in the header. They can be placed in a single line, but it is common to separate the magic number, image dimensions, and maximum value into different lines. Also, the image data can be separated into single lines, but it doesn't have to be. A maximum line length of 76 in the file is recommended for readability, but once again, this recommendation does not have to be obeyed when we are only interested in storing the data for computers to read.

Listing 12.2 A simple PGM file with comments in its header

```
P2 10 14 # PGM in ASCII with 10x14 pixels
9          # Values from 0 (black) to 9 (white)
9 6 3 4 9 9 9 9 9 9
8 4 2 2 6 9 9 9 9 9
8 6 9 5 4 9 9 9 9 9
8 9 9 9 4 9 9 9 9 9
9 9 9 9 4 7 9 9 9 9
9 9 9 9 3 6 9 9 9 9
9 9 9 6 1 3 9 9 9 9
9 9 9 4 0 3 8 9 9 9
9 9 7 0 4 4 8 9 9 9
9 9 4 1 7 5 6 9 9 9
9 7 1 3 9 6 5 9 9 8
9 5 0 7 9 8 3 8 9 6
8 1 2 8 9 8 3 3 4 4
5 2 5 9 9 9 7 2 1 7
```

The image result from the PGM file shown in the following listing is shown in figure 12.2. Using the *Netpbm* and *ImageMagick* tools, we can easily convert these files to and from other more common file formats, like jpeg or png.

Figure 12.2 Example portable grayscale upscaled by 150%

Now that we have an idea how these file formats work, we can think about how to read these files in our program.

12.1.2 *How to parse a file*

Reading information, be it files, network packets, or data from a serial port, requires us to describe an expected structure. This is true, whether we read CSV files, source code for a programming language, or (in our case) image files. Describing this structure is often achieved using parsers. Parsers are programs, or parts of a program, that translate a string of characters or bytes into data that can be interpreted within said program. A parser has two core responsibilities:

- Validate the structure of the data and report errors if validation fails.
- Transform strings of characters or bytes into native data types.

In theory, we can achieve these goals by writing simple functions that do this, as we have done in chapter 8 when we parsed CSV files. This has the disadvantage of it being hard to comprehend the expectations the parser has just from looking at its definition. As we do not want to repeat this and we are tackling parsing with Haskell, we additionally have a couple of goals:

- Parsing functionalities should be composable.
- The definition of the parser should give insights into the expected structure.

So let us write a general parser in Haskell. We start a new project using `stack new` and add the following default language extensions:

```
default-extensions:
- OverloadedStrings
- RecordWildCards
- NamedFieldPuns
```

To start with our parser, we have to come up with a type for it. As we go along, this type will transform as the need arises.

Since a parser transforms an input to some native datatype, a parser could be just a simple function:

```
type Parser a = Text -> a
```

For our simplified parser, we are going to work on the `Text` data type from `Data.Text`. If we wanted to write a parser for the PNM format's magic numbers, we could do that like so:

```
module Graphics.PNM.Types where

import Parser.Core

data MagicNumber = P1 | P2 | P3 | P4 | P5 | P6 deriving (Eq, Show)

magicNumberP :: Parser MagicNumber
magicNumberP "P1" = P1
magicNumberP "P2" = P2
magicNumberP "P3" = P3
```

```
magicNumberP "P4" = P4
magicNumberP "P5" = P5
magicNumberP "P6" = P6
```

Our parser, called `magicNumberP`, can read a magic number from `Text`. For the rest of this chapter, we assume that the `OverloadedStrings` language extension is enabled on the whole project. However, it is apparent that our parser uses nonexhaustive pattern matching and would crash our program if parsing failed. So our type should encode the possibility of failure.

> **NOTE** Just like it's common to prefix `Maybe` and `Either` values for `m` in the variable name, it's common to put a postfix `P` on parsers!

As we have learned in previous chapters, this can be done with the `Either` type. This also gives us the possibility to return an error message in our parser. We can update the type like this:

```
type ErrorMessage = String

type Parser a = Text -> Either ErrorMessage a
```

Using this new parser for magic numbers looks like this:

```
magicNumberP :: Parser MagicNumber
magicNumberP "P1" = Right P1
magicNumberP "P2" = Right P2
magicNumberP "P3" = Right P3
magicNumberP "P4" = Right P4
magicNumberP "P5" = Right P5
magicNumberP "P6" = Right P6
magicNumberP t =
  Left $
    "Could not parse \""
      ++ T.unpack t
      ++ "\" as magic number"
```

This function now does not crash when parsing fails but returns an error message:

```
ghci> magicNumberP "P3"
Right P3
ghci> magicNumberP "Not a magic number"
Left "Could not parse \"Not a magic number\" as magic number"
```

While that seems to work, we encounter a problem: How do we compose this parser with other parsers to fully read the header of PNM files? We need to be able to parse different parts of the header into different types, while ignoring whitespaces, newlines, and comments. This is shown in figure 12.3.

Our `magicNumberP` parser is capable of parsing the first part of the header, but from this, we are not capable of parsing further parts of the file. That's because our

Each part of the data parses to a specific
Haskell type. While the magic number, width,
and height are expected to exist, the same
is not true for the maximum value, which is
why it is a `Maybe` of a value. Whitespace
and comments are ignored, so they do not
result in a type that holds information.

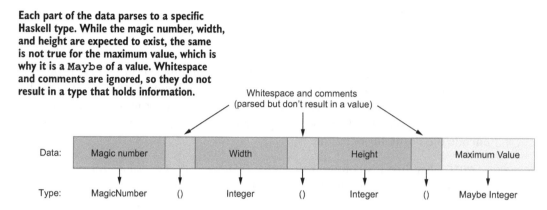

Figure 12.3   A mapping showing the parsed information from a file, which parts of it result in a value, and which are ignored

parser does not return the rest of the input for us to further parse it. We can resolve this problem by letting our parser not just return a result but also the rest of the input that is left after parsing. That way, we can pass it to another parser. The final type for our parser is shown in the following listing. The `ParseResult` contains the rest of the input and the parse result from running the parser. Also, we wrap the parser in a `new-type` with a field for accessing the internal function.

Listing 12.3   A data type for parsers

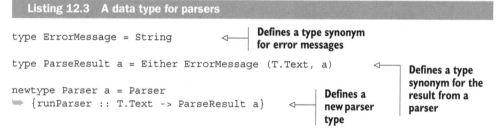

```
type ErrorMessage = String
```
Defines a type synonym for error messages

```
type ParseResult a = Either ErrorMessage (T.Text, a)
```
Defines a type synonym for the result from a parser

```
newtype Parser a = Parser
   {runParser :: T.Text -> ParseResult a}
```
Defines a new parser type

For the rest of this chapter, we assume that our modules contain an import of `Data.Text` with the qualified name `T`. We could now rewrite our `magicNumerP`, but before we go through that, we should think about more basic building blocks for our parser. We already know that we have to parse fixed strings for our magic numbers, so why not create a general parser for strings?

We can do this by creating a function that reads as many characters as a specified string and comparing them to that string. If the comparison succeeds, we can drop these characters from the input and return the result. This function is shown in the following listing.

Listing 12.4   A parser for fixed strings

```
string :: T.Text -> Parser T.Text
string str =
```

```
    Parser $ \t ->
      if T.take (T.length str) t == str
        then Right (T.drop (T.length str) t, str)
        else Left $ "failed to parse \""
 ⇨  ++ T.unpack str ++ "\""
```

← Compares the beginning of the input with the specified string

← Returns the parsed string and the rest of the input without the characters that were parsed

← Returns the full input and an error message

This parser can now parse the magic numbers of a header:

```
ghci> runParser (string "P1") "P1 100 100"
(" 100 100",Right "P1")
ghci> runParser (string "P1") "P2 100 100"
("P2 100 100",Left "failed to parse \"P1\"")
```

We can see how the parser fails if the input does not start with the specified string and how it returns the rest of the input on a successful parse. However, this isn't enough to define a parser for `MagicNumber` because we still need to transform the parsed string to a Haskell type. What we would like to do is transform our `Parser Text` to `Parser MagicNumber`. This looks similar to what a `Functor` can do, and indeed, an instance for `Functor Parser` is exactly what is needed here, since we want to transform the internal value of the parser.

In our definition for `fmap`, which is needed for the instance, we can use the fact that the `Functor Either` and `Functor ((,) a)` instances already exist. The definition for this instance is shown in the following listing.

Listing 12.5 A functor instance for parsers

```
instance Functor Parser where
  fmap f p = Parser $ \t -> fmap (fmap f) (runParser p t)
```

← Runs the parser on some input and maps the specified function only to valid results

Why does this work? Since `fmap` works on the `Right` values of `Either` and on the last value of a tuple, we can transform the type and value of our parse result:

```
ghci> fmap (+1) (1,1) :: (Int, Int)
(1,2)
ghci> fmap (+1) (Right 1) :: Either Int Int
Right 2
ghci> fmap (+1) (Left 1) :: Either Int Int
Left 1
```

Remember that `Right` signifies that our parser has succeeded in parsing, and the second value of the tuple is the parse result. Therefore, the outer `fmap` is applied on the `Either` type, and the inner `fmap f` is applied to the tuple within the `Right` constructor.

For our magic numbers, we can now define parsers:

```
ghci> p1P = fmap (const P1) $ string "P1"
ghci> :t p1P
p1P :: Parser MagicNumber
ghci> runParser p1P "P1 100 100"
Right (" 100 100",P1)
ghci> runParser p1P "P2 100 100"
Left "failed to parse \"P1\""
```

Whenever we want to apply an expression like `fmap (const X)`, we can simplify it to an operator from the `Functor` type class that does exactly that. The (`<$`) operator is used to provide a constant value for a functorial mapping. Using this operator, we can define our parsers:

```
magicNumberP1P :: Parser MagicNumber
magicNumberP1P = P1 <$ string "P1"

...

magicNumberP6P :: Parser MagicNumber
magicNumberP6P = P6 <$ string "P6"
```

Now, we have a parser for each magic number. To parse the whole header of our files, we should worry about combining parsers next. How can we take these disparate parts to build a bigger structure?

12.1.3 Composing effects

Let's assume that we are not trying to parse files starting with a general magic number but a fixed one. We will choose P1. In this header, there is no maximum value for the image data, so the header only consists of a magic number, a width, and a height. For the sake of simplicity, we do not worry about comments and assume that the header consists of a single line with spaces between the values. So a header might look like this:

```
P1 100 100
```

Parsing an arbitrary amount of spaces can be achieved by constructing a parser that has the `takeWhile` functionality we know from `Data.List` and `Data.Text` that reads the input while some predicate holds on the characters of the input. Since our functions operate on `Text` values, we can use the functions from `Data.Text` to build a parser. This is shown in the following listing.

Listing 12.6   A parser that reads input as long as a predicate holds

```
takeWhile :: (Char -> Bool) -> Parser T.Text
takeWhile p = Parser $ \t -> Right
➡   (T.dropWhile p t, T.takeWhile p t)     ◄─────
```

Reads characters as long as the specified predicate holds, removing the read characters from the rest of the input that still needs to be parsed

Using this, we can construct parsers for spaces as well as strings consisting of digits:

```
spaces :: Parser T.Text
spaces = takeWhile (' ' ==)
```

Using `takeWhile` and `fmap`, we can also define a parser for integers:

```
integer :: Parser Integer
integer = read . T.unpack <$> takeWhile (`elem` ['0' .. '9'])
```

A problem with this parser is that it crashes the program on empty inputs. We will write a better parser for numeric values later.

Now, we can define a type for the header:

```
data Header = Header
  { width :: Integer,
    height :: Integer
  }
  deriving (Show)
```

We would like to create a `Parser Header` and to have a way to combine our `spaces` and `integer` components to then build a parser for the actual data type. To specify the expected structure of the header, it could look something like this:

```
Header <_> (string "P1" <_> spaces <_> integer) <_> (spaces <_> integer)
```

This would enable us to indicate how to read the magic number, width, and height and which parse results will be used as fields in the `Header` data type. The `(<_>)` operator is just a placeholder. We will need to come up with operators in its place. Whatever these operators are, they need to propagate errors from any of the parsers to the completed parsers.

To better understand this problem, let us look at what `Header` is. It is a constructor, but it is also a function of type `Integer → Integer → Header`. Let's imagine for a moment that we could change the type to `Parser Integer → Parser Integer → Parser Header`. This would enable us to plug in `integer` as both arguments, and we would end up with `Parser Header`.

From this, we can infer that what we want is to sequence the application of parsers and gather the results. By *gather*, we mean any kind of aggregation of the results, which could include ignoring some results or somehow combining them. We essentially want to apply a function on (`Header`, in this case) to multiple `Parser` values.

The `Functor` class already provides us with `fmap` to apply a unary function to a `Parser`. So what would happen if we applied `Header` to `integer`?

```
ghci> :t Header <$> integer
Header <$> integer :: Parser (Integer -> Header)
```

It results in a `Parser` with a function as its internal type (remember that the `<$>` operator is just an infix version of `fmap`). How do we continue from here? How can we apply this parser? This is where a new type class comes into play: the `Applicative`.

Applicative functors, or *applicatives* for short, are an extension of functors by allowing the application of a function in the functorial context to another value in the context, thus making it possible to sequence these operations. To make this more clear, let us look at the class definition for `Applicative`:

```
class Functor f => Applicative f where
  pure :: a -> f a
  (<*>) :: f (a -> b) -> f a -> f b
  liftA2 :: (a -> b -> c) -> f a -> f b -> f c
  (*>) :: f a -> f b -> f b
  (<*) :: f a -> f b -> f a
  {-# MINIMAL pure, ((<*>) | liftA2) #-}
```

The most important functions of this type class are `pure` and `(<*>)`. `pure` is used to take a value and put it into the functorial context denoted by `f`. `(<*>)` is used to apply a function in this context to a value in it. Essentially, we could rewrite the type of this operator to `f (a → b) → (f a → f b)`, which would mean that the operator transforms a function inside the context into a function outside it. This is what makes *applicatives* so special. A *functor* can transform a normal function to a function working with functorially wrapped values, as shown in figure 12.4.

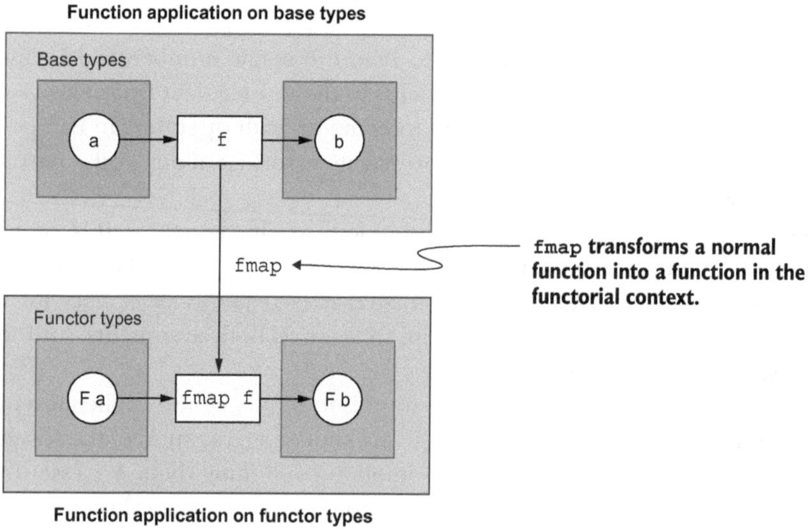

Figure 12.4   An abstract view of the functionality of functors

Applicatives, however, take a function in the functorial context and unlift them into a normal context, where we can compose it. This is shown in figure 12.5.

**The applicative can transform a function
in the functorial context to a normal function,
which we can compose.**

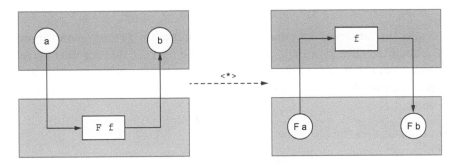

Figure 12.5 **An abstract view of the functionality of applicatives**

Before we start worrying about the other functions, let us look at an example. The
Maybe type has an instance for Applicative, where (<*>) applies a function if it is
wrapped in the Just constructor on a value inside the Just constructor. If any of the
Maybe values are Nothing, the end result is also nothing:

```
ghci> Just (+1) <*> Just 1 :: Maybe Int
Just 2
ghci> Just (+1) <*> Nothing :: Maybe Int
Nothing
ghci> Nothing <*> Just 1 :: Maybe Int
Nothing
ghci> Nothing <*> Nothing :: Maybe Int
Nothing
ghci> pure 100 :: Maybe Int
Just 100
```

Since we can now happily compose functions, we can apply them to even more values
in the Maybe context:

```
ghci> add3 x y z = x + y + z
ghci> pure add3 <*> Just 1 <*> Just 2 <*> Just 3 :: Maybe Int
Just 6
```

Using pure to lift a function into the context is seen quite often, but using partial
function application (just like we have seen with our Header example) and fmap, we
can achieve a bit cleaner syntax:

```
ghci> add3 <$> Just 1 <*> Just 2 <*> Just 3 :: Maybe Int
Just 6
```

But what are the rest of the functions in the `Applicative` class? `liftA2` is used to lift any binary function to work on arguments in the functorial context:

```
ghci> liftA2 (+) (Just 1) (Just 2) :: Maybe Int
Just 3
```

`(<*)` and `(*>)` are special, in that they discard either the first or second argument but still evaluate its effects. By that, we mean that the result of that argument is relevant to the end result. For `Maybe`, if any argument evaluates to `Nothing` while sequencing them, then the whole term evaluates to `Nothing`. This is also true for these discarding versions of `(<*>)`:

```
ghci> Just (1 :: Int) <* Just (2 :: Int)
Just 1
ghci> Just 1 <* Nothing :: Maybe Int
Nothing
```

Why is that relevant for us? The `Applicative` class gives us the possibility to sequence our parsers. This input will be sequentially parsed by calling later parsers in the sequence on the input that the other parsers left over. While at first, it might seem strange that we have to construct a function for a `Parser` of a function value, it makes sense once we apply it. The code for the `Applicative` `Parser` instance is shown in the following listing.

Listing 12.7   An `Applicative` instance for the parser type

```
instance Applicative Parser where
  pure x = Parser $ \t -> Right (t, x)        ◁——  Returns a parser that does not consume
  (<*>) a b =                                       input but returns a fixed value
    Parser $ \t ->
      case runParser a t of                   ◁——  Applies the first parser to the input
        Left msg -> Left msg                  ◁——  If the first parser failed while
        Right (rest, f) -> runParser (fmap f b) rest   ◁——  parsing, a failing result is returned.
```

Returns a parser that does not consume input but returns a fixed value

Applies the first parser to the input

If the first parser failed while parsing, a failing result is returned.

If the first parser succeeded, the second parser is applied to the rest of the input, applying the resulting function of the first parser to the result of the second.

`pure` creates a parser that does not consume any input and returns a fixed value. The `(<*>)` operator first runs the input on the first parser; if the result of this parsing step is unsuccessful, we return the `ErrorMessage` and the rest of the message. Otherwise, we run the second parser on the rest, applying the function returned by the first parser with `fmap`.

Now, we can play around with sequencing our `Parser`. For example, we can normalize the spaces between two words:

```
ghci> :{
ghci| helloWorldP = (\x _ z -> x <> " " <> z)
ghci|        <$> string "Hello"
```

```
ghci|        <*> spaces
ghci|        <*> string "World"
ghci| :}
ghci> runParser helloWorldP "Hello World"
Right ("","Hello World")
ghci> runParser helloWorldP "Hello        World"
Right ("","Hello World")
ghci> runParser helloWorldP "Helloooo World"
Left "failed to parse \"World\""
```

Here we see how each parser works with the input that is left by the previous parser. The same definition could have been made with (<*):

```
ghci> :{
ghci| hw = (\x y -> x <> " " <> y)
ghci|        <$> string "Hello"
ghci|        <* spaces
ghci|        <*> string "World"
ghci| :}
```

This brings us to finally finishing our parser for the example header. We can complete it with `Header` and (<$>) from before by using (<*>):

```
ghci> :{
ghci| headerP = Header
ghci|             <$> (string "P1" *> spaces *> integer)
ghci|             <*> (spaces *> integer)
ghci| :}
ghci> runParser headerP "P1 100 200"
Right ("",Header {width = 100, height = 200})
ghci> runParser headerP "P2 100 200"
Left "failed to parse \"P1\""
ghci> runParser headerP "P1 100 "
Right ("",Header {width = 100, height = *** Exception:
⮕ Prelude.read: no parse
```

This *applicative* style of writing down parsers is common and, therefore, worth studying a bit. `Applicative` (just like `Functor`) is a common class to encounter when reading Haskell code. It is used simply for its ability to combine effects, which helps us to write code that is still freely composable but follows strict rules about its semantics. All of this is ensured through the type system alone! Many of the types we have encountered so far, like `Maybe`, `Either`, and even `IO`, have instances of this class.

Exercise: Monoidal functors and applicative functors

Applicative functors are equivalent to so-called *(lax) monoidal functors*. We can use them to combine two functorial values into a tuple, thus combining them:

```
class Functor f => Monoidal f where
  unit :: f ()
  (**) :: f a -> f b -> f (a, b)
```

(continued)

For this class to be equivalent to `Applicative`, it must be possible to transform any instance of one class into the other. Show that this is possible!

Now, we have built a parser for a simplified header. What we have not managed so far is to make the parser accept more than one magic number. In our example, we also could have allowed `P4` as the magic number, but that would make our parser fail. We have to find a way of encoding alternatives in our parser. The answer comes to us in yet another type class.

12.1.4 *Choosing alternatively*

The `(<*>)` implementation for our parser can be understood as an *and then* semantic. The first parser parses the input and then the second does too. To encode alternatives for our parser, we need to implement an *or else* semantic. This means that if the first parser fails, the original input (without having anything consumed) must be passed to the second parser, which then, hopefully, won't fail.

This exact semantic is required for instances of the `Alternative` type class. Let's look at its definition:

```
class Applicative f => Alternative f where
  empty :: f a
  (<|>) :: f a -> f a -> f a
  some :: f a -> f [a]
  many :: f a -> f [a]
  {-# MINIMAL empty, (<|>) #-}
```

The minimal definition (consisting of `empty` and `(<|>)`) look suspiciously similar to the definition for `Monoid`, and indeed, they are similar! `empty` is the identity element for `(<|>)`, which is the associative binary operation for `Alternative`. In fact, `Alternative` is a monoid on applicative functors!

While `(<*>)` fails when a single argument fails, `(<|>)` only fails if both arguments fail. We can quickly experiment with this semantic, again using `Maybe`:

```
ghci> Just 1 <|> Just 2 :: Maybe Int
Just 1
ghci> Just 1 <|> Nothing :: Maybe Int
Just 1
ghci> Nothing <|> Just 2 :: Maybe Int
Just 2
ghci> Nothing <|> Nothing :: Maybe Int
Nothing
```

If we think of `Nothing` as "failure," we now have an understanding of how our parser should behave. To give our parser some more meaningful error messages, we can write a function to modify the error message of a parser. This is shown in the following listing.

Listing 12.8 A function to modify the error message of a parser on a failed parse

```
modifyErrorMessage ::
  (ErrorMessage -> ErrorMessage) ->
  Parser a ->
  Parser a
modifyErrorMessage f p =
  Parser $ \t -> case runParser p t of        ◁── Runs the parser on
    Left msg -> Left $ f msg          ◁──────       the given input
    result -> result        ◁──────
```

Runs the parser on the given input

Modifies the error message if the parser is unsuccessful

Returns a successful result unchanged

With this function, we can create an instance for `Alternative Parser`, which is shown in listing 12.9. For `empty` to be the identity element, it always has to fail, so we can write a parser, which doesn't even consume input but always returns some `Left` value as its result. For `(<|>)`, we have to run the first parser, and in the case of failure, we run the second one, using our new `modifyErrorMessage` function to modify a possible error message by prepending the error message of the first parser.

Listing 12.9 An instance of `Alternative` for the custom parser

```
instance Alternative Parser where
  empty = Parser $ \_ -> Left "empty alternative"
  (<|>) a b =
    Parser $ \t ->
      case runParser a t of
        Left msg -> runParser (modErr msg b) t        ◁──
        right -> right        ◁──
    where
      modErr msg =
        modifyErrorMessage
➥     (\msg' -> msg ++ " and " ++ msg')        ◁──
```

Runs the first parser

Runs the second parser, modifying its error message in the case of failure

Returns a result if the first parser succeeded

Appends the given error message the error message of the parser to be modified

---

With this instance, we are now able to encode a choice in our parser. The interesting thing about this is that this can be done with highly nested parsers. So if a parser succeeds in parsing large parts of the input only to then find out that parsing can't succeed the `(<|>)` makes it possible to roll back to have another try with another parser. Let's look at an example:

```
ghci> import Control.Applicative
ghci> runParser (string "A" <|> string "B") "A"
Right ("","A")
ghci> runParser (string "A" <|> string "B") "B"
Right ("","B")
ghci> runParser (string "A" <|> string "B") "C"
Left "failed to parse \"A\" and failed to parse \"B\""
```

Notice the import of `Control.Applicative`. The type classes we have discussed so far (`Functor`, `Applicative`, and `Alternative`) are all defined there. For us to use `(<|>)`, its import is required.

While the `Alternative` instance is incredibly useful in its own right, it also features two more functions: `some` and `many`. Both functions repeatedly apply the given applicative functor until it can't be applied anymore, in our case, meaning that the parser fails. The results are then collected in a list. The only difference between them is that `many` never fails. If the first application fails, an empty list is returned. `some`, however, needs at least one successful application to be successful. In this sense, `some` means *one or more* and `many` means *zero or more*.

> **Exercise: Many and some**
>
> `many` can be defined like so:
>
> ```
> many f = some f  <|> pure []
> ```
>
> Either we get one or more elements or we return an empty list. However, how could we define `some`? Try to come up with an implementation for it.

Using these two functions, we can now make a parser that parses some token arbitrarily often:

```
ghci> runParser (many $ string "A") "AAA"
Right ("",["A","A","A"])
ghci> runParser (many $ string "A") ""
Right ("",[])
ghci> runParser (some $ string "A") "AAA"
Right ("",["A","A","A"])
ghci> runParser (some $ string "A") ""
Left "failed to parse \"A\""
```

Think back to our definition of `spaces`, which was implemented with the `takeWhile` parser. If we wanted to create a parser that makes sure that at least one space exists in the input, we could very easily do so with `some`, as is shown in the following listing.

Listing 12.10   Parser that parses at least one space

```
someSpaces :: Parser T.Text
someSpaces = T.concat <$> some (string " ")    ◁——
```
Parses at least one space and concatenates the resulting strings to a larger one, failing otherwise

The last thing we have to discuss is how to write down cases with many alternative parsers. Do we really want to combine them with the `(<|>)` operator in a large term? It would be nicer to just specify a list of parsers, which are then tried one by one. This can be achieved using the `asum` function from `Data.Foldable`. It folds over a given structure using the semantics of the `Alternative` instance for the given type:

```
ghci> :i asum
asum :: (Foldable t, Alternative f) => t (f a) -> f a
ghci> runParser (asum [string "A", string "B"]) "A"
```

```
Right ("","A")
ghci> runParser (asum [string "A", string "B"]) "B"
Right ("","B")
ghci> runParser (asum [string "A", string "B"]) "C"
Left "failed to parse \"A\" and failed to parse \"B\" and
➥ empty alternative")
```

Notice how the error message ends in `empty alternative`. That is the error message of the identity element of our `Alternative Parser` implementation! `asum` really combines all elements of the structure with the monoid semantics given by `Alternative`, folding them with `(<|>)` with the last element being `empty` (which is the default for an empty structure).

> **WARNING** `some` and `many` are defined in terms of the functions defined in `Alternative` and `Applicative`. If you pass an argument to them, which is constant and always succeeds, you cause an endless loop! One example could be `some (Just 1)`.

Using this handy function, we can create a function serving as an alias to make our code easier to understand:

```
choice :: [Parser a] -> Parser a
choice = asum
```

With alternatives out of the way, we only have one puzzle piece left. Parsing a header for PNM files is almost possible. We can encode a choice of magic numbers in our parser, skip arbitrarily many spaces, and read integers. What we are lacking is a tiny bit of logic that tells us that we only have to parse the maximum value for data points if the magic number is not `P1` or `P4`. To solve our problems of composability and error handling, we upgraded from `Functor` to `Applicative`. However, this problem that we want to tackle now will require us to go one step further.

12.1.5 *Introducing monads*

So far, a parser is only dependent on the input it reads but not on the results of previous parsers. This makes it virtually impossible to make a parser act on the context and additional information provided by already parsed data. Let's review the problem in parsing the header for PNM files:

```
P2 3 2 1
1 0 1
0 1 0
```

The header shown here specifies a graymap file with a maximum value of 1. Therefore, the only values that are possible are it and 0. A parser for this file needs to read the magic number, infer from it that it needs to read a maximum value, and then proceed to read the data. In the case of the magic number being `P1`, the magic number is skipped and data is read immediately. Here, we have to do a case distinction on the magic number that was read. First, let us create a more specific type for the PNM headers, which is shown in the following listing.

Listing 12.11 Type for PNM file headers

```
data Header = Header
  { magicNumber :: MagicNumber,
    width :: Integer,
    height :: Integer,
    maxVal :: Maybe Integer
  }
  deriving (Eq, Show)
```

Defines a field for the header's magic number

Defines fields for the width and height of the image

Defines a field for the optional maximum value for data points

Derives instances for Eq and Show

We have to parse the magic number, width, and height of the header. Then, we have to make a choice. Either we do not parse the maximum value because it is not needed or we read it. We make this choice based on the magic number that was parsed.

However, *applicatives do not allow this*! It turns out that they enable us to compose parsers but not to do case distinctions. We cannot change our behavior based on the already read values. To solve this problem, we have to introduce another concept. Just as *applicatives* were an extension to *functors*, we now take a look at an extension to *applicatives*: the *Monad*.

Monads are a central concept in Haskell and might be one of the most useful and interesting concepts in functional programming. They allow for values to be wrapped into a monadic type and for arbitrary functions to act on them. Just as we have seen with *applicatives*, *monads* allow for the composition of these functions adhering to rules we can define for our use case. Let us take a look at the type class:

```
class Applicative m => Monad m where
  (>>=) :: m a -> (a -> m b) -> m b
  (>>) :: m a -> m b -> m b
  return :: a -> m a
  {-# MINIMAL (>>=) #-}
```

In Haskell, all monads are also *applicatives*. The most important, and only required function for a `Monad` instance, is `(>>=)`, colloquially called *bind*. It receives a monadic value `m a` and a function that acts on the value inside of that monadic value, returning a new monadic value, possibly of a different type, `m b`. This value is then returned from the bind function. The second function `(>>)` is similar to `(>>=)`. It evaluates the first monadic value but ignores its result and returns the second argument. `return` does not just look like `pure` in the `Applicative` class, but it, essentially, is `pure`, wrapping a value into a monadic value.

> **NOTE** Previously, we referred to the results of `pure` as values in the functorial context. Now, we refer to them as monadic values, as these terms are interchangeable. Sometimes, we refer to monadic values `m a` as *actions*, since they

can potentially change some state in the underlying monad structure. These actions can produce *effects*. It's important to distinguish between evaluating or not evaluating an action, since it can make a drastic difference.

To get a feel for this class, we again look at an example instance—Monad Maybe:

```
ghci> return 1 :: Maybe Int
Just 1
ghci> (Just 1) >>= (\x -> return (x + 1)) :: Maybe Int
Just 2
ghci> (Just 1) >>= (\x -> return (x + 1)) >>= (\x -> return (x * 2))
➥ :: Maybe Int
Just 4
ghci> Nothing >>= (\x -> return (x + 1)) :: Maybe Int
Nothing
```

Just like (<*>) produced Nothing if an argument was Nothing, (>>=) does the same for the first argument! Here, we can see how we can use the bind function to access values inside a monad (in this case, Maybe). The function passed to bind can have arbitrarily complex behavior, using any language features we like, as long as the type signatures check out. This means that we can use bind within the function passed to bind, which allows us to combine an arbitrary number of values that were wrapped in a monadic type. As an example, we can take a look at the function shown in the following listing.

Listing 12.12 Function to monadically add numeric values

```
monadd :: (Num a, Monad m) => m a -> m a -> m a
monadd xm ym =
  xm >>=
    (\x ->               Binds the value inside the monadic value xm to x
      ym >>=
        (\y ->           Binds the value inside the monadic value ym to y
          return $ x + y    Returns the sum of x and y
        )                   as a new monadic value
    )
```

This function receives two monad values, unwrapping them using (>>=) and returning their sum in a new monadic value:

```
ghci> monadd (Just 1) (Just 2) :: Maybe Int
Just 3
ghci> monadd Nothing (Just 2) :: Maybe Int
Nothing
ghci> monadd (Just 1) Nothing :: Maybe Int
Nothing
ghci> monadd Nothing Nothing :: Maybe Int
Nothing
```

By using the bind function, we can construct and compose arbitrary logic when dealing with the aforementioned values. Something of note is that we don't have to worry about failure states. As we can see from the example in listing 12.12, we do not have to worry about a value being `Nothing` (in the case, using `Maybe`). The bind function makes sure we have access to a value or else our term simply evaluates to `Nothing`. This property makes our monads a wonderful candidate to handle *side effects*.

> **NOTE**   Sometimes, we say that Haskell is free of side effects. This is not true. If Haskell had no side effects, it would have no `IO`. Haskell simply doesn't have arbitrary side effects, but instead, it has controlled side effects that are clearly separated from pure code by the type system!

As a matter of fact, we have been working with monads since chapter 3! It turns out that `IO` is a monad. The side effects being produced in `IO` are controlled and handled within the bind function. The `return` function we have used with `IO` is precisely the `return` from the `Monad` type class. It also turns out that we used the bind function for `IO`, without knowing it. The `do` notation provided by Haskell is syntactic sugar for the bind functions!

```
m >>= f
```

This simple term is equivalent to

```
do x <- m
   f x
```

The other bind function is even easier to translate:

```
m1 >> m2
```

This term becomes

```
do _ <- m1
   m2
```

Note how this snippet makes it clear that the first argument will be evaluated. From knowing the relation between `bind` and `do` notation, we can quickly rewrite our example from listing 12.12 to using the `do` notation:

```
monadd' :: (Num a, Monad m) => m a -> m a -> m a
monadd' xm ym = do
  x <- xm
  y <- ym
  return $ x + y
```

The `do` notation makes it clear when and how values from the evaluation of monadic values are being used.

Before we go into a deeper discussion of monads, we first should take a look at how we can use them with our parser. To create a `Monad Parser` instance, we have to define the functions `return` and `(>>=)`. For the implementation of `return`, we can simply use pure from our `Applicative` instance. The `bind` function needs to evaluate the parser given as a first argument and then evaluate the function given as a second argument with the result of this parser and run the resulting parser (from the evaluation of the function) on the rest of the input. This is shown in the following listing. In the case of failure for the first parser, we have to short-circuit, since no value for the function exists, so we simply fail at that point.

Listing 12.13 A `Monad` instance for the parser type

```
instance Monad Parser where
  return = pure              ◄─── Defines return to be pure from
  (>>=) p f =                     the Applicative instance
    Parser $ \t ->
      case runParser p t of  ◄─── Runs the first parser on the given input
        Left msg -> Left msg ◄─── Returns the failed parse result in the
        Right (rest, x) -> runParser (f x) rest  ◄───  case of failure of the first parser
```

Applies the given function to the result from the first parser and runs the resulting parser

---

Using this, we can now use `do` notation to write our parsers!

```
helloWorldP = do
  h <- string "Hello"
  _ <- someSpaces
  w <- string "World"
  return $ h <> " " <> w
```

Compare this to the applicative notation earlier in the chapter; the functionality is still the same. As expected, a failure to parse within the `do` block causes the whole parser to fail:

```
ghci> runParser helloWorldP "Hello World"
Right ("","Hello World")
ghci> runParser helloWorldP "Hello     World"
Right ("","Hello World")
ghci> runParser helloWorldP "Bye Bye World"
Left "failed to parse \"Hello\""
```

However, we did not introduce monads to replace *applicatives* but to extend them. Specifically, we want to be able to make decisions based on parsed values. This could include converting a parsed string, which allows us to improve our `integer` parser from before.

By using `do` notation, we can read the numeric values, just like we did before. Then, by using `readMaybe`, we can detect whether conversion to an `Integer` value failed or succeeded. This would look something like the code shown in the following listing.

Listing 12.14   A parser for integer values

```
import Text.Read (readMaybe)

...

integer :: Parser Integer
integer = do
  intStr <- takeWhile (`elem` ['0' .. '9'])
  case readMaybe (T.unpack intStr) of
    Just value -> return value
    Nothing ->
      Parser $ \_ ->
        Left $
          "Could not convert \""
            ++ T.unpack intStr
            ++ "\" as an integer"
```

Reads numeric characters from the input

Tries to convert the read string to an Integer

Returns the converted value if the conversion was successful

Returns an error message if the conversion was not successful

This parser now safely reads characters from the input and converts a failure in conversion to a failure of the parser. We can do this because monads allow us to act on the value that resulted from the evaluation of a previous action.

Now, we are finally able to construct a parser for our header. We read the magic number, at least one space, the width, at least one space, the height, and then optionally some more spaces and the maximum value based on the magic number. This is achieved with the parser shown in the following listing.

Listing 12.15   A parser for PNM headers

```
headerP :: Parser Header
headerP = do
  magicNumber <-
    choice
      [ magicNumberP1P,
        magicNumberP2P,
        magicNumberP3P,
        magicNumberP4P,
        magicNumberP5P,
        magicNumberP6P
      ]
  _ <- someSpaces
  width <- integer
  _ <- someSpaces
  height <- integer
  maxVal <-
    if magicNumber == P1 || magicNumber == P4
      then return Nothing
      else Just <$> (someSpaces *> integer)
  return Header {..}
```

Parses any of the magic numbers

Parses at least one space and ignores the result

Parses numeric values for the image width and height

Parses at least one space and ignores the result

Parses numeric values for the image width and height

Returns Nothing if the magic number indicates that no magic number should be present in the header

Parses at least on space and then an Integer, which is wrapped in the Just constructor

Constructs the full value for the Header type from the parsed data

The parser for headers presented here uses all the concepts we have discussed so far. The magic number parsers, introduced earlier in this chapter, are combined by `choice`. The first parser in the list that parses the magic number is chosen. Since they parse distinct strings without ambiguity, it doesn't matter in which order we write them down. However, if one parser were to parse only the prefix of another parser, the order would matter. We use `someSpaces` to parse but ignore spaces between the values.

> **NOTE** We use `_ ← someSpaces` to ignore spaces by indicating that the resulting value should not be assigned to any name, thus we are using `_`. We have to do this because the result of `someSpace` is not `()`; otherwise, we could forfeit binding the value. This can be simplified by the `void` function from `Control .Monad` to map the result to `()`. Therefore, it can be rewritten to `void some-Spaces`, which makes it explicit that we are ignoring the result of the action.

Width and height are parsed by the `integer` parser from listing 12.14. The parser for the maximum values is constructed in a new do block. There, we can make a case distinction in relation to a value that was parsed earlier. In the case where we need to parse the maximum value, we also parse some spaces but ignore them, using `(*>)` from the `Applicative` instance. It's worth noting that if any of these parsers fail, the whole parser fails. This is the important property of monads that makes it simpler and easier for us to build more complex applications, all the while not having to think about effects and errors, since they are handled by the `Monad` instance's definition.

12.1.6 A discussion on monads

This section would not be complete without a bit of further discussion on monads. A few things need to be noted about functors, applicatives, and monads:

- They help us separate pure from effectful code with the type system.
- They are only one method of handling effects.
- They are not always referential transparent.
- They follow specific rules.

One of the most important attributes of applicatives and monads is how they help us manage and control effects with pure code. Just from their definitions, the classes we have seen are pure, but what they can do does not have to be pure. The `IO` monad is a prime example. Within the `IO` monad, we can interact with the environment. That is an effect! However, it is not what we typically consider a side effect, since it doesn't happen within our pure functions but outside of them in the `IO` monad. Of course, for Haskell programs to do anything useful, a logical conclusion has to be made: all of our code has to live within the `IO` monad. That is why `main` is of type `IO ()`.

This should make us wonder: Why can't we break out of monads? Why is there no function with type `(Monad m) => m a -> a` that would allow us to access a value inside a monad within pure code? Because it would invalidate the reason we use the monad! The methods given by the `Monad` class only allow us to bring values into the monadic context (using `return`) but not to extract them except for using the bind functions.

This is deliberate. We should not be able to break out of monads without carefully handling whatever state we might manage.

> **NOTE**   A structure that explicitly allows breaking out of it is the *comonad* for which its own package exists on Hackage.

As an example, let us look at the `Maybe` monad. In the case of failure, typically, it assumes the `Nothing` value. A function `Maybe a -> a` cannot be constructed for this type without making the function partial. `fromMaybe`, indeed, gives us the same functionality but requires a default value. So we can break out of the `Maybe` monad, but we need to make sure we can handle a possible error state ourselves. The function that allows unsafely breaking out of a `Maybe` is `fromJust`, which will fail if the value is `Nothing`.

   This property is almost true for `IO`. The function `unsafePerformIO` is able to break out of the `IO` monad. However, using it can lead to unexpected effects, like effects being produced out of order or applied more than once. In more complicated code, `unsafePerformIO` can even lead to type errors at run time.

> **WARNING**   It almost goes without saying, but you should not use `unsafe-PerformIO`. Most problems that can be solved by it can also be solved by some other means. If you are using it, you should really know what you are doing and make sure that its usage will not lead to problems for your program.

Monads are not the be-all and end-all of handling effects; they are one possible way of dealing with effects. Other languages implement their own effect systems, often with partial support. Java requires the programmer to specify which exceptions can be thrown from a method. A calling function is then required to either specify that it could also throw that exception or handle the exception. This is a system of handling effects in the realm of exceptions.

   One reason we want our functions to be pure is *referential transparency*. In short, it means that we can replace a function application with its resulting value without changing the result of the program. Here is a little example:

```
f x = x + 1
```

The term `f 1` will always evaluate to `2`, so it makes no difference whether we substitute `f 1` with the value `2`. All occurrences of `f 1` in our program can be changed to `2`. If all of our functions were referentially transparent, we could replace all of their applications with the result of the same application that happened earlier. Sadly, not everything we do can be referentially transparent. The `IO` monad and actions like `getLine` are a trivial example. Reading user input or data from a file, interacting with the network or other interfaces, or generating random numbers are all not referentially transparent. Luckily, we can (and do) isolate these in the `IO` and other monads. While monads like the `Maybe` monad are referentially transparent, other monads do not have to be.

NOTE It turns out that `Applicative` has more instances than `Monad`. This is important to keep in mind when writing general functions for monadic structures. Sometimes, we can keep functions more general and only have to assume an `Applicative` instance, which enables us to use our code on more types.

12.1.7 How to fail

The last thing we want to deal with is failing. Failure is a part of human nature, and so is the nature of our parsing efforts. Parsing simply might fail. In fact, we have already modeled failed parsing in our functions. `string` and `integer` can fail. Can we generalize this behavior? It turns out that we can through the help of more type classes.

The first is given to us in the `Control.Monad.Fail` module and is called `Monad-Fail`. It was introduced to fix a problem that arises when pattern matching inside a monad. Here is an example:

```
mhead :: (Monad m) => m [a] -> m a
mhead m = do
  (x : _) <- m
  return x
```

This definition of a monadic version of `head` does not compile! The reason is the implicit and incomplete pattern match performed on the list. The pattern match might fail. In this case, it's not clear how to enter an internal failure state in the monad. This is where the `MonadFail` type class comes in, to provide exactly this functionality with the `fail` method. The class is rather simple:

```
class Monad m => MonadFail m where
  fail :: String -> m a
```

`fail` receives an error message (which it can choose to completely ignore) and has to provide a monadic value that responds to the failure. For `Maybe`, this is rather trivial. `fail` simply ignores the message and results in `Nothing`.

We can now change the type of our monadic `head` function:

```
mhead :: (MonadFail m) => m [a] -> m a
mhead m = do
  (x : _) <- m
  return x
```

It now compiles, and we can try it out:

```
ghci> mhead (return [1]) :: Maybe Int
Just 1
ghci> mhead (return []) :: Maybe Int
Nothing
ghci> mhead (return [1]) :: IO Int
1
ghci> mhead (return []) :: IO Int
*** Exception: user error (Pattern match failure in 'do' block at ...
```

In the case of the IO monad, we receive an exception. We have not yet covered how to handle exceptions but will do so in chapter 14.

To handle this and to treat failure more generally, we can provide a MonadFail instance for our Parser type, as shown in the following listing. We have already seen how to encode such a failure state in the definition of empty and the error in the integer parser.

Listing 12.16   A MonadFail instance for the parser type

```
instance MonadFail Parser where
  fail s = Parser $ \t -> Left s
```
◁─┤ Defines a method for failure that wraps an error message in the result type of a parser

This will allow us to use fail whenever we cannot continue parsing. Using this, we can clean up our integer parser:

```
integer :: Parser Integer
integer = do
  intStr <- takeWhile (`elem` ['0' .. '9'])
  case readMaybe (T.unpack intStr) of
    Just value -> return value
    Nothing ->
      fail $
        "Could not convert \""
          ++ T.unpack intStr
          ++ "\" as an integer"
```

Another way of giving monads the capability of failure is the MonadPlus type class. Similar to how Alternative is a monoid for applicatives, MonadPlus is a monoid for monads! Its definition is very similar to Alternative:

```
class (Alternative m, Monad m) => MonadPlus m where
  mzero :: m a
  mplus :: m a -> m a -> m a
```

It turns out that the default implementation for mzero is empty and the default implementation for mplus is (<|>), both from the Alternative type class. If we want to use these default implementations when defining an MonadPlus Parser instance, we can do this in a single line:

```
instance MonadPlus Parser
```

However, we might want to change the error message for the mzero method. This is shown in the following listing.

Listing 12.17   A MonadPlus instance for the parser type

```
import Control.Monad

instance MonadPlus Parser where
  mzero = modifyErrorMessage (const "mzero") empty
```
◁─┘ Returns a parser that defaults to an error message

Using `empty` in this definition is deliberate, since we want to reflect changes in the definition of `empty` in `mzero`. Both should behave similarly. `MonadPlus`, similar to `Alternative`, allows us to implement a failure, the choice between monads (`msum`), and filters on the results of actions (`mfilter`):

```
ghci> import Control.Monad
ghci> smallerTen = mfilter (< 10) integer
ghci> greaterTwenty = mfilter (> 20) integer
ghci> px = msum [smallerTen, greaterTwenty]
ghci> px' = modifyErrorMessage (const "value not < 10 or > 20") px
ghci> runParser px' "1"
("",Right 1)
ghci> runParser px' "100"
("",Right 100)
ghci> runParser px' "15"
("15",Left "value not < 10 or > 20")
```

Note how these functions don't just work for our `Parser` type. They work for *all monads*. Many functions, like `msum` and `mfilter`, are defined in `Control.Monad` and `Control.Applicative`, helping you to compose functionality better.

This concludes our discussion on monads. While it seems like an extraneous diversion, it is very important to understand them. Monadic programming is a paradigm that helps us get our effects under control, and Haskell is unique in that it has support for it in its core language.

So far, our parser can handle the header of our image files. Now, it is time to extend it to finally read the full image data.

12.2 Parsing on a bigger scale

We have covered how to write a composable and failure-resistant parser. Also, we have seen how to implement one for the header of PNM files. Now, it is time to build a parser for the whole image file, meaning parsing the header and continuing to parse the image data. During parsing, we have to validate if there is enough or too much data and if the optional maximum value found in the header is being exceeded.

Furthermore, we need to discuss a problem we have been ignoring so far. Depending on the magic number, the data might not be given to us as `Text` but as bytes. Our parser does not support that. Furthermore, our parser has limitations and lacks support for several things:

- `Parser` does not keep track of the location in the parsed input.
  - Therefore, it does not know how much data has been parsed.
  - Its error messages do not include the position of a syntax error.
- The full input has to be present when parsing.
  - Streamed inputs (from files or a network) are, thus, not supported.
  - We are required to load the full input into memory before we can start parsing.
- We copy all remaining data when taking a slice of the input.

- Only `Text` is supported as input.
  - Binary data cannot be parsed.
  - The parser cannot detect encoding problems and fails with a generic error message.

Solving these problems is not trivial, which is why we want to turn our attention to a new kind of parser that solves all of them. The topic of parsing has been extensively studied in the world of Haskell. A few libraries have come out of this work. Maybe the most influential is the *Parsec* library, which features a parser very similar to the one we have written. The main idea of the library is that monadic parsers can be built from *parser combinators*. These combinators are simply first-class functions. We have already used parser combinators without knowing it, like `takeWhile`, `choice`, and the monadic bind functions.

> ### Exercise: Implementing combinators
> A library that features many useful parser combinators is the *parser-combinators* library. It features functions like `between`, which applies parsers to the beginning, middle, and end of an input, and `skipMany`, which skips zero or more successful applications of a parser. Here are some examples:
>
> ```
> ghci> import Control.Monad.Combinators
> ghci> parenInteger = between (string "(") (string ")") integer
> ghci> runParser parenInteger "(123)"
> ("",Right 123)
> ghci> runParser parenInteger "(123"
> ("",Left "failed to parse \")\"")
> ghci> skipSpaces = skipMany $ string " "
> ghci> integerWithSpaces = between skipSpaces skipSpaces integer
> ghci> runParser integerWithSpaces "  123   "
> ("",Right 123)
> ```
>
> Look up the functions that the library provides, and try to reimplement them yourself!

State-of-the-art parser combinator libraries for Haskell include *Megaparsec* and *Attoparsec*. Megaparsec is the Swiss Army Knife of parser combinator libraries. It can be used to parse text or bytes, features great support for detailed error messages, and features a wide variety of methods to better control how a parser behaves. Attoparsec, on the other hand, is a highly specialized library for constructing parsers for raw byte data with a focus on performance. A notable feature is the built-in support for incremental input, so parsing large files can be achieved without loading the complete file contents into memory before beginning parsing. However, it should be noted that since the parsers support arbitrary backtracking, the whole input will reside in memory once it is fully supplied to the parser.

For our purposes, we want to shift our attention to Attoparsec and construct a parser for PNM files with it. In fact, this should be an easy switch, since the parsers in the library behave just like our parser, for the most part. Just like our library, Attoparsec features a `string` function. However, the parsers are not working with `Text` but the `ByteString` type. This type has similar functions to `Text`, provided by the `bytestring` package, so we can treat it as a drop-in replacement to how we usually worked with text data.

A `ByteString` is a list-like data structure with values of type `Word8` as its elements, which are 8-bit unsigned integers. This means that single characters are just integers between `0` and `255`. The `Data.ByteString.Internal` module provides us with the functions `c2w` and `w2c` to transform `Char` to `Word8` and back if we want to use our normal `Char` type in conjunction with `ByteString`. Luckily for us, the instance `IsString ByteString` already exists, so we can write down normal strings and have them reinterpreted as `ByteString`.

12.2.1 *An introduction to Attoparsec*

For us to use the new type and new library, we will have to add `bytestring` and `attoparsec` to our dependencies in package.yaml. With that done, let us experiment with the new types. An Attoparsec parser consists of very simple building blocks. Its central type is the `Parser` type, which is used to parse `ByteString` values. This type and most functions needed for parsing can be imported from the `Data.Attoparsec.ByteString` module. There also exists the `Data.Attoparsec.Text` module that exposes equivalent functions and types that work with `Text` values, just like our parser did. However, since we need to deal with binary data, we will choose the former:

```
ghci> import Data.Attoparsec.ByteString as AP
ghci> AP.parse (AP.string "Hello") "Hello"
Done "" "Hello"
ghci> AP.parse (AP.string "Hello") "hello"
Fail "hello" [] "string"
ghci> AP.parse (AP.string "Hello") "He"
Partial _
```

We import the module in GHCi with a qualified name so that we can use it without its names clashing with the module of our own parser. As we can see, the module exports a `string` function of type `ByteString -> Parser ByteString` that works just like our `string` function before. `parse` is a function of type `Parser a -> ByteString -> Result a` that applies a parser to a given input. The `Result` type is slightly different from what we have built in our parser. It has three constructors: `Done` for a successful parse, `Fail` in the case of failure, and `Partial` if a parser did not strictly fail but did not have enough input to finish the parse. `Done` and `Fail` carry the rest of the unparsed input in their first field. However, `Partial` holds a continuation function that can be used on the rest of the input:

```
ghci> Partial c = AP.parse (AP.string "Hello") "He"
ghci> Partial c2 = c "l"
ghci> c2 "lo"
Done "" "Hello"
```

In this example, we ignore the compiler warnings from our incomplete pattern matches. As we can see, the functions in the partial result can be used for incrementally parsing input. In this chapter, we are largely uninterested in this feature and only parse whole inputs. For this, we can use the `parseOnly` function of type `Parser a -> ByteString -> Either String a`, which is incredibly similar to our `runParser` function. They both work the same. The result from `parseOnly` cannot be `Partial` and either succeeds or fails.

We have a nice collection of functions for building a parser:

- `word8 :: Word8 -> Parser Word8`—Reads a specific byte from the input
- `anyWord8 :: Parser Word8`—Reads any byte from the input
- `string :: ByteString -> Parser ByteString`—Reads a specific string of bytes
- `skipWhile :: (Word8 -> Bool) -> Parser ()`—Skips bytes as long as a given predicate is valid
- `take :: Int -> Parser ByteString`—Reads a specific number of bytes
- `takeWhile :: (Word8 -> Bool) -> Parser ByteString`—Reads bytes as long as a given predicate is valid

As we can see, most of these functions are specialized to deal with `Word8`. If we want to use `Char` instead, we can alternatively use the `Data.Attoparsec.ByteString.Char8` module, which exposes functions for parsing ASCII letters and digits and generally makes it easier to work with `Char` values.

12.2.2 Parsing images

Now, we can get serious about parsing our image data. First, let us define the data types we are working with. We already have a type for our header, but we want to provide a small adjustment. The absolute maximum value for any data in PNM files is **65535**, which is the maximum value of a 16-bit unsigned integer. This can be represented with `Word16` from the `Data.Word` module. Therefore, we will switch out the `Maybe Integer` for our optional maximum value with `Maybe Word16`. The actual raw data is just a bunch of `Word16` values. We could aim for a more compact way of storing the pixel values, since it is somewhat wasteful to use 16 bits for a bitmap, but we are not optimizing our framework at this point. The types are shown in the following listing.

Listing 12.18   Types for parsing PNM files

```
data MagicNumber = P1 | P2 | P3 | P4 | P5 | P6      ◁──┐  Defines a type for
  deriving (Eq, Show)                                   │  the magic numbers

data Header = Header                           ◁──┐  Defines a type
  { magicNumber :: MagicNumber,                    │  for the header
    width :: Integer,                              │  of PNM files
    height :: Integer,
    maxVal :: Maybe Word16
  }
  deriving (Eq, Show)
```

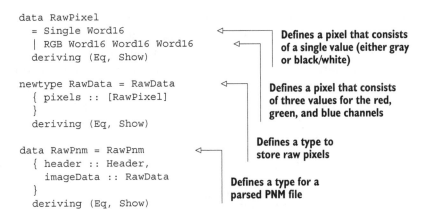

```
data RawPixel
  = Single Word16
  | RGB Word16 Word16 Word16
  deriving (Eq, Show)

newtype RawData = RawData
  { pixels :: [RawPixel]
  }
  deriving (Eq, Show)

data RawPnm = RawPnm
  { header :: Header,
    imageData :: RawData
  }
  deriving (Eq, Show)
```

Defines a pixel that consists of a single value (either gray or black/white)

Defines a pixel that consists of three values for the red, green, and blue channels

Defines a type to store raw pixels

Defines a type for a parsed PNM file

To construct a parser for the header using Attoparsec, we have to make a small adjustment to our initial parser for the header. We will take the opportunity to replace the functions we have written ourselves with the ones provided by the library. In the following code listings, we will assume these modules to be imported:

```
import Data.Attoparsec.ByteString
import qualified Data.Attoparsec.ByteString.Char8 as C8
import qualified Data.ByteString as BS
```

With these modules covered, we can get to work on parsing our header. Parsing the magic number has not changed from our previous implementation of a parser. Since the library's `Parser` type has a `Functor`, `Applicative`, and `Monad` instance equivalent to our definitions, we can use the `(<$)` operator to parse input and return a `Magic-Number`, as we can see in the following listing.

Listing 12.19 Parsers for PNM magic numbers

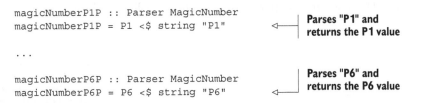

```
magicNumberP1P :: Parser MagicNumber
magicNumberP1P = P1 <$ string "P1"
```

Parses "P1" and returns the P1 value

```
...
```

```
magicNumberP6P :: Parser MagicNumber
magicNumberP6P = P6 <$ string "P6"
```

Parses "P6" and returns the P6 value

This way, we can parse a fixed string and instantly translate it to a Haskell value.

NOTE Using the `OverloadedStrings`, we can omit using `string` for fixed string parsers. It suffices to just write down the string like so: `P1 <$ "P1"`. However, this might not be as readable as using `string` explicitly, which is why we choose to not take this shortcut in this chapter.

The `Data.Attoparsec.ByteString.Char8` module also provides us with a replacement for the `integer` parser with the `decimal` parser of type `Integral a => Parser a` that parses decimal values. One problem we have to solve is skipping whitespace. In the PNM format, a whitespace is any of the following characters: ' ', \n, \r, \f, \v, and \t. Similar to before, we can use `satisfy` and check if a given `Char` is one that we consider whitespace. However, at certain points, we want to parse at least one whitespace character. For this, we can use `skipMany1`, which applies a given parser at least once and ignores the read values entirely. This is shown in the following listing.

Listing 12.20   A parser to skip whitespaces

```
import Control.Monad (void)

. . .

whitespace :: Parser ()              Ignores the result,
whitespace =                         mapping it to ()
  void $
    C8.satisfy $                     Reads a single character
      \c ->                          that satisfies a predicate
        c == ' '
           || c == '\n'              Defines a predicate
           || c == '\t'              for whitespaces in
           || c == '\r'              PNM files
           || c == '\v'
           || c == '\f'

whitespaces :: Parser ()             Skips at least
whitespaces = skipMany1 whitespace   one whitespace
```

Next, we also want to be able to parse (and then ignore) comments that might occur in the header. Such a comment starts with the % character and ends at some point in a newline. We can translate this into a parser by using the `char :: Char -> Parser Char` parser to read the character and `takeWhile` to read characters until a newline has been found. This code for the parser is shown in the following listing.

Listing 12.21   A parser for comments

```
                                                          Reads a % character and then
                                                          continues to read characters
comment :: Parser BS.ByteString                           until a newline is found,
comment = C8.char '%' >> C8.takeWhile (/= '\n')           returning the string that was
                                                          read after the % character
```

Of note is that this parser requires to read a comment, so if we want to use it to optionally parse a comment, we need to ignore failures. In our header, we want to ignore whitespaces and comments. Sadly, we don't know when they will occur in the header, so we need to ignore them in between the magic number and other values we are reading. For this, we can construct another parser, to skip this extraneous information.

Listing 12.22 A parser to skip whitespaces and comments

```
skipWhitespace :: Parser ()
skipWhitespace =
  option () $
    choice
      [ comment >> skipWhitespace,
        whitespaces >> skipWhitespace
      ]
```

Makes the parser optional, always returning ()

Runs the following parsers and applies the effects of the one that succeeded in parsing

Parses a comment and makes a recursive call to the parser

Parses a whitespace and makes a recursive call to the parser

As we can see in listing 12.22, we can construct this parser that skips whitespace by providing a choice of either reading a comment or whitespaces and then recursively calling the parser again to read another comment or set of whitespaces. However, what if we encounter real data and parsing of these things fails? To cover this, we are using `option :: Alternative f => a -> f a -> f a`, which tries to apply the action from the second argument and if that fails, provides a default value given by the first argument.

We can now combine all of these parsers to parse our new header type from listing 12.18. Between the elements of the parser, we allow arbitrary comments and whitespaces, using `skipWhitespace`. At the end of the header, we also parse a single whitespace, since the specification requires a header to end on one. This time, we are using `decimal` from `Data.Attoparsec.ByteString.Char8` to parse `Word16` values. Apart from this, not much has changed from our last implementation. The code for the new parser is shown in the following listing.

Listing 12.23 A parser for PNM headers with Attoparsec

```
headerP :: Parser Header
headerP = do
  skipWhitespace
  magicNumber <-
    choice
      [ magicNumberP1P,
        magicNumberP2P,
        magicNumberP3P,
        magicNumberP4P,
        magicNumberP5P,
        magicNumberP6P
      ]
  skipWhitespace
  width <- C8.decimal
  skipWhitespace
  height <- C8.decimal
  maxVal <- do
    if magicNumber == P1 || magicNumber == P4
      then return Nothing
      else Just <$> (skipWhitespace *> C8.decimal)
  whitespace
  return Header {..}
```

Parses the magic number of the PNM file

Parses decimal values for width and height

Parses another decimal value on demand as the maximum value

With the header taken care of, we can now go to parsing image data.

12.2.3 *Choosing between formats*

The different formats in the PNM file format all encode their data differently. Let us review the different formats. For the magic numbers P1 (bitmap), P2 (graymap), and P3 (pixmap), the data is encoded in ASCII. For bitmaps, there are only two possible values, which are 1 and 0 and for graymaps and pixmaps, the accepted values depend on the maximum value given in the header. Pixel values are single-decimal values for graymaps and three-decimal values for each pixel in the pixmap. The magic numbers P4 (bitmap), P5 (graymap), and P6 (pixmap) have similar rules. However, the data is encoded in binary. For the binary bitmap, each *bit* corresponds to a single pixel, where the pixels appear in the same order the bits do, meaning the file has to be read byte by byte, parsing the bits from most-significant bit to least-significant bit. When the number of pixels that have to be read is not cleanly divisible by 8, the superfluous bits are ignored. For binary graymaps and pixmaps, the same rules apply as for their ASCII counterparts. However, a special rule applies based on the maximum value. By default, a single byte constitutes a value. If the maximum value is greater than 255, the value cannot fit into a single byte, and thus, two bytes have to be read for each pixel value.

Let us begin by writing parsers for the ASCII-encoded files. For now, we are only interested in parsing single pixels, and we will use them later to parse the full data. From our previous discussion, we know that the pixel data for bitmaps comes down to parsing constants (1 and 0). Parsing graymaps and pixmaps requires us to parse decimal values. In our parser, we do not immediately check whether the maximum value given in the header is exceeded or not. We are just interested in parsing the raw data present in the files. The code for these parsers is shown in the following listing.

Listing 12.24 Parsers for ASCII-encoded PNM image data

```
p1PixelP :: Parser RawPixel
p1PixelP =
  Single
    <$> choice
      [ 1 <$ C8.char '1',
        0 <$ C8.char '0'
      ]
```
Parses only 1 and 0 characters and maps them to the appropriate values

```
p2PixelP :: Parser RawPixel
p2PixelP = Single <$> C8.decimal
```
Parses a single decimal value

```
p3PixelP :: Parser RawPixel
p3PixelP = do
  r <- C8.decimal
  whitespaces
  g <- C8.decimal
  whitespaces
  b <- C8.decimal
  return $ RGB r g b
```
Parses three decimal values as an RGB pixel value

The `decimal` parser of type `Integral a => Parser a` can parse any integral values. Haskell can infer that the value being parsed in our instances is of type `Word16`, since these are the types given for the constructors. In the implementation for `p1PixelP` and `p2PixelP`, we are using `(<$>)` to apply the constructor for a single value to the parsed data. For `p3PixelP`, we make use of the `do` notation to parse an arbitrary amount of whitespaces between decimal values, since the specification for the file format does not enforce a fixed amount of whitespaces between values.

With the ASCII-encoded pixels taken care of, we can tackle the binary formats next. First, let us discuss graymaps and pixmaps, since bitmaps are somewhat special. For these two formats, we actually need two parsers for each magic number, since we either need to read a single byte (`Word8`) or two bytes (`Word16`) to get the values. Attoparsec already provides us with the `anyWord8 :: Parser Word8` parser that reads a single byte. However, there is no `anyWord16` parser for us to use, meaning we have to construct our own.

To write this parser, we have to think a bit about how to combine multiple bytes into a larger word. Assume we have two bytes, which are immediately next to each other. We want to read them as a `Word16`. What we can do is read the first and then the second byte consecutively. To combine them, we have to reinterpret them as 16-bit words and shift the first byte 8 places to the left. That way, the byte will fill up the first 8 bits of the 16-bit word and make room in its lower half for the byte that was read after it. Assuming that shifting the values to the left only leaves 0 behind, where the first byte was written down, we can insert the second byte by doing a bitwise OR operation. This way, the values that are 0 in the second byte stay 0 and the values that are 1 become 1.

Such *low-level* operations are given to us by the `Data.Bits` module. There, we find the `Bits` type class, which defines bit-wise operations for various datatypes, among which are our word types `Word8` and `Word16`. In this class, we also find the methods `shift :: a -> Int -> a`, which shifts a value to the left and the `(.|.) :: a -> a -> a` operator, which performs a bitwise OR operation. Let's quickly experiment:

```
ghci> import Data.Word
ghci> import Data.Bits
ghci> byte1 = 1 :: Word8
ghci> byte2 = 1 :: Word8
ghci> shift byte1 8
0
ghci> shift (fromIntegral byte1 :: Word16) 8
256
ghci> byte1_16 = fromIntegral byte1 :: Word16
ghci> byte2_16 = fromIntegral byte2 :: Word16
ghci> shift byte1_16 8 .|. byte2_16
257
```

As we can see, shifting a `Word8` with a single bit (as its least significant bit) by 8 places results in 0, since we are running out of space in a single byte. Converting it to a

Word16 by using fromIntegral, however, makes space for the bit to be shifted. As we can also see, shifting one byte by 8 places and performing a bitwise OR with a second byte effectively combines the two in the order we want. This is shown in figure 12.6.

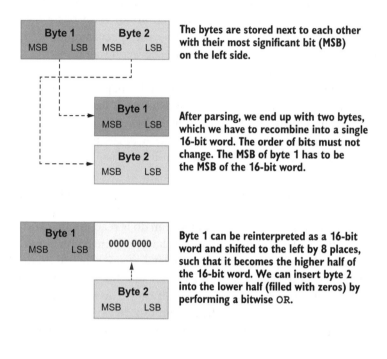

Figure 12.6 The process of combining two bytes into a 16-bit word

We can use this to build our anyWord16 parser by reading two bytes and combining them in the aforementioned way. Its implementation is shown in the following listing.

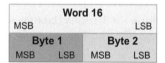

Listing 12.25 Parser for 16-bit words

```
import Data.Bits

...

anyWord16 :: Parser Word16
anyWord16 = do
  h <- fromIntegral <$> anyWord8
  l <- fromIntegral <$> anyWord8
  return $ shift h 8 .|. l
```

Reads an 8-bit word and converts it to a 16-bit word

Combines both values into a single 16-bit word

Again, we are using `fromIntegral` to convert our `Word8` values to `Word16` for the bit-wise operations to work. With this functionality taken care of, we can construct parsers for gray- and pixmaps in an 8-bit and 16-bit variety. Their implementation, shown in the following listing, is straightforward enough, since we do not have to worry about whitespaces this time.

Listing 12.26   Parsers for binary encoded PNM files in 8-bit and 16-bit variants

```
p5PixelWord8P :: Parser RawPixel
p5PixelWord8P = Single <$> (fromIntegral <$> anyWord8)      ◁──┐  Reads a single
                                                               │  8-bit word

p5PixelWord16P :: Parser RawPixel
p5PixelWord16P = Single <$> anyWord16        ◁──┐  Reads a single
                                                │  16-bit word

p6PixelWord8P :: Parser RawPixel
p6PixelWord8P = RGB <$> p <*> p <*> p       ◁──┐  Reads three
  where                                        │  8-bit words
     p = fromIntegral <$> anyWord8


p6PixelWord16P :: Parser RawPixel
p6PixelWord16P = RGB <$> anyWord16 <*>          ┐  Reads three
➡ anyWord16 <*> anyWord16                 ◁─────┘  16-bit words
```

Now, all that is left is to work with binary bitmaps. As mentioned earlier, we have to parse these files bitwise, meaning each bit is a pixel value. We are not able to parse a file bitwise, so we have to rethink how to extract the values from the bytes we read. Again, the `Bits` type class from `Data.Bits` provides us with a helpful function to achieve this, called `testBit :: a -> Int -> Bool`, which lets us check the bit of a value at a certain offset. Using this function, we can parse a single byte and return eight pixel values from it. This is shown in the following listing, where we can see the implementation for the parser for pixel values in the binary pixmap format.

Listing 12.27   A parser for binary-encoded bitmaps

```
p4PixelP ::
  Parser
    ( RawPixel,
      RawPixel,
      RawPixel,
      RawPixel,
      RawPixel,
      RawPixel,
      RawPixel,
      RawPixel
    )
p4PixelP = do                        ┐  Reads a single
  w <- anyWord8            ◁──────────┘  8-bit word              ┐  Defines a function to
  let parseBitAtIndex n =                                        │  parse a specific bit
       Single $ if testBit w n then 1 else 0   ◁────────────────┘  from an 8-bit word
```

```
return
  ( parseBitAtIndex 7,
    parseBitAtIndex 6,
    parseBitAtIndex 5,
    parseBitAtIndex 4,          Returns each bit of
    parseBitAtIndex 3,          the parsed word
    parseBitAtIndex 2,          separately
    parseBitAtIndex 1,
    parseBitAtIndex 0
  )
```

In this implementation, we parse each bit separately in a tuple, as we already know how many bits are in a `Word8` value. We parse these values from the most significant to the least significant bit as specified for PNM files. This way, we have access to each bit value. However, when parsing the full file, we need to make sure we ignore superfluous bits that are not part of the image anymore (if the total amount of pixels for the image is not cleanly divisible by 8). With parsers constructed for single-pixel values, we can now construct a parser for the body of our image files.

12.2.4 *Putting parsers together*

The parser for our image file bodies can be constructed by doing a case distinction on the already parsed header and based on the magic number and maximum value given, we select one of the parsers from the previous subsection to read the data. Since all parsers except for the binary bitmap parser read a single `RawPixel` value, we can simply repeat its application as many times as we need pixels (the width times the height of the image). Additionally, we construct an optional whitespace parser that we can use for our ASCII-encoded data. For bitmaps, whitespaces are not necessary in the data, but we will still allow them to catch newlines, for example. For binary graymaps and pixmaps, we have to select the correct parser based on the maximum value given. Otherwise, we ignore it. We do this because our parser should not fail at this stage if a value is larger than the maximum value from the header. We want to check such properties later. The only special case is the handling of binary bitmaps, which have to be parsed a bit differently. We will cover this case soon. For now, let us discuss the implementation of the image data parser given in the following listing.

Listing 12.28 A parser for image data in PNM files

```
dataP :: Header -> Parser RawData
dataP (Header {..}) = do
  pixels <- case (magicNumber, maxVal) of
    (P1, _) -> count' $ whitespaces' *> p1PixelP
    (P2, _) -> count' $ whitespaces' *> p2PixelP
    (P3, _) -> count' $ whitespaces' *> p3PixelP
    (P4, _) -> p4DataP width' height'
    (P5, Just mv) ->
      count' $
```

Parses the image data in the appropriate format defined by the headers magic number, repeating a specific parser a fixed amount of times

```
        if mv <= 255
          then p5PixelWord8P
          else p5PixelWord16P
    (P6, Just mv) ->
      count' $
        if mv <= 255
          then p6PixelWord8P
          else p6PixelWord16P
    _ ->
      error $
        "Internal error: "
          ++ show magicNumber
          ++ " without maximum value in header!"
  return $ RawData pixels
  where
    whitespaces' = option () whitespaces
    count' = count (width' * height')
    width' = fromInteger width
    height' = fromInteger height
```

Parses single pixels with the appropriate bit width

Throws an error if the header is malformed

Defines a parser that optionally skips whitespaces

Defines a combinator that runs a parser as many times as there should be pixels in the image data

Parses the image data in the appropriate format defined by the headers magic number, repeating a specific parser a fixed amount of times

The count' function applies a given parser as many times as we need. The case on the magic number and maximum value provides the correct action that is evaluated to read the pixels value. Our type permits that P5 and P6 can occur without a maximum value. However, this is not allowed and should result in an internal error. If this happens, the header parser should have failed. So if we run into this problem, it means that our header parser is somehow exhibiting incorrect behavior.

As we can see, all of our parsers are used with count', except for the parser for binary bitmaps. That's because we never read a single RawPixel value from the parser but eight at a time. We have to construct an algorithm that parses the values from a byte but stops once enough values have been parsed. Furthermore, these binary bitmaps contain a raster of values. Each row is defined by as many bits as the width of the image specifies. However, these rows are packed in bytes! This means each row can contain some extra bits, which have to be ignored. According to the specification, we can simply ignore these extraneous bits. To achieve this, we can define a recursive action that parses each row separately by recursively reading as many bits as needed and ignoring the rest. Then, we can concatenate the rows into one large list of RawPixel values. This implementation is shown in the following listing.

Listing 12.29 A parser for image data in binary bitmap files

```
p4DataP :: Int -> Int -> Parser [RawPixel]
p4DataP width height = do
  rows <- count height (reverse <$> readRow width [])
  return $ concat rows
  where
    readRow n pxs
```

Read as many rows as the height of the image.

```
 | n <= 0 = return pxs                                         ◄──────────┐  Returns the
 | otherwise = do                                                         │  read pixels when
     (b7, b6, b5, b4, b3, b2, b1, b0) <- p4PixelP        ◄───────┐        │  finished reading
     case n of                                                   │
       1 -> return $ b7 : pxs                                    │           Parse a byte with the
       2 -> return $ b6 : b7 : pxs                               │           parser and extract the
       3 -> return $ b5 : b6 : b7 : pxs                          │           single-pixel values.
       4 -> return $ b4 : b5 : b6 : b7 : pxs
       5 -> return $ b3 : b4 : b5 : b6 : b7 : pxs
       6 -> return $ b2 : b3 : b4 : b5 : b6 : b7 : pxs
       7 -> return $ b1 : b2 : b3 : b4 : b5 : b6 : b7 : pxs
       8 -> return $ b0 : b1 : b2 : b3 : b4 : b5 : b6 : b7 : pxs
       _ ->
         readRow                                          ◄──────────────┐  Recursively parses
           (n - 8)                                                       │  more bytes until the
           (b0 : b1 : b2 : b3 : b4 : b5 : b6 : b7 : pxs)                 │  specified amount of
                                                                         │  pixels in a row has
  Returns the correct amount of bits if there is less                    │  been read
  than one byte to be read from the parser source
```

Here, we have to be careful when considering the order of bits. We parse the bits from most- to least-significant bit, but we add them in reverse order to the resulting list for each row. These lists are then reversed. We keep track of how many elements we need to read in `readRow` so that once we need less than nine, we can just the right amount of values to the result.

NOTE   We add the values in the reversed order for performance. Otherwise, we couldn't prepend elements using the `(:)` constructor but would need to use the append function `(++)`. The append function is very expensive, since it needs to traverse the whole list before adding new elements. Doing this recursively quickly becomes infeasible for large lists. It is cheaper to add elements in the reverse order and then reverse the whole result afterward.

After all rows have been read, we can concatenate all values to receive our full data of `[RawPixel]`. With the parsing for all formats taken care of, we can put all the pieces together!

With `headerP` and `dataP`, we have constructed parsers for both the header and body of our image files. Now, we put them together to construct a parser for generic PNM files. This is shown in the following listing.

Listing 12.30   A parser and function to parse PNM files

```
pnmP :: Parser RawPnm                          Parses the header
pnmP = do
  header <- headerP                       ◄────┤  Parses the image data
  imageData <- dataP header               ◄────┘  based on the header
  option () whitespaces                   ◄──────  Skips any
  return RawPnm {..}                              trailing spaces          Parses a PNM image from a
                                                                           bytestring expecting the
parsePnm :: BS.ByteString -> Either String RawPnm                         parser to reach the end of
parsePnm = parseOnly (pnmP <* endOfInput)                          ◄────── the string, failing otherwise
```

```
readPnmFile :: FilePath -> IO (Either String RawPnm)
readPnmFile path = parsePnm <$> BS.readFile path
```
◁── **Parses a PNM file expecting the parser to reach the end of the file, failing otherwise**

After reading the header and data, we additionally skip any whitespace that potentially still exists in the file. We do this so that we can be sure that we have reached the end of the file. In `parsePnm`, we actively enforce that a parse has to fail if we have not read the full input, which we do by using `endOfInput`. If the application of `pnmP` has not resulted in the parser halting at the end of the file, `endOfInput` will simply fail.

> ### Exercise: Parsing multiple images
> The parser we have shown in this chapter is only capable of reading a single PNM image from a file. However, the specification allows for multiple images to be present in a single file. Can you modify our parsing functions to allow this?

If you want to try out our newly built parser, the repository for this book provides sample images in different sizes and formats.

We have built a parser for the PNM file format and can read image data from files. In the next chapter, we will worry about processing this data using parallelism to speed up execution.

Summary

- Functors are used to modify a value that results from the evaluation of an effect in a referentially transparent way.
- Applicatives can be used to compose effectful actions, like processing input or parsing contents from files.
- `Alternative` gives an applicative the possibility to choose between succeeding and failing actions, like, for example, giving a parser the possibility to return an error message from deep within a recursively structured parse.
- Monads can be used to compose effectful actions, while making the results of previous actions influence the new result, effectively chaining the actions while still keeping consistent handling of errors.
- `MonadFail` is used to give a monadic type the possibility to fail, which is used to make the monad go into a failure state explicitly.
- `MonadPlus` is the monadic counterpart to `Alternative`, giving monads the capability of choosing between succeeding and failing actions.
- Bit-level operations can be achieved with functions from `Data.Bits` when we need to manipulate numbers and byte strings on a low level.

Parallel image processing 13

This chapter covers

- Working with generalized algebraic data types
- Safely avoiding return-type polymorphism
- Writing a generic algorithm for transforming image data
- Improving performance using parallelism

In the last chapter, we built a parser for PNM files, a simple image format. While we have covered the possibility of reading these files, we have not yet created a way of transforming them and writing them back to the filesystem. That will change with this chapter.

We want to cover using Haskell's type system to create a data type that can dynamically store data of various types without needing to use parametric polymorphism while still being able to retrieve type information on this data later on. Then, we define a validation for our parsed data as well as a generic way of mapping data of different types. Finally, we cover how to perform work in parallel and more than double our program's performance by using one single line of code.

13.1 Providing type information to the caller

The last chapter was all about parsing images in the portable anymap format (PNM). Now that we have these images in our program, we should do something with them. Let's process them! More specifically, we want to build a generic way of changing the pixels of our image programmatically. This will enable us to write different filters, like

- Grayscale
- Pixelation
- Blur

To speed things up, we will use parallelism to make use of multicore CPUs. Ultimately, we want to store our images (processed or not) in the PNG format on the drive, for which we are going to use the *JuicyPixels* library.

13.1.1 Problems with return-type polymorphism

First, let us recap where we left off. We have written a parser to read files in the PNM format, which reads the file data and produces a representation in Haskell using the RawPnm type. The type we have introduced is shown in the following listing.

Listing 13.1 Types for parsing PNM files

```
data MagicNumber = P1 | P2 | P3 | P4 | P5 | P6        ◁──┐  Defines a type for
   deriving (Eq, Show)                                    │  the magic numbers

data Header = Header                          ◁──┐  Defines a type for the
   { magicNumber :: MagicNumber,                  │  header of PNM files
     width :: Integer,
     height :: Integer,
     maxVal :: Maybe Word16
   }                                                 Defines a pixel that consists
   deriving (Eq, Show)                               of a single value (either
                                                     gray or black/white)
data RawPixel
   = Single Word16                            ◁──┐  Defines a pixel that consists
   | RGB Word16 Word16 Word16                 ◁──┤  of three values for the red,
   deriving (Eq, Show)                             green, and blue channels

newtype RawData = RawData                     ◁──┐  Defines a type to
   { pixels :: [RawPixel]                          │  store raw pixels
   }
   deriving (Eq, Show)

data RawPnm = RawPnm                          ◁──┐  Defines a type for
   { header :: Header,                             │  a parsed PNM file
     imageData :: RawData
   }
   deriving (Eq, Show)
```

These types are a representation of the raw data that was read from a file. The values of these types come straight from the parser, meaning no validation has been done on them. This is the first thing we should take care of. From the last chapter, we are left with the module structure shown in the following listing for our PNM parsing code.

> **Listing 13.2   The module structure found in chapter 12**

```
src/
└── Graphics
    ├── PNM
    │   ├── Parsing.hs
    │   └── Types.hs
    └── PNM.hs
```

We now want to create a `Graphics.PNM.Validation` module, which will provide functions to take care of validation. To recap, PNM files can be in bitmap, graymap, and pixmap format and can be encoded in ASCII or binary. This is signified by a magic number given in the file's header. Based on the format, pixels are either encoded as single numbers (bitmap or graymap) or by three numbers (pixmap). Additionally, the format specifies a maximum value in its header that specifies what the maximum numerical value for a color value should be.

The parser written in the previous chapter does not validate the data it parses. Validation needs to include a few steps to check the following:

- The number of pixels read is equal to the width times the height from the header
- The type of pixels read matches the magic number in the header
- The color values of pixels never exceed the maximum value given in the header

This process should return us some type that we can safely work with. How would that type look? First, how would a type for our pixels look? Since we know that PNM files are either 8- or 16-bit encoded, we want to keep this differentiation. In our parser, we encoded 8-bit values with a `Word16`, which is a bit wasteful, so let's not continue doing this. Types for our pixels could look like this:

```
import Data.Word (Word8, Word16)

data Pixel8Bit = Pixel8Bit Word8 Word8 Word8

data Pixel16Bit = Pixel16Bit Word16 Word16 Word16
```

However, we don't have to reinvent the wheel. These types are already provided by the JuicyPixels package, which we will use for converting PNM data to PNG images later! Therefore, it makes sense to incorporate the types of this package into our image type.

For this, we add `JuicyPixels` to dependencies in our package.yaml file. Now, we can use the `PixelRGB8` and `PixelRGB16` types from the `Codec.Picture` module. Additionally, the module provides the `Pixel8` and `Pixel16` types for grayscale pixels, which will also come in handy:

```
ghci> :t PixelRGB8
PixelRGB8 :: Pixel8 -> Pixel8 -> Pixel8 -> PixelRGB8
ghci> :t PixelRGB16
```

```
PixelRGB16 :: Pixel16 -> Pixel16 -> Pixel16 -> PixelRGB16
ghci> :i Pixel8
type Pixel8 :: *
type Pixel8 = Word8
ghci> :i Pixel16
type Pixel16 :: *
type Pixel16 = Word16
```

How will we later use this package to write our data as a PNG? For this, the library provides a `DynamicImage` type, which internally encodes the type of image that is being saved in terms of bit depth, color, or grayscale and color model. To correctly use this type later, we need to keep track of the type of pixels we are using.

Now, we can ask the question of how we can construct our image type. A simple type containing basic information on the image could look like this:

```
import qualified Codec.Picture as P

data PnmImage = PnmImage
  { width :: Int,
    height :: Int,
    pixels :: Either [P.PixelRGB8] [P.PixelRGB16]
  }
```

However, if we also want to store grayscale pixels, we need some type similar to `Either` that gives us four choices. Doing so might leave us with the following type:

```
data ArbitraryPixels
  = Pixels8Bit [P.PixelRGB8]
  | Pixels16Bit [P.PixelRGB16]
  | GrayPixels8Bit [P.Pixel8]
  | GrayPixels16Bit [P.Pixel16]

data PnmImage = PnmImage
  { width :: Int,
    height :: Int,
    pixels :: ArbitraryPixels
  }
```

This solution seems fine at first but isn't really practical. First of all, it is impossible to specify that a certain function only accepts images with a certain pixel type, since the type `Image` has no parameter. Working with this type will always result in us having to match on the constructor of `pixels` to figure out the internal type. Furthermore, the PNM format has an extension to also use 32-bit pixel values. If we ever wanted to support that, we would need to further extend this type and all functions that match on it. So our solution isn't really practical.

We can solve this by adding a parameter to our `Image` type. This way, we can specify what type of image we are dealing with in the type system:

```
data PnmImage px = PnmImage
  { width :: Int,
```

```
    height :: Int,
    pixels :: [px]
  }
```

However, this raises a new problem. How should the validation function we are trying to build look? What is the type of this function? They might look something like this:

```
validatePnm :: RawPnm -> Either String (PnmImage px)
```

This looks fine until we think about where the type variable px is being decided. We cannot decide the type of px inside validatePnm, since Haskell uses return-type polymorphism, as we have covered in chapter 9. This means that the *caller* of a function decides the return type of a function! However, that is completely backward for our purposes. The caller cannot know what type of image is expected before validation. The validatePnm function should decide what kind of image it is, check it for validity, and then produce the fitting value. How can we shift the responsibility of choosing the type to this function?

13.1.2 *Generalized algebraic data types*

Our problem is a very simple one. The caller has no way of deciding the type of the validation function before calling it, so its type should be polymorphic. However, when we want to work with the parsing result, we need a way of *refining* the type. This means we need a way to take the polymorphic type and *refine* it to a concrete type. This functionality is provided by an extension to Haskell's type system, called *generalized algebraic data types* (GADTs). We can enable them with the language extension GADTs.

GADTs are largely equivalent to the usual algebraic data types we work with. They consist of constructors that consist of fields. However, the first difference we encounter is the syntax we use for GADTs:

```
{-# LANGUAGE GADTs #-}

...

data MyAdt a
  = AdtCons1 Int Float String
  | AdtCons2 Bool a

data MyGADT a where
  GadtCons1 :: Int -> Float -> String -> MyGADT a
  GadtCons2 :: Bool -> a -> MyGADT a
```

These two data types are equivalent. MyAdt and MyGadt have equivalent constructors with equivalent fields and (most importantly) equivalent types. As we can see, both constructors for our GADT have the type MyGADT a. This is exactly how it works for our ADTs, as they are always of type MyAdt a.

However, GADTs can have a type that is dependent on the constructor being used! Let's change the definition a bit:

```
data MyGADT a where
  GadtCons1 :: Int -> Float -> String -> MyGADT Bool
  GadtCons2 :: Bool -> a -> MyGADT String
```

Now, the constructor decides what the polymorphic type (a) will be.

```
ghci> :t GadtCons1 1 1.0 "Hi!"
GadtCons1 1 1.0 "Hi!" :: MyGADT Bool
ghci> :t GadtCons2 True (1 :: Int)
GadtCons2 True (1 :: Int) :: MyGADT [Char]
```

How is this helpful? It allows for definitions of functions that are polymorphic but restricted by the type of the GADT:

```
data GiveMe a where
  SomeString :: GiveMe String
  SomeInt :: GiveMe Int

giveMe :: GiveMe a -> a
giveMe SomeString = "Hello"
giveMe SomeInt = 1
```

The definition for giveMe is completely legal, even though it returns *different types* based on the matched constructor. This is possible because of the type of GiveMe. Since SomeString is of type GiveMe String, that means giveMe SomeString must be of type String, as the a of GiveMe a is replaced by the String from GiveMe String. Haskell is smart enough to statically figure out the necessary type based on the matched constructor. That's why the definition type checks and works as expected:

```
ghci> giveMe SomeString
"Hello"
ghci> giveMe SomeInt
1
```

GADTs are an important counterpart to type classes. While type classes *map types to terms*, GADTs *map terms to types*. Type classes are used to allow us to write polymorphic code and still use concrete implementations. GADTs are able to *refine the polymorphic type* when their constructors are being matched. That's why our definition of giveMe works as intended.

We can use this in our code to let the caller of the validation function figure out what kind of pixel type is being used. Let's assume we were using an image type like this:

```
data Image px where
  Image8Bit ::
```

```
    Int ->
    Int ->
    [P.PixelRGB8] ->
    Image P.PixelRGB8
Image16Bit ::
    Int ->
    Int ->
    [P.PixelRGB16] ->
    Image P.PixelRGB16
```

Now, we can create functions for values of this type that match on the constructors. The difference to ADTs is that matching on a GADT refines the type inside the match case. Let's look at an example:

```
to16Bit :: Image px -> Image P.PixelRGB16     | Matches on the input
to16Bit img =                                 | argument of type Image px
    case img of
        Image8Bit w h pxs -> Image16Bit w h      | Matches on the Image8Bit constructor,
→    (map pixel8To16 pxs)                         | refining the type of pxs (Haskell now statically
        Image16Bit {} -> img                     | knows that the type of pxs is [PixelRGB8])
    where
        pixel8To16 :: P.PixelRGB8 -> P.PixelRGB16   | Matches on the Image16Bit
        pixel8To16 (P.PixelRGB8 r g b) =            | constructor (ignoring its fields)
            let f x = 256 * fromIntegral x          | and returns the matched
            in P.PixelRGB16 (f r) (f g) (f b)       | argument, since it already
                                                    | matches the needed type

                            Scales a Word8 to       Defines a function to map
                              a Word16              PixelRGB8 to PixelRGB16 values
```

As we can see in this example, the argument (of type `Image px`) is polymorphic. However, our function can coalesce this polymorphic type to `PixelRBG16` without sacrificing any type safety. Haskell is able to statically figure out which constructors exist, which types they imply, and if we are using these types correctly. s

13.1.3 *The Vector type*

Now, we can think about designing a type for our images. It should be able to hold the width and height of our image as well as the image data encoded as some type for our pixel values. In the last chapter, we used a simple list to store our pixels. While lists are fine for smaller amounts of data, they have bad performance characteristics, when it comes to accessing their elements. Since this will be important later, we would like to use some other data structure.

For our use case, we can use the `Vector` data type from the `vector` package. The `Vector` is comparable to arrays in other languages, where the indexing of values can be performed in constant time. Also, usual operations, like `take`, `drop`, or `splitAt`, can be performed in constant time. However, the `Vector` type is slower for operations, such as adding new elements or appending multiple `Vector` values. Again, this type is very similar to normal arrays in other languages, where dynamically scaling arrays have to be copied in memory, over and over again.

In our library, we want to store image data and later efficiently map over it. For this, we also want to be able to read single pixels of the image to later combine them. Therefore, most of the work we are performing is *reading* data, instead of *writing* it, which makes the `Vector` type a good candidate for us.

We can add the package by adding `vector` to our dependencies section in our package.yaml. `Vector` values can be created by either using `cons` and `snoc` to prepend and append values or simply by converting a normal list with the `fromList` function:

```
ghci> import Data.Vector as V
ghci> :t V.empty
V.empty :: Vector a
ghci> :t V.cons
V.cons :: a -> Vector a -> Vector a
ghci> V.cons 1 V.empty :: V.Vector Int
[1]
ghci> V.fromList [1..10] :: V.Vector Int
[1,2,3,4,5,6,7,8,9,10]
```

It's a good idea to first lazily build a list and later convert it to a vector. That way, we can take advantage of the many functions that allow us to build lists from simpler functions (think of the parser combinators in the last chapter) and then build a more compact representation that is much faster to index and read from.

> **NOTE** Vectors are not always structurally lazy. This means we typically cannot create infinite `Vector` values, like we can with normal lists. The following code will eat up memory until your program crashes: `V.take 100 $ V.concat [V.empty, (V.fromList [1..])]`.

Now, we can add a new type to our `Graphics.PNM.Types` module from the previous chapter. This type will provide four constructors to encode grayscale and color images in 8-bit and 16-bit variations. Each constructor will hold information on the width, height, and pixels. The latter will be encoded with the `Vector` type.

Listing 13.3 Type to store PNM images

```
{-# LANGUAGE GADTs #-}
```
← Enables the GADTs language extension to enable GADTs in the file

```
module Graphics.PNM.Types where

import qualified Codec.Picture as P
import qualified Data.Vector as V
```
Imports the needed modules

```
...

data PnmImage px where
```
← Defines a data type for encoding validated PNM images

```
  PnmGray8Bit ::
```
← Defines constructors for the different kinds of PNM images

```
    Int ->
    Int ->
    V.Vector P.Pixel8 ->
    PnmImage P.Pixel8
```

```
PnmGray16Bit ::          ◁─┐
  Int ->
  Int ->
  V.Vector P.Pixel16 ->
  PnmImage P.Pixel16              Defines constructors
PnmColor8Bit ::          ◁─┤      for the different kinds
  Int ->                           of PNM images
  Int ->
  V.Vector P.PixelRGB8 ->
  PnmImage P.PixelRGB8
PnmColor16Bit ::         ◁─┘
  Int ->
  Int ->
  V.Vector P.PixelRGB16 ->
  PnmImage P.PixelRGB16
```

Couldn't we have used the record syntax in this definition? While, in theory, it is possible to use it when defining GADTs, we cannot use it in this context, since the third field (the pixels) are of different type for each constructor and don't match with a polymorphic type px. However, we should write a few functions to access widths, heights, and pixel data. For our pixels, the function now actually works, since it is polymorphic over the px type variable. These functions are shown in the following listing.

Listing 13.4   Functions to access fields of PNM images

```
pnmWidth :: PnmImage px -> Int        ◁─┐
pnmWidth (PnmGray8Bit w _ _) = w          Defines a function
pnmWidth (PnmGray16Bit w _ _) = w         to extract the width
pnmWidth (PnmColor8Bit w _ _) = w         of a PnmImage
pnmWidth (PnmColor16Bit w _ _) = w

pnmHeight :: PnmImage px -> Int       ◁─┐
pnmHeight (PnmGray8Bit _ h _) = h         Defines a function to
pnmHeight (PnmGray16Bit _ h _) = h        extract the height of
pnmHeight (PnmColor8Bit _ h _) = h        a PnmImage
pnmHeight (PnmColor16Bit _ h _) = h

pnmPixels :: PnmImage px -> V.Vector px   ◁─┐
pnmPixels (PnmGray8Bit _ _ pixels) = pixels    Defines a function to
pnmPixels (PnmGray16Bit _ _ pixels) = pixels   extract the pixels of
pnmPixels (PnmColor8Bit _ _ pixels) = pixels   a PnmImage
pnmPixels (PnmColor16Bit _ _ pixels) = pixels
```

You might wonder why we haven't derived Show or Eq for our new type. That's because we cannot use the usual deriving keyword with GADTs. To still derive type class instances for them, we have to use the StandaloneDeriving extension and provide single expressions that do the work.

Listing 13.5   Deriving type class instances for a GADT

```
{-# LANGUAGE StandaloneDeriving #-}       ◁─┐   Activates the StandaloneDeriving
                                                language extension
...
```

```
deriving instance (Show px) => Show (PnmImage px)
```
◁─┐ **Derives the Show instance**
    | **for PnmImage px where a**
    | **Show px instance exists**

```
deriving instance (Eq px) => Eq (PnmImage px)
```
◁─
  ┌─ **Derives the Eq instance for**
  | **PnmImage px where a Eq px**
  | **instance exists**

With the code in listing 13.5, we have the field selectors and instances taken care of and we can consider our `PnmImage` type definition complete for the time being. Now that this type is taken care of, can we finally write our validation function?

13.1.4 *Dynamic types with existential quantification*

Sadly, we aren't ready to write our validation function just yet. The whole reason we introduced our GADT was so that the validation function could decide the type of the pixels. However, return-type polymorphism still forces our hand when we have a function that returns a `PnmImage px`. Using a GADT was only the first part of the solution to the puzzle, as it allows the caller of our function to refine the polymorphic type.

Now, we also have to find a way to disallow the caller from ever choosing that type. We need a way of hiding the type parameter from the return value in the function. A nifty trick we have already discussed in chapter 11 is *yet another* extension to Haskell's type system: `ExistentialQuantification`.

As a short recap, with this extension, we can create data types that effectively hide their type variables from their own type. This enables us to create a type that can hold polymorphic types, while itself not being polymorphic. The only thing we need to worry about is retrieving information from this type again. While we would usually solve this with type constraints, we are a bit luckier in our current situation

> **Listing 13.6 The definition of a dynamic data type for PNM images**

```
{-# LANGUAGE ExistentialQuantification #-}
```
◁─┐ **Activates the StandaloneDeriving**
   | **language extension**

```
...

data DynamicPnmImage = forall px.
➥ DynamicPnmImage (PnmImage px)
```
◁─┐ **Defines a type that can hold PnmImage**
  | **px values of arbitrary px type**

Looking at listing 13.6, we see that we do not actually need a type constraint. Why is that? Won't our value be useless in the end? Not quite, since we still know that whatever we put inside the `DynamicPnmImage` constructor is the GADT `PnmImage`, and as we have discussed earlier, matching on a GADT's constructor refines its type. This means that after matching on whatever the value inside the constructor is, we know what kind of image we are dealing with. We don't lose the information on types! Now, we are finally able to write a validation function that takes an arbitrary parse result and creates a `DynamicPnmImage`, which we can later use to figure out what kind of image type was stored inside by the validation function.

13.2   *Validation of parsed data*

Let us start by reminding ourselves what our validation function should do. It should check the following:

- The amount of pixels read is equal to the width times the height from the header.
- The type of pixels read are matching the magic number in the header.
- The pixel values of pixels never exceed the maximum value given in the header.

The parser we wrote in the last chapter performs no validation when producing RawPnm values. We can now write a function that transforms RawPnm to DynamicPnmImage values, while checking that the preceding assertions hold. We want to put this function inside a new module called Graphics.PNM.Validation, which we will later re-export from our Graphics.PNM module.

We can start our validation process by thinking about how to transform (and validate) single pixels. For bitmap pixels, the parser should return us RawPixel values with the Single constructor, using either 0 or 1 as a color value, as bitmap images are in black and white. We will map these pixels to the Pixel8 type from the JuicyPixels package, as they stand for an 8-bit grayscale pixel value. This type is just an alias for Word8 values, so we can return a simple number. Remember that 1 in PNM represents black. A function to validate a single bitmap pixel is shown in the following listing.

Listing 13.7   A function to transform a raw pixel to a bitmap pixel

```
module Graphics.PNM.Validation where

import Graphics.PNM.Types
import qualified Codec.Picture as P

bitmapPixel :: RawPixel -> Either String P.Pixel8
bitmapPixel (Single 1) = Right 0            Returns either a black or white pixel
bitmapPixel (Single 0) = Right 255          value based on the given RawPixel
bitmapPixel p =
  Left $                              Returns an error message
    "Could not convert "             if the RawPixel does not
      <> show p                       represent a bitmap pixel
      <> " to a bitmap pixel"
```

As in previous chapters, we are using the Either type to encode our validation errors. Note that we do not check whether the pixel values exceed the maximum value, as bitmap images should not have a maximum value set. We will check this property later.

The maximum value does matter when we want to work with graymap pixels. Depending on the maximum value, we will have to either return a Pixel8 or Pixel16, but that will be decided outside of the function. Since Pixel16 is an alias for Word16, we can return an arbitrary type. After checking if the value is smaller or equal to the maximum value, we can scale the pixel value by the ratio between the given value and maximum value. This is shown in the following listing

Listing 13.8 A function to transform a raw pixel to a graymap pixel

```
import Data.Word

...

graymapPixel ::
  (Integral px) =>
  Word16 ->
  RawPixel ->
  Either String px
graymapPixel maxVal pixel@(Single g)
  | g > maxVal =
    Left $
      "The pixel "
        <> show pixel
        <> " exceeds the maximum value "
        <> show maxVal
  | otherwise = Right v
  where
    factor = fromIntegral g / fromIntegral maxVal
    v = round $ fromIntegral maxVal * factor
graymapPixel _ p =
  Left $
    "Could not convert "
      <> show p
      <> " to a graymap pixel"
```

Checks whether the given pixel exceeds the maximum value and returns an error message

Returns the scaled value

Computes the ratio between the given value and the maximum value

Scales the maximum value by the ratio between the given value and maximum value

Returns an error message if the RawPixel does not represent a graymap pixel

To use `round`, we have to add the `Integral` class as a type constraint to our code. How the value will be rounded is decided by the return-type, which is decided by the caller.

For the pixmap pixels, we essentially do the same, but we do the transformation on the `RawPixel` type for RGB values. The result type is also much different from before, as we now have to either return a `PixelRGB8` or `PixelRGB16` value. Both of these constructors receive three values (either of `Pixel8` or `Pixel16` type):

```
ghci> import Codec.Picture
ghci> :t PixelRGB8
PixelRGB8 :: Pixel8 -> Pixel8 -> Pixel8 -> PixelRGB8
ghci> :t PixelRGB16
PixelRGB16 :: Pixel16 -> Pixel16 -> Pixel16 -> PixelRGB16
```

To keep our validation function as generic as possible, we can require an argument that matches a polymorphic version of these constructors. The caller can then pass the fitting constructor to the function to specify what the result type should be. The function is shown in the following listing.

Listing 13.9 A function to transform a raw pixel to a pixmap pixel

```
pixmapPixel ::
  (Integral val) =>
  Word16 ->
```

```
(val -> val -> val -> px) ->
RawPixel ->
Either String px
pixmapPixel maxVal f pixel@(RGB r g b)
  | r > maxVal || g > maxVal || b > maxVal =
    Left $
      "The pixel "
        <> show pixel
        <> " exceeds the maximum value "
        <> show maxVal
  | otherwise =
    Right $
      f (transform r) (transform g) (transform b)
  where
    factor x = fromIntegral x / fromIntegral maxVal
    transform x = round $ fromIntegral maxVal * factor x
pixmapPixel _ _ p =
  Left $
    "Could not convert "
      <> show p
      <> " to a pixmap pixel"
```

Checks whether the given values for red, green, and blue exceed the maximum value and returns an error message

Returns the scaled values for the red, green, and blue values and wraps them with the function, given as an argument, to produce the final result

Computes the ratio between the given value and the maximum value

Returns an error message if the RawPixel does not represent a pixmap pixel

Scales the maximum value by the ratio between the given value and the maximum value

For the construction of our validation function, it would be helpful to infer what kind of image we are dealing with from the magic number. We can create a few simple helper functions (shown in the following listing) to help us with that.

Listing 13.10 Helper functions for validation

```
indicatesBitmap :: MagicNumber -> Bool
indicatesBitmap P1 = True
indicatesBitmap P4 = True
indicatesBitmap _ = False
```

Defines a function that checks whether the given magic number indicates a bitmap image

```
indicatesGraymap :: MagicNumber -> Bool
indicatesGraymap P2 = True
indicatesGraymap P5 = True
indicatesGraymap _ = False
```

Defines a function that checks whether the given magic number indicates a graymap image

```
indicatesPixmap :: MagicNumber -> Bool
indicatesPixmap P3 = True
indicatesPixmap P6 = True
indicatesPixmap _ = False
```

Defines a function that checks whether the given magic number indicates a pixmap image

```
imageSizeCorrect :: RawPnm -> Bool
imageSizeCorrect RawPnm {header, imageData} =
  let expectedNumPixels =
        fromIntegral $ width header * height header
      numPixels = length $ pixels imageData
  in numPixels == expectedNumPixels
```

Defines a function that checks whether the image sizes suggested by the header match the number of pixels

For convenience, we also add a function to check whether the number of pixels present in the value is equal to the number suggested by the header. Note that for this definition to be legal, the NamedFieldPuns extension has to be enabled. Let us think about how to check that the pixels in our image are correct. We have already written functions to check a single pixel, but we need to check all the pixels of the raw image. Additionally, we want to return the first error (`Left` value) that happens while transforming our pixels. Luckily, we do not have to write a special function for this, as we can use the fact that `Either a` is a *monad*.

Thinking back to the last chapter, we learned that the `Maybe` monad will always coalesce down to a `Nothing` if at any point in the computation, a `Nothing` occurs. It is similar to `Either a` and the `Left` constructor. So we have to map our pixel transforming functions on the list of pixels and treat these computations in the `Either a` monad. As it turns out, we have already seen a function in chapter 4 that does exactly that, `mapM`:

```
ghci> :t mapM
mapM :: (Traversable t, Monad m) => (a -> m b) -> t a -> m (t b)
ghci> :{
ghci| f :: Int -> Either String Int
ghci| f 0 = Left "zero is not allowed"
ghci| f x = Right x
ghci| :}
ghci> mapM f [1..10]
Right [1,2,3,4,5,6,7,8,9,10]
ghci> mapM f [0..10]
Left "zero is not allowed"
```

Something we have not discussed earlier is the full type for the `mapM` function, as we didn't know about type constraints and monads back then. `mapM` operates on a `Traversable` (which lists are) in a monadic context. The function given to `mapM` evaluates to a monad action (`m b`) for each element whose results are collected in the result `m (t b)`. `mapM` essentially traverses our list and applies the monad actions one by one. As the `Either a` monad short-circuits to `Left`, our whole computation does too!

NOTE Strictly speaking, we could have switched the usage of `mapM` with `traverse`, which is of type `Applicative f => (a -> f b) -> t a -> f (t b)`. `mapM` is essentially equivalent in functionality but uses a `Monad` constraint instead of `Applicative`. For `Either a`, it makes no difference.

We now have all the puzzle pieces taken care of, and we are ready to write our validation function. It should check all assertions and wrap the correct type of `PnmImage` inside a `DynamicPnmImage` if validation succeeds. The function is shown in the following listing.

Listing 13.11 The validation function for PNM parse results

```
import qualified Data.Vector as V

...

validatePnm :: RawPnm -> Either String DynamicPnmImage
validatePnm img@(RawPnm {header, imageData})
```

```
  | not $ imageSizeCorrect img =
    Left $
      "The number of pixels given does not match "
        <> "the expected size inferred from the header"
  | indicatesBitmap magicNum =
    case maxVal header of
      Nothing -> PnmGray8Bit `withTransform`
⇒ bitmapPixel
        Just _ ->
          Left $
            "Image seems to be a bitmap image "
              <> "but has a maximum value set"
  | indicatesGraymap magicNum =
    case maxVal header of
      Nothing ->
        Left $
          "Image seems to be a graymap image "
            <> "but has no maximum value set"
      Just maxVal ->
        if maxVal <= 255
          then
            PnmGray8Bit
              `withTransform` graymapPixel maxVal
          else
            PnmGray16Bit
              `withTransform` graymapPixel maxVal
  | indicatesPixmap magicNum =
    case maxVal header of
      Nothing ->
        Left $
          "Image seems to be a pixmap image "
            <> "but has no maximum value set"
      Just maxVal ->
        if maxVal <= 255
          then
            PnmColor8Bit
              `withTransform` pixmapPixel maxVal P.PixelRGB8
          else
            PnmColor16Bit
              `withTransform` pixmapPixel maxVal P.PixelRGB16
  | otherwise = Left "Image seems to be of unknown type"
  where
    magicNum = magicNumber header
    width' = fromIntegral $ width header
    height' = fromIntegral $ height header

  withTransform ::
    (Int -> Int -> V.Vector px -> PnmImage px) ->
    (RawPixel -> Either String px) ->
    Either String DynamicPnmImage
  withTransform c f =
    let mConvertedData = mapM f $ pixels imageData
      in fmap mkRes mConvertedData
```

Returns a PnmGray8Bit with raw data converted into bitmap pixels

Returns an error message if an assertion isn't holding true

Returns a PnmGray8Bit or PnmGray16Bit based on the maximum value with the raw data converted into graymap pixels

Returns a PnmColor8Bit or PnmColor16Bit based on the maximum value with the raw data converted into pixmap pixels

Returns an error message if an assertion isn't holding true

Converts the pixels of the image data using the given argument for conversion, stopping early if conversion fails

Creates a final result from a successful conversion

```
    where
      mkRes = DynamicPnmImage . c width' height'
⇨ . V.fromList
```
Converts pixel data to a Vector and wraps the data in a DynamicPnmImage, using a constructor given as an argument

While the definition might look intimidating at first, it becomes manageable once the `withTransform` function is understood. It receives two arguments: `c` is a function to build a `PnmImage`. This is only used with constructors from the `PnmImage` type. `f` is the conversion function used to translate the raw image data to the pixel type needed for the constructor given as the `c` argument. `withTransform` is used in an infix style to make the code more readable. A constructor is used with a given function to perform the pixel data transformation.

As we can see, `validatePnm` can fully determine the kind of `PnmImage` by the data we pass to it (magic number and image data), returning specific constructors wrapped inside the `DynamicPnmImage`. The pixels are converted appropriately. Note how the caller of this function is not able to determine what `PnmImage` is being returned. `validatePnm` has full responsibility.

13.3 A generic algorithm for image conversion

Since we now have a way of validating and encoding our images, we want to be able to actually do something with them. We might want to pixelate our images or even create a blur filter, but how would we do that? Since the pixel data is of different type based on the constructor of our `PnmImage`, we might need to write multiple versions of our filter to work on the different types of pixels. Can we provide a way of generically mapping pixels inside an image?

Doing so forces us to generically work with pixels. We will need to transform a concrete pixel type (like `Pixel8` or `PixelRGB16`) to something more generic. That means mapping a type to some kind of function to provide a conversion. As we have already discussed, type classes are used for exactly this purpose. Therefore, we define a type that represents a generic pixel and a type class that provides conversion functions to and from such a generic pixel, as shown in the followng listing.

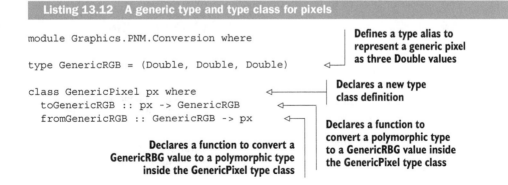

Listing 13.12 A generic type and type class for pixels

```
module Graphics.PNM.Conversion where

type GenericRGB = (Double, Double, Double)

class GenericPixel px where
  toGenericRGB :: px -> GenericRGB
  fromGenericRGB :: GenericRGB -> px
```

Defines a type alias to represent a generic pixel as three Double values

Declares a new type class definition

Declares a function to convert a GenericRBG value to a polymorphic type inside the GenericPixel type class

Declares a function to convert a polymorphic type to a GenericRBG value inside the GenericPixel type class

We can put the code in listing 13.12 into a new module, which we will call `Graph-ics.PNM.Conversion`. The `GenericRGB` type represents the red, blue, and green channels of a pixel in a range from `0` to `1`. This will make it easier to perform calculations with the pixel values, as we do not have to cast integral values to `Double` and back again inside our mapping.

On that note, since our pixels are integral types, we need a way of scaling them down to the range inside the `GenericRGB` type. All of our pixel types either consist of `Word8` or `Word16`, so we can provide functions to scale these values appropriately. These are shown in the following listing.

Listing 13.13 Helper functions for converting integral types to and from `Double`

```
import Data.Word

...

clamp :: Double -> Double
clamp = max 0 . min 1                     ◁── Clamps a value to an
                                              interval of 0 and 1

scaleDown8Bit :: Word8 -> Double
scaleDown8Bit v = clamp $ (fromIntegral v) / 255.0   ◁── Scales a Word8 to an
                                                         interval of 0 to 1

scaleUp8Bit :: Double -> Word8
scaleUp8Bit v = round $ 255 * (clamp v)   ◁── Scales an interval of 0 to 1 to a Word8

scaleDown16Bit :: Word16 -> Double
scaleDown16Bit v = clamp $ (fromIntegral v) / 65535.0   ◁── Scales a Word16 to an
                                                            interval of 0 to 1

scaleUp16Bit :: Double -> Word16
scaleUp16Bit v = round $ 65535 * (clamp v)   ◁── Scales an interval of 0 to 1 to a Word16
```

Using these functions, we can define instances for the different pixel types. However, we have to keep in mind that `Pixel8` and `Pixel16` are type synonyms, and we have to use the `TypeSynonymInstances` language extension to allow instances for them. The instance declarations themselves are straightforward. Since we technically have a red, green, and blue channel, we have to combine these channels and normalize them to get a single grey channel. In theory, we could have used a more elaborate generic type to differentiate between color and gray pixels, but we want to keep our code simple to have an easier time defining mappings.

Listing 13.14 Instances for the `GenericPixel` type class

```
import qualified Codec.Picture as P

...

instance GenericPixel P.Pixel8 where
  toGenericRGB p = (p', p', p')              ◁── Returns a GenericRGB
    where                                        from a single integral value
      p' = scaleDown8Bit p
  fromGenericRGB (r, g, b) = p              ◁── Returns a single integral value
    where                                      from a GenericRGB value
```

```
        p = scaleUp8Bit $ (r + g + b) / 3

instance GenericPixel P.Pixel16 where
  toGenericRGB p = (p', p', p')
    where
      p' = scaleDown16Bit p / 3
  fromGenericRGB (r, g, b) = p
    where
      p = scaleUp16Bit $ (r + g + b) / 3

instance GenericPixel P.PixelRGB8 where
  toGenericRGB (P.PixelRGB8 r g b) =
    (scaleDown8Bit r, scaleDown8Bit g, scaleDown8Bit b)
  fromGenericRGB (r, g, b) =
    P.PixelRGB8
      (scaleUp8Bit r)
      (scaleUp8Bit g)
      (scaleUp8Bit b)

instance GenericPixel P.PixelRGB16 where
  toGenericRGB (P.PixelRGB16 r g b) =
    (scaleDown16Bit r, scaleDown16Bit g, scaleDown16Bit b)
  fromGenericRGB (r, g, b) =
    P.PixelRGB16
      (scaleUp16Bit r)
      (scaleUp16Bit g)
      (scaleUp16Bit b)
```

Returns a GenericRGB from a single integral value

Returns a single integral value from a GenericRGB value

Returns a GenericRGB from an RGB pixel

Returns an RGB pixel from a GenericRGB value

Returns a GenericRGB from an RGB pixel

Returns an RGB pixel from a GenericRGB value

With the conversion taken care of, we can think about what our mapping function should look like. While it would be fine to simply provide an interface to apply some pure function on a single pixel, this is not necessarily powerful enough to facilitate more interesting operations on images. What we want to implement is a way of mapping *kernels*.

13.3.1 *Image algorithm for conversion matrices*

Kernels, sometimes called *convolution matrices*, are used in image processing to combine pixels into a single pixel. The kernel can be considered a matrix that "slides" over the image, where the center of the matrix is placed on each individual pixel to compute a new one. This is visually shown in figure 13.1. Applying this convolution to an image produces a new one. Different matrices produce different effects, such as sharpening and blurring. Even more involved techniques, such as edge detection, are possible using kernels.

However, we do not just want to create a boring kernel. We want to generalize the kernel to a function that can freely read any pixel from the image to produce a new value. This way, we can emulate kernels but also write functions that would be impossible using kernels alone.

To do this, we create a type alias for a function that will be able to perform this task. It receives the coordinates of the current pixel as well as a function to retrieve an arbitrary pixel from the image. If this function is given coordinates outside of the image, it should return a Nothing instead of a value. Finally, the function receives the current pixel. This is shown in listing 13.15.

A kernel is a matrix laid over the image. The matrix decides how the pixels are being combined into a new value based on weights.

The kernel is a function from a pixel's neighborhood to that pixel. The function can decide how to arbitrarily combine pixels.

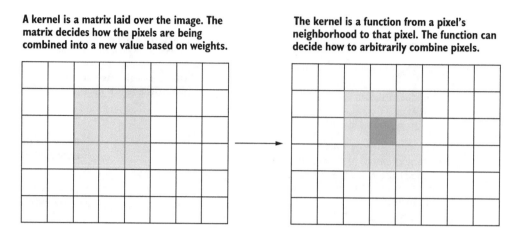

Figure 13.1   The functionality of image kernels interpreted as functions

Listing 13.15   Type synonym for generic pixel mappings

```
type PixelMapping =
  ( Int ->                              The position of the current pixel in the x direction
    Int ->                              The position of the current pixel in the y direction
    (Int -> Int -> Maybe GenericRGB) ->
    GenericRGB ->                       A function to retrieve a pixel from
    GenericRGB                          the image given a coordinate
  )                                     (x and y values)
```

The resulting pixel at the current position after the mapping

The currently mapped pixel in the image

With this definition, we can create a simple mapping for each pixel, a kernel, or something even more elaborate. To construct our mapping function, we can use `imap` from `Data.Vector` to have the current index for our mapping present when going through all pixels:

```
ghci> import qualified Data.Vector as V
ghci> vec = V.fromList [1..10] :: V.Vector Int
ghci> V.imap (\i x -> (i, x)) vec
[(0,1),(1,2),(2,3),(3,4),(4,5),(5,6),(6,7),(7,8),(8,9),(9,10)]
```

Using `imap` with the functions from our `GenericPixel` class, we can create a map function that receives a `PixelMapping` and applies it to the pixels inside a `DynamicPnmImage`, keeping the type of `PnmImage` intact. This is shown in the following listing.

Listing 13.16   Generic function to map image data

```
import qualified Data.Vector as V
import Graphics.PNM.Types


...
```

```
mapImagePixels ::
  PixelMapping ->
  DynamicPnmImage ->
  DynamicPnmImage
mapImagePixels f (DynamicPnmImage img) =
  case img of
    PnmGray8Bit _ _ pxs ->
      PnmGray8Bit `withPixels` mapping pxs        ◁─┐
    PnmGray16Bit _ _ pxs ->
      PnmGray16Bit `withPixels` mapping pxs       ◁─┤
    PnmColor8Bit _ _ pxs ->
      PnmColor8Bit `withPixels` mapping pxs       ◁─┤
    PnmColor16Bit _ _ pxs ->
      PnmColor16Bit `withPixels` mapping pxs      ◁─┘
  where
    w = pnmWidth img
    h = pnmHeight img

    withPixels ::
      (Int -> Int -> V.Vector px -> PnmImage px) ->
      V.Vector px ->
      DynamicPnmImage
    withPixels c pxs = DynamicPnmImage $ c w h pxs   ◁─┘

    mapping :: GenericPixel px => V.Vector px -> V.Vector px
    mapping pixels =
      flip V.imap pixels $ \i px ->
        let x = i `mod` w
            y = i `div` w
            getPixel x' y' =
              toGenericRGB <$> pixels V.!? (y' * w + x')    ◁─
            result = f x y getPixel $ toGenericRGB px    ◁─┐
        in fromGenericRGB result   ◁─┐
```

Matches on the PnmImage and creates a new DynamicPnmImage with mapped pixels

Wraps a PnmImage constructor and pixels of fitting type inside a DynamicPnmImage with the correct width and height

Computes the x and y coordinates from the current index of a pixel

Defines a function that accesses a pixel in the Vector safely and converts it into a GenericRGB

Calls the PixelMapping function with the current coordinate, the function to retrieve arbitrary pixels from the image, and the current pixel

Converts the result back to the correct pixel type

We use `withPixels` in a similar manner as we did previously with `withTransform` in the `validatePnm` function. Note the usage of `V.!?`, which is the safe variant of the normal indexing of the `Vector` type, returning a `Maybe` of the vectors type:

```
ghci> import Data.Vector as V
ghci> vec = V.fromList [1..10] :: V.Vector Int
ghci> (V.!?) vec 0
Just 1
ghci> (V.!?) vec (-1)
Nothing
ghci> (V.!?) vec 10
Nothing
```

13.3.2 *Exporting images as PNG*

Now that we are able to work with our PNM images, we have to take care of one last step: writing them back to the filesystem. We could serialize our data in the PNM format again, but we want to use the power of the JuicyPixels package to write our image data as PNG files. Doing so will require us to transform our `DynamicPnmImage` into the `DynamicImage` type of the package.

This type is very similar to our `DynamicPnmImage`, as it holds different image types differentiated by their internal pixel type. However, it's neither a GADT nor existentially quantified but a simple ADT containing different constructors for different pixel types. Among these constructors are `ImageY8` and `ImageY16`, which are used for grayscale images, while `ImageRGB8` and `ImageRGB16` are used for color images. The `Codec.Picture` module features the `generateImage` function to construct images from a function; its signature is `Pixel px ? (Int -> Int -> px) -> Int -> Int -> Image px`. It receives a function to return a pixel at a given coordinate as well as a width and height for the image. The signature for that first argument looks suspiciously similar to the signature of the function that retrieved an arbitrary pixel inside our image mapping, so we already have an idea of how to write that function. The width and height of our image are also known, so all that's left is to differentiate on our image types and build the correct image from it. The function is shown in the following listing.

Listing 13.17 The function to transform PNM images to JuicyPixels image values

```
dynamicPnmToDynamicImage :: DynamicPnmImage -> P.DynamicImage
dynamicPnmToDynamicImage (DynamicPnmImage img) =
  case img of
    PnmGray8Bit {} -> P.ImageY8 $ pnmToImage img       Matches on the
    PnmGray16Bit {} -> P.ImageY16 $ pnmToImage img     PnmImage constructor
    PnmColor8Bit {} -> P.ImageRGB8 $ pnmToImage img    and returns the
    PnmColor16Bit {} -> P.ImageRGB16 $ pnmToImage img  appropriate image
  where
    pnmToImage :: P.Pixel px => PnmImage px -> P.Image px
    pnmToImage pnmImg =                                 Builds the
      P.generateImage build (pnmWidth pnmImg) (pnmHeight pnmImg)  image from
      where                                             the PnmImage
        build x y =                                     pixel data
          pnmPixels pnmImg V.! (y * (pnmWidth pnmImg) + x)   Defines a function
                                                         to retrieve pixels
                                                         from a coordinate
```

Here, we use the (`!`) operator from `Data.Vector`, since we can be sure that the index will be in the vector's length. Otherwise, we would have made a mistake in our programming. You might wonder why we are repeating `pnmToImage img` in each matched case. Couldn't we have just written something like this?

```
dynamicPnmToDynamicImage (DynamicPnmImage img) =
  let img' = pnmToImage img
   in case img of
        PnmGray8Bit {} -> P.ImageY8 img'
```

```
PnmGray16Bit {} -> P.ImageY16 img'
PnmColor8Bit {} -> P.ImageRGB8 img'
PnmColor16Bit {} -> P.ImageRGB16 img'
```

The answer is no! That's because case matches on a GADT are special. Not only do they refine their type, but this type refinement is *only valid* inside the expression of the case match, not in an outside let binding or where binding. We are using this refinement to use determine the type of the result of pnmToImage.

Finally, we can now write an action that finally writes our image data as a PNG to the filesystem. To do this, we can use writeDynamicPng with the type FilePath -> DynamicImage -> IO (Either String Bool). As we already have a function to convert our DynamicPnmImage to a DynamicImage, we can simply combine the two functions. This is shown in the following listing.

Listing 13.18 An action to save dynamic PNM images as PNGs

```
writeAsPng ::
  FilePath ->
  DynamicPnmImage ->
  IO (Either String Bool)
writeAsPng path img =
  P.writeDynamicPng path $
    dynamicPnmToDynamicImage img
```

writeDynamicPng returns errors encoded as Either if conversion or saving is not possible. Our Graphics.PNM.Conversion module is, thus, complete. We can add our new functions to our Graphics.PNM module, which re-exports data types and functions from our internal modules.

Listing 13.19 Module to re-export definitions of internal modules

```
module Graphics.PNM
  ( module PNMC,        Exports the
    module PNMP,        definitions of the
    module PNMT,        imported modules
    module PNMV,
  )
where

import Graphics.PNM.Conversion as PNMC    Imports the
import Graphics.PNM.Parsing as PNMP       modules
import Graphics.PNM.Types as PNMT         with aliases
import Graphics.PNM.Validation as PNMV
```

We can now get to the fun part and start writing mapping functions for our library, since so far, we have only built the tools. Now, it's time to use them.

13.4 *Using parallelism to transform data*

Let's have some fun writing different mappings for our image processing library. We will test them on the image shown in figure 13.2. This book's code repository features this image for you to play with.

Figure 13.2   An image used for manipulation

Let's first write a very simple mapping that turns a color image into a grayscale one by summing the red, green, and blue channels and normalizing the resulting value. This mapping, shown in the following listing, ignores most of the features our `PixelMapping` is capable of.

Listing 13.20   A grayscale mapping

```
module Main where

import Graphics.PNM

grayScale :: PixelMapping
grayScale _ _ _ (r, g, b) = (v, v, v)
  where
    v = (r + g + b) / 3
```

Returns the grayscale pixel

Adds the color channels and normalizes the value

Now to something more interesting: a mapping to pixelate the image. When pixelating, we want to increase the size of certain pixels and overwrite other ones. Since our `PixelMapping` knows its current position, it can check on which enlarged pixel it is being called and then retrieve that pixel. But how do we determine the enlarged pixel? We can compute the remainder of a division with a fixed constant for our coordinates. Using this, we can retrieve the pixel at the negative offset of our current position, as shown in the following listing.

Listing 13.21   A pixelation mapping

```
import Data.Maybe

...

pixelate :: Int -> PixelMapping
pixelate pixelSize x y getPx curPx =
  let xDiff = x `mod` pixelSize
      yDiff = y `mod` pixelSize
  in fromMaybe curPx $ getPx (x - xDiff) (y - yDiff)
```

Computes the difference between the current pixel and the pixel to be enlarged

Retrieves the pixel to be enlarged and defaults to the current pixel

This mapping, shown in listing 13.21, allows us to specify the pixel size, which determines the size of the enlarged pixels. Applying this mapping to our original image with different pixel sizes results in the images shown in figure 13.3.

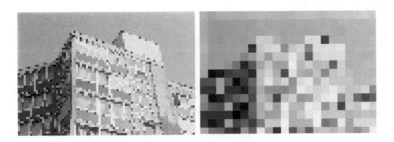

Figure 13.3   Image pixelated with `pixelate 16` **and** `pixelate 64`

The last mapping we will introduce in this chapter is the *blur effect*. While there are many ways of blurring an image, we will take a look at the most straightforward implementation: the box blur. It is called a *box* blur because the blur is achieved by drawing a box of predefined size around the pixel that should be blurred and computing the average pixel from all the pixels in that box. In our `PixelMapping`, this can be achieved by enumerating the pixels inside that box and calculating the average for each color channel. This mapping is shown in the following listing.

Listing 13.22   A box blur mapping

```
boxBlur :: Int -> PixelMapping
boxBlur boxSize x y getPx _ =
  let nbrs =
        catMaybes
          [ getPx (x + dx) (y + dy)
            | dx <- [(-boxSize) .. boxSize],
              dy <- [(-boxSize) .. boxSize]
          ]
      (rx, gx, bx) = unzip3 nbrs
```

Discards pixels that could not be retrieved because the coordinate was outside of the image's dimensions

Enumerates the pixels inside the box around the current coordinate

Splits the list of (Double, Double, Double) into three lists for the different color channels

```
      numPixs = fromIntegral $ length nbrs        ┌── Counts the number of
  in ( sum rx / numPixs,    ┌─────────────────┐  │   pixels that could be
       sum gx / numPixs,    │ Computes an averaged │  retrieved from the
       sum bx / numPixs     │ pixel by averaging the │ image
     )                      │ color channels       │
                            └─────────────────┘
```

Applying this mapping creates an image, as shown in figure 13.4. In the preceding definition, we used `unzip3`, which is a version of `unzip` that operates on a list of tuples with three elements and returns three lists containing the elements of the tuples at first, second, and third place.

Figure 13.4   Image blurred by `boxBlur 8`

The amount of time it takes to run this mapping is worth noting, as it takes considerably longer than the other mappings. Accordingly, we will now spend the rest of the chapter speeding it up, using *parallelism*.

13.4.1 *Measuring time*

For testing, we use the following main module. To make the code simpler, the program expects that a single argument is given to it and crashes if any errors during validation or parsing happen. We hardcode the program to perform a box blur.

Listing 13.23   Example main module for testing

```
module Main (main) where

...
import Graphics.PNM
import System.Environment (getArgs)

main :: IO ()
main = do
  [filePath] <- getArgs
  Right rawImg <- readPnmFile filePath
  let Right pnmImg = validatePnm rawImg
```

```
    pnmImg' = mapImagePixels (boxBlur 8) pnmImg
  _ <- writeAsPng "test.png" pnmImg'
  return ()
```

Running this program on the example image large/p6.ppm from the book's code repository takes about 33 seconds on a 2021 MacBook Pro. We can check so by adding the runtime option -s, by running our program like so: stack run—<path to the pnm image> +RTS -s. The output will contain information on the time it took to run the program:

```
INIT    time    0.000s  (  0.004s elapsed)
  MUT     time   23.866s  ( 28.727s elapsed)
  GC      time    2.794s  (  4.578s elapsed)
  EXIT    time    0.002s  (  0.009s elapsed)
  Total   time   26.662s  ( 33.318s elapsed)
```

That's … slightly underwhelming. Can we speed things up, and if so, how would we do that? To start things off, let us review what steps we are performing in our program:

1 Parse the file contents.
2 Validate the parsed result.
3 Map the image data to produce a new image.
4 Write the new image to a file.

Validation and writing the image are not expensive enough to warrant us improving their design. Parsing can take some time, but it also isn't the culprit, which we can quickly check by swapping boxBlur with pixelate in our main module. Now, the program runs in under 2 seconds! Clearly, the expensive part is our mapping.

Let's take a step back and analyze what our PixelMapping is. At its core, it is nothing but a simple *pure* function, which we have dealt with from chapter 2 onward. This pure function is being applied to each pixel in the image, which means a mapping on a 1,000-by-1,000-pixel image results in 1 million computations. Since pure functions do not produce side-effects, it is largely irrelevant in which order they are evaluated. Furthermore, the single computations in our pixel mapping do not interfere with each other. So why not run these computations in parallel?

13.4.2 *How parallelism works*

When we compile a Haskell program, the resulting binary does not just contain our code but an extensive *runtime system*. This system not only contains the garbage collector but a scheduler for *green threads* (sometimes called *virtual threads*). These are not actual threads that run on our processor but lightweight processes within our program's runtime system. This has many advantages:

- Threads can be scheduled and disposed of quickly.
- The maximum number of threads is much higher than what would be permissible by the operating system.

- Concurrency and shared resources can be handled by the runtime system in a safe way.
- The runtime system can decide how to schedule threads with the available resources.
- Options allow the runtime system to be tweaked.
- Different concurrency models are available.

It's only logical that a language like Haskell, where almost everything that has to do with side effects is managed, provides us with abstractions to facilitate safe multithreading. For concurrency, we have a few packages that provide us with a way to asynchronously perform computations:

- `async` *package*—High-level interface for safe asynchronous computations
- `stm` *package*—Software transactional memory inside Haskell's runtime system
- `Control.Concurrent` *module*—Low-level access to threads

While these possibilities are interesting, they don't fully apply to us, as we do not require *concurrency* but *parallelism*. The difference is that the computations we want to run in parallel are the same for each invocation. For this kind of multithreaded model, we can use the `parallel` package.

This package provides us with the `Control.Parallel.Strategies` module, which provides us with ways of expressing parallel execution simply. The central concept of the module is the `Strategy` type, which defines how something should be evaluated. A `Strategy` is a type synonym for a function of type `a -> Eval a`. `Eval` is a monad that specifies how certain computations should be performed, specifying what should be evaluated in parallel and which computations should forcibly be performed sequentially.

To define evaluation orders, we have a few prebuilt strategies we can use:

- `r0`—Perform *no* evaluation.
- `rseq`—Evaluate the argument.
- `rpar`—Spark a parallel evaluation of the argument.
- `rdeepseq`—Fully evaluate the argument.

What is the difference between `rseq` and `rdeepseq`? Don't both evaluate the argument? The difference is that evaluation in Haskell does not imply a full evaluation but an evaluation to the so-called *weak head normal form*. While we will not go too deep into this subject, the quick gist is that an expression is evaluated to weak head normal form if it has been evaluated up to at least the first data constructor. That means that a list is in weak head normal form if it has been evaluated up to the first (`:`) or the `[]` constructor. However, values in the list don't have to be evaluated for this! This is possible thanks to a concept called *thunks*, which are pieces of data that are not evaluated. These thunks are only evaluated once they are needed. That's what makes Haskell lazy.

In contrast to `rseq`, `rdeepseq` forces evaluation to *normal form*, which means data has to be fully evaluated. The most important strategy for our use case however is `rpar`, since it sparks parallel evaluation.

13.4.3 *All about sparks image process HECs (Haskell execution contexts)*

Sparks are a concept similar to thunks. While thunks make up our unevaluated data, sparks point to these thunks. Evaluating a spark means evaluating a thunk. However, the difference is that sparks can be evaluated in parallel. To do this the runtime system uses so-called *Haskell execution contexts* (HECs). Roughly speaking, each of these execution contexts lives in its own operating system thread and is managed by the runtime system.

HECs are able to evaluate sparks. For this, they have access to a *spark pool*, which is filled with sparks by `rpar`. Scheduling of this parallel execution is done via *work stealing*, which means any HEC that can take on a new spark simply "steals" it from the spark pool to evaluate it. This idea is shown in figure 13.5.

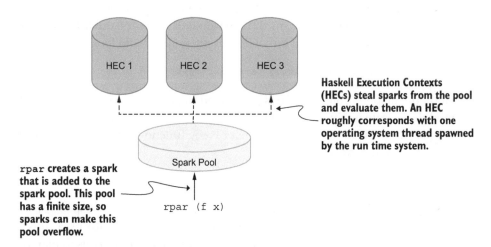

Figure 13.5   Haskell execution contexts and spark pools

Of course, the story is slightly more complicated, as sparks can be prematurely evaluated or garbage collected before a HEC can touch them. However, these are messy details that the runtime system luckily takes care of for us.

With this knowledge under our belt, let us write our first parallel evaluation. To do this, we need to add the `parallel` package to our dependencies in the package.yaml file. The evaluation is controlled by the `Eval` monad and kicked off using `runEval` to retrieve a value from this monad. Let's look at an example:

```
runEval $ do
  x' <- rpar x
  return x'
```

This invocation sparks the parallel computation of x, putting it into the spark pool. However, the `return` does not wait for the evaluation to finish. This means that if the resulting value is evaluated by the code calling `runEval`, the spark becomes invalid.

We then say that the spark *fizzled*. If x has already been evaluated prior to the rpar evaluation, we consider it a *dud*. Can we somehow force the evaluation before return?

```
runEval $ do
  x' <- rpar x
  rseq x'
  return x'
```

In this version, we first create the spark and then force a sequential evaluation before return is called. However, this makes no sense, as the whole point was to perform a parallel evaluation. Let's extend our evaluation to a whole list. The Control.Parallel.Strategies module provides us with a few helper functions to do just that.

One such helper function is evalList, which is of type Strategy a -> Strategy [a]. We can pass a strategy to use on the individual elements of the list, producing a new strategy that can then be used with a list. An invocation could look something like this:

```
map (^ 100) [1 .. 1000] `using` evalList rpar
```

Here, the mapped computation is performed in parallel. using is a function from the module to evaluate the data structure using the specified strategy. We could have also written this expression using the withStrategy function, which is just another way of writing down the evaluation:

```
withStrategy (evalList rpar) $ map (^ 100) [1 .. 1000]
```

Evaluating list-like structures in parallel makes a lot of sense, especially when performing very expensive mappings on them. This is important for us, as this is exactly what our PixelMapping is! However, we do not have a list of pixels to map over but a Vector, so how can we specify a fitting strategy? The module provides us with the evalTraversable function, which defines a way of applying a strategy to each element of a Traversable, as can be surmised from its type Traversable t ? Strategy a -> Strategy (t a). Luckily for us, the Traversable Vector instance exists!

Let's use this to fully evaluate our PixelMapping in parallel! To do so, we have to add a single line of code to our mapping helper function in mapImagePixels. This can be seen in the following listing.

Listing 13.24   A faulty parallel mapping strategy

```
import Control.Parallel.Strategies as S

...

mapping :: GenericPixel px => V.Vector px -> V.Vector px
mapping pixels =
  S.withStrategy (S.evalTraversable S.rpar) $        ⟵┐  Evaluates the vector
    flip V.imap pixels $ \i px ->                      │  of pixels completely
      let x = i `mod` w                                │  in parallel
```

```
      y = i `div` w
      getPixel x' y' =
        toGenericRGB <$> pixels V.!? (y' * w + x')
      result = f x y getPixel $ toGenericRGB px
  in fromGenericRGB result
```

Now, we can rerun our program. We will run it with the following runtime options: `+RTS -N8 -s -RTS`. `-N8` tells the runtime system to use eight processors for evaluation, which correlates with eight HECs that will be used. Using `-s`, we will also receive statistics on how sparks were evaluated.

NOTE We can run the program in parallel because it was compiled with the `-threaded` option, as `stack` adds this option to the build configuration by default.

When we run the program with these options, we will receive the following statistics in the output:

```
SPARKS: 1318768 (10163 converted, 1210301 overflowed, 0 dud, 0 GC'd, 0 fizzled)

  INIT    time    0.000s  (  0.003s elapsed)
  MUT     time   23.793s  ( 27.440s elapsed)
  GC      time    2.758s  (  3.972s elapsed)
  EXIT    time    0.000s  (  0.011s elapsed)
  Total   time   26.552s  ( 31.427s elapsed)
```

As it turns out, our program's performance only marginally improved. This wasn't really worth it after all! But wait, what does the SPARKS statistic actually tell us? We can see that, in total, 1,318,768 sparks were created. As the image we are feeding into the program is 1,397 by 944 pixels, that checks out to *exactly* one spark per pixel, so our mapping seems to work. 10,163 of these sparks were *converted*, which means that a HEC took them from the pool and evaluated them. Also, no sparks *fizzled*, were garbage collected, or were classified as *duds*, so that means that our mapping does not produce unnecessary sparks. A spark is *garbage collected* (GC'd) if it turns out that the spark's evaluation was never needed before a HEC could get to it. The most staggering number is the number of 1,210,301 sparks that *overflowed*. What does that mean?

The answer is simple: spark pools have a fixed size. If too many sparks are created in a short time, the pool can fill up completely and eventually overflow. In this case, the sparks simply get discarded and no parallel evaluation will happen. That is where we messed up! Our program doesn't actually compute the mapping in parallel.

So how do we avoid filling up the spark pool? Of course, we need to create fewer sparks but still want to perform the evaluation in parallel. We need to do *more work* in each single spark. This can be done by splitting the work into larger *chunks* that we then evaluate as sparks.

The `Control.Parallel.Strategies` module provides us with the `parListChunk` function, which defines a `strategy` for lists that operates on chunks of a specified size.

However, this function only operates on lists. To apply this strategy, we will have to convert our `Vector` to a list, perform the parallel computation, and then convert the list back to a `Vector`. Let's write this function in a new `Data.Vector.Strategies` module, which is shown in its entirety in the following listing.

Listing 13.25   A module for chunked parallel execution of the `Vector` type

```
module Data.Vector.Strategies (parVectorChunk) where

import Control.Parallel.Strategies          Imports necessary
import qualified Data.Vector as V           modules

parVectorChunk :: Int -> Strategy (V.Vector a)           Defines a strategy
parVectorChunk size =                                    to evaluate chunks
  fmap V.fromList . parListChunk size rseq . V.toList     of a vector of size,
                                                          size, in parallel
```

Why do we use the `rseq` strategy? Because `parListChunk` already evaluates in parallel. Using `rpar` would cause the strategy to spark a spark, which is useless work!

Now, we can use `parVectorChunk` in our `mapping` function. But how do we decide how many chunks we want to use? That's sadly an inexact science, as sparks are not without a cost. Management and garbage collection mean that creating more sparks (even when they don't overflow the pool) does not result in faster but slower execution. This also heavily depends on how much work can be done in a single spark. In the end, the programmer has to tweak such parameters and verify performance gains, using benchmarking.

For our purposes, we create around 1,000 sparks. We can do so by calculating how big a chunk should be from the total amount of pixels in the image.

Listing 13.26   A parallelized mapping function for mapping pixels in an image

```
import Control.Parallel.Strategies as S           Imports the module for
import qualified Data.Vector as V                 parallel strategies
import qualified Data.Vector.Strategies as V
                                                   Imports Data.Vector and
                                                   Data.Vector.Strategies in
...                                                the same namespace
  mapping :: GenericPixel px => V.Vector px -> V.Vector px
  mapping pixels =
    S.withStrategy (V.parVectorChunk
 ((w * h) `div` 1000)) $                Chunks the image data into
     flip V.imap pixels $ \i px ->      approximately 1,000 chunks
       let x = i `mod` w                and evaluates them in parallel
           y = i `div` w
           getPixel x' y' =
             toGenericRGB <$> pixels V.!? (y' * w + x')
           result = f x y getPixel $ toGenericRGB px
         in fromGenericRGB result
```

With this modification in place, we can test our mapping with the previously introduced box blur. Looking at the statistics after running it presents us with a wonderful view:

```
SPARKS: 1001 (1001 converted, 0 overflowed, 0 dud, 0 GC'd, 0 fizzled)

    INIT    time      0.000s  (   0.004s elapsed)
    MUT     time     27.682s  (   5.502s elapsed)
    GC      time      3.085s  (   2.180s elapsed)
    EXIT    time      0.000s  (   0.000s elapsed)
    Total   time     30.767s  (   7.686s elapsed)
```

Not only don't we have any more overflowing sparks, but we have slashed the execution time from 33 seconds to about 8 seconds *with just a single line of code changed!*

This concludes building our parallel image processing library. We have successfully built a validation for PNM files, using a type-safe dynamic encoding for our data. Also, we have created a generic method of mapping pixels of an image to create different filters and effects. Finally, we have improved the performance of our generic algorithm considerably by using Haskell's built-in support for parallelism.

Summary

- *Generalized algebraic data types* are used to *refine* a polymorphic type to a concrete type, by defining concrete types for constructors for otherwise polymorphic type variables.
- `Vector` is a high-level type similar to lists with performance characteristics similar to arrays, providing very fast access but suffering from slower dynamic allocation, which is used to efficiently store data that has to be read from often.
- Existentially quantified types in conjunction with GADTs can be used to circumvent return-type polymorphism, while still using parametrically polymorphic types, which enables us to decide the type of a result inside a called function instead of letting the caller decide.
- A pure function that is applied uniformly to a collection of data can easily be parallelized, using evaluation strategies in the `Control.Parallel.Strategies` module.
- Haskell features built-in support for parallel execution, using sparks, which can be created using the `Eval` monad and `rpar` or any prebuilt parallel strategies, which enables us to transparently introduce deterministic parallelism into our programs without having to change our algorithms.
- Creating too many sparks causes the spark pool to overflow and parallelism not to be effective, which can be fixed by first splitting our work into larger chunks, which are then evaluated in parallel.

Files and exceptions

This chapter covers

- Working with files on a low level
- Reading byte-level data from a file
- Exploring the filesystem and dealing with exceptions
- Defining, throwing, and catching exceptions

So far in this book, we have covered projects that dealt with reading data, transforming it, and providing some kind of output. We were mostly interested in the "happy path," keeping interactions with the environment to a minimum, so we didn't have to worry about dealing with erroneous behavior. That will change with this chapter.

The project we want to take a look at is a file syncing utility that will copy files and directory structures from one directory to another, only copying files that are not already present at the target directory. This will require us to learn about *exceptions* and how to handle them, which is what this chapter is about.

14.1 Opening and reading files

Sometimes, we want to keep two directory structures in sync, whether as a backup, as a way of keeping files on a network-attached storage, or to sync files between staging and production environments. A common tool for this task is rsync. However, we want to try our hand at creating such a tool ourselves. It should be capable of traversing a directory structure as well as copying missing and changed files to a destination, which is shown in figure 14.1. If a file is present at the destination but not the source, we simply ignore it and do not delete or move it.

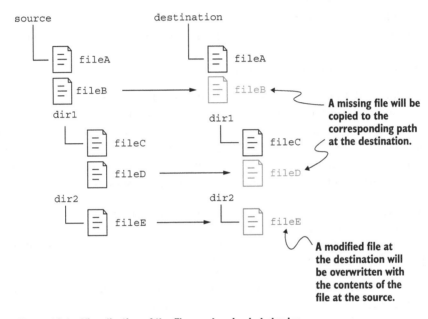

Figure 14.1 Visualization of the file synchronizer's behavior

To set our file synchronization tool apart from others, we will additionally try to determine the file type of files to limit our synchronization to certain types. Writing this tool requires us to interact with the environment in a few ways:

- Copy files
- Read metadata from files
- Create directories
- Partially read files to determine the file type

To start our project, we first have to review how dealing with files in Haskell works.

14.1.1 *System.IO and Handle*

So far, we have seen only basic file handling in our projects. For the most part, we have only either read a whole file into our program to operate on or have written some content to a new file.

Now, we want to go in more depth. First, let's take a look at the `System.IO` module, which defines many operations to read and write files. An important type inside this module is the `Handle`, which describes a *file handle* opened by our process and its associated properties, such as

- Whether it is readable or writable
- Whether it is opened or closed
- What position in the associated file the process is currently reading from or writing to
- What kind of buffering behavior is exhibited on writing

The operations defined for this type are similar to operations that can be performed on file descriptors on Unix-like systems. In Unix fashion, `stdout`, `stderr` and `stdin` are handles that are always open at the start of our program, and we have implicitly interacted with them before (e.g., by using `putStrLn`, we wrote to `stdout`). However, it is important to keep in mind that Haskell's runtime system manages these `Handle` values and they are generally independent of the operating system.

> **NOTE** When working with the `Handle` type, some default behaviors are *platform dependent*, meaning our code will assume different defaults, depending on the system your program is running on. Therefore, we need to be careful when working with files on such a low level.

So how do we work with this type? The module provides us with the function `openFile` of type `FilePath -> IOMode -> IO Handle`, which creates a `Handle` that manages access to the file at the given path. `IOMode` controls how we can interact with the `Handle`:

- `ReadMode`—Open the file to be read from.
- `WriteMode`—Open or create the file to write to and truncate its contents to zero length if it exists.
- `AppendMode`—Open or create the file to write to and set the handle's position to the end of the file.
- `ReadWriteMode`—Open or create the file to support reading and writing to it without truncating its contents.

Now that we can open a handle, we can use them. Here is an example in GHCi:

```
ghci> import System.IO
ghci> h <- openFile "test.txt" WriteMode
ghci> hPutStrLn h "Hello World"
ghci> hClose h
ghci> h2 <- openFile "test.txt" ReadMode
```

```
ghci> hGetLine h2
"Hello World"
ghci> hClose h2
```

Assuming `test.txt` did not exist before, it now contains a little message. `hPutStrLn` writes a given string to a given `Handle`, and `hClose` closes it. We close these handles for two reasons:

- Closing a `Handle` flushes its buffer.
- Multiple handles to the same file can cause exceptions.

Such an exception can easily be caused by simply opening the same file twice—once for reading and once for writing:

```
ghci> import System.IO
ghci> h1 <- openFile "test.txt" ReadMode
ghci> h2 <- openFile "test.txt" WriteMode
*** Exception: test.txt: openFile: resource busy (file is locked)
```

Therefore, it's important to not keep handles open for longer than needed. But what about the buffers? Let's take a look at how they work.

14.1.2 *Buffering and Seeking*

Every `Handle` has a buffer associated with it that records changes to a file before writing them out to the filesystem. A simple `hPutStrLn` does not necessarily write the `String` to the file but only to the buffer, which can be flushed by `hFlush` or by closing the handle, using `hClose`. The buffering behavior can be influenced by using `hSetBuffering`, using a `BufferMode` argument:

- `NoBuffering`—Disables buffering, meaning data is immediately written.
- `LineBuffering`—The buffer is flushed when a newline is written to it.
- `BlockBuffering`—Buffer a set amount of elements or use an implementation-dependent default.

Note that specifying this buffering behavior means setting an *upper limit* on the buffer. It may be flushed more often. Also, different handles have their own defaults:

```
ghci> import System.IO
ghci> h <- openFile "test.txt" ReadMode
ghci> hGetBuffering stdout
NoBuffering
ghci> hGetBuffering h
BlockBuffering Nothing
```

When interacting with a handle that is *seekable*, be it reading or writing, it keeps track of a position within the file it is attached to. This position advances automatically when reading or writing and can be modified manually. Handles like `stdout` are not seekable, as you cannot roll back to an earlier position, since everything you write to it is eventually printed.

Handles that are associated with a file, however, are seekable. We can use hTell and hSeek to get and set the position, respectively:

```
ghci> import System.IO
ghci> h <- openFile "test.txt" WriteMode
ghci> hTell h
0
ghci> hPutStr h "Hello"
ghci> hTell h
5
ghci> hPutStr h " "
ghci> hTell h
6
ghci> hPutStr h "World"
ghci> hTell h
11
ghci> hSeek h AbsoluteSeek 6
ghci> hPutStr h "Haskell"
ghci> hClose h
```

This will write "Hello Haskell" to a file, as we *seek* the position of the first character of "World" before overwriting it with hPutStr. hSeek supports different modes of seeking using a SeekMode parameter:

- AbsoluteSeek—The position of the handle is set exactly to the specified offset.
- RelativeSeek—The position of the handle is set to the specified offset from the current position.
- SeekFromEnd—The position of the handle is set to the specified offset from the end of the file.

While we do cover these details for completeness, we shouldn't have to deal with these technical details too often, as buffering and seeking are examples of something we try to avoid as much as possible: side effects! When working with handles, we are almost always dependent on the internal state of them. Operations on handles are not referential transparent, which makes their use dangerous if we don't keep track of positions, buffering behavior, and the status of the handle, as we might run into exceptions. We will discuss handling these exceptions later. For now, we want to work with handles to determine file types.

14.2 *Reading bytes from a file*

Many file formats carry a signature, in the form of a magic number, to make it easy to figure out what kind of data a program is working with. We now want to write an IO action that can determine the file type of a given file by parsing this magic number so that we can use it later in our tool.

We first start with a new project using `stack new` and adding `bytestring` to our dependencies, as we want to parse the singular bytes from files and need the `Data.ByteString` module for it. Then, we create a new `System.FileType` module inside the src directory.

NOTE `System.IO` offers actions to work with `Handle` and `String` values. As `String` is not the most efficient data type, performance-critical software should rather work with `Data.ByteString` from the `bytestring` package or `Data.Text.IO` from the `text` package to work with handles directly.

We could spend a lifetime gathering magic numbers of the most common file types, but for our use case, we will restrict ourselves to just a few different files, shown in 14.1.

Table 14.1 Magic numbers of a selection of formats

File format	File extension	Magic number (hexadecimal)	Category
Bitmap	`.bmp`	`42 4d`	Image
PNG	`.png`	`89 50 4e 47 0d 0a 1a 0a`	Image
JPEG	`.jpg, .jpeg`	`ff d8 ff`	Image
bzip2	`.bz2`	`42 5a 68`	Compressed
gzip	`.gz`	`1f 8b`	Compressed

Now, we can start writing our module. We can start by defining a type to define categories of file types.

```
data FileType
  = Other
  | Image
  | Compressed
  deriving (Show, Eq)
```

For our `IO` action, we need some functionality from `Data.ByteString` and `System.IO`. We can import them like so:

```
import qualified Data.ByteString as BS
import System.IO (IOMode (ReadMode), hClose, openFile)
```

The `Data.ByteString` module provides us with a few `IO` actions that can deal with the `Handle` values we have discussed. We will use `hGet`, which is of type `Handle → Int → IO ByteString`. The action reads up to the specified number of bytes from the `Handle` in a `ByteString`. Most importantly, it does not fail when the end of file (EOF) is being encountered. Using this, we can read the minimum amount of bytes we need to check for magic numbers and then provide a pattern match on the byte representation of the `ByteString` as a `[Word8]`. The conversion is handled by `unpack`. In the following listing, we can see an initial version of how our action could look.

Listing 14.1   An insecure example of reading from a file handle

```
determineFileType :: FilePath -> IO FileType
determineFileType path = do
  hdl <- openFile path ReadMode              ⊲──────   Opens a Handle to the file
  signature <- BS.hGet hdl 8                           at the specified file path
  let fileType = case BS.unpack signature of   ⊲───    Reads the first
        0x42 : 0x4d : _ -> Image                       eight bytes from
        0x89 : 0x50 : 0x4e : 0x47 : 0x0d : 0x0a : 0x1a : 0x0a   the Handle
      : _ -> Image                                  Determines the
        0xff : 0xd8 : 0xff : _ -> Image              filetype by matching
        0x42 : 0x5a : 0x68 : _ -> Compressed         the read bytes
        0x1f : 0x8b : _ -> Compressed
        _ -> Other
  hClose hdl             ⊲─────── Closes the Handle
  return fileType        ⊲─── Returns the result
```

Closing the `Handle` is technically not necessary, as the garbage collector will close it for us once it is collected. However, that is considered bad style, as we cannot be sure when exactly the GC will choose to do so. In the meantime, we might want to open another `Handle`, which can cause problems.

> **NOTE** Using `unpack` is not necessary when matching prefixes of `ByteString` values. We could have alternatively used `isPrefixOf` provided by `Data.Byte-String`. For larger chunks of data, this is important for performance.

Another problem is one of exceptions. What if our code throws an exception before calling `hClose`? This is a general problem of resource acquisition and release.

14.2.1 *Resource acquisition and bracket*

The problem is so common that Haskell provides us with a nifty function to solve this problem, called `bracket`. It is imported from the `Control.Exception` module and has the type `IO a → (a → IO b) → (a → IO c) → IO c`. The three actions provided to `bracket a r w` are

- `a`—Acquires a resource and passes it to `w` and then `r`
- `w`—Uses the acquired resource and produces some result
- `r`—Releases the acquired resource

`bracket` is special, in that it guarantees that the resource release action is called, even if the action doing the actual work throws an exception. We can use this to rewrite `determineFiletype` using this function and finalize our new module.

Listing 14.2   The full `System.FileType` module

```
module System.FileType          ⊲─── Defines an export list
  ( FileType (..),                    for the module
```

```
            determineFileType,
    )
where

import Control.Exception (bracket)                          Imports necessary
import qualified Data.ByteString as BS                      functions and types
import System.IO (IOMode (ReadMode), hClose, openFile)

data FileType                 ◁──┐  Defines a type for
  = Other                          │  filetype categories
  | Image
  | Compressed
  deriving (Show, Eq)

determineFileType :: FilePath -> IO FileType               Wraps opening and
determineFileType path =                                   closing a file handle
  bracket (openFile path ReadMode) hClose $ \hdl -> do  ◁──  with bracket
    signature <- BS.hGet hdl 8                          ◁──  Reads the first
    return $ case BS.unpack signature of                ◁──  eight bytes from
      0x42 : 0x4d : _ -> Image                                the opened file
        0x89 : 0x50 : 0x4e : 0x47 : 0x0d : 0x0a : 0x1a : 0x0a
  ➥    : _ -> Image                                     Determines the
        0xff : 0xd8 : 0xff : _ -> Image                 filetype by matching
        0x42 : 0x5a : 0x68 : _ -> Compressed            the read bytes and
        0x1f : 0x8b : _ -> Compressed                   returns the result
        _ -> Other
```

We can see how `bracket` cleans up our code in the module shown in listing 14.2. The argument order of the function makes it possible to quickly write wrappers for different resources. This way, we can (more) safely write code that deals with external resources, such as files, network connections, or databases.

> **NOTE** `bracket (openFile path mode) hClose` is commonly used and can be replaced with the `withFile path mode` function from `System.IO`, which is equivalent but easier to read.

Now that we have an understanding of how to read and write files, we should start to investigate how to deal with directories containing them.

14.3 Working with the filesystem and exceptions

So far, we have seen only a single method of referencing files, using `FilePath` to describe a path to wherever a file resides. However, the tool we are trying to construct primarily deals with directories. We need a way of creating and listing them.

To do so, we will use the `System.Directory` and `System.FilePath` modules, which are made available by adding `directory` and `filepath` to our package.yaml. The first module contains system-independent functions to create, remove, move, and list directories, while the second provides us with utility functions to create and split filepaths.

14.3.1 *System.Directory and System.FilePath*

Let's take a look at some basic usage of the aforementioned modules `System.Directory` and `System.FilePath`. Suppose we have a directory structure like this:

```
foo
├── bar
│   ├── fileB.txt
│   └── fileC.txt
├── baz
│   ├── fileD.txt
│   └── fileE.txt
└── fileA.txt
```

This is how we can interact with it using the functions from the modules:

```
ghci> import System.Directory as Dir
ghci> import System.FilePath as FP
ghci> Dir.listDirectory "foo"
["fileA.txt","baz","bar"]
ghci> Dir.listDirectory ("foo" </> "bar")
["fileB.txt","fileC.txt"]
ghci> Dir.listDirectory ("foo" </> "baz")
["fileD.txt","fileE.txt"]
ghci> map FP.dropExtension <$> Dir.listDirectory "foo"
["fileA","baz","bar"]
```

`listDirectory` will list the contents of a directory but only returns the base names for files and directories. The `(</>)` operator helps us to join these base names without having to worry about path separators. `System.FilePath` features many functions to work with files and their extensions, like `dropExtension` and `takeExtension`. In the last line, we see an important limitation of the `System.FilePath` functions: they are unaware of what is a file and what isn't. The module purely manipulates strings, and it is up to us to correctly use them.

14.3.2 *Listing files and directories*

A functionality we need for our program is to list files and directories separately and then to copy the files and traverse the directories. How can do know which path is a file, and which is a directory? That can be achieved with `doesFileExist` and `doesDirectoryExist` from the `System.Directory` module:

```
ghci> Dir.listDirectory "foo"
["fileA.txt","baz","bar"]
ghci> Dir.doesFileExist ("foo" </> "fileA.txt")
True
ghci> Dir.doesFileExist ("foo" </> "bar")
False
ghci> Dir.doesDirectoryExist ("foo" </> "bar")
True
```

Both functions are of type `FilePath -> IO Bool`, so we can't use a simple `filter` when working with a list of paths we need to check. We need the monadic equivalent of this function, which is given to us by the `Control.Monad`. Similar to how `mapM` is the monadic version of `map`, the monadic version of `filter` is called `filterM`, and its type is `Applicative m => (a -> m Bool) -> [a] -> m [a]`.

Listing 14.3   An action to list files and directories separately

```
module System.Directory.Safe where

import System.Directory as Dir
import System.FilePath ((</>))
import Control.Monad (filterM)

listFilesAndDirectories :: FilePath -> IO ([FilePath], [FilePath])
listFilesAndDirectories pathPrefix = do
  paths <- Dir.listDirectory pathPrefix        ◁─┤ Lists all files and directories
                                                    at the specified path
  files <-
    filterM                                     ◁─┐ Filters file paths
      (Dir.doesFileExist . (pathPrefix </>))        that point to files
      paths
  dirs <-
    filterM                                     ◁─┤ Filters file paths that point to directories
      (Dir.doesDirectoryExist . (pathPrefix </>))
      paths
  return (files, dirs)                          ◁─┤ Returns file paths for files
                                                    and directories separately
```

Now, we can use this function to traverse our sample file tree and retrieve the files within it. The paths are *relative*, meaning a path retrieved with `listFilesAndDirectories` is only valid if it is prepended with the path it was retrieved from:

```
ghci> listFilesAndDirectories "foo"
(["fileA.txt"],["baz","bar"])
ghci> listFilesAndDirectories $ "foo" </> "bar"
(["fileB.txt","fileC.txt"],[])
ghci> listFilesAndDirectories $ "foo" </> "baz"
(["fileD.txt","fileE.txt"],[])
ghci> listFilesAndDirectories $ "foo" </> "foo"
*** Exception: foo/foo: getDirectoryContents:openDirStream:
⇒ does not exist (No such file or directory)
```

Notice the important attribute of the function. It throws an exception when the specified path is not present. This brings us to an inconvenient part of working with the filesystem: exceptions.

Exercise: All files in a directory

Use the functions from `System.Directory` and `System.FilePath` to write an IO action that lists all files in a given directory recursively. Running it on our `foo` example should return a flat list of files in arbitrary order:

(continued)
```
ghci> listFilesRecursively "foo"
["foo/fileA.txt","foo/baz/fileD.txt","foo/baz/fileE.txt",
   "foo/bar/fileB.txt","foo/bar/fileC.txt"]
```

14.3.3 *The basics of exceptions*

In this book, we have seen a few ways of dealing with errors. We have encoded optional values and results from failed computations by returning either a `Maybe` value or an `Either` value. We have also used `fail` from the `MonadFail` type class in chapter 12, where we implemented the instance to make our parser fail gracefully.

To reiterate, the `MonadFail` class is used to provide an action called `fail` to make a monadic computation fail, using some given error message:

```
class Monad m => MonadFail m where
  fail :: String -> m a
```

Notice that the action returns `m a` for any arbitrary `a`. How can the implementation invent a value? In the case of our parser, we returned an `Either String a` type, which was constructed by using the `Left` constructor with a `String` value. However, what kind of failure can the `IO` monad produce?

```
ghci> fail "Whoops" :: IO ()
*** Exception: user error (Whoops)
```

It turns out that `fail` in the `IO` monad simply throws an exception, which makes sense when we look at the type signatures of the usual functions to throw exceptions:

```
ghci> import Control.Exception
ghci> :t throw
throw :: Exception e => e -> a
ghci> :t throwIO
throwIO :: Exception e => e -> IO a
```

`throw` and `throwIO` are seemingly able to invent values of arbitrary type. This is similar to two other functions we have seen that can raise exceptions:

```
ghci> :t error
error :: GHC.Stack.Types.HasCallStack => [Char] -> a
ghci> :t undefined
undefined :: GHC.Stack.Types.HasCallStack => a
```

Exceptions are a tricky subject in a purely functional programming language, such as Haskell. Arguably, exceptions don't fit into the pure functional design, as they are *side effects*. They completely disrupt the control flow of our program, since they immediately get rethrown from a function to its caller. Until now, we have completely circumvented dealing with exceptions, since we mostly constricted ourselves to using pure functions.

However, exceptions are a part of dealing with the system outside of our program. Files, networks, and other processes are examples of dealing with the environment in a way that could at any point fail. Files could vanish, networks could lose connection, and other processes could crash. Exceptions are just a part of working with the outside world, so we should get to know them.

14.4 Throwing and catching exceptions

Let's take a look at the `Control.Exception` module, which defines types and functions for using exceptions. `Exception` is a type class that defines how to transform a value into a `SomeException` and back as well as how to display it:

```
class (Typeable e, Show e) => Exception e where
  toException :: e -> SomeException
  fromException :: SomeException -> Maybe e
  displayException :: e -> String
```

`SomeException` is an existentially quantified type similar to our `DynamicPnmImage` type from the last chapter:

```
ghci> :i SomeException
type SomeException :: *
data SomeException = forall e. Exception e => SomeException e
```

We will soon get to know some common exception types, but for now, let's create our own. We can define a new type and derive the `Exception` type class by also deriving `Show` for the type. To do so, we need the `DeriveAnyClass` language extension, which will tell the compiler to create instances of classes like `Exception` with an empty definition. This works because `Exception` has no minimal definition, so `DeriveAnyClass` will produce a usable instance:

```
ghci> :set -XDeriveAnyClass
ghci> data SomeFailure = SomeFailure String deriving (Show, Exception)
ghci> throw (SomeFailure "Whoops")
*** Exception: SomeFailure "Whoops"
```

Great! We can throw exceptions! But that also means we need some way of catching and reacting to them. The most basic function to catch an exception is `catch`, which is of type `Exception e => IO a -> (e -> IO a) -> IO a`:

```
ghci> :t catch
catch :: Exception e => IO a -> (e -> IO a) -> IO a
ghci> throw (SomeFailure "Whoops") `catch` \(SomeFailure s)
 -> putStrLn ("Caught " ++ s)
Caught Whoops
```

Note that we explicitly only catch exceptions of type `SomeFailure`—not any others. This means that an exception thrown by `error` or `undefined` will not be caught by the `catch` function, and generally, any exception that is not of type `SomeFailure` will not be caught:

```
ghci> catchSomeFailure act = act `catch` \(SomeFailure s)
  -> putStrLn ("Caught " ++ s)
ghci> catchSomeFailure (throw $ SomeFailure "Whoops")
Caught Whoops
ghci> catchSomeFailure (error "Whoops")
*** Exception: Whoops
CallStack (from HasCallStack):
  error, called at <interactive>:15:19 in interactive:Ghci6
ghci> catchSomeFailure undefined
*** Exception: Prelude.undefined
CallStack (from HasCallStack):
  undefined, called at <interactive>:16:18 in interactive:Ghci6
```

However, it is possible to catch *all* exceptions by providing `catch` with a function handling `SomeExcpetion`, which is the existentially quantified type that can hold any exception. This is generally discouraged, since handling all exceptions is too broad to be meaningful in most cases, as exceptions can be thrown for all sorts of reasons, such as user interruptions or asynchronous control flow. We will later see some of the different kinds of exceptions that exist.

> **NOTE** When catching more than one exception type, it might seem sensible to use a chain of `catch` applications with different types. However, that has the negative effect: exceptions thrown by an exception handler, called by an earlier `catch`, will then be caught by a later `catch`. This means that we catch too many exceptions, not just the ones from the expression we want to catch exceptions for but also some of the exception handlers, which leads to confusing control flow. A solution to this problem is the `catches` function from `Control.Exception`, which lets you define multiple handlers for a single expression.

Another function that helps us work with exceptions is the `try` function of type `Exception e => IO a -> IO (Either e a)`. It runs an `IO` action and returns an encountered exception inside the `Left` constructor of the `Either` type. If no exception occurs, we receive the value from the action in the `Right` constructor. This way, we can take unsafe operations, which potentially throw exceptions, and make them into safer versions that encode exceptions in their return type.

Now, we can take our `listFilesAndDirectories` function and turn it into a safe function, using `try`. The important thing to determine is which type of exceptions to catch. Since `listFilesAndDirectories` is an action in the `IO` monad, the exception we expect is of type `IOException`. This type of exception could *always* be thrown from the `IO` monad and encodes errors related to the filesystem and networks. By catching this type of exception and encoding in it our return type, we create a safe version of our function. Therefore, we can give it a name that properly specifies that this function is safe to use, as shown in the following listing.

> **Listing 14.4   A safe listing function that encodes exceptions in the return value**

```
import Control.Exception

...

safeListFilesAndDirectories ::
  FilePath -> IO (Either IOException ([FilePath], [FilePath]))
safeListFilesAndDirectories = try .
  listFilesAndDirectories
```
Calls the listFilesAndDirectories function and catches exceptions of type IOException

The code for this function is shown in listing 14.4. It is important to understand that the return type of the function specifies which kinds of exceptions are caught by `try`. Only exceptions of type `IOException` are being caught, and all other exceptions will just be rethrown by this function.

As we will later use this function in our implementation, we can put these functions inside a module that specifically contains and exports safe functions for working with the filesystem. Therefore, we can call the module `System.Directory.Safe`.

14.4.1 Handling an error

We have created a function to list files and directories. Another functionality we need for our synchronization tool is the ability to copy files from one location to another. `System.Directory` provides us with two actions that can copy a file. One is `copyFile`, which copies a file, keeping its permissions on the operating system intact but without copying other metadata with it. The other action is `copyFileWithMetadata`, which copies a file with all of its metadata. For our application, we want to preserve the metadata to better compare the files we are synchronizing.

Neither action creates a target directory if it doesn't exist, so that is what we have to do. A good candidate for this purpose is `createDirectoryIfMissing`, which does what its name implies. It receives a file path and a `Boolean` that specifies whether the action should also create the parent directories of the file path. Using `createDirectoryIfMissing` and `copyFileWithMetadata`, we can write an action that creates the target directory (if missing) and copies a file to it:

```
safeCopyFileAndCreateDir ::
  FilePath -> FilePath -> IO (Either IOException ())
safeCopyFileAndCreateDir src dst = try $ do
  Dir.createDirectoryIfMissing True $ takeDirectory dst
  Dir.copyFileWithMetadata src dst
```

We use `takeDirectory` to remove the filename from the destination path. This action is fine, but it has one problem. Let's say our application copies a larger file and the user interrupts the execution. In this case, whatever was already copied by the action will remain. This is hardly the behavior we expect from a synchronization tool!

> **NOTE** copyFileWithMetadata does not copy files atomically, meaning copying can partially succeed before failing, leaving behind a corrupted file. However, copyFile ensures that the file is either being copied or not. If you need more control over atomicity when working with files, you can take a look at the UnliftIO.IO.File module from the unliftio package.

We can specifically catch interrupts from the user, by catching a specific subtype of so-called *asynchronous exceptions*. They are the foil to *synchronous exceptions*, which are being thrown by the code that runs on the specific thread to itself. Asynchronous exceptions, however, are being thrown by code in other threads. Usually, they are used by one thread in our program to specifically stop the execution of another thread by throwing an asynchronous exception to it (using throwTo). While we will not cover this in this book, we will still have to work with these when it comes to user interrupts, as asynchronous exceptions can also be initiated by the operating system.

The type AsyncException has four constructors:

- StackOverflow—Raised when a thread exceeds its stack size limit
- HeapOverflow—Raised when the program's heap has reached its limit
- ThreadKilled—Raised when a thread should be stopped (usually thrown by other threads)
- UserInterrupt—Raised when the user cancels the execution of the program (e.g., by using Ctrl-C)

We want to specifically catch exceptions with the UserInterrupt constructor and delete the file that has been partially copied. To catch exceptions with such fine-grained control, we can use catchJust and tryJust, which let us decide whether we want to catch an exception by a predicate. catchJust has the type Exception e => (e -> Maybe b) -> IO a -> (b -> IO a) -> IO a, with the first argument being the predicate that receives the exception, which might be returned from the action in the second argument, and it returns Just of some value to pass to the exception handler, which is the third argument. The predicate can specify which type of exception it generally receives and then make a choice based on the exception's data if the handler should work with whatever data could be extracted from it.

Inside this predicate, we can match on the AsyncException value we expect and check if it is an UserInterrupt. This is shown in the following listing.

Listing 14.5 A function safely copying a file with metadata

```
safeCopyFileAndCreateDir ::
  FilePath -> FilePath -> IO (Either IOException ())      Catches exceptions
safeCopyFileAndCreateDir src dst = try $ do         ◄─┘  of type IOException
```

```
Dir.createDirectoryIfMissing True $ takeDirectory dst                ◁──   Creates the path for
catchJust                                                                  the file destination
   ( \(ex :: AsyncException) -> case ex of                                 if it isn't already
       UserInterrupt -> Just ()                          ◁───┐             present
       _ -> Nothing                                           │
   )
   (Dir.copyFileWithMetadata src dst)       ◁──       Returns a Just () in case a
   (const $ Dir.removeFile dst >>                      UserInterrupt exception was thrown
➡ throwIO UserInterrupt)                       ◁──┐
                                                   └──  Copies the file from the source path to the
                                                        destination path, preserving metadata
```

In case a UserInterrupt exception was caught, removes the file that was partially copied and then rethrows the UserInterrupt

If we catch the `UserInterrupt`, we remove the file at the destination and then rethrow a `UserInterrupt` exception, as we may want it to halt the rest of the program. Note that we require the `ScopedTypeVariables` extension to specify the type inside the predicate.

The functions we have talked about can happily live in the aforementioned `System.Directory.Safe` module. To make its usage clear, the beginning of the module should look like the following outline:

```
{-# LANGUAGE ScopedTypeVariables #-}

module System.Directory.Safe
  ( safeListFilesAndDirectories,
    safeCopyFileAndCreateDir,
  )
where

import Control.Exception
import Control.Monad (filterM)
import qualified System.Directory as Dir
import System.FilePath (takeDirectory, (</>))
```

With our two modules, `System.FileType` and `System.Directory.Safe`, we can now build our application. This will make us think about how to handle configuration, state, and output across multiple IO actions.

Summary

- `Handle` gives us low-level control over files that can be used to read specific bytes from a file.
- `bracket` is used to safely acquire and then release a resource, even when exceptions are thrown.
- Similar to how `mapM` is the monadic version of `map`, the monadic version of `filter` is called `filterM` and its type is `Applicative m =\> (a -> m Bool) -> [a] -> m [a]`.
- Exceptions are normal types that have an instance of the `Exception` type class and can be used to change the control flow of our programs.

- The `DeriveAnyClass` language extension allows the compiler to derive instances of type classes for any type, as long as the minimal set of definitions for the instance is empty.
- Exceptions can be caught with `catch` or `try`, but when we want to catch multiple exceptions, we should use `catches`.
- Asynchronous exceptions are being thrown by code to other threads to change their control flow.

Transformers for synchronizing

This chapter covers

- Using monad transformers to extend the abilities of monads
- Structuring an application using a monad-transformer stack with a read-only environment, an event log, and state
- Providing the application with command-line arguments, using the `optparse-applicative` package

In the last chapter, we began building an application to synchronize directory structures. We have also dealt with reading and writing files as well as handling exceptions. Now, we want to use this functionality to build the application.

To structure our program, we want to use *monad transformers* to more easily construct effectful computations that have access to read-only data, modify state, and collect output instead of simply relying on the IO monad. We also provide command-line arguments, using the `optparse-applicative` package.

347

15.1   *Monad transformers*

Let's first define what features our file synchronization application should have. In general, the user can specify one source and one destination path but also needs to be able to limit the type of files being copied. Additionally, the user should be able to limit the synchronization to a certain recursive directory depth and an upper bound to the number of files that should be copied. While the synchronization is in progress, we will have to manage some state that will be used to check against the limits set by the user, which includes the recursion depth and the number of already transferred files.

It would be nice to get some kind of report listing the files the application looked at and whether copying the file was successful, as we might have encountered exceptions while working with them. Alternatively, it's possible to ignore files when they are unchanged from the file we have already copied. After all, this is the whole point of our application.

We can identify three different ways of interacting with data. The configuration given by the user is data that doesn't change but should be read from anywhere in our application. We can consider it a static environment we want to read from. Information on recursion depth and synchronized files is some kind of state that our program needs to operate on. The listing of files and what we did with them is some output we want to accumulate while running our application. To interact with data in these different ways, we want to use a technique called *monad transformers*, which will help us to create a powerful abstraction for our application.

15.1.1   *Reading an environment with ReaderT*

Let's first review how we normally implement something like a configuration we can read from. We will start implementing different types for our application in a new module, called App.Types. This is where a type for our configuration can live.

As we have already discussed, the configuration for our application needs a source and destination path as well as a file type we want to restrict the synchronization on and bounds on recursion depth and number of files. A type for this configuration might look like the one shown in the following listing.

> **Listing 15.1   A type for configuring the file synchronization application**

```
module App.Types where                          Imports the
                                                 FileType type
import System.FileType (FileType)        ⭠

data Config = Config
  { configFromPath :: FilePath,
    configToPath :: FilePath,                   Defines fields for the file paths
    configRequiredFileType :: Maybe FileType,   ⭠  Defines a possibly required file
    configMaxRecursionDepth :: Maybe Int,          type for synchronization
    configMaxTransferredFiles :: Maybe Int
  }                                              Defines optional limits on recursion
  deriving (Show, Eq)                            depth and the amount of transferred files
```

Now comes the question of how to read from this configuration inside of our actions. A simple solution is to pass the `Config` as an argument and then use the `RecordWild-Cards` language extension to easily access the fields of the configuration:

```
action :: Config -> ... -> IO ()
action cfg@(Config {..}) ... = ...
```

In this action, we can access all fields of our configuration and pass it down to other actions by using `cfg` as an argument. While this seems fine at first, it is a bit messy. We have to specify the configuration and its type in every action we want to use it in, leading to a lot of repetition.

What we would rather have is a way of reading a read-only environment without having to specify this environment for every action. This behavior is enabled by something called the `Reader` monad. As its name suggests, the `Reader` has the special capability of being able to *read from an environment* but not change it.

To use it, we have to add the transformers package to our package.yaml and import the `Control.Monad.Trans.Reader` module:

```
ghci> import Control.Monad.Trans.Reader
ghci> :{
ghci| withConstantAdded :: Int -> Reader Int Int
ghci| withConstantAdded x = do
ghci|   env <- ask
ghci|   return $ env + x
ghci| :}
ghci> runReader (withConstantAdded 1) 10
11
```

A `Reader r a` has two type variables: the first (`r`) for the environment it reads from and the second (`a`) the return type of running the `Reader`. The `runReader` function executes a `Reader` with a given environment. In the preceding example, we pass a simple `Int` to it, and using `ask`, we can read the environment inside the `Reader` monad:

```
ghci> :{
ghci| addIfNotNeg :: Int -> Reader Int Int
ghci| addIfNotNeg x = do
ghci|   env <- ask
ghci|   if env < 0
ghci|     then return env
ghci|     else withConstantAdded x
ghci| :}
ghci> runReader (addIfNotNeg 10) 1
11
ghci> runReader (addIfNotNeg 10) (-1)
-1
```

The clear advantage of using the `Reader` monad is that we do not have to pass the environment from action to action but are still able to access it. However, the `Reader` monad is rather boring. It does not possess the capabilities of IO, so we cannot possibly use it for our purposes! Wouldn't it be nice if we could somehow take the IO monad and infuse it with the capabilities of the Reader monad?

This is exactly what the transformers package is here for! It defines *monad transformers* that can be used to give existing monads new features. One of these is ReaderT, which allows us to fuse Reader with other monads, like IO.

> **NOTE** Monad transformers usually carry a T at the end of their name, so we can see from a type that another base monad was extended by it.

The type ReaderT r m a carries the following type variables:

- r—The environment the ReaderT has access to
- m—The underlying monad of ReaderT
- a—The result of running the ReaderT

When m satisfies the Monad m type constraint, the whole ReaderT satisfies it. Therefore, ReaderT Config IO a is a monad that uses IO as its underlying monad and has access to a Config value as its environment. Using ask (which is of type Monad m => ReaderT r m r), we can query the environment:

```
ghci> import Control.Monad.Trans.Reader
ghci> type App a = ReaderT Config IO a
ghci> import Control.Monad.IO.Class (liftIO)
ghci> :{
ghci| example :: App ()
ghci| example = do
ghci|   env <- ask
ghci|   let toPath = configToPath env
ghci|       fromPath = configFromPath env
ghci|     in liftIO $ putStrLn (fromPath <> " -> " <> toPath)
ghci| :}
ghci> cfg = Config "src" "dst" Nothing Nothing Nothing
ghci> runReaderT example cfg
src -> dst
```

In this example, we define a new type, App, that represents our application. The example action reads the paths from the given Config and prints them. Note that here, we have to use liftIO. That's because putStrLn is an IO action, but we are inside of App, not IO. If we want to use IO actions inside App, we first have to *lift* them to an App action, which is given to us by liftIO, which is defined in the MonadIO type class:

```
ghci> import Control.Monad.IO.Class
ghci> :i MonadIO
type MonadIO :: (* -> *) -> Constraint
class Monad m => MonadIO m where
  liftIO :: IO a -> m a
  {-# MINIMAL liftIO #-}
```

Monads that implement an instance of `MonadIO` can run any `IO` action using `liftIO`. `ReaderT` implements `MonadIO` if the underlying monad implements `MonadIO` and `IO` implements `MonadIO`.

But what if our underlying monad isn't `IO`? Would we be able to lift actions from it into the transformer? As it turns out, this is a core concept for monad transformers, which is codified by the `MonadTrans` type class:

```
ghci> import Control.Monad.Trans.Class
ghci> :i MonadTrans
type MonadTrans :: ((* -> *) -> * -> *) -> Constraint
class MonadTrans t where
  lift :: Monad m => m a -> t m a
  {-# MINIMAL lift #-}
```

As we can see, the `lift` function is the function that takes a monad and *lifts* it into the transformer context (denoted by `t`).

So `ReaderT` will enable us to read the `Config` inside our `IO` actions, but what about handling state inside these actions? Is there a transformer for that?

15.1.2 *StateT and WriterT*

As it turns out, there is a transformer that allows us to handle state, called `StateT`. It works very similarly to `ReaderT`. The type `StateT s m a` uses these variables:

- `s`—The state the `StateT` manages
- `m`—The underlying monad of `StateT`
- `a`—The result of running the `StateT`

`StateT` behaves similarly in defining the instances for `Monad` and `MonadIO`. The difference between `ReaderT` and `StateT` mainly comes in the functions we can use to access whatever data they manage. While `ReaderT` has its `ask` function, `StateT` mainly provides us with three different functions:

- `get :: Monad m => StateT s m s`—Retrieves the current state in the `StateT` monad
- `put :: Monad m => s -> StateT s m ()`—Sets a new value as the state in the `StateT` monad
- `modify :: Monad m => (s -> s) -> StateT s m ()`—Modifies the existing state in the `StateT` monad

There are a few more functions we can use, but these three are the most essential. With them, we can freely modify some state inside arbitrary monads. Of course, in our case, we will use `IO`:

```
ghci> import Control.Monad
ghci> import Control.Monad.Trans.State.Strict
ghci> import Control.Monad.IO.Class (liftIO)
ghci> import System.Directory.Safe
ghci> import System.FilePath
```

```
ghci> type App a = StateT Int IO a
ghci> :{
ghci| example :: FilePath -> App ()
ghci| example path = do
ghci|   mFilesAndDirs <-
ghci|     liftIO $ safeListFilesAndDirectories path
ghci|   case mFilesAndDirs of
ghci|     Left _ -> return ()
ghci|     Right (_, dirs) -> do
ghci|       modify (\x -> x + (length dirs))
ghci|       if null dirs
ghci|         then return ()
ghci|         else forM_ (map (path </>) dirs) example
ghci| :}
ghci> execStateT (example "foo") 0
2
```

Now comes the question of what the state for our application should look like. As mentioned previously, we need to keep track of our recursion depth and the number of files already transferred. A type that does that is shown in the following listing.

Listing 15.2   A type and helper functions for runtime statistics

```
data Stats = Stats                          ◁———┐  Defines a type for
  { statsRecursionDepth :: Int,                  │  runtime statistics
    statsTransferredFiles :: Int
  }
  deriving (Show, Eq)


modifyRecursionDepth :: (Int -> Int) -> Stats -> Stats
modifyRecursionDepth f (Stats recDepth files) =
  Stats (f recDepth) files                        ◁———┐  Defines functions
                                                       │  to modify single
modifyTransferredFiles :: (Int -> Int) -> Stats -> Stats  │  fields of the Stats
modifyTransferredFiles f (Stats recDepth files) =      │  type
  Stats recDepth (f files)                        ◁———┘
```

Additionally, we define modification functions for the different fields, mainly to make it easier to work with the modify function. Since we later want to start our application with an empty state, it would be nice to have a definition for mempty, so we can also implement instances for Semigroup and Monoid for this type. This is shown in the following listing.

Listing 15.3   Semigroup and Monoid instances for the Stats type

```
instance Semigroup Stats where
  a <> b =
    Stats                                      Computes the
      { statsRecursionDepth = max `on`         maximum of two
⇨ statsRecursionDepth,                 ◁———    recursion depths
```

```
         statsTransferredFiles = (+) `on`
⮕ statsTransferredFiles
     }
   where
     f `on` field = f (field a) (field b)
```

	Computes the sum of the transferred files

Defines a helper function to use function on a given field for both arguments

```
instance Monoid Stats where
  mappend = (<>)
  mempty =
    Stats
      { statsRecursionDepth = 0,
        statsTransferredFiles = 0
      }
```

Uses the associative function from the Semigroup instance as mappend

Defines an empty Stats value

With these definitions in place, we have a state for our application. The last puzzle piece is the report of what happened to the files while processing them. Our monad needs some way to accumulate this report "on the side," while doing its normal computation. You might assume that this can be done through the aforementioned state again, and that is technically correct. However, once again, there is another transformer that allows us to do this in a much nicer way: `WriterT`.

`WriterT` is yet another monad transformer that allows accumulating some output while running other effectful computations. The `WriterT w m a` type is made up of the following types:

- w—The output being collected by `WriterT`
- m—The underlying monad for `WriterT`
- a—The result of running `WriterT`

For this to work, the output typically needs to have a `Monoid` instance, as different parts of the output are being collected one at a time and combined using `mappend`, which we covered in chapter 7:

```
ghci> import System.Directory.Safe
ghci> import Control.Monad
ghci> import Control.Monad.IO.Class (liftIO)
ghci> import Control.Monad.Trans.Writer.Strict
ghci> type App a = WriterT [FilePath] IO a
ghci> :{
ghci| example path = do
ghci|   mFilesAndDirs <- liftIO $ safeListFilesAndDirectories path
ghci|   case mFilesAndDirs of
ghci|     Left _ -> return ()
ghci|     Right (_, dirs) -> do
ghci|       tell dirs
ghci|       if null dirs
ghci|         then return ()
ghci|         else forM_ (map (path </>) dirs) example
ghci| :}
ghci> runWriterT (example "foo")
((),["baz","bar"])
```

This type features the `tell` function of type `Monad m => w -> WriterT w m ()` to add output to the accumulation. With that, we can think about how our report should look as a type. In general, file synchronization can succeed, fail, or not be required (as a file could have already been synced). Thus, our log should contain these different types with their respective parameters.

Listing 15.4   Definitions for log entries for the output of the file synchronisation application

```
import Control.Exception

...

data SuccessEntry = SuccessEntry        Defines a type
  { successFromPath :: FilePath,        for a successfully
    successToPath :: FilePath           synchronized file
  }
  deriving (Show, Eq)
                                        Defines a type
data FailureEntry = FailureEntry        for failure during
  { failureFilePath :: FilePath,        synchronization
    failureException :: IOException
  }
  deriving (Show, Eq)
                                        Defines a type
data SkipEntry = SkipEntry              for a skipped file
  { skipFilePath :: FilePath,
    skipReason :: String
  }
  deriving (Show, Eq)
                                        Defines a type for a
data LogEntry                           generic log entry
  = Success SuccessEntry
  | Failure FailureEntry
  | Skipped SkipEntry
  deriving (Show, Eq)
```

Here, we can see that even exceptions like `IOException` are just data, which can be stored in values and passed around. We can then define a simple type for our log, which is a `newtype` definition for `[LogEntry]`:

```
newtype Log = Log [LogEntry]
```

However, now, we have to manually define instances for `Semigroup` and `Monoid` for this new type, even though the list type already has these instances defined. The definition for the functions of these instances would only consist of unwrapping the `Log` type, calling the appropriate functions, and then wrapping them inside the `Log` constructor. Luckily for us, Haskell provides us with a technique to automatically derive such instances from `newtype` definitions. To do that we need to add two language extensions to our file:

```
{-# LANGUAGE DerivingStrategies #-}
{-# LANGUAGE GeneralizedNewtypeDeriving #-}
```

The first one allows us to tell Haskell how type classes should be derived from a type by providing a *deriving strategy* after `deriving`. Here is an example:

```
ghci> :set -XDerivingStrategies
ghci> newtype Foo = Foo String deriving newtype Show
ghci> show $ Foo "Hey, where did Foo go?"
"\"Hey, where did Foo go?\""
```

By specifying the `newtype` strategy by writing `deriving newtype`, we tell the compiler to use the instance of the underlying type of the `newtype` to construct a new instance. In our example, we use the `Show` instance of `String` to get a `Show Foo` instance. Because of this, the constructor is not shown. If we want to use the default deriving strategy, we can either not specify one or use the `stock` strategy, to make it more clear that we want Haskell's default behavior.

> **NOTE** Haskell also provides the `anyclass` and `via` deriving strategies, which are used in combination with the `DeriveAnyClass` and `DerivingVia` language extensions to provide strategies for classes that have an empty minimal definition set and deriving instances for types with identical runtime representations.

By default, Haskell can only derive instances for `Eq`, `Ord`, `Enum`, and `Bounded` with the `newtype` strategy. To enable the compiler to derive more instances, we need the `GeneralizedNewtypeDeriving` language extension. With it, we are finally able to derive `Semigroup` and `Monoid` for our `Log` type, which is shown in the following listing.

Listing 15.5   A type definition for a log that can be used with the `WriterT` transformer

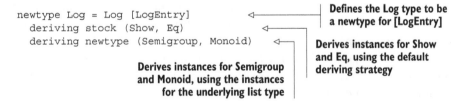

```
newtype Log = Log [LogEntry]        ◄────────────   Defines the Log type to be
  deriving stock (Show, Eq)          ◄─────────      a newtype for [LogEntry]
  deriving newtype (Semigroup, Monoid)   ◄────
                                                     Derives instances for Show
         Derives instances for Semigroup             and Eq, using the default
         and Monoid, using the instances             deriving strategy
         for the underlying list type
```

Exercise: Sequence for performance

While this almost seems fine, we have sadly introduced a performance problem to our application. When using the `tell` action, we know that some data is being added to the collected output of the `WriterT` using `mappend`, which, for a normal list, is the append function (`++`). As we want to add single elements to the end of the previously collected results, the whole list needs to be traversed, so to collect the output of n elements, we have to traverse the list n times, which leads to a quadratic blowup. A plain list is, therefore, not suitable for larger amounts of data. As an alternative, we

> **(continued)**
> can use the `Seq` type from the `containers` package's `Data.Sequence` module. It
> supports appending values to the end of a sequence of values in constant time,
> which allows us to avoid the quadratic blowup. While the rest of this chapter will still
> use lists, try to use the `Seq` type. (Hint: You will not have to touch a lot of code.)

Now, we can happily use functions from both type classes with the new type. Therefore, we can use it as the accumulated output in our `WriterT`!

15.1.3 *Stacking multiple transformers with RWST*

As we have seen, we can use `ReaderT` to enable a monad to read from an environment,
`StateT` to manage some state that can be accessed from within the monad, and
`WriterT` to enable the monad to collect some output while it is computing some other
output. However, we want to combine all of these functionalities into one monad. Is
that possible?

As we have become accustomed to, it indeed is. As a monad transformer transforms a `Monad` and also produces a `Monad`, we can combine multiple transformers. This
is also often referred to as a *transformer stack*:

```
ghci> import Control.Monad.Trans.Class (lift)
ghci> import Control.Monad.Trans.Reader
ghci> import Control.Monad.Trans.Writer
ghci> type Foo a = ReaderT Int (WriterT String IO) a
ghci> foo = (ask >>= lift . tell . show) :: Foo ()
ghci> runWriterT (runReaderT foo 1)
((),"1")
```

As we can see, to use `tell` from `WriterT`, we first have to *lift* it into the `ReaderT`
monad. Now, imagine we wanted to use a transformer stack of all three transformers
we have seen. This would force us to use `lift` twice at times when using actions from
the innermost monad.

Luckily for us, using the three transformers we have seen is rather common, which
is why the `transformers` package exposes another transformer called `RWST`, which is a
combination of the three that does not rely on a stack of transformers.

> **NOTE** The monad transformers we have covered here are very common.
> However, many others exist, and it is quite common to see more complicated
> transformer stacks in the wild.

The `RWST r w s m a` definition is a combination of the transformers we have seen
before:

- `r`—The environment the `RWST` has access to
- `w`—The output being collected by the `RWST`
- `s`—The state the `RWST` manages

- ▪ m—The underlying monad of RWST
- ▪ a—The result of running the RWST

So the type for our application can now be a simple RWST using the types we wanted to work within our transformer stack. As we are working with the filesystem, our underlying is IO. This final type is shown in the following listing.

Listing 15.6   Definition for the application monad

```
import Control.Monad.Trans.RWS.Strict          ◁─┐   Imports the
                                                  │   definition for RWST
...

type App a = RWST Config Log Stats IO a        ◁─┐   Defines a type for the
                                                      application in terms of RWST
```

Note that since RWST is itself a monad, we can simply use App in the same way we used the other transformers so far. With this type finally set in stone, we can start implementing our application logic.

15.2   *Implementing an application*

Our implementation will live in a separate module, called App.Impl. Where the other module was meant to provide type definitions, the new module will contain the actual implementation. This module will use the following imports:

```
import App.Types
import Control.Exception (SomeException, catch)
import Control.Monad (forM_, when)
import Control.Monad.IO.Class
import Control.Monad.Trans.RWS.Strict
import qualified System.Directory as Dir
import qualified System.Directory.Safe as Dir
import System.Exit (ExitCode (ExitFailure), exitWith)
import System.FilePath ((</>))
import System.FileType (determineFileType)
import System.IO (hPutStrLn, stderr)
```

Note that we import System.Directory and System.Directory.Safe with identical qualified names. By referencing the single qualified name Dir, we can reference symbols from both modules simultaneously.

First things first: How can we run an App? Since App is an RWST, we can use runRWST, which is of type RWST r w s m a -> r -> s -> m (a, s, w). It takes an RWST, an environment to read from, and a state, and it returns the result, the state, and the accumulated output in the underlying monad. Let's use that! However, what will a, the result, be in our case? As our actions do not compute a meaningful result (and only serve to produce side effects by copying files), we can keep it as the unit type (). With that, we already know the types we can pass to runRWST. Since Stats, our state type, has an instance of Monoid, we can use mempty to supply an initial state. The environment (which is our Config) will need to be passed from the outside. With this, we can write a helper to run an `App` with a given `Config` and return a `Log` in the `IO` monad. The full code is shown in the following listing.

Listing 15.7 A function to execute an `App` in the `IO` monad

```
runApp :: App () -> Config -> IO Log
runApp app config = do
  (_, _, syncLog) <-
    runRWST app config mempty
      `catch` exceptionHandler
  return syncLog
  where
    exceptionHandler :: SomeException -> IO a
    exceptionHandler ex = do
      hPutStrLn stderr $
        "Syncing interrupted by exception: "
          ++ show ex
      exitWith $ ExitFailure 1
```

Executes the App with an empty state and the given config

Catches all exceptions

Returns the accumulated Log

Prints an exception to stderr

Exits the program with code 1, indicating a failure

In our code, we take the extra precaution of catching exceptions and exiting the program as well as logging the error to `stderr` so that the user has some diagnostic of what was going on when the program crashed.

Now, we can think of the actions our `App` needs to be able to perform:

- Check if two file locations need synchronization.
- Check the file type of a file.
- Copy a file from one location to another and count number of files transferred.
- Traverse a directory structure and keep track of recursion depth.

Let's go through these one by one. Two file locations need synchronization when the destination file either does not exist or has a different modification time. We can check the modification time of a file, using `getModificationTime` from the `System.Directory` module. As this action is in `IO`, we have to use `liftIO` to use it in our `App` monad. The same goes for `doesFileExist`, which we can use to check if the destination file exists. The code for the action is shown in the following listing.

Listing 15.8 An action to check if two files have an identical modification time

```
data FileDiff
  = Matching
  | ModificationTimeDiff
  | DestinationMissing
  deriving (Show, Eq)

checkFileDiff :: FilePath -> FilePath -> App FileDiff
checkFileDiff src dst = do
  dstExists <- liftIO $ Dir.doesFileExist dst
  if not dstExists
    then return DestinationMissing
    else do
```

Defines a type that represents if and what kind of difference between files exists

Checks if the destination file exists

```
srcModTime <- liftIO $ Dir.getModificationTime src
dstModTime <- liftIO $ Dir.getModificationTime dst
if srcModTime == dstModTime
  then return Matching
  else return ModificationTimeDiff
```

Checks if the modification times of the two files differ

Using this action, we can check whether we should synchronize two files.

TIP Just checking modification times is not enough to ensure that two files are identical. In theory, we would need to check that the size of the files match and additionally compute checksums to make sure the contents were not changed. To keep things simple, we will stick with the modification time heuristic.

However, we also have to check the file type of the source file matches the file type restriction that might be given in our `Config` type. First, we have to read the `config-RequiredFileType` from the `Config` in our `App`. We have already seen the `ask` function to query the environment, but a nicer way to read just a single field from a type is the `asks` function of type `(Monoid w, Monad m) => (r -> a) -> RWST r w s m a`. Using this function, we can transform code like this:

```
config <- ask
let mRequiredFileType = configRequiredFileType config
```

Or more concisely written, our code looks like this:

```
mRequiredFileType <- configRequiredFileType <$> ask
```

And we turn it into this:

```
mRequiredFileType <- asks configRequiredFileType
```

Similar to what `asks` is to `ask`, there exists a dual for `get`, which enables us to read single fields from the state of our `App`. Using `asks`, we can now write our function that checks if the file type for a file matches the required file path. The code for this is shown in the following listing.

Listing 15.9 A function to check whether a file has an optionally required file type

```
checkFileType :: FilePath -> App Bool
checkFileType path = do
  mRequiredFileType <- asks configRequiredFileType      ◁── 
  case mRequiredFileType of
    Just requiredFileType -> do
      fileType <- liftIO $ determineFileType path
      return (requiredFileType == fileType)
    Nothing -> return True
```

Retrieves the configRequiredFileType field from the Config

Checks whether the file type of the given file path matches the required file type

Now that we can check if we should synchronize files, we should write an action that actually does synchronize files. Since we will need to log successes, failures, and reasons why we skipped synchronizing, we first write a few helpers that will help us log our different log entry types:

```
logSingleEntry :: LogEntry -> App ()
logSingleEntry x = tell $ Log [x]

logFailure :: FailureEntry -> App ()
logFailure = logSingleEntry . Failure

logSuccess :: SuccessEntry -> App ()
logSuccess = logSingleEntry . Success

logSkipped :: SkipEntry -> App ()
logSkipped = logSingleEntry . Skipped
```

Our synchronization action should first check how many files have already been transferred and what the maximum amount of transferrable files is. After that, it has to check the file type and if files match and log accordingly. Then, it has to copy the file using our `safeCopyFileAndCreateDir` action and log successes and failures as well as increment the number of transferred files. This is shown in the following listing.

Listing 15.10   Action to synchronize a file from one path to another

```
syncFile :: FilePath -> FilePath -> App ()          Reads the current state
syncFile src dst = do                               and environment
  curFiles <- gets statsTransferredFiles              Checks if the limit
  mMaxFiles <- asks configMaxTransferredFiles         of file transfers has
  when (maybe True (curFiles <) mMaxFiles) $ do       already been met
    fileTypeCorrect <- checkFileType src
    if not fileTypeCorrect                            Checks if the file has
      then                                            the required file type
        logSkipped $
          SkipEntry dst "Required filetype did not match"    Checks
      else do                                                whether two files
        filesMatch <- checkFileDiff src dst                  differ and need
        if filesMatch == Matching                            synchronization
          then logSkipped $ SkipEntry dst "Files matched"
          else do
            mDidCopy <-                         Safely copies
              liftIO $                          the source file
  Dir.safeCopyFileAndCreateDir src dst
              case mDidCopy of
                Left ex -> logFailure $         Logs the exception, in case it
                                                was thrown while copying
  FailureEntry dst ex
                Right () -> do                    Increments the number
                  modify (modifyTransferredFiles (+ 1))   of transferred files
                  logSuccess $ SuccessEntry src dst    Logs the successfully
                                                       synchronized file
```

Here, we can see the `when` function from `Control.Monad`, which allows us to only run an action when a certain condition is met. In our action, we use it to only perform any further checking and copying if the amount of transferred files is smaller than the maximum amount of transferred files or if no maximum has been set. If we can continue, we call our `checkFileType` and `checkFileDiff` actions and log results accordingly. If all checks succeed, we copy the file and increment the number of transferred files using `modify (modifyTransferredFiles (+ 1))` and log the success.

Now, we define the last building block for our application: the directory traversal. It is similar to `syncFile`, as it first has to check a predicate (whether the maximum recursion depth has been reached), log information when appropriate, modify our state, and recursively traverse subdirectories. The code for this action is shown in the following listing.

Listing 15.11 An action to traverse a directory structure and synchronize all found files

```
traverseAndCopy :: FilePath -> App ()
traverseAndCopy pathSuffix = do
  fromPath <- asks configFromPath
  toPath <- asks configToPath
  mMaxRecDepth <- asks configMaxRecursionDepth
  curRecDepth <- gets statsRecursionDepth
  let path = fromPath </> pathSuffix
  when (maybe True (curRecDepth <=) mMaxRecDepth) $ do
    mFilesAndDirs <-
      liftIO $ Dir.safeListFilesAndDirectories path
    case mFilesAndDirs of
      Left ex -> logFailure $ FailureEntry path ex
      Right (files, dirs) -> do
        forM_ files $ \fileName ->
          syncFile
            (fromPath </> pathSuffix </> fileName)
            (toPath </> pathSuffix </> fileName)
        modify (modifyRecursionDepth (+ 1))
        forM_ dirs $ traverseAndCopy . (pathSuffix </>)
        modify (modifyRecursionDepth (\x -> x - 1))
```

Reads configuration and state

Checks whether the maximum recursion depth has been reached

Lists all files and directories at the current path

Logs a failure in the case of an exception

Synchronizes a file

Increments the current recursion depth

Recursively calls traverseAndCopy on all subdirectories

Decrements the current recursion depth

The action receives the current path suffix to operate on as an argument. As we can see, we modify the recursion depth before and after recursively calling `traverseAndCopy`, keeping track of the recursion depth.

With all of these actions ready, we can define our main app, which will receive the paths it needs to operate on through its environment. `traverseAndCopy` is only parametrized by the path suffix added to the `configFromPath`. So the initial start has to be with an empty path. This leads to our final definition in the `App.Impl` module: the App to run, shown in the following listing.

Listing 15.12 The definition for the main application

```
mainApp :: App ()
mainApp = traverseAndCopy ""
```

Our program will simply consist of a call of `runApp`, using `mainApp`. The only other argument that `runApp` requires is the `Config`. As we want to supply this configuration using the CLI, we have to write a parser for the options, which the user can provide. This time we will use a commonly used parser for this task and take a look at the `optparse-applicative` module.

15.3   Providing a CLI

Our file synchronization application is almost finished. We just have to provide a way for the user to set the configuration for our `App` so that we can run it. In the previous chapters, we have often resorted to writing our own parsing functions to read the arguments given to the program, but now, we want to use a better solution, brought to us by the `optparse-applicative` package.

As always, we add it to our package.yaml so that our final dependencies section looks like this:

```
dependencies:
- base >= 4.7 && < 5
- bytestring
- directory
- filepath
- transformers
- optparse-applicative
```

With this package added to our project, let's review what it can do.

15.3.1   *Parsing arguments with optparse-applicative*

The `optparse-applicative` package provides us with parsers for options and arguments we can read from the command line, using an *applicative* style. It also automatically generates a help text for our application, deals with parsing different types of arguments, and checks if all required arguments exist.

Let's look at an example of a parser for arguments. For this example, we assume that we have the following type we want to parse from the arguments given to us by the user:

```
data Args = Args
  { arg1 :: String,
    arg2 :: Int,
    arg3 :: Bool,
    arg4 :: Maybe String
  }
  deriving (Show)
```

We want to parse strings and integers for `arg1` and `arg2`. `arg3` can be represented by a simple flag, which is either switched on or not. `arg4` is an optional argument. Let's examine how a parser would look for this type.

Listing 15.13   An example of an argument parser

```
import Options.Applicative

...

argsParser :: Parser Args
argsParser = Args <$> strArg <*> intArg <*>
  boolArg <*> maybeArg                    ◁──┐ Constructs the
  where                                       result type in an
    strArg =                          ◁──┐    applicative style
      strOption $                         │
        long "string"                 Defines a parser for
          <> short 's'                a string argument
          <> metavar "STRING"
          <> help "An example string"
    intArg =                          ◁──┐ Defines a parser for
      option auto $                        an integer argument
        long "integer"
          <> short 'i'
          <> metavar "INTEGER"
          <> help "An example integer"
    boolArg =                         ◁──┐ Defines a parser for
      switch $                             a Boolean switch
        long "boolean"
          <> short 'b'
          <> help "An example boolean switch"
    maybeArg =                        ◁──┐ Defines a parser for
      optional $                           an optional string
        strOption $                        argument
          long "optional"
            <> short 'o'
            <> metavar "OPTIONAL"
            <> help "An example optional string"
```

Our parser uses the package's `Parser` type. Each argument uses its own parser, which
we define separately. `strOption` denotes a string argument, while `option auto` can be
used to define a parser for any type for which a `Read` instance exists.

> **NOTE**   When we want to parse a `String`, we need to use `strOption` (or `option`
> `str`) instead of `option auto`, since the `Read String` instance requires quotes
> around the value, so `ABC` won't parse, but `"ABC"` will. `strOption` corrects that
> for us.

Optional arguments are modified, using the `optional` function to create an optional
parser. Using `long` and `short`, we supply the parser long and short argument names,
which the user will use to specify the argument. `metavar` and `help` are used for documentation in the help text. Note that these functions are used to combine the description of each option using in a *monoid* style by using (`<>`). In this case, their order is
irrelevant and most are optional. We are only forced to either provide `short` or `long`,
as the option can otherwise not be referenced.

The aforementioned *applicative* style can be seen in the actual definition of the parser, which uses this style to build the actual `Args` value from the parsing results. We explored this style in chapter 12 when we examined how parsers can be defined as applicatives and monads.

Now that the `Parser` is defined, we have to define a `ParserInfo` that we can then execute. This `ParserInfo` combines a parser with additional information, which, just like the information for our options, is relevant for generating the help text.

Listing 15.14   An example `ParserInfo`

```
                                          Creates a ParserInfo from
                                          a Parser and additional
argumentParser :: ParserInfo Args         information
argumentParser =
  info
    ( argsParser          ◄────────────   Adds a parser that parses a --help
        <**> helper        ◄───────────   option and displays the help text
        <**> simpleVersioner "v1.0"  ◄───
    )                                           Adds a parser that
    ( fullDesc           ◄────────────         parses a --version
        <> progDesc "This is an example"       option and displays
        <> header "OPTPARSE APPLICATIVE EXAMPLE"   the option
        <> footer "Thanks for checking this example out!"   Provides additional
    )                                                        information for the
                                                             help text
```

As with the options before, `progDesc`, `header`, and `footer` are completely optional. Here, we combine our `argsParser` with an additional `helper` parser, which will provide the user with a `--help` option to display the full help text and a `simpleVersioner` parser that parses a `--version` option and displays the provided version.

With the `ParserInfo` constructed, we can execute it in the `IO` monad:

```
main :: IO ()
main = do
  args <- execParser argumentParser
  print args
```

Let's observe how the program now responds:

```
shell $ stack run
Missing: (-s|--string STRING) (-i|--integer INTEGER)

Usage: optparse-exe (-s|--string STRING) (-i|--integer INTEGER) [-b|--boolean]
                    [-o|--optional OPTIONAL]

  This is an example
```

As we can see, the parser correctly identifies that two required arguments are missing. The previously defined `progDesc` is also printed along the program name, which is optparse-exe in this case (given by stack, in this example). Let's supply the program with the required arguments:

```
shell $ stack run -- -s "Foo" -i 10
Args {arg1 = "Foo", arg2 = 10, arg3 = False, arg4 = Nothing}
```

As we can see, the switch (for arg3) is not required, as it is False when omitted:

```
shell $ stack run -- -s "Foo" -i 10 -b -o "Bar"
Args {arg1 = "Foo", arg2 = 10, arg3 = True, arg4 = Just "Bar"}
```

optparse-applicative chooses to use a *applicative* style for its parsing for two reasons:

- The help text is automatically generated from the parser, no matter how complicated our parsing logic becomes.
- The order in which arguments appear is irrelevant.

First, let us look at the help text in action:

```
shell $ stack run -- --help
OPTPARSE APPLICATIVE EXAMPLE

Usage: optparse-exe (-s|--string STRING) (-i|--integer INTEGER) [-b|--boolean]
                    [-o|--optional OPTIONAL]

  This is an example

Available options:
  -s,--string STRING       An example string
  -i,--integer INTEGER     An example integer
  -b,--boolean             An example boolean switch
  -o,--optional OPTIONAL   An example optional string
  -h,--help                Show this help text
  --version                Show version information

Thanks for checking this example out!
```

And now, let's look at the order of arguments again:

```
shell $ stack run -- -o "Bar" -i 10 -b -s "Foo"
Args {arg1 = "Foo", arg2 = 10, arg3 = True, arg4 = Just "Bar"}
```

The package provides us with more ways of building rich command-line interfaces by, for example, providing parsers for commands with their own arguments. For the sake of brevity, we exclude these extra features from our discussion.

15.3.2 *Enumerating custom types*

Now that we know the basics, we can provide a parser for arguments that will result in the Config type we have defined earlier. Let's remind ourselves what the type looked like:

```
data Config = Config
  { configFromPath :: FilePath,
    configToPath :: FilePath,
    configRequiredFileType :: Maybe FileType,
    configMaxRecursionDepth :: Maybe Int,
    configMaxTransferredFiles :: Maybe Int
  }
  deriving (Show, Eq)
```

We can determine that the two `FilePath` arguments should be required results from `strOption`. The rest of our arguments are optional. One question might be how we can parse `FileType`, as that is a custom type that we defined. As was mentioned earlier, when creating a parser with `auto`, we can parse any datatype with an instance of the `Read` type class. We briefly covered its usage in chapter 8 when parsing integers.

Now, we want to parse `FileType`. More precisely, we want to parse the values of this type. If we don't mind that they are parsed as capitalized words (the exact same way we write the constructors in the source code), we can simply derive `Read` for the type:

```
data FileType
  = Other
  | Image
  | Compressed
  deriving (Show, Read, Eq)
```

After adding `Read` to the `deriving` clause, we can happily parse the values from strings:

```
ghci> read "Image" :: FileType
Image
ghci> read "Compressed" :: FileType
Compressed
ghci> read "Foobar" :: FileType
*** Exception: Prelude.read: no parse
```

This is fine, but we need some way of telling the user which kinds of values they can provide and how they should be written. When deriving `Show` and `Read`, they are dual, meaning the strings `Show` produces are the strings `Read` expects for parsing. It would be helpful if we could somehow enumerate all constructors of `FileType` to show the user all possible values. We can provide a simple list of the constructors like so:

```
allFileTypes :: [FileType]
allFileTypes = [Other, Image, Compressed]
```

This is fine, but what if we ever extend the type? We must keep this new constant and the type in sync, which seems error prone. Is there an automatic way?

15.3.3 *The Enum class*

It turns out there is an automatic way, since `FileType` is a *enumeration type*. Such types only consist of *nullary constructors*, simply meaning that the constructors have no fields.

Therefore, all possible values of the type can be enumerated by deriving an instance of Enum. The Enum type class provides us with a number of functions to compute a range of values of said type and to give each constructor a corresponding numeric value (starting from 0). Lets look at an example:

```
ghci> :i Enum
type Enum :: * -> Constraint
class Enum a where
  succ :: a -> a
  pred :: a -> a
  toEnum :: Int -> a
  fromEnum :: a -> Int
  enumFrom :: a -> [a]
  enumFromThen :: a -> a -> [a]
  enumFromTo :: a -> a -> [a]
  enumFromThenTo :: a -> a -> a -> [a]
  {-# MINIMAL toEnum, fromEnum #-}
ghci> data EnumType = A | B | C deriving (Show, Enum)
ghci> enumFromTo A C
[A,B,C]
ghci> toEnum 0 :: EnumType
A
ghci> toEnum 1 :: EnumType
B
ghci> map fromEnum $ enumFromTo A C
[0,1,2]
```

Notice the enumFromTo function that computes the range from a start value and ends at another value. This might remind us of the ranges syntax for lists we have seen in previous chapters, and as it turns out, that syntax is just syntactic sugar for this exact function!

```
ghci> [A .. B]
[A,B]
ghci> [B .. C]
[B,C]
ghci> [A .. C]
[A,B,C]
```

We can evaluate [1 ..] and ['a' .. 'z'] because Int and Char have instances for this type class.

While this helps us to enumerate our constructors, we still have to manually write the first and last constructors, don't we? Once again, I have deceived you, dear reader! It turns out that we don't, since there is another type class we can derive and use that supplies us these values—the Bounded class:

```
ghci> :i Bounded
type Bounded :: * -> Constraint
class Bounded a where
  minBound :: a
```

```
  maxBound :: a
  {-# MINIMAL minBound, maxBound #-}
ghci> data EnumType = A | B | C deriving (Show, Enum, Bounded)
ghci> minBound :: EnumType
A
ghci> maxBound :: EnumType
C
ghci> enumFromTo minBound maxBound :: [EnumType]
[A,B,C]
```

For enumeration types, it is customary to derive `Bounded` and `Enum`. These will now allow us to automatically determine all possible constructors we might have for our type. The changes that have to be made to our `FileType` type are shown in the following listing.

Listing 15.15   The `FileType` and a helper function that enumerates all of its constructors

```
data FileType
  = Other
  | Image
  | Compressed                                     ◄── Derives instances for
  deriving (Show, Read, Eq, Enum, Bounded)             serialization, parsing,
                                                       comparison, and
                                                       enumeration

allFileTypes :: [FileType]                         ◄── Enumerates all constructors
allFileTypes = enumFromTo minBound maxBound            for the FileType type as a list
```

Now, we can create the parser for our `Config` type.

15.3.4   A CLI for App

As our `App` produces a `Log`, it would be nice if we could have a switch, that enables printing it once the `App` is done executing. We can define a new type that contains the actual `Config` as well as this `verbose` flag. This is shown in the following listing.

Listing 15.16   A parser for CLI arguments

```
data CliArgs = CliArgs          ◄── Defines a type for
  { cliArgsConfig :: Config,         the CLI arguments
    cliArgsVerbose :: Bool
  }
                                                    Constructs the
                                                    Parser CliArgs
cliArgsParser :: Parser CliArgs                     value
cliArgsParser = CliArgs <$> config <*> isVerbose  ◄──
  where
    config =
      Config          ◄── Constructs the
        <$> fromPath      Parser Config value
        <*> toPath
        <*> onlyFileType
        <*> maxRecDepth
        <*> maxFiles
```

```
  fromPath =                      <—┐
    strOption $                      │  Parses the required
      long "from-path"               │  filepath arguments
        <> metavar "PATH"            │
        <> help "Path to sync files from"
  toPath =                        <—┘
    strOption $
      long "to-path"
        <> metavar "PATH"
        <> help "Path to sync files to"    Creates a textual representation
  fileTypeMetaVar = L.intercalate "|" $    of the different FileType values
➡ map show allFileTypes         <—        the user can supply
  onlyFileType =
    optional $                 <—————————┐
      option auto $                       │
        long "only-filetype"              │
          <> help "Only consider files of a certain filetype"
          <> metavar fileTypeMetaVar      │
  maxRecDepth =                           │      Parses the
    optional $               <————————————┤      optional
      option auto $                       │      arguments
        long "max-rec-depth"              │
          <> help "Limit maximum recursive depth to traverse"
          <> metavar "NUMBER"             │
  maxFiles =                              │
    optional $              <—————————————┘
      option auto $
        long "max-files"
          <> help "Limit number of files to sync"
          <> metavar "NUMBER"
  isVerbose =
    switch              <——————— Parses the --verbose flag
      ( short 'v'
          <> long "verbose"
          <> help "Enable verbose output"
      )
```

Here, we can see how we use the *applicative* style to build a parser for a more complex type. Based on this parser, we can now construct our ParserInfo. This is shown in the following listing.

Listing 15.17 A ParserInfo for the application's CLI arguments

```
argumentParser :: ParserInfo CliArgs    Creates a ParserInfo from a Parser
argumentParser =
  info                                   Combines the normal parser for CLI arguments
    (cliArgsParser <**> helper)          with an additional parser for the --help flag
    ( fullDesc                                             Provides a
        <> progDesc "A simple file synchronization tool"   rudimentary
    )                                                      description of
                                                           the program
```

We complete our program by an IO action that prints the Log type. In the following listing, we can see this action as well as the main action that executes the argument parser, then we see the `mainApp` we introduced earlier, and then it optionally prints the log.

Listing 15.18   An action to print the log produced from running an `App`

```
printLog :: Log -> IO ()
printLog (Log xs) = forM_ xs (putStrLn . prettyEntry)        | Prints each
  where                                                       | entry in the Log
    prettyEntry (App.Success (SuccessEntry _ toPath)) =
      "[*] " ++ takeFileName toPath                            Shows the filename
    prettyEntry (App.Failure (FailureEntry path exc)) =       of the successfully
      "[!] " ++ takeFileName path ++ ": " ++ show exc         copied file
    prettyEntry (App.Skipped (SkipEntry path reason)) =
      "[s] " ++ takeFileName path ++ ": " ++ reason            Shows the filename
                                                               as well as the
main :: IO ()                            Executes the         exception in case
main = do                                argument             of a failure
  args <- execParser argumentParser      parser
  result <- runApp mainApp $ cliArgsConfig args                Shows the filename as
  when (cliArgsVerbose args) $ printLog result                 well as the reason in
                                                               case of a skipped file

                   Prints the resulting log if     Executes the mainApp,
                   the --verbose flag was set       using the config from
                                                    the argumentParser
```

Here, we specifically prefix the `Success`, `Failure`, and `Skipped` constructors to not cause name clashes with `Options.Applicative`.

Exercise: Removing missing files

Our application only supports copying files from a source to a destination. However, it completely ignores files that are present at the destination but *not* the source.

Extend the application such that files that are not present at the source are deleted from the destination. Additionally, define a new command-line argument to turn this functionality off

---

Now, let's test our application. Let's assume we find the following *foo* directory in our project's directory:

```
shell $ tree foo
foo
├── bar
│   ├── fileB.txt
│   └── fileC.txt
├── baz
│   ├── fileD.txt
│   └── fileE.txt
└── fileA.txt
```

We can sync this directory to another by using our tool like so:

```
shell $ stack run -- --from-path "foo" --to-path "/tmp/bar" --verbose
[*] fileA.txt
[*] fileD.txt
[*] fileE.txt
[*] fileB.txt
[*] fileC.txt
shell $ tree /tmp/bar
/tmp/bar
├── bar
│   ├── fileB.txt
│   └── fileC.txt
├── baz
│   ├── fileD.txt
│   └── fileE.txt
└── fileA.txt
```

And with that, we conclude our file synchronization experiment.

Summary

- Monad transformers are used to extend a monad's functionalities.
- The `ReaderT` transformer is used to give a monad the capability of reading a read-only environment.
- The `StateT` transformer is used to give a monad the capability of modifying and accessing some state, while the monad is executing.
- The `WriterT` transformer is used to give a monad the capability of producing output "on the side," while producing other values as actual return values.
- The `RWST` transformer is a combination of `ReaderT`, `StateT`, and `WriterT` that does not require stacking transformers.
- `optparse-applicative` defines parsers and combinators to define rich argument parsing for CLIs.

JSON and SQL

This chapter covers

- Parsing and serializing JSON
- Deriving typeclasses, using `Generic`
- Using SQLite databases with our programs

In previous chapters, we have gotten to know many techniques and concepts in Haskell and built quite a few tools using them. Now, it is time to use everything we learned to realize a larger project. This and the following chapter function as a showcase for building an application with Haskell talking to a database and the network, providing a type-safe HTTP/JSON API. Additionally, we will automatically derive a client application for our API to safely interface with it. We will get to know a few new packages that will help us realize this.

This chapter starts with a discussion on working with JSON data using the aeson library and how to generically derive type classes. Then, we will dive into using SQLite in our programs and how to pass data to and from the database. We will use this knowledge in the following chapter to construct our application.

16.1 Encoding values as JSON

For our last project, we want to create an application that will allow us to manage a todo list, using an API to do so. This means we want some kind of *server application* to communicate about the state of this list using JSON-encoded data over the *Hypertext Transfer Protocol* (HTTP). Additionally, we would like a fitting *client application* that can communicate with the server as a CLI tool. The server application should also provide an HTML page that renders our todo list for easier inspection.

What we are building in this project is considered a *create, read, update, delete* (CRUD) API, which could be used to implement all kinds of use cases:

- Questionnaire services
- Appointment planners
- Booking platforms
- Store backends

We will start our implementation by defining a structure for the data to be sent over the wire.

16.1.1 Aeson and JSON parsing

Let's start by creating a new project using `stack new todolist`.

Since we are dealing with a JSON API, we need some way to serialize our data type and parse it from JSON data. How do we do that in Haskell? The most famous and widely used package for this is `aeson`. After adding it as a dependency to our package.yml file, we can test it out in GHCi using `stack repl`:

```
ghci> import Data.Aeson as J
ghci> :set -XOverloadedStrings
ghci> :i J.Value
type Value :: *
data Value
  = Object !Object
  | Array !Array
  | String !Text
  | Number !Scientific
  | Bool !Bool
  | Null
ghci> J.decode "{\"a\":\"Hello\", \"b\": [1,2,3]}" :: Maybe J.Value
Just (Object (fromList [("a",String "Hello"),("b",Array
➥ [Number 1.0,Number 2.0,Number 3.0])]))
ghci> :t J.decode
J.decode :: FromJSON a => ByteString -> Maybe a
```

Here, we see the `Value` type, which is the Haskell representation for possible JSON values. As we can see, the `decode` function takes a lazy `ByteString` (which is why we needed to enable `OverloadedStrings`) and parses it to some value that satisfies the

FromJSON constraint. This allows us to get a simple JSON representation from a string. Using the encode function, we can then turn values into a JSON representation:

```
ghci> J.decode "[1,2,3]" :: Maybe [Int]
Just [1,2,3]
ghci> J.encode ([1,2,3] :: [Int])
"[1,2,3]"
ghci> :t J.encode
J.encode :: ToJSON a => a -> ByteString
```

As we can see, encode is constrained by ToJSON, which is the type class that lets us serialize values. If we want to support JSON for a type, we need to create instances of ToJSON and FromJSON for it.

First, let us worry about creating our type, which we can do in an appropriate Todos.Types module. Since we are building a todo list, we need a way to represent an entry in that list. What kinds of fields does such an entry need? As we want to reference them within our API, we need an ID to reference them. Also, an entry needs some text on whatever the entry is about and whether it has been checked. As we later want to display the list, we also need a way of sorting them. We will use an optional rank to do this. After adding *text* to our dependencies in package.yml, this type might look like this:

```
import qualified Data.Text as T

data TodoEntry = TodoEntry
  { entryId :: Maybe Int,
    text :: Text,
    checked :: Bool,
    rank :: Maybe Int
  }
  deriving (Eq, Show)
```

Now, we can worry about providing our JSON instances. The FromJSON instance requires a parseJSON function of type Value -> Parser a. Building such a Parser value can be done using a host of helper functions provided to us by Data.Aeson. Some of them include

- withObject :: String -> (Object -> Parser a) -> Value -> Parser a
- withText :: String -> (Text -> Parser a) -> Value -> Parser a
- withArray :: String -> (Array -> Parser a) -> Value -> Parser a
- withScientific :: String -> (Scientific -> Parser a) -> Value -> Parser a
- withBool :: String -> (Bool -> Parser a) -> Value -> Parser a

These functions create a parser by first receiving a name as a first argument (used for generating better error messages) and a function as well as a JSON Value to apply the function. The resulting parsers fail if the Value is not of the expected JSON value, so withObject fails if the Value is not an object:

```
import qualified Data.Aeson as J
import qualified Data.Aeson.Types as J
import qualified Data.Text as T
import qualified Data.ByteString.Lazy as BSL

myParser :: BSL.ByteString -> J.Parser T.Text
myParser string =
  case J.decode string of
    Nothing -> fail "failed to decode value as JSON"
    Just json -> J.withText "a simple string" pure json
```

Here, we define a simple parser, that decodes a lazy `ByteString` as JSON and parses a single string literal. In case we are unable to decode the string into valid JSON, we use `fail` to make the parser fail. This is possible, since the `MonadFail Parser` instance exists:

```
ghci> import qualified Data.Aeson.Types as J
ghci> J.parse myParser "\"Hello\""
Success "Hello"
ghci> J.parse myParser "1"
Error "parsing a simple string failed, expected String,
➥ but encountered Number"
ghci> J.parse myParser ""
Error "failed to decode value as JSON"
```

By using `withText`, we get an error message that precisely tells us what was expected and what we actually got. Now, comes the more interesting part: parsing a JSON object. These objects contain key–value pairs, using strings as keys mapping to arbitrary JSON values. `Data.Aeson` provides us with a few operators to parse these:

- `(.:) :: FromJSON a => Object -> Key -> Parser a`—Requires a key to be present in an object and retrieves the value
- `(.:?) :: FromJSON a => Object -> Key -> Parser (Maybe a)`—Looks up a key in an object and provides the value if it is present and not `Null`
- `(.:!) :: FromJSON a => Object -> Key -> Parser (Maybe a)`—Like `(.:?)` but tries to parse `Null` as a value
- `(.!=) :: Parser (Maybe a) -> a -> Parser a`—Can be used with `(.:?)` and `(.:!)` to provide a default value

With these operators, we can define a parser that takes a JSON `Value` and tries to parse a `TodoEntry` from it. It makes sense to require our JSON representation for a `TodoEntry` to be an object with keys with the same names as the Haskell type. `Text`, `Int`, and `Bool` have direct representations in JSON, so we know what kinds of values we expect from the corresponding keys. Fields that result in a `Maybe` are optional. All this can neatly be written down in a simple parser shown in the following listing.

Listing 16.1   A JSON parser for `TodoEntry`

```
{-# LANGUAGE RecordWildCards #-}

...

todoEntryParser :: J.Value -> J.Parser TodoEntry
todoEntryParser = J.withObject "TodoEntry" $
  \object -> do
    entryId <- object J..:? "entryId"
    text <- object J..: "text"
    checked <- object J..: "checked"
    rank <- object J..:? "rank"
    return TodoEntry {..}
```

Expects a JSON object for the parser to continue

Parses optional fields in the JSON object

Parses required fields in the JSON object

Parses optional fields in the JSON object

Builds the completed TodoEntry (uses the RecordWildCards language extension)

Now, we can write a new parsing function that takes a `ByteString` and produces a `Parser` for our `TodoEntry` type:

```
parseTodoEntry :: BSL.ByteString -> J.Parser TodoEntry
parseTodoEntry string =
  case J.decode string of
    Nothing -> J.parseFail "failed to decode value as JSON"
    Just json -> todoEntryParser json
```

Using this function, we can parse strings of JSON as our TodoEntry type:

```
ghci> J.parse parseTodoEntry "{\"text\":\"Do something\",\"checked\":false}"
Success (TodoEntry {entryId = Nothing, text = "Do something",
  checked = False, rank = Nothing})
ghci> J.parse parseTodoEntry "{\"text\":\"Do something\",
  \"checked\":false,\"rank\":100}"
Success (TodoEntry {entryId = Nothing, text = "Do something",
  checked = False, rank = Just 100})
ghci> J.parse parseTodoEntry "{\"text\":\"Do something\"}"
Error "key \"checked\" not found"
```

However, the `parseTodoEntry` function is not necessary, as `decode` can automatically parse `ByteString` values if a `FromJSON` instance for a type exists. We can define this instance by using our `todoEntryParser`, which is shown in the following listing.

Listing 16.2   A `FromJSON` instance for `TodoEntry`

```
instance J.FromJSON TodoEntry where
  parseJSON = todoEntryParser
```

Defines the parseJSON function for the FromJSON instance

With this instance defined, we can directly parse `TodoEntry` values, without going through our little helper function:

```
ghci> J.decode "{\"text\":\"Do something\",\"checked\":false}"
➥ :: Maybe TodoEntry
Just (TodoEntry {entryId = Nothing, text = "Do something",
➥ checked = False, rank = Nothing})
```

Now that we can parse JSON as our `TodoEntry` values, we also need to be able to serialize the values to JSON. We can do so by implementing a `ToJSON` instance.

16.1.2 Serializing to JSON

When converting Haskell values to JSON, we can simply use `toJson` to turn a Haskell value into a JSON `Value` and `encode` to turn it into a lazy bytestring. Using `toJSON`, we can easily turn strings, numbers, and Booleans into JSON values:

```
ghci> J.toJSON ("Hello" :: String)
String "Hello"
ghci> J.toJSON (100 :: Int)
Number 100.0
ghci> J.toJSON (True :: Bool)
Bool True
```

It becomes more complex when we want to construct an object with keys and values:

- `object :: [Pair] -> Value`—Constructs an object `Value` from a list of `Pair` values
- `(.=) :: (KeyValue kv, ToJSON v) => Key -> v -> kv`—Constructs a JSON `KeyValue` from a key and a value that can be serialized as JSON

Using these two functions, we can write a serializer function to turn our `TodoEntry` values into JSON.

Listing 16.3 A `ToJSON` instance for `TodoEntry`

```
todoEntrySerializer :: TodoEntry -> J.Value
todoEntrySerializer TodoEntry {..} = do          ◁── Constructs an object Value
  J.object                                            from key–value pairs
    [ "entryId" J..= entryId,
      "text" J..= text,             ◁── Defines key–value
      "checked" J..= checked,           pairs using the fields
      "rank" J..= rank                  from the argument
    ]

instance J.ToJSON TodoEntry where      ◁── Defines the toJSON function
  toJSON = todoEntrySerializer             for the ToJSON instance
```

With this instance defined, we can test that `encode` and `decode` provide us with a successful round trip, encoding a value and then parsing it again into the same value:

```
ghci> e = TodoEntry Nothing "Do Something" False (Just 1)
ghci> J.encode e
"{\"checked\":false,\"entryId\":null,\"rank\":1,\"text\":\"Do Something\"}"
ghci> J.decode $ J.encode e :: Maybe TodoEntry
Just (TodoEntry {entryId = Nothing, text = "Do Something",
➥ checked = False, rank = Just 1})
```

Wonderful! We have successfully written functions to turn our values into JSON and back. But let us ask a question: Isn't this boilerplate and a bit annoying? When looking at our instances, we see that we manually have to add queries and key–value pairs for each field in our record. Imagine we want to add another field. We then would need to add the field to the parsing and serialization functions, even though this could be figured out statically by the compiler, as it is known what fields the type has.

16.2 *Deriving type classes with Generic*

To avoid all of this manual labor, we can use the help of the GHC.Generics module. Haskell has a built-in deriving mechanism to provide library developers with a way of accessing a generic datatype representation that can be used to define instance implementations. We will not go into detail about what these representations look like or how we could use them when implementing our type classes. Instead, we will focus on using this mechanism to avoid writing boilerplate code.

The main interface for this mechanism is the Generic type class, which features a function to turn a value into its *representation* and a function to turn this representation back into the actual value:

```
ghci> import GHC.Generics
ghci> :i Generic
type Generic :: * -> Constraint
class Generic a where
  type Rep :: * -> * -> *
  type family Rep a
  from :: a -> Rep a x
  to :: Rep a x -> a
  {-# MINIMAL from, to #-}
```

This representation can be used by the aeson library to automatically provide us with JSON representations for our values. For this purpose, it defines the functions genericToJSON and genericParseJSON that are used as the default implementations for the toJSON and parseJSON functions from the ToJSON and FromJSON type classes. Therefore, all we need to do is to provide an instance of Generic for our type and we get the ToJSON and FromJSON instances for free!

Luckily, this can be done by the compiler automatically. We enable this functionality by using the DeriveGeneric language extension and then deriving Generic for our data type. After that, we can instantiate ToJSON and FromJSON, using an empty definition. We can do this in a new module, which is shown in the following listing.

Listing 16.4 A ToJSON instance for TodoEntry

```
{-# LANGUAGE DeriveGeneric #-}        ◁       Enables the DeriveGeneric language extension
                                              to allow deriving the Generic type class
module Todos.Types where

import qualified Data.Aeson as J    |  Imports Data.Aeson and
import qualified Data.Text as T     |  Data.Text with qualified names
```

```
import GHC.Generics (Generic)
```
⊲ ┐ **Imports the Generic type**
     class from GHC.Generics
```
data TodoEntry = TodoEntry
  { entryId :: Maybe Int,
    text :: T.Text,
    checked :: Bool,
    rank :: Maybe Int
  }
  deriving (Eq, Show, Generic)
```
⊲ **Defines the TodoEntry type**

Derives Eq, Show, and
⊲ **Generic for TodoEntry**

```
instance J.ToJSON TodoEntry
```
⊲ **Defines instances for ToJSON and**
   FromJSON, using the datatype-
```
instance J.FromJSON TodoEntry
```
⊲ **generic implementation for both**

Using this definition we can test whether the roundtrip (encoding and decoding should not change the value) still works:

```
ghci> e = TodoEntry Nothing "Do Something" False (Just 1)
ghci> J.encode e
"{\"checked\":false,\"entryId\":null,\"rank\":1,
⇒ \"text\":\"Do Something\"}"
ghci> J.decode $ J.encode e :: Maybe TodoEntry
Just (TodoEntry {entryId = Nothing, text = "Do Something",
⇒ checked = False, rank = Just 1})
```

So how exactly will aeson derive instances? Here are a few general rules:

- Named fields in ADTs are represented by key–value pairs in an object.
- Multiple constructors are represented by tag key containing the name of the constructor.
- Contructors with a single unlabeled field convert to that field.
- Constructors with multiple unlabeled fields are converted to JSON arrays.
- Types that only consist of contructors without fields will be serialized into a string only containing the constructor name.
- Maybe values are encoded as optional values that will be serialized as null if missing.
- Types containing other types that can be serialized to JSON will be nested in the JSON output recursively.

In general, we can assume that the instances for ToJSON will generate JSON values that can be parsed by FromJSON. The logic between serialization and parsing stays the same.

> **NOTE** Using the Generic instance for FromJSON and ToJSON is mostly fine, but we have to keep in mind that changing the data type will also change the implementations for these type classes. If we write software that stores JSON persistently, this might break backward compatibility. For data serialization that can be made backward compatible, you could have a look at the safecopy or proto-lens packages.

And so we can conclude our excursion into JSON serialization. Next, we want to look into putting our values into a database.

16.3   *Using a SQLite database*

We want to persist our todo list entries in a database so that our list can survive a restart of our server. While there are many different database systems, like Postgresql, MySQL, or MariaDB, that we could integrate into our project, we will use *SQLite*, since it is generally easier to set up. SQLite is a low-level library that stores the database as a normal file on the filesystem but still enables us to write queries in SQL to retrieve and modify data. It has bindings to many languages, and luckily for us, Haskell is no exception. There isn't just one library to deal with SQLite but a large number of them, each of them featuring unique qualities.

For this chapter, we will stick with the `sqlite-simple` package, as it is (like the name suggests) simple to use. While other libraries feature domain-specific languages or type-safe modeling, `sqlite-simple` features a more direct approach to interfacing with a database.

16.3.1   *The basics of sqlite-simple*

To use the package, we have to add `sqlite-simple` to the dependencies section in our `package.yml`. Then, we can use `stack repl` to play around with it:

```
ghci> :set -XOverloadedStrings
ghci> :set -XScopedTypeVariables
ghci> import Database.SQLite.Simple
ghci> dbConn <- open ":memory:"
ghci> execute_ dbConn "CREATE TABLE myTable (id INTEGER PRIMARY KEY,
⇨ data TEXT)"
ghci> execute dbConn "INSERT INTO myTable VALUES (?,?)" (1 :: Int, "hello" ::
      String)
ghci> res :: [(Int, String)] <- query_ dbConn "SELECT * FROM myTable"
ghci> res
[(1,"hello")]
```

Here, we see the basic usage of opening a database connection, creating a table, writing data to it, and retrieving it. We use `open :: String -> IO Connection` to connect to a database, creating it if it does not exist. While the first argument is usually the path to a local file, we can use `":memory:"` to specify that a temporary in-memory database should be created, which will automatically be cleaned up after use.

The simplest functions to interact with a database connection are the `query` and `execute` functions:

- `query :: (ToRow q, FromRow r) => Connection -> Query -> q -> IO [r]`
- `query_ :: FromRow r => Connection -> Query -> IO [r]`
- `execute :: ToRow q => Connection -> Query -> q -> IO ()`
- `execute_ :: Connection -> Query -> IO ()`
- `executeMany :: ToRow q => Connection -> Query -> [q] -> IO ()`
- `executeNamed :: Connection -> Query -> [NamedParam] -> IO ()`

Both functions have two flavors, either using some data q to insert into the query or not providing any data. query is used for queries that return data, like SELECT, while execute is used for queries that do not return data, like INSERT, UPDATE, or DELETE. We can use the changes function to check how many rows have been affected by a query:

```
ghci> rows = [(i :: Int, "hello" :: String) | i <- [2..10]]
ghci> executeMany dbConn "INSERT INTO myTable VALUES (?,?)" rows
ghci> execute_ dbConn "UPDATE myTable SET data = 'updated' WHERE id > 5"
ghci> changes dbConn
5
ghci> executeNamed dbConn "UPDATE myTable SET data = :data WHERE id =
⮞ :id" [":data" := "HELLO" :: String, ":id" := 1 :: Int]
ghci> res :: [(Int, String)] <- query_ dbConn "SELECT * FROM myTable"
ghci> res
[(1,"hello"),(2,"hello"),(3,"hello"),(4,"hello"),(5,"hello"),(6,"updated"),
⮞ (7,"updated"),(8,"updated"),(9,"updated"),(10,"updated")]
```

Here, we see the special syntax used for executeNamed, which receives a list of named parameters. The meaning of (:=) will be covered later. For now, let us look at how to get data from our program into the database.

16.3.2 *ToRow and FromRow*

We use ? to define placeholders where our data should be inserted into the query. To turn Haskell values into something the library can use, we have the ToRow type class, which turns a value into data for SQL. Conversely, FromRow is used to turn this data back into Haskell values. Let's investigate these classes:

```
ghci> :i ToRow
type ToRow :: * -> Constraint
class ToRow a where
  toRow :: a -> [SQLData]
  default toRow :: (Generic a, GToRow (Rep a)) => a -> [SQLData]
ghci> :i FromRow
type FromRow :: * -> Constraint
class FromRow a where
  fromRow :: RowParser a
  default fromRow :: (Generic a, GFromRow (Rep a)) => RowParser a
ghci> :i SQLData
type SQLData :: *
data SQLData
  = SQLInteger Int64
  | SQLFloat Double
  | SQLText Text
  | SQLBlob ByteString
  | SQLNull
```

Here, we see the (heavily simplified) output from GHCi. The toRow function from ToRow is used to turn a value into a list of SQLData, which is a simple sum type. fromRow from `FromRow` defines a parser for said data. The `RowParser` type is a bit more complex, but in general, we can assume it to be a parser that parses `SQLData` to some value. N-tuples (up to a size of 10) have instances for `ToRow` defined as well as lists of values but only if the containing elements satisfy the `ToField` constraint:

```
ghci> import Database.SQLite.Simple.ToField
ghci> :i ToField
type ToField :: * -> Constraint
class ToField a where
  toField :: a -> SQLData
ghci> toField ("hello" :: String)
SQLText "hello"
ghci> toField (1 :: Int)
SQLInteger 1
ghci> toField (Nothing :: Maybe Int)
SQLNull
ghci> toField (Just 1 :: Maybe Int)
SQLInteger 1
```

`toField` is the actual function to turn a Haskell value to `SQLData`. The `ToField` constraint is necessary for the `(:=)` operator to turn data into named parameters:

```
ghci> :t (:=)
(:=) :: ToField v => Text -> v -> NamedParam
ghci> "param" := 1
("param",SQLInteger 1)
```

Luckily for us, instances for the `ToField` type class are already defined for the types we usually deal with:

```
ghci> toRow (1 :: Int, "hello" :: String)
[SQLInteger 1,SQLText "hello"]
ghci> toRow [1,2,3,4,5 :: Int]
[SQLInteger 1,SQLInteger 2,SQLInteger 3,SQLInteger 4,SQLInteger 5]
ghci> toRow (Only "hello" :: Only String)
[SQLText "hello"]
```

We require the `Only` value when we want to use a single value in our query, as tuples with only a single element do not exist:

```
ghci> res :: [(Int, String)] <- query dbConn "SELECT * FROM myTable
➥ WHERE id = ?" (Only 1 :: Only Int)
ghci> res
[(1,"hello")]
```

Now that we know how `sqlite-simple` deals with Haskell data, we can write instances for our `TodoEntry` type. We can start with the `TodoRow TodoEntry` instance shown in the following listing.

Listing 16.5 A `ToRow` instance for `TodoEntry`

```
import Database.SQLite.Simple.ToRow        ◄─────  Imports the ToRow type class
import Database.SQLite.Simple.ToField      ◄─┐
                                             │      Imports the ToField type class

...

instance ToRow TodoEntry where                      ┐  Defines the
  toRow (TodoEntry entryId text checked rank) =     │  toRow function
    [ toField entryId,                        ◄──────┘
      toField text,                    Defines a row of SQLData
      toField checked,                 from a TodoEntry
      toField rank
    ]
```

This simple definition allows us to turn a `TodoEntry` into a list of `SQLData`:

```
ghci> toRow (TodoEntry Nothing "Hello" False (Just 1))
[SQLNull,SQLText "Hello",SQLInteger 0,SQLInteger 1]
ghci> toRow (TodoEntry (Just 10) "Hello" True Nothing)
[SQLInteger 10,SQLText "Hello",SQLInteger 1,SQLNull]
```

Notice how a `Bool` gets turned into an integer. That's because SQLite does not have a dedicated type for Boolean values.

Now that we can turn our `TodoEntry` into a row, we have to also be able to read it again from a row. To define a parser, we first need a parser for a single field. This is handled by the `FromField` type class:

```
ghci> import Database.SQLite.Simple.FromField
ghci> import Database.SQLite.Simple.FromRow
ghci> :i FromField
type FromField :: * -> Constraint
class FromField a where
  fromField :: FieldParser a
ghci> :i FieldParser
type FieldParser :: * -> *
type FieldParser a = Field -> Ok a
```

`fromField` defines a `FieldParser`, which takes field and returns a type similar to `Maybe` with the parsed result. We won't go into defining a `FieldParser`, as they are already defined for the types we usually use. How do we then define a `RowParser` from multiple `FieldParser`? That's where the `field` function of type `FromField a => RowParser a` comes in, which defines a `RowParser` for values that have a `FieldParser` defined. We can then use *applicative* style we have seen in chapter 12 and chapter 14 to combine multiple `RowParser` to a single parser. This is shown in the following listing.

Listing 16.6   A `FromRow` instance for `TodoEntry`

```
import Database.SQLite.Simple.FromRow          ◁⎯┐    Imports the FromRow type
                                                     class and field function
...

instance FromRow TodoEntry where       Defines the
  fromRow =                            fromRow function
    TodoEntry                 ◁⎯⎯⎯⎯⎯⎯
      <$> field
      <*> field        Defines a RowParser, parsing
      <*> field        every field in the TodoEntry
      <*> field        type from a SQL row
```

With these instances defined, we can now first create a table that holds the values of our datatype and then insert a value as a row and retrieve it again:

```
ghci> execute_ dbConn "CREATE TABLE IF NOT EXISTS entries (
➥ id INTEGER PRIMARY KEY, text TEXT, checked INTEGER, rank INTEGER)"
ghci> execute dbConn "INSERT INTO entries (id, text, checked, rank)
➥ VALUES (?,?,?,?)" (TodoEntry Nothing "Hello" False (Just 1))
ghci> res :: [TodoEntry] <- query_ dbConn "SELECT * FROM entries"
ghci> res
[TodoEntry {entryId = Just 1, text = "Hello", checked = False, rank = Just 1}]
```

However, don't the repeated usages of `toField` and `field` seem a bit like boilerplate? Couldn't this be somehow generically derived? As it turns out, we can derive instances for `ToRow` and `FromRow` automatically, when we have a `Generic` instance for our type. For this to work, the fields of the data type need to have `ToField` and `FromField` instances defined, but as we have already covered, this is given for our `TodoEntry` type. So we can derive the necessary instances in the same way we did for `FromJSON` and `ToJSON`. This is shown in the following listing.

Listing 16.7   A generic `FromRow` and `ToRow` instance for `TodoEntry`

```
import qualified Database.SQLite.Simple.FromRow as SQL   │ Imports necessary modules
import qualified Database.SQLite.Simple.ToRow as SQL     │ under the qualified name SQL

...

instance SQL.FromRow TodoEntry        ◁⎯┐    Derives instances for the FromRow
                                             and ToRow classes for TodoEntry
instance SQL.ToRow TodoEntry          ◁⎯┘
```

Our type as well as the instances will live in a `Todos.Types` module. Now that we can convert entries to SQL and back, we can write a few functions to interact with the database for our purpose.

16.3.3   Defining actions for database access

Our API will consist of the following functionality:

- List all entries.
- Add an entry.
- Update a single entry.

We now want to implement functions to deal with communication with the database so that all code with it is bundled in a single module. For this purpose, we will create a new `Todos.Database` module. Since our server will first create a `Connection` and all further communication with the database will be done using it, it makes sense to have functions that receive this connection as an argument and modify the database using it.

When the database is first created, it does not contain any data, especially not a table we could write to. So we have to provide a function to set up the database. This function should create the table using CREATE TABLE IF NOT EXISTS so that we ensure the table is created and just kept intact if it already exists. This function is shown in the following listing.

Listing 16.8   A function to set up the database

```
module Todos.Database where

import Database.SQLite.Simple

setupDb :: Connection -> IO ()          Executes a
setupDb dbConn =                        query on the
  execute_          <─────┘             database
    dbConn
      "CREATE TABLE IF NOT EXISTS entries \      Specifies a query that
      \ (id INTEGER PRIMARY KEY AUTOINCREMENT, \  creates a table if it does not
      \ text TEXT, checked INTEGER, rank INTEGER)"  exist for the todo list entries
```

We specify the `id` as an INTEGER PRIMARY KEY AUTOINCREMENT so that it automatically gets created with a unique integer if it does not exist on our `TodoEntry`. Additionally, this specifies that inserting a row with the same `id` will cause an exception. This will be important when we add new entries to the database.

With the set up taken care of, we can now write a function to retrieve entries. On the SQL side, this will be a simple SELECT * FROM entries query. Luckily for us, this is *all* we have to do, as the parsing from the database is already taken care of by the `FromRow TodoEntry`. The full definition is shown in the following listing.

Listing 16.9   A function to retrieve all entries from the database table

```
import Todos.Types

...
```

```
getEntries :: Connection -> IO [TodoEntry]
getEntries dbConn = query_ dbConn                          Queries the database for
   "SELECT * FROM entries"                                 all entries in the table
```

Now, it's time to provide a function to modify the database by adding a `TodoEntry` to it. While the basic mechanism consists of using `execute` and an `INSERT INTO` statement, we have to be careful, as we have introduced a `PRIMARY KEY` when defining our table. Inserting the same `id` twice will result in `execute` throwing an `SQLError`, so we have to take care of the possibility of producing a failing query. To do so, we can use `try`, which we know from the `Control.Exception` module introduced in chapter 14. However, how can we make the database itself a bit more resilient against failures? For this purpose, the `Database.SQLite.Simple` provides the `withTransaction :: Connection -> IO a -> IO a` function that runs an action by first starting a transaction on the database (using `BEGIN TRANSACTION`), then running the action, and then commiting the transaction (using `COMMIT TRANSACTION`). If the action throws an exception, the transaction will be rolled back (using `ROLLBACK TRANSACTION`), meaning the database will remain unchanged. Using these two functions, we can create a function to add the `TodoEntry` to the database. The code is shown in the following listing.

Listing 16.10   A function to add a `TodoEntry` to the database

```
import Control.Exception (try)

...

addEntry :: Connection -> TodoEntry -> IO (Either SQLError Int)    Catches
addEntry dbConn entry = try $                                      exceptions of
  withTransaction dbConn $ do                                      type SQLError
    execute
      dbConn
      "INSERT INTO entries (id, text, checked, rank) \
      \ VALUES (?,?,?,?)"
      entry
    newIdx <- lastInsertRowId dbConn
    return $ fromIntegral newIdx
```

Catches exceptions of type SQLError

Wraps the action in a database-level transaction that is automatically rolled back in case of an uncaught exception

Executes the INSERT statement on the database

Retrieves the id of the last inserted row

Converts the row id to an Int and returns it

We return `SQLError` if it was thrown during execution so that the callee of the function has more information to present to the user, or we return the last inserted row `id`. Since our `CREATE TABLE` statement specified `id` as `INTEGER PRIMARY KEY`, the `lastInsertRowId` will return exactly this value of the last inserted row. This way, we know what `id` was created if it was not explicitly set by the `TodoEntry` value that was inserted. `lastInsertRowId` is of type `Connection -> Int64`, which is why we need to convert the value into an `Int`.

The last thing we need is to provide a way of negating the `checked` field of a single entry. For this, we first define a function that retrieves a single entry by `id` and then a function that updates the `checked` property for an `id` given by a `TodoEntry`. This can be used by our API to first check that a given `TodoEntry` does exist and then update it. The two functions are shown in the following listing.

Listing 16.11 Functions to retrieve a `TodoEntry` from the database and update it

```
getEntryById :: Connection -> Int -> IO (Maybe TodoEntry)
getEntryById dbConn rowId = do
  entries <- query dbConn "SELECT * from entries          Retrieves entries by id
  where id = ?" (Only rowId)                              from the database
  case entries of
    [x] -> return $ Just x            Returns a Just if there was
    _ -> return Nothing               exactly one entry found

updateEntry :: Connection -> TodoEntry -> IO ()
updateEntry dbConn entry =
  withTransaction dbConn $           Wraps the action in a database-level
    executeNamed                     transaction that is automatically rolled
      dbConn                         back, in case of an uncaught exception
      "UPDATE entries SET checked =
  :checked WHERE id = :id"           Executes the query with
      [":checked" := checked entry,  named parameters
  ":id" := entryId entry]
                                     Builds a query with named
                                     parameters, updating the checked
                                     field for entries with a given id
```

Here, we see the `executeNamed` function in action used to build a query using fields from the `TodoEntry` value selectively. Parameters are either prefixed with : or @. If a parameter occurs in the query but not in the data, the function will raise a `FormatError` exception.

To conclude our creation of the `Todos.Database`, we export the functions as well as the `Database.SQLite.Simple` module to have access to types like `Connection` when we import `Todos.Database` into other modules. The header for the module should look like this:

```
{-# LANGUAGE OverloadedStrings #-}

module Todos.Database
  ( module Database.SQLite.Simple,
    setupDb,
    getEntries,
    addEntry,
    getEntryById,
    updateEntry,
  )
where

import Control.Exception (try)
import Database.SQLite.Simple
import Todos.Types
```

Now that our database is taken care of, we can get to defining the heart of our API. We will do this in the next chapter, using `servant`.

Summary

- Using `aeson`, we can define parsers and serializers for JSON data.
- `ToJSON` and `FromJSON` are the type classes used to provide serialization and parsing of JSON data.
- `Generic`, which can be automatically derived, can help derive other type classes (like `ToJSON` and `FromJSON`).
- Deriving using `Generic` will create implementations for type classes that are dependent on the datatype's definition.
- `ToField`, `ToRow`, and `FromRow` are the type classes used to provide serialization and parsing of data in the database.
- `Generic` can be used to derive the typeclasses for interaction with the database (`ToField`, `ToRow`, and `FromRow`).
- Inserting rows into the database can result in an `SQLError` if a constraint is not satisfied, such as a primary-key constraint.

APIs using Servant

This chapter covers

- Providing typesafe APIs, using Servant
- Implementing a WAI application
- Automatically deriving clients for the API

In the last chapter, we discussed how to implement the conversion of Haskell data to and from JSON and how to store that data in a database. We also provided a few types for the todo list API we want to use.

In this chapter, we will complete the project by first exploring the Servant ecosystem of libraries and packages to define a typesafe API and define a server for it. After doing so, we extend the server to also serve HTML to the client. We then wrap things up by automatically deriving a client application for the API server.

17.1 Defining a typesafe API

For our server, we will write an HTTP/JSON API, meaning we will use HTTP as our protocol and JSON as the data serialization format. JSON is something we have already taken care of, so now it's time to worry about the network. While there are many ways of talking to the network, we don't want to work on a low level but, rather, focus on the definition of the API instead of worrying about pesky network details. A large list of libraries and packages exist to help us work with the network, but we will focus on a well-known, industry-hardened library that is known for its type safety: *Servant.*

Servant is not just a simple library but a family of packages to allow for modeling of APIs, the automatic generation of clients for that API, and even the generation of documentation. It provides us with a way to first specify the general "signature" of the API (which endpoints are served, using which methods, and with what data) and then provide an implementation that is checked against it.

Let's start by adding Servant to our project. As we will require a large number of dependencies, we will keep it concise and list all of them:

```
dependencies:
- base >= 4.7 && < 5
- aeson
- sqlite-simple
- bytestring
- text
- wai
- warp
- http-types
- http-client
- servant
- servant-server
- servant-client
- blaze-markup
- blaze-html
- optparse-applicative
```

This is the complete list of dependencies that will need to be used in our package.yml file. It also includes `aeson` and `sqlite-simple` but, more importantly, many network-related packages. We will cover them as they come up!

17.1.1 *Typed APIs with Servant*

First, let us cover Servant's API declaration. We can start a new module called `Todos.Api`, which will define which endpoints in our API exist, including which HTTP verbs they accept and what data they return. This API is encoded as a single type that we built from a few *type operators* that help us combine different types into a bigger type. To create such a definition, we need the two language extensions: `DataKinds` and `TypeOperators`. We will not go into depth about what these extensions do, as it is not relevant to the general usage of the library.

The two operators that are used to create APIs are (`:>`) and (`:<|>`). (`:>`) is used to combine information about the path and the request into a description for a single API subroutine. (`:<|>`) combines these subroutine descriptions into a larger definition for a library. Let's start with a simple example:

```
type Api = "simple" :> "example" :> GetNoContent
```

This type describes an API with a single endpoint found under the /simple/example route. The accepted HTTP verb is GET, which then results in no content being delivered on successful handling of the request. Let's say we want to deliver some JSON data as a response. Then, we have to encode this in our type:

```
type Api = "simple" :> "example" :> Get '[JSON] SomeType
```

Now, the API would need to return a JSON-encoded value of type SomeType. While it is possible to specify more than just JSON as a response, we will not need that for our project.

If an API has more than one endpoint, we use (:<|>) to combine them:

```
type TodoApi =
  "simple" :> "example" :> Get '[JSON] SomeType
   :<|> "another" :> "example" :> Get '[JSON] AnotherType
```

This API would now serve two endpoints. GET requests to /simple/example, serving a JSON of SomeType, and GET requests to /another/example, serving a JSON of Another-Type. This way, we can combine an arbitrary number of endpoints into one large API.

So far, we have only seen endpoints for GET requests, but we can also freely define endpoints for other HTTP verbs, like POST, PATCH, DELETE, and others. For POST requests, we want to specify what kind of request body we expect a client to send us. This can be achieved with ReqBody:

```
type Api = "send" :> ReqBody '[JSON] SomeType :> PostNoContent
```

This requires a JSON representation of SomeType to be sent to the /send endpoint, resulting in an empty response. If the request body does not conform to the specification, Servant will automatically reject it.

When specifying an entry point, we might want to keep a part of the route variable. This can be done by *capturing* a part of the route, using Capture:

```
type Api = "select" :> Capture "id" String :> Get '[JSON] SomeType
```

If the requested route is /select/this, the captured part of the route would be this. This will be passed to our implementation when a request's route matches the type.

NOTE Servant allows many more modifiers to a route, like Summary and Description, to document the endpoints. We will only cover the necessary ones in this chapter. Feel free to look up the library's documentation (https://hackage.haskell.org/package/servant) to see the full range of possibilities.

With this knowledge under our belts, we can start defining our API. To reiterate, we want to have three endpoints that do the following things:

- List all entries.
- Add an entry.
- Update a single entry.

Listing all elements should return all `TodoEntry` rows we find in our database, so a fitting type would be `[TodoEntry]`. Luckily for us, a `FromJSON` instance exists for lists with elements that also implement `FromJSON`, so we do not have to do any extra work. We will call the endpoint /entries and respond to `GET` requests. The type for this endpoint looks like this:

```
"entries" :> Get '[JSON] [TodoEntry]
```

The endpoint that adds a new entry to our list should respond to `POST` requests, as we are creating a whole new entity on the server side. The data for the entry should be sent in the request body as a JSON-encoded `TodoEntry` value. On successful creation of the resource, we answer the client with the `id` of the newly created entry and HTTP status code 201, which signifies the successful creation of a resource. This can be encoded with the `PostCreated` type. We will call the endpoint /add and model it like this:

```
"add" :> ReqBody '[JSON] TodoEntry :> PostCreated '[JSON] Int
```

Now comes the update for a single entry. In this chapter, we restrict ourselves to only toggling the `checked` value of the entry, meaning it's only possible to check or uncheck an entry but not, for example, change its text. The client can do this with a `PATCH` request to an endpoint that captures the `id` of the entry to toggle in the URL. For this, we can define a /toggle/<id> endpoint, where <id> is a placeholder for the `id` of the entry to be updated. The server will not need to respond with content if the request was successful, so again, we will provide no content to client:

```
"toggle" :> Capture "id" Int :> PatchNoContent
```

Here, we specify to capture the `id` part of the endpoint as an `Int`. If this is not possible because the endpoint contains letters, for example, Servant will automatically reject the request. Putting all of these endpoints together leads us to the following API definition.

Listing 17.1   A type for the todo list API server

```
{-# LANGUAGE TypeOperators #-}          Activates necessary
{-# LANGUAGE DataKinds #-}              language extensions
module Todos.Api where

import Servant.API                              Defines an /entries endpoint to
import Todos.Types                              retrieve all TodoEntry values

type TodoApi =                                  Defines an /add endpoint to
  "entries" :> Get '[JSON] [TodoEntry]          add new entries, using POST
    :<|> "add" :> ReqBody '[JSON] TodoEntry :>
⇒ PostCreated '[JSON] Int                       Defines a /toggle
    :<|> "toggle" :> Capture "id" Int :> PatchNoContent    endpoint to check
                                                            or uncheck an
                                                            entry, given an id
                                                            in the URL
```

Something that we will later need for defining our API is a so-called `Proxy` value of our API. This type and its constructor can be imported from `Data.Proxy`, and as it is quite interesting, we will spend a paragraph talking about it.

17.1.2 *Phantom types*

The definition for the `Proxy` type roughly looks like this:

```
data Proxy a = Proxy
```

This looks boring, doesn't it? It's a type with only a single constructor. However, what is the type variable a doing in the definition? The `Proxy` constructor does not have any fields, so a cannot occur on the right side of the definition. This is known as a *phantom type*. The variable a will be known to Haskell's type system but not actually be linked to any runtime values:

```
ghci> data Proxy a = Proxy
ghci> :t Proxy
Proxy :: Proxy a
ghci> :t Proxy :: Proxy Float
Proxy :: Proxy Float :: Proxy Float
ghci> :t Proxy :: Proxy [Int]
Proxy :: Proxy [Int] :: Proxy [Int]
```

Why is such a type helpful? We can use it to pass type information to functions, by providing a `Proxy` value with a fitting phantom type:

```
readProxy :: Read a => Proxy a -> String -> a
readProxy _ = read

intProxy :: Proxy Int
intProxy = Proxy

stringProxy :: Proxy String
stringProxy = Proxy
```

Note how we completely ignore the `Proxy` value in the `readProxy` function. Using these definitions, we can now parse different data based on the type of the `Proxy`:

```
ghci> :t readProxy stringProxy
readProxy stringProxy :: String -> String
ghci> :t readProxy intProxy
readProxy intProxy :: String -> Int
ghci> readProxy stringProxy "\"abcde\""
"abcde"
ghci> readProxy intProxy "\"abcde\""
*** Exception: Prelude.read: no parse
```

With this little detail taken care of, we can also define a `Proxy` for our API, as Servant requires that to define the implementation. The complete module that will hold our type and `Proxy` is shown in the following listing.

> **Listing 17.2 A module to define the type for our Servant API together with a `Proxy` value**

```
{-# LANGUAGE DataKinds #-}
{-# LANGUAGE TypeOperators #-}
```
Enables language extensions that are needed to define the TodoApi type

```
module Todos.Api
  ( TodoApi,
    todoApi,
  )
where
```

```
import Data.Proxy (Proxy (..))
import Servant.API
import Todos.Types (TodoEntry)
```
Imports needed types and constructors

```
type TodoApi =
  "entries" :> Get '[JSON] [TodoEntry]
    :<|> "add" :> ReqBody '[JSON] TodoEntry :>
  PostCreated '[JSON] Int
    :<|> "toggle" :> Capture "id" Int :>
  PatchNoContent
```
Defines a type for the todo list server API

```
todoApi :: Proxy TodoApi
todoApi = Proxy
```
Defines a Proxy value for the TodoApi type

Now that we have defined the type of our API, we are ready to implement it.

17.1.3 *Implementing the API*

For the implementation, we can define a list of handlers that will respond to requests. Servant knows two types that are used for defining an implementation:

- `Handler`—An action to handle a single endpoint in the API definition
- `Server`—A combination of handlers to serve the full specification of an API

We will put all of our definitions into a new module, called `Todos.Handlers`. This module will need quite a few imports, so we will specify them right now to save us time later:

```
import Control.Monad.IO.Class
import qualified Data.ByteString.Lazy as BSL
import Data.String (fromString)
import qualified Data.Text as T
import qualified Data.Text.Encoding as T
import Servant
import qualified Text.Blaze.Html5 as H
import Todos.Api
import Todos.Database
import Todos.Types
```

Additionally, we will need the following language extensions:

```
{-# LANGUAGE NamedFieldPuns #-}
{-# LANGUAGE OverloadedStrings #-}
```

So now, let us think about the `Handler` for the `/entries` endpoint. The `Handler` will need to return a value of type `[TodoEntry]`, as the conversion to JSON will be handled automatically by Servant. Retrieving `[TodoEntry]` from our database is simple, as it is the result of the `getEntries` action from our `Todos.Database` module. The only thing we have to do is provide a `Connection` to `getEntries` and embed the `IO` action of our database into the `Handler` action. As all of our handlers will need to be able to talk to our database, it makes sense to provide them with `IO` actions that already have the connection. We will construct them in a single definition later.

For now, we can assume our handler will receive an `IO [TodoEntry]` action, so the full signature should look like this:

```
entriesHandler :: IO [TodoEntry] -> Handler [TodoEntry]
```

How can we convert `IO` to `Handler`? We have seen similar embeddings of `IO` actions in other monads in chapter 14, when discussing `liftIO` and `MonadIO`. It turns out that a `MonadIO Handler` instance is given, so a simple `liftIO` will do the trick and transform our database query into a handler for our API.

> **Listing 17.3 A `Handler` that returns a list of `TodoEntry` values**

```
entriesHandler :: IO [TodoEntry] -> Handler [TodoEntry]
entriesHandler = liftIO          ◁─────  Lifts the IO action into
                                         the Handler monad
```

For this to become a `Handler` that Servant can use, all arguments need to be applied, so the actual definition of this handler looks more like this:

```
entriesHandler (getEntries dbConn)
```

Given a `dbConn` of type `Connection`, we can provide the `entriesHandler` with the appropriate `IO` action. We will define the rest of our handlers in the same fashion. This way, we can make sure the handlers do not accidentally interact with our database connection and only use the actions we supply them. An additional benefit of abstracting it this way is that creating mocks with "fake" databases becomes easier, as the `IO` actions can also interact with files in place of the actual database.

Now, let's define the handler for adding a new `TodoEntry`. As we have specified the request body to contain a JSON-encoded `TodoEntry`, the handler will need to have this type as an argument for the `Handler`. So the final type that Servant expects from us is `TodoEntry → Handler Int`. However, we also need the `IO` action to interact with the database. The fitting database action is `addEntry`, which had the type `Connection → TodoEntry → IO (Either SQLError Int)`. Partially applying the `Connection` and passing the resulting action to the handler leads us to conclude that the final type for the handler looks like this:

```
addHandler ::
  (TodoEntry -> IO (Either SQLError Int)) ->
  TodoEntry ->
  Handler Int
```

In case our action returns an error, we will need to report that to the client. Inside the `Handler` monad, we are provided with the `throwError` action that lets us abort the handling with an error. Additionally, Servant provides us with a `ServerError` type that we can throw, using this action:

```
ghci> import Servant
ghci> :i ServerError
type ServerError :: *
data ServerError
  = ServerError {errHTTPCode :: Int,
                 errReasonPhrase :: String,
                 errBody :: ByteString,
                 errHeaders :: [Header]}
```

It allows us to set an appropriate HTTP response code as well as the headers, body, and reason phrase. The library also offers many premade errors that have a code and fitting reason phrase set:

```
ghci> err403
ServerError {errHTTPCode = 403, errReasonPhrase = "Forbidden",
⇒  errBody = "", errHeaders = []}
ghci> err404
ServerError {errHTTPCode = 404, errReasonPhrase = "Not Found",
⇒  errBody = "", errHeaders = []}
ghci> err418
ServerError {errHTTPCode = 418, errReasonPhrase = "I'm a teapot",
⇒  errBody = "", errHeaders = []}
ghci> err500
ServerError {errHTTPCode = 500, errReasonPhrase = "Internal Server Error",
⇒  errBody = "", errHeaders = []}
```

However, as we can see, the body as well as the headers are empty. This allows us to provide further information in the body to let the client know what happened.

So how do we turn our `SQLError` into something human readable? It turns out that this type already contains a description of the error in a field called `sqlErrorDetails`:

```
ghci> import Database.SQLite.Simple
ghci> :i SQLError
type SQLError :: *
data SQLError
  = SQLError {sqlError :: Error,
              sqlErrorDetails :: Text,
              sqlErrorContext :: Text}
```

So we can take this description and combine it with a fitting error. The full code for this is shown in the following listing.

Listing 17.4 A `Handler` that adds a `TodoEntry` and returns descriptive errors

```
addHandler ::
  (TodoEntry -> IO (Either SQLError Int)) ->
  TodoEntry ->
  Handler Int
addHandler addAct entry = do
  mSqlError <- liftIO $ addAct entry
  case mSqlError of
    Right idx -> pure idx
    Left exc ->
      let errBody =
            BSL.fromStrict
              (T.encodeUtf8 $ sqlErrorDetails exc)
      in throwError $ err422 {errBody}
```

Lifts the action to add an entry into the Handler monad and evaluates it on the TodoEntry argument

In case no exception was thrown, returns with an empty response

Encodes the error description as a lazy bytestring

Throws an error with status code 422 and the error description as its body

Just like before, we use `liftIO` to lift the `IO` action into the `Handler` monad. Since the error details of the `SQLError` are given as `Text`, we first have to transform it to a `ByteString`. However, Servant requires a lazy `ByteString`, which is why we use `fromStrict` to provide the conversion. We chose to use HTTP status code 422, as it signifies a request that was correctly understood but could not be processed. This happens when the `TodoEntry` passed in the request has an `id` set that is already present in the database.

Now comes our last handler, which toggles the `checked` attribute of an entry. We do not have a single database query that would do this. However, we have an action that retrieves a single entry by `id` and one that updates it.

So our handler will need these two actions as arguments. Additionally, since we specified the `Capture "id" Int` part in our type for the endpoint, the handler needs an `Int` as its argument. This handler will also need to return the special `NoContent` type, since we have specified the endpoint to not return any data in the response body. The type will look something like this:

```
toggleHandler ::
  (Int -> IO (Maybe TodoEntry)) ->
  (TodoEntry -> IO ()) ->
  Int ->
  Handler NoContent
```

The implementation is rather straightforward. If the `TodoEntry` with the given `id` cannot be found, we return the classic HTTP 404 status code with a little description that the `id` could not be found. Otherwise, we negate the `checked` field on the `TodoEntry` and pass it to our update action, as shown in the following listing.

Listing 17.5 A `Handler` that negates the `checked` value of a `TodoEntry`

```
toggleHandler ::
  (Int -> IO (Maybe TodoEntry)) ->
  (TodoEntry -> IO ()) ->
```

```
                     Int ->
                     Handler NoContent                         Retrieves a
                   toggleHandler queryAct updateAct rowId = do  TodoEntry by
                     mEntry <- liftIO $ queryAct rowId          the given id
                     case mEntry of
                       Nothing ->
                         let errBody =
                               fromString $
                                 "Couldn't find entry with id \""
                                   <> show rowId               Throws an error with HTTP
                                   <> "\""                     status code 404 if the entry
                         in throwError $ err404 {errBody}       cannot be found
                       Just entry -> do
                         let newEntry = entry                  Negates the checked field
 ➥  {checked = not $ checked entry}                           for the found entry
                         liftIO $ updateAct newEntry
                         pure NoContent                        Performs the update
                                                               of the TodoEntry

                                                               Returns no content
```

In this definition, we use `fromString` to create a lazy `ByteString` from a normal `String`. `NoContent` is the only value of the `NoContent` type, which serves as a more descriptive alternative to `()`.

With the definitions for our handlers taken care of, we can now define a `Server` for our `TodoApi` type. As mentioned previously, this server will need to be constructed with a database `Connection` to define the actions we pass to our handlers. After this is done, we need to combine the `Handler` functions to a `Server`. This is achieved using an operator that should feel familiar: `(:<|>)`. The same operator that we used on the *type level* to combine endpoint descriptions to a full API description is used on the *term level* to let us combine our handlers to a server.

Listing 17.6   A function to create a `Server` for the `TodoApi`

```
mkTodoApiServer :: Connection -> Server TodoApi
mkTodoApiServer dbConn =
   entriesHandler getEntries'                      Combines the different
     :<|> addHandler addEntry'                      handlers into a full
     :<|> toggleHandler getEntryById' updateEntry'  implementation for the server
   where
     getEntries' = getEntries dbConn
     addEntry' = addEntry dbConn                    Partially applies the database
     getEntryById' = getEntryById dbConn            actions with their necessary
     updateEntry' = updateEntry dbConn              Connection argument
```

The truly wonderful thing about this definition is that Servant's type definitions are all statically checked against the implementation we provide, meaning the compiler would automatically reject our implementation if we forgot to implement an endpoint, did not accept the correct parameters, or were returning the wrong types of data. If this function compiles, we can be sure that our implementation adheres to the specification given in the `TodoApi` type. Furthermore, a lot of heavy lifting is done by Servant for us. Notice how we never had to specify HTTP status codes (except for error cases) and how we never needed to manually transform our data to and from JSON. This behavior is all derived for us, without requiring us to do anything. We simply need to define a type for our API and implement the core logic. The library takes the type information and automatically derives the API's behavior from it, only relinquishing control to our code once it is needed (to provide the actual logic of the API).

17.2 Running the application

Now that our API implementation is essentially finished, at this point, we want to build an executable that we can run. This project is somewhat unique as we will want to be able to build two independent executables with the same library: one executable for the server and one for the client. Therefore, we will change the executables section of our package.yml like so:

```
executables:
  todolist-server:
    main:              Server.hs
    source-dirs:       app
    ghc-options:
    - -main-is Server
    - -threaded
    - -rtsopts
    - -with-rtsopts=-N
    dependencies:
    - todolist
```

This will allow us to use a Server.hs file in the app directory to build the server. The executable name will be `todolist-server`. Importantly, we are using the `-main-is` option of GHC to tell it that our main module is named `Server`. Otherwise, the Server.hs would need to create a `Main` module, which does not match the file's name.

We can now delete the Main.hs file and create a new Server.hs file in our app directory. The imports of the file should look like this:

```
module Server (main) where

import Network.Wai
import Network.Wai.Handler.Warp
import Servant
import Todos.Api
import Todos.Database
import Todos.Handlers
```

We can now define a function that will turn our `Server TodoApi` into a web application interface `Application`.

17.2.1 *The WAI application*

A *web application interface* defines types and functions for web frameworks to interface with web server implementations. The most common server implementation to be used with WAI is Warp, which we have also imported into our file. We will explore the possibilities of this interface in a short time, but for now, we are interested in connecting our Servant `Server` with Warp to finally get a server running.

To do this, Servant provides us with the `serve` function, which takes a `Proxy` of our API as well as the `Server` and produces an application.

Listing 17.7 A function to create a WAI `Application` from the API implementation

```
mkApiServer :: Connection -> Application          Creates the Server, using the
mkApiServer = serve todoApi . mkTodoApiServer  ⊲─  given Connection, and turns it
                                                   into an Application
```

Now, we can write a `main` that will finally start our server:

```
main :: IO ()
main = do
  let port = 9001
  withConnection ":memory:" $ \dbConn -> do
    setupDb dbConn
    putStrLn $
      "Running todo list server on port " ++ show port
    run port (mkApiServer dbConn)
```

Since we are testing our application, we will use a preset port to start the server on and keep the database in memory, so we do not persist anything between restarts. Using `withConnection`, we can acquire a `Connection` that is automatically closed. We first do the needed setup for our database and then run our API. To start our application, we can use `stack run todolist-server`. We should be greeted with `Running todo list server on port 9001`.

Now, we can use a tool to communicate with our API. Friends of the terminal might be inclined to use `curl`, which is fine. We will use *Restman*, which is an extension to Chromium-based browsers, as it is easy to use and cross-platform. It allows us to make requests to our API and properly format JSON responses that our API will send to us.

We can send a simple GET request to our `localhost` on port `9001` on the `/entries` endpoint. The result is an empty JSON list, as expected and as seen in figure 17.1.

Now, we can add an entry. We will have to switch from GET to POST and now send our data to the `/add` endpoint. Also, we will need to set the `Content-Type` header to `application/json`. Then, we are ready to send an entry, which is shown in figure 17.2.

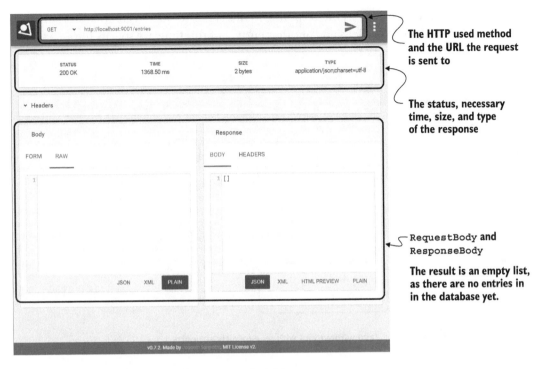

The HTTP used method and the URL the request is sent to

The status, necessary time, size, and type of the response

`RequestBody` **and** `ResponseBody`

The result is an empty list, as there are no entries in in the database yet.

Figure 17.1   A GET request to /entries on an empty database

We are now using the POST method as the add endpoint only responds to POST.

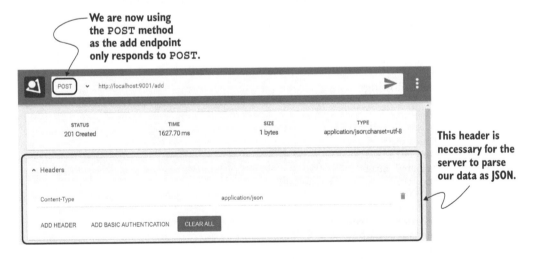

This header is necessary for the server to parse our data as JSON.

Figure 17.2   Necessary header data for a POST request to /add

As we can see, we get 1 as the response, as this is the id that was used to store the entry in the database. Now, let's add another entry, but this time, we specify the id and rank, as shown in figure 17.3.

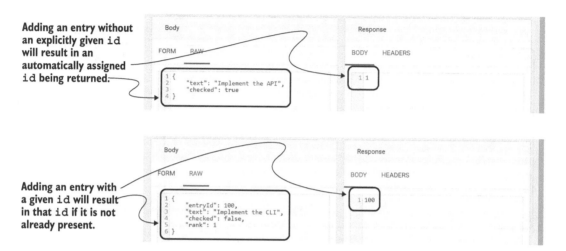

Figure 17.3   POST **requests to** /add **without and with an explicitly set entry** id

When we try to add another entry with the same id, we receive a response with code 422 and an error message (UNIQUE constraint failed: entries.id). Sending a malformed JSON to the endpoint will also result in an error, which is automatically served. The full error looks like this when the checked key is missing:

```
Error in $: parsing Todos.Types.TodoEntry(TodoEntry) failed,
⇨ key "checked" not found
```

Now, we can retrieve the stored entries again. Another GET request to /entries will result in the following:

```
[
    {
        "checked": true,
        "entryId": 1,
        "rank": null,
        "text": "Implement the API"
    },
    {
        "checked": true,
        "entryId": 100,
        "rank": 1,
        "text": "Implement the API"
    }
]
```

Now, we may toggle an entry in figure 17.4.

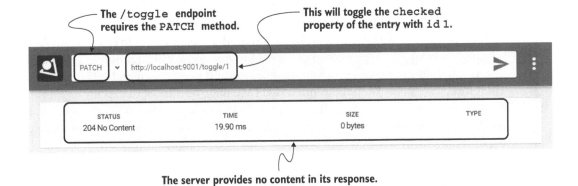

Figure 17.4 A PATCH request to /toggle switching the checked property of the entry with id1

We can then see that the entry has changed after querying the entries:

```
[
    {
        "checked": true,
        "entryId": 1,
        "rank": null,
        "text": "Implement the API"
    },
    {
        "checked": true,
        "entryId": 100,
        "rank": 1,
        "text": "Implement the API"
    }
]
```

Great! We have successfully created an API server that we can query using HTTP/JSON. However, since we are working with a web server, couldn't we also pass some HTML to the user?

Exercise: Deleting entries

We have implemented endpoints to create, read, and update our entries. For a full CRUD API, we still need a way to delete entries from the database. Implement this endpoint yourself! It makes sense to model the endpoint similarly to the toggle endpoint. The URL should look like this: /delete/<id>.

Now, we want to implement another endpoint that exists outside of our API to list the entries of our todo list.

17.2.2 *Application middleware*

While our server has a usable JSON API, it lacks a frontend for humans to directly inspect. We want to change this by rendering the todo list as HTML on the root endpoint (/). This will lead us to a design decision. How should we model this endpoint?

In general, we have two choices. We could model the endpoint in our Servant API, by using a special HTML type instead of JSON. However, as we will later derive a client for this API, it does not make sense that the client would need to query the HTML page. Therefore, we want to keep the rendered HTML page outside of our API.

So how do we inject this additional route into our web server if we cannot touch the API type? As Servant will produce an Application, we need some way of modifying it. What exactly is a WAI Application? The type is rather simple:

```
type Application = Request -> (Response -> IO ResponseReceived) ->
➥ IO ResponseReceived
```

The Application is a simple function that receives a request and response callback. If we want to implement this function, we can take a Request, compute a Response, and call the response callback. When we want to modify an Application, we have to wrap the function in a new function. A mapping from Application to Application is called a Middleware:

```
type Middleware = Application -> Application
```

When defining a Middleware, it is a good starting point to have three arguments:

```
myMiddleware :: Middleware
myMiddleware app req responseAct = ...
```

The first is the Application to be wrapped, and the second and third are the arguments an Application requires. This will give us the type Application -> Application.

Our Middleware should check whether the Request is a GET request to the application's root (/). In that case, we want to return our HTML. Otherwise, we will just use the app we are wrapping (which will be our API server). We can retrieve the important attributes of the request using requestMethod and pathInfo to determine whether we should respond with our HTML:

```
import Network.HTTP.Types (methodGet)

...

mkAppRoot :: Connection -> Middleware
mkAppRoot dbConn app req responseAct
  | isRootRequest = ...
  | otherwise = app req responseAct
  where
    isRootRequest =
      requestMethod req == methodGet
        && null (pathInfo req)
```

Now, we have to generate some HTML to respond with. First, we should think about the order we want to display our entries. After all, we have the rank field for a reason! We will sort the entries based on their rank. A lower rank means a higher position in our list, and ranked entries will always come before unranked entries. Sadly, the Ord instance for Maybe Int will sort Nothing values before any Just value, so we need to write a function that separates entries by the existence of a rank and sorts the ranked ones. This is shown in the following listing, which we can add to the Todos.Types module.

Listing 17.8 A function to sort todo list entries

```
import qualified Data.List as L
import qualified Data.Maybe as M

...

sortTodoEntries :: [TodoEntry] -> [TodoEntry]          Sorts ranked entries
sortTodoEntries entries = L.sortOn rank ranked         and appends unranked
  ++ unranked                                          entries
  where
    (ranked, unranked) = L.partition        Partitions entries with
  (M.isJust . rank) entries                 and without ranks
```

We will also need to create qualified imports of Data.List and Data.Maybe as L and M, respectively. Now, we can define another an IO action that takes a Connection and returns HTML.

17.2.3 *Producing HTML from data*

To build HTML from Haskell values, we are going to use the blaze-html library. It features combinators to build an HTML document, using do notation.

We can import Text.Blaze.Html5 with the qualified name H in our Todos.Handlers module to now define the root handler. The basics of the library are relatively straightforward. It provides combinators named after HTML elements. Using do notation, we can nest these combinators, which will be reflected in the rendered HTML output:

```
H.body $ do
  H.h1 "Title"
  H.p "Foobar"
```

This definition will result in the following output:

```
<body>
    <h1>Title</h1>
    <p>Foobar</p>
</body>
```

We can also use functions we would normally use with monads. For example, we can use mapM_ to produce elements in a list from a list of strings:

```
mkHtmlList xs = H.ul $ mapM_ (H.li . H.string) xs
```

The output of `mkHtmlList ["Foo", "Bar", "Baz"]` is

```
<ul>
    <li>Foo</li>
    <li>Bar</li>
    <li>Baz</li>
</ul>
```

With these combinators, we can build our web page. The following handler, shown in the following listing, is a recommendation by yours truly, but you can come up with your own design.

Listing 17.9   An action to retrieve all entries from the todo list and render them as HTML

```
rootHandler :: Connection -> IO H.Html
rootHandler dbConn = do
  entries <- sortTodoEntries <$> getEntries dbConn
  let listHtml
        | null entries = H.p $ H.text "No entry found"
        | otherwise = H.ul $ mapM_
  (H.li . mkTodoEntryHtml) entries
      fullHtml = H.docTypeHtml $ do
        H.head $ do
          H.title "TODOs"
          H.style $ H.text style
        H.body $ do
          H.h1 "TODOs"
          listHtml
  return fullHtml
  where
    style :: T.Text
    style =
      "body {font-family: sans-serif} \
      \ ul {list-style: none} \
      \ li {margin-bottom: 5px}"

    mkTodoEntryHtml :: TodoEntry -> H.Html
    mkTodoEntryHtml (TodoEntry _ text checked _) =
      let mark =
            if checked
              then "\x2713"
              else "\x2718"
      in H.text (mark <> " " <> text)
```

- Retrieves and sorts all entries
- Provides a placeholder if no entry was found
- Renders the found entries as an unordered list
- Defines the doctype of the document
- Defines the head of the HTML document, providing a title and a style
- Defines the body of the HTML document, consisting of a heading and the rendered list
- Defines a style for the document
- Either provides a check mark (U+2713) or cross mark (U+2718) in UTF-8 encoding
- Concatenates the check or cross mark with the text of the entry

Notice that we are using UTF-8-encoded characters here. When turning this definition into data we are sending as a response, it will be important to keep this in mind.

We can now finish our `Middleware`. `rootHandler` computes the HTML, which then needs to be rendered into a `ByteString`. In our `Server` module, we can import `Text.Blaze.Html.Renderer.Utf8` to have access to the `renderHTML` function that will compute an UTF-8-encoded bytestring. To respond with it as data, we can use `response-LBS` from `Network.WAI`. For our definition to work, we will need a few imports:

```
import Network.HTTP.Types.Header
import Network.HTTP.Types.Method
import Network.HTTP.Types.Status
import qualified Text.Blaze.Html.Renderer.Utf8 as H
```

Now, we can complete our `Middleware` in the following listing.

Listing 17.10   A `Middleware` to render the todo list as HTML on the application's root

```
mkAppRoot :: Connection -> Middleware
mkAppRoot dbConn app req responseAct
  | isRootRequest = do
      html <- rootHandler dbConn            ◁───┐  Computes HTML from the todo list
      responseAct $ responseLBS ok200 headers      entries read from the database
      (H.renderHtml html)                    ◁───   Renders the HTML as a UTF-8 encoded
  | otherwise = app req responseAct          ◁──    ByteString, which is used to build a
  where                                             response with HTTP status code 200
    headers = [(hContentType,
    "text/html; charset=utf-8")]             ◁──   If the request was not a GET request to
    isRootRequest =                                our application's root, we relinquish
      requestMethod req == methodGet               control to the wrapped Application.
        && null (pathInfo req)
```

Computes HTML from the todo list entries read from the database

Renders the HTML as a UTF-8 encoded ByteString, which is used to build a response with HTTP status code 200

If the request was not a GET request to our application's root, we relinquish control to the wrapped Application.

Defines a header, setting the content type to text/HTML with the utf-8 charset

Checks whether a request is a GET to our application's root

It's important to note that we lose some static guarantees modifying our `Application` this way. If our Servant API was to later implement an endpoint for GET requests to /, we would have no way of guaranteeing that this `Middleware` wasn't interfering with it. However, as our application is rather simple, this is fine, and using this `Middleware`, we can modify our `main` from before:

```
main :: IO ()
main = do
  let port = 9001
  withConnection ":memory:" $ \dbConn -> do
    setupDb dbConn
    putStrLn $
      "Running todo list server on port " ++ show port
    run port (mkAppRoot dbConn $ mkApiServer dbConn)
```

Let's say that we have the following data in our database that we can access using /entries:

```
[
    {
        "checked": true,
        "entryId": 1,
        "rank": null,
```

```
            "text": "Specify JSON and Database serialization"
        },
        {
            "checked": true,
            "entryId": 2,
            "rank": null,
            "text": "Specify API type"
        },
        {
            "checked": true,
            "entryId": 3,
            "rank": null,
            "text": "Implement API"
        },
        {
            "checked": true,
            "entryId": 4,
            "rank": null,
            "text": "HTML rendering for list"
        },
        {
            "checked": false,
            "entryId": 5,
            "rank": 2,
            "text": "CLI arguments"
        },
        {
            "checked": false,
            "entryId": 6,
            "rank": 1,
            "text": "Implement client application"
        }
    }
]
```

Then, the resulting HTML will be rendered as shown in figure 17.5.

Figure 17.5 An example rendering of the
root endpoint showing the created todo
list entries

Note that the check and cross marks might look different on your system, depending on your operating system and browser. With this addition to our server, we can finally finish it by providing our server with some CLI arguments. As we already covered `opt-parse-applicative` in chapter 14, we will not discuss how to provide these arguments in detail. We provide the user to specify the port to connect to as well as the database file to use (using the in-memory database by default). The code for this is shown in the following listing.

Listing 17.11   CLI arguments for the todo list server executable

```
import Options.Applicative

...

data CliArgs = CliArgs            │ Provides a type for the
  { cliArgsPort :: Int,           │ server's CLI arguments
    cliArgsDatabaseFile :: String
  }

cliArgsParser :: Parser CliArgs
cliArgsParser = CliArgs <$> port <*> databaseFile
  where
    port =
      option auto $          ◄────┤ Provides a parser for the port
        long "port"               │ argument, using 9001 as the default
          <> value 9001
          <> metavar "PORT"
          <> help "Port to connect to"
          <> showDefault
    databaseFile =
      strOption $            ◄────┤ Provides a parser for the database
        long "database"           │ file, using :memory: as the default
          <> value ":memory:"
          <> metavar "PATH"
          <> help "Database file to use"
          <> showDefaultWith
            ( const
                "none, using in-memory database"
            )

argumentParser :: ParserInfo CliArgs
argumentParser =
  info                      ◄────┤ Defines parser info for
    (cliArgsParser <**> helper)   │ the CLI arguments
    ( fullDesc
        <> progDesc "A todo list API server"
    )
```

Modifiers here we have not previously seen are `value`, `showDefault`, and `showDefault-With`, which are used to show default values in the help text. Using these arguments, we can augment our `main` once more, which is shown in the following listing.

Listing 17.12   The todo list server's `main`

```
main :: IO ()
main = do
  args <- execParser argumentParser              Parses the CLI
  let port = cliArgsPort args                    arguments
  withConnection (cliArgsDatabaseFile args) $    Creates a database
  \dbConn -> do                                  connection
    setupDb dbConn                               Sets up the database
    putStrLn $
      "Running todo list server on port " ++ show port   Generates and runs
    run port (mkAppRoot dbConn $ mkApiServer dbConn)      the Application from
                                                          mkApiServer with
                                                          the mkAppRoot
                                                          Middleware
```

Now, let's test our server, using a local database file and the default port:

```
shell $ stack run todolist-server -- -h
Usage: todolist-server [--port PORT] [--database PATH]

  A todo list API server

Available options:
  --port PORT              Port to connect to (default: 9001)
  --database PATH          Database file to use
                           (default: none, using in-memory database)
  -h,--help                Show this help text
shell $ stack run todolist-server -- --database todolist.db
Running todo list server on port 9001
```

Now, we can use Restman or `curl` again to test our server. However, we now want to shift our focus to implementing the client for this API server to provide us with a simple command-line tool to interface with this server.

17.3 Deriving a client

With our server taken care of, we will now start a new file called Client.hs in our app directory. Additionally, we will add the following executable to the executables section in our package.yml file:

```
todolist-client:
  main:           Client.hs
  source-dirs:    app
  ghc-options:
  - -main-is Client
  - -threaded
  - -rtsopts
  - -with-rtsopts=-N
  dependencies:
  - todolist
```

With this taken care of, we can start of by providing the following header for our new file:

```
module Client (main) where

import qualified Data.Text as T
import Network.HTTP.Client
  ( defaultManagerSettings,
    newManager,
  )
import Options.Applicative
import Servant
import Servant.Client
import Todos.Api
import Todos.Types
```

17.3.1 Using servant-client

The most important module we are importing here is `Servant.Client`, which is provided by the `servant-client` package. It provides us with an important type called `ClientM`, which models actions for our clients. It also provides us with two functions. The first is `client`, which is of type `HasClient ClientM api => Proxy api -> Client ClientM api`. Given a `Proxy` for an API, it *automatically derives* the client functions for said API. We can then use `runClientM` of type `ClientM a -> ClientEnv -> IO (Either ClientError a)`, which executes the `ClientM` monad in the `IO` monad.

So how do we use `client`? Let's look at our full derivation for our API client, shown in the following listing, to get a sense of it.

Listing 17.13 Derivation of client functionality from the API's `Proxy`

```
getEntries :: ClientM [TodoEntry]
addEntry :: TodoEntry -> ClientM Int        Defines the types of
toggleEntry :: Int -> ClientM NoContent     the client's actions
getEntries :<|> addEntry :<|> toggleEntry =
⇨ client todoApi        ◁───   Derives the definition of the client's
                               actions from the API's Proxy
```

These four lines of code are the complete definition for our client! We first define the types of our actions. Notice the similarity from the `TodoApi` type. `"entries" :> Get '[JSON] [TodoEntry]` is matched by `ClientM [TodoEntry]`, as the resulting type is the same. `"add" :> ReqBody '[JSON] TodoEntry :> PostCreated '[JSON] Int` is matched by `TodoEntry -> ClientM Int`, since the request needs a `TodoEntry` for its request body, so the action also needs this type as an argument. Notice, again, that the JSON encoding is completely irrelevant for the client definition. Servant handles all of this automatically.

17.3.2 *Defining commands for the CLI*

Now, we can define a CLI for this client. Something new we want to introduce for this application is the concept of *commands*. So far, our CLIs have only had options but not commands, which we might know from tools like git, where we can use some identifier after the binary name to access some specific functionality:

```
git pull --rebase
git commit -m "Cool work"
git push --force-with-lease
```

The options we see here are only available (or have different meanings) based on the previous identifier. Our tool should feature three commands:

- `list`—Lists entries
- `add`—Adds new entries
- `toggle`—Toggles entries

Additionally, we need to add information about the host and the port the client should connect to. We can first define types for our arguments:

```
data CliArgs = CliArgs
  { cliArgsHost :: String,
    cliArgsPort :: Int,
    cliArgsCommand :: CliCommand
  }

data CliCommand
  = GetEntries
  | AddEntry TodoEntry
  | ToggleEntry Int
```

Now, we define a `Parser` and a fitting `ParserInfo` for our `CliArgs`. We purposefully leave out the definitions for the command parsers.

Listing 17.14 Parser for the API client's CLI arguments

```
cliArgsParser :: Parser CliArgs
cliArgsParser =
  CliArgs
    <$> host
    <*> port
    <*> commandParser
  where
    host =
      strOption $                    ◁──  Defines a parser for
        long "host"                       the hostname, using
          <> value "localhost"            localhost as a default
          <> metavar "HOST"
          <> help "host to connect to"
          <> showDefault
```

```
port =
    option auto $
        long "port"
            <> value 9001
            <> metavar "PORT"
            <> help "port to connect to"
            <> showDefault
commandParser =
    subparser
        ( command "list" getEntriesCommandParser
            <> command "add" addEntryCommandParser
            <> command "toggle" toggleEntryCommandParser
        )
```

⟵ **Defines a parser for the port, using 9001 as a default**

Defines a parser for the command

Defines commands using an identifier and a fitting parser for further options

```
argumentParser :: ParserInfo CliArgs
argumentParser =
    info
        (cliArgsParser <**> helper)
        ( fullDesc
            <> progDesc "A todo list API client"
        )
```

⟵ **Defines the ParserInfo for the client's CLI**

The code shown in listing 17.14 presents us with `subparser`, which is used to create a nested parser for commands, which are built by `command`. This function requires an identifier (a name for the command) and a `ParserInfo` for its options and arguments. We can define these just like we did before; there is nothing special about them when used in this context.

Implementations for `getEntriesCommandParser` and `toggleEntryCommandParser` are relatively straightforward and shown in listing 17.15. While we usually have separate definitions for `Parser` and `ParserInfo`, we have combined definitions here, as they are so small. Since the `getEntriesCommandParser` does not have any options, we return the `GetEntries` constructor immediately. `toggleEntryCommandParser`, however, needs an `Int` for the `id`.

Listing 17.15 The parser for the API client's CLI arguments

```
getEntriesCommandParser :: ParserInfo CliCommand
getEntriesCommandParser =
    info
        (pure GetEntries <**> helper)
        ( fullDesc
            <> progDesc "Retrieves and lists all todo list entries"
        )


toggleEntryCommandParser :: ParserInfo CliCommand
toggleEntryCommandParser =
    info
        ((ToggleEntry <$> idParser) <**> helper)
        ( fullDesc
            <> progDesc "(Un)checks the entry with the given id"
        )
```

⟵ **Defines the ParserInfo for the list command**

⟵ **Defines the ParserInfo for the toggle command**

```
where
  idParser =
    option auto $
      long "id"
        <> metavar "INT"
        <> help "Row id to toggle"
```

←——| Defines the parser for a
      single Int without a default

As the add command requires to have a `TodoEntry` as its data, we have to implement a
`Parser TodoEntry`, shown in listing 17.16. It's important to note how almost all of our
definitions revolve around the definition of `TodoEntry`. Since types are checked statically,
even across the boundaries of server and client, we can be sure that a client will always be
compatible with a server if they stem from the same version of our project. This, of
course, assumes that the logic of the server and client are correctly implemented.

Listing 17.16   Parser for the API client's CLI arguments

```
addEntryCommandParser :: ParserInfo CliCommand
addEntryCommandParser =
  info
    ((AddEntry <$> todoEntryParser) <**> helper)
    ( fullDesc
        <> progDesc "Adds a new entry to the todo list"
    )

todoEntryParser :: Parser TodoEntry
todoEntryParser =
  TodoEntry
    <$> teEntryId
    <*> (T.pack <$> teText)
    <*> teChecked
    <*> teRank
  where
    teEntryId =
      optional $
        option auto $
          long "id"
            <> metavar "INT"
            <> help "Row id to use (optional)"
    teText =
      strOption $
        long "text"
          <> metavar "TEXT"
          <> help "What is there to do?"
    teChecked =
      option auto $
        long "checked"
          <> metavar "BOOL"
          <> help "Is it done?"
    teRank =
      optional $
        option auto $
          long "rank"
            <> metavar "INT"
            <> help "Sorting rank (optional)"
```

←——| Defines the ParserInfo
      for the add comman

←——| Defines a parser for
      the optional id

←——| Defines a parser for
      the entry's text

←——| Defines a parser for the
      entry's checked property

←——| Defines a parser for
      the optional rank

17.3.3 *Implementing the client*

Now that we have taken care of argument parsing, we can finish our client's definition by providing the `main` action. We have our `ClientM` actions and have to run them using `runClientM`. To do so, we need a `ClientEnv`, for which we can use the `mkClientEnv` function of type `Manager -> BaseUrl -> ClientEnv`. The `Manager` is used to handle keep alives, which is not important for us. We can use `newManager defaultManager-Settings` to generate a `Manager` with sensible default values. `BaseUrl`, however, is important, as it specifies the base URL our client is operating on:

```
ghci> import Servant.Client
ghci> :i BaseUrl
type BaseUrl :: *
data BaseUrl
  = BaseUrl {baseUrlScheme :: Scheme,
             baseUrlHost :: String,
             baseUrlPort :: Int,
             baseUrlPath :: String}
```

It specifies the scheme, host, port and default path for all requests. For our client, the `Scheme` is `Http` and the path is empty, while host and port information will come from the parsed arguments.

Listing 17.17   The todo list client's `main`

```
main :: IO ()
main = do
  args <- execParser argumentParser              Parses the executables
  clientManager <- newManager defaultManagerSettings   arguments and command
  let url = BaseUrl Http (cliArgsHost args)
            (cliArgsPort args) ""
      clientEnv = mkClientEnv clientManager url
      runClientM' :: ClientM a -> (a -> IO ()) -> IO ()
      runClientM' clientAct resAct = do
        res <- runClientM clientAct clientEnv
        case res of
          Left err -> putStrLn $ "Error: " ++ show err
          Right x -> resAct x
  case cliArgsCommand args of
    GetEntries ->
      runClientM' getEntries $ mapM_ print .
        sortTodoEntries
    AddEntry entry ->
      runClientM' (addEntry entry) print
    ToggleEntry rowId ->
      runClientM' (toggleEntry rowId) (const $ pure ())
```

- Parses the executables arguments and command
- Defines a default Manager for the client
- Specifies the BaseUrl for the API server
- Creates a ClientEnv for the client
- Defines an action that runs runClientM on a ClientM and runs a second action on the result or prints the error if the client failed
- Retrieves all entries using getEntries and then sorts and prints them
- Adds a new entry using addEntry and prints the resulting id
- Toggles an entry and ignores the result

Putting everything together results in the definition shown in listing 17.17. We specify the `runClientM'` function to have `runClientM` always use our `clientEnv` and also handle errors the same way. Now that we have this executable ready, we can test it!

Let's say we are running our server in one shell on port `9001`. We can then run our client:

```
shell $ stack run todolist-client -- list
TodoEntry {entryId = Just 6, text = "Implement client application",
➦ checked = False, rank = Just 1}
TodoEntry {entryId = Just 5, text = "CLI arguments", checked = False,
➦ rank = Just 2}
TodoEntry {entryId = Just 1, text = "Specify JSON and Database
➦ serialization", checked = True, rank = Nothing}
TodoEntry {entryId = Just 2, text = "Specify API type", checked = True,
➦ rank = Nothing}
TodoEntry {entryId = Just 3, text = "Implement API", checked = True,
➦ rank = Nothing}
TodoEntry {entryId = Just 4, text = "HTML rendering for list",
➦ checked = True, rank = Nothing}
```

It seems like we should check the entries with ids 5 and 6:

```
shell $ stack run todolist-client -- toggle --id 5
shell $ stack run todolist-client -- toggle --id 6
shell $ stack run todolist-client -- list
TodoEntry {entryId = Just 6, text = "Implement client application",
➦ checked = True, rank = Just 1}
TodoEntry {entryId = Just 5, text = "CLI arguments", checked = True,
➦ rank = Just 2}
TodoEntry {entryId = Just 1, text = "Specify JSON and Database
➦ serialization", checked = True, rank = Nothing}
TodoEntry {entryId = Just 2, text = "Specify API type", checked = True,
➦ rank = Nothing}
TodoEntry {entryId = Just 3, text = "Implement API", checked = True,
➦ rank = Nothing}
TodoEntry {entryId = Just 4, text = "HTML rendering for list",
➦ checked = True, rank = Nothing}
```

Looks good! Now, let's add one final todo:

```
shell $ stack run todolist-client -- add --text "Celebrate learning
➦ Haskell!" --checked False --rank 0
7
```

Solving this todo is left as an exercise to the reader!

Summary

- Servant allows us to specify typesafe APIs, using the type operators `(:>)` and `(:<|>)` to combine path information on an endpoint and combining multiple endpoints in one API, respectively.
- A phantom type is a type that contains at least one type variable that does not appear on the right-hand side of the definition and is used to pass additional type information to functions, without having to construct explicit values of a type.

- `Proxy` from `Data.Proxy` is an often-used phantom type.
- Inside a `Handler`, we can throw a value of type `ServerError` to return a fitting response to the client, indicating an error.
- A WAI `Application` can be modified using `Middleware`, which is a function that takes an `Application` and returns a modified `Application`.
- Using the `client` function from `Servant.Client`, we can automatically derive the functions to speak with a `servant` API.
- We can define commands for the CLI, using `subparser`.

appendix A
The Haskell Toolchain

Like any modern language, Haskell comes with a variety of tools. Here is a short overview of the essentials:

- *GHC*—The *Glasgow Haskell Compiler*, the standard compiler for the Haskell language.
- *GHCi*—GHC's interactive environment. It can be used to tinker with functions, test out certain code snippets, and get some information on types and definitions.
- *Cabal*—A tool for building Haskell applications. It can be used for downloading dependencies, compiling programs, and even bundling code into packages. It uses Hackage, the Haskell package repository, as a source for dependencies and GHC for compiling.
- *Stack*—A tool for organizing projects and resolving their dependencies with a high guarantee for build success. In normal use, it replaces the need to interact with cabal. It uses Hackage, Cabal, GHC, and the Stackage package collection, which consists of curated Hackage packages tested for compatibility.
- *HLS*—The Haskell language server. It can be used in conjunction with editors and IDEs to provide real-time information on types, compiler errors, and warnings.

Some other tools are also useful:

- *GHCup*—A tool for installing the essentials. It can install different versions of GHC, Cabal, Stack, and HLS for you.
- *HLint*—Suggests improvements to your Haskell code. It can point out ways to make the code simpler (e.g., by suggesting eta reductions).
- *Ormolu*—A formatter for Haskell code. It uses very readable and sensible defaults and is used throughout this book!

- *hasktags*—Generates tag files for Haskell code. Tag files are used to store locations of definitions for faster jumping to definitions inside your editor or IDE.
- *Shake*—A library for configuring build systems for Haskell projects.

A.1 Choosing tools and editor

Throughout this book, we are using GHCi and Stack, so these tools are necessary. GHCup is a great tool for installing other tools, making it highly recommended. When using Visual Studio Code, HLS might be a good addition to your workflow; however, HLS struggles with larger code bases. For such projects, hasktags is the faster, and arguably more sane, choice.

Largely, the choice of tools is up to you. I would recommend checking out HLint, especially as a beginner, to get a few more hints on how to improve your code. Ormolu (or any other code formatter) also tends to help a lot, since you don't have to worry about spaces and indentations.

A.2 Installing Haskell tools

For specific links to these tools, please check the code repository's README! The essential tools can be installed using GHCup. It can be installed on a variety of operating systems. From the command line, an interactive menu can be invoked:

```
ghcup tui
```

This will let you install GHC, Stack, Cabal, and HLS. Note that GHCi comes with GHC, so you can call it from your shell:

```
shell $ ghci
```

A.2.1 Running Stack and GHCi

The first time you run Stack, you need to update its package index:

```
stack update
```

If you want to make sure you have the newest version of Stack, you can do so using GHCup. There are two ways of starting ghci. You can do it directly with Stack, using one of the two following commands:

```
stack repl
stack ghci # Just an alias for stack repl
```

However, on some systems, this does not necessarily install the binaries to a directory that is in your PATH variable. To check which path Stack uses for installing your programs, you can use stack path and search for the *programs* path. This is where Stack copies the installed binaries. After you have added ghc and ghci to your PATH, you will be able to call these programs directly!

A.2.2   *Installing other tools*

Many tools can be installed globally with Stack. Note that installing them this way will put them in your PATH:

```
stack install <tool name>
```

A.3   *All in one Docker file*

If you don't want to install any parts of the Haskell toolchain on your computer locally, don't panic! The code repository for this book contains a Docker file that can be used to build a docker image that has the Haskell toolchain already installed!

When located in the repository, you can build an image from the Docker file, like so:

```
shell $ docker build -t haskell-bookcamp .
```

After building the image, you can get a container running that mounts the repository into /root/repo, where the code can be run. You could also mount your own Haskell projects into the container for ease of use!

```
shell $ docker run \
  -ti \
  --mount type=bind,source="$(pwd)",target=/root/repo \
  haskell-bookcamp \
  bash
```

appendix B
Lazy evaluation

Haskell does not strictly evaluate its values but uses *lazy evaluation*. The short explanation of lazy evaluation is that values are only evaluated once they are needed; it's *call by need*. However, this doesn't tell the full story.

First of all, *why is lazy evaluation useful?* Let's look at the const function:

```
const :: a -> b -> a
const x _ = x
```

As we can see, the second argument is always discarded. So what if the value of the second argument is very expensive to compute? The answer is *it does not matter*, since the value is not needed! This also extends to case distinction (e.g., if-then-else or pattern matching). Let's say we have code like this:

```
expensive1 :: Int
expensive1 = ... -- something terribly expensive

expensive2 :: Int
expensive2 = ... -- something terribly expensive

f :: Bool -> Int
f b = if b then expensive1 else expensive2
```

In the evaluation of f, we only ever need to evaluate one of the two values. The other one is simply ignored!

B.1   Lazy data structures

In chapter 5, we exploit lazy evaluation in our search algorithm. We construct a graph lazily and also search it lazily (since everything in Haskell is lazy by default). This enables us to evaluate only the searched part of the graph.

A prime example of lazy data structures is *infinite lists*. Yes, you heard correctly:

```
nat :: Int
nat = [1..]
```

Just like this, we can construct a list with all natural numbers. Why does that work? Let's look at an alternative implementation:

```
natRec :: [Int]
natRec = go 1
  where
    go n = n : go (n+1)
```

A call of go n evaluates to n : go (n+1) but *only if it is needed*! So when we need to evaluate the first 15 elements of a list, this is possible without evaluating the whole list:

```
ghci> take 15 natRec
[1,2,3,4,5,6,7,8,9,10,11,12,13,14,15]
ghci> take 15 (drop 15 natRec)
[16,17,18,19,20,21,22,23,24,25,26,27,28,29,30]
```

B.2   *How it works*

Lazy evaluation is implemented with *thunks*. A thunk represents a deferred computation. We can inspect which parts of a data structure are evaluated by using GHCi:

```
ghci> x = [1..10] :: [Int]
ghci> y = map (+1) x
ghci> :print y
y = (_t1::[Int])
ghci> take 5 y
[2,3,4,5,6]
ghci> :print y
y = 2 : 3 : 4 : 5 : 6 : (_t2::[Int])
```

Using :print, we can print a value *without* forcing its evaluation. We see that at first, y is simply not evaluated at all, but after we force the computation of the first five elements (since we are printing them to the screen), the list is evaluated up to the fifth element:

```
ghci> x = [1,1,1,1,1] :: [Int]
ghci> y = map (+1) x
ghci> :print y
y = (_t1::[Int])
ghci> length y
5
ghci> :print y
y = [(_t2::Int),(_t3::Int),(_t4::Int),(_t5::Int),(_t6::Int)]
```

It's important to note that there is a difference between evaluating constructors and actual values. Since the length function is only concerned with the list's constructors, not its values, it fully evaluates the constructors but not the thunks making up the values!

B.3   *Leaking space and time*

Lazy evaluation comes with a few issues. The first might be unpredictable performance, since you never know when an expression is fully evaluated. You don't know *when* work is done.

A much larger issue, however, is the fact that thunks are an extra step between the expression and its value. Let's look at a simple application of the `foldl` function:

```
foldl (+) 0 [1,2,3]
-> foldl (+) (0 + 1) [2,3]
-> foldl (+) ((0 + 1) + 2) [3]
-> foldl (+) (((0 + 1) + 2) + 3) []
-> (((0 + 1) + 2) + 3)
-> ((1 + 2) + 3)
-> (3 + 3)
-> 6
```

→ represents a single step of evaluation. `foldl` first builds a progressively larger term made of thunks, which only gets reduced once the recursion is finished. A better way to deal with this is the strict version of this function: `foldl'`.

Lazy evaluation can also lead to something much more sinister, called *space leaks*. Let's look at a very simple function to compute the average of a numeric list:

```
avg :: (Fractional a) => [a] -> a
avg xs = sum xs / fromIntegral (length xs)
```

This looks simple enough. The `avg` function should require constant memory, since we are only computing the sum of all elements in a list and also figuring out the length of the list in the process. However, if we try to evaluate this function, we will see that the space usage is many times higher than expected. Even for lists where neither `sum` nor `length` need a lot of memory, the `avg` function will take many gigabytes of memory! Why is that? This is because xs is shared between the two function calls. *Sharing* refers to the fact that if two expressions point to the same thunk, the thunk is only evaluated once, since a new evaluation wouldn't change the result. However, in this case, this means that after we have evaluated the sum, the whole huge list is kept in memory until `length` is finished. Remember that `sum` and `length` are lazy! They create huge collections of thunks, which are only forced on the evaluation of (/), causing a huge space leak in this simple function.

To avoid this problem, we are forced to compute the sum and length at the same time. This is not too complicated, as we can use a single `foldl'` to do that:

```
avg :: (Fractional a) => [a] -> a
avg xs =
  let (sum, count) = L.foldl' f (0,0) xs
  in sum / count
  where
    f (sum, count) x = (sum + x, count + 1)
```

However, this will not fix the problem, as `foldl'` will evaluate to *weak head normal form*, meaning the terms are only evaluated to their first constructor. In our case, this is the tuple constructor `(,)`, not the actual values inside those tuples, so thunks will still build up during the fold. To fix this, we have to also make the values of the accumulator strict. We can do so using the `BangPatterns` language extension and adding exclamation marks in front of the arguments inside the matching of the accumulator:

```
avg :: (Fractional a) => [a] -> a
avg xs =
  let (sum, count) = L.foldl' f (0,0) xs
   in sum / count
  where
    f (!sum, !count) x = (sum + x, count + 1)
```

This will cause `sum` and `count` to be evaluated to weak head normal form before calling `f`. For numeric types, this means they will be fully evaluated. This fixes the memory consumption and the function now runs in constant space, consuming the list as a lazy stream.

B.4   *undefined and newtype*

`undefined` is an error state, since something that we seemingly want to compute is undefined. However, `undefined` has a type:

```
ghci> x = undefined :: Int
ghci> :t x
x :: Int
ghci> :t undefined
undefined :: a
```

`undefined` does not just have a single type but can be of *any type*! So every type can be of the `undefined` value! This value is often referred to as *bottom* and signifies "undefinedness." In general, when `undefined` is encountered, our program crashes, but lazy evaluation sometimes changes this rule:

```
ghci> case undefined of _ -> print "I did not crash!"
"I did not crash!"
```

Why doesn't this crash? It avoids crashing because the pattern _ does not force any evaluation of the undefined thunk!

```
ghci> :print undefined
undefined = (_t1::GHC.Stack.Types.HasCallStack => a)
```

Since the `undefined` did not get evaluated, we had no reason to crash:

```
ghci> data X = X
ghci> case undefined of X -> print "I did not crash!"
*** Exception: Prelude.undefined
```

However, everything changes once we introduce a pattern that forces the thunk to be evaluated to its first constructor. Now, the `undefined` thunk is evaluated and the program crashes, but this isn't *always* true!

```
ghci> newtype Newtype = Newtype Int
ghci> data Data = Data Int
ghci> case undefined of Newtype _ -> print "I did not crash!"
"I did not crash!"
ghci> case undefined of Data _ -> print "I did not crash!"
*** Exception: Prelude.undefined
```

`newtype` seems to break the rules! Why is that? In chapter 5, we learned that `newtype` lets the compiler optimize the constructor away, since there is a one-to-one correspondence between the field of the `newtype` and its constructor. So `newtype` is more lazy! The constructor is never checked, and only the _ pattern remains, producing the same behavior as before!

index

427